70052792

338.4791
DAL

AS Level **Double Award**

D0587797

AS Level for.**Edexcel**

Travel &
Tourism

Gillian Dale • Malcolm Jefferies • Alan Marvell • Helen Oliver

www.heinemann.co.uk
✓ Free online support
✓ Useful weblinks
✓ 24 hour online ordering

01865 888058

Heinemann
Inspiring generation

Heinemann Educational Publishers
Halley Court, Jordan Hill, Oxford OX2 8EJ
Part of Harcourt Education

Heinemann is the registered trademark of
Harcourt Education Limited

Text © Gillian Dale, Helen Oliver, Alan Marvell, Malcolm Jefferies, 2006

First published 2006

09 08 07 06 05 04
10 9 8 7 6 5 4 3 2 1

British Library Cataloguing in Publication Data is available
from the British Library on request.

10-digit ISBN: 0 435 44643 6
13-digit ISBN: 978 0 435 44643 7

Copyright notice
All rights reserved. No part of this publication may be reproduced in
any form or by any means (including photocopying or storing it in any
medium by electronic means and whether or not transiently or
incidentally to some other use of this publication) without the written
permission of the copyright owner, except in accordance with the
provisions of the Copyright, Designs and Patents Act 1988 or under
the terms of a licence issued by the Copyright Licensing Agency,
90 Tottenham Court Road, London W1T 4LP. Applications for the
copyright owner's written permission should be addressed to the publisher.

Typeset and illustrated by 🐦 Tek-Art, Croydon, Surrey, UK

Original illustrations © Harcourt Education Limited, 2006
Cover design by Wooden Ark Studio, Leeds, UK
Printed in the UK by CPI Bath
Cover photo: © Robert Harding

Contents

Acknowledgements

The publishers wish to thank the following for their kind permission to reproduce the photos in this book.

Alamy 241, 250; Alton Towers 170; Jean Pierre Amet/Bel Ombra/Corbis UK Ltd 120; BAE Systems 12; British Airways Plc/Newscast Limited 51; Britain on View (BTA) 151; CDC/PHIL/Corbis UK Ltd 219; Ashley Cooper/Corbis UK Ltd 168; Corbis 44, 107, 109; Howard Davies/Corbis UK Ltd 152; Demetrio Carrasco/Jon Arnold Images/Alamy 108; Club Med 98; Empics 159; Britt Erlanson/Stone/Getty Images 254; Robert Estall/Collections 147; Everett/The Flight Collection/Alamy 202; Randy Faris/Corbis UK Ltd 252; Jeff Greenberg/Alamy 211; Jason Hawkes/Corbis UK Ltd 154; Michael Heuberger/Europa-Park Freizeit-und Familienpark Mack KG 107; Richard Klune/Corbis UK Ltd 93; Danny Lehman/Corbis UK Ltd 129; Murdo McLeod/Sygma/Corbis UK Ltd 190; Martial Colomb/Getty Images/PhotoDisc/60012 126; D. Maxwell/Robert Harding Picture Library Ltd/Alamy 94; UIF Michaelson/Reuters/Corbis UK Ltd 231; Pawel Libera/Corbis UK Ltd 157; Graeme Peacock/Alamy 146; Dave Penman/Rex Features 131; Richard Philpott/Zooid Pictures 206; Norman Price/Alamy 135; Tibor Rozsahegyi/Rex Features 137; A C Searle/Rex Features 155; Neil Setchfield/Lonely Planet 187; Skyscan/Corbis UK Ltd 202; SPA Photos/The Flight Collection/Alamy 202; Liba Taylor/Corbis 214; Thermae Bath Spa 195; Thorpe Park 21; John Wang/Getty Images/PhotoDisc/60032 171; Adam Woolfitt/Corbis UK Ltd 135; Yiorgos Karahalis/Reuters/Corbis UK Ltd 191; Zooid Pictures 62.

Every effort has been made to contact copyright holders of material reproduced in this book. Any omissions will be rectified in subsequent printings if notice is given to the publishers.

Introduction

Travel and tourism is one of the world's fastest growing industries, with over two million people employed in tourism-related industries in the UK. The AS GCE Travel and Tourism (Double Award) has been designed as a qualification that provides an appreciation of the diversity and complexity of this dynamic industry. You will develop a range of practical and technical skills and gain an understanding of the issues affecting the travel and tourism industry. The qualification will enable you to progress to the GCE A2 Advanced Level Travel and Tourism qualification and other qualifications in further and higher education, training or employment.

This book has been produced to meet the requirements of the Edexcel AS GCE Travel and Tourism (Double Award) qualification. It has been specifically written by a team of experienced authors to enable you to get the most from your course.

The book is set out in the order of the units that you will be studying:

* Unit 1 The Travel and Tourism Industry
* Unit 2 The Travel and Tourism Customer
* Unit 3 Destination Europe
* Unit 4 Destination Britain
* Unit 5 Travelling Safely
* Unit 6 Resort Operations

Each unit in this book has been written with essential information that you need to know along with a range of examples, case studies, activities and practice questions:

* Key terms – these provide concise definitions of important words and phrases.
* Key points – these are a summary and reminder of important points covered in sections of the text.
* Case study – these are detailed examples to show you how key ideas relate to the travel and tourism industry.

* Think it over – these provide you with an opportunity to think, discuss and reflect on important questions affecting the industry.
* Skills practice – these allow you to research and investigate ideas related to the information that has been discussed and to begin working towards your portfolio.
* Knowledge check – these allow you to check your understanding of what you have learnt before you start work on your portfolio.
* Portfolio practice – these provide you with examples of the type of work that you will be expected to produce as part of this course and helps you to build your own assessment portfolio.

How will I study?

You will be researching and investigating a wide range of issues relating to travel and tourism. These will be based around a series of assignments that are agreed with your tutor. You will be expected to use a variety of different sources, some of which can include:

* Libraries and information centres
* Internet searches
* Travel brochures and guidebooks
* News reports and advertisements from a variety of different media
* Visiting and talking to people in the travel and tourism industry
* Using industry reports and trade journals
* Learning from guest speakers
* If it is possible, work experience with a travel and tourism company.

How will I be assessed?

Two-thirds of the qualification is assessed by a portfolio of activities that are set out in the

Edexcel specification. Your tutor will give you a copy. The portfolio is based on coursework and other activities as specified by your tutor. You must make sure that you follow the instructions carefully and that the portfolio is all your own work. For some of the units, you will be able to choose the type of organisation or sector of the industry you want to study in more depth. This book provides you with examples and suggestions on where to find information.

The other third of the qualification is assessed by two written exams consisting of short answer questions. The exams are based on Unit 1 The Travel and Tourism Industry and Unit 5 Travelling Safely. This book prepares you for the exams with hints, suggestions and practice questions.

We hope you enjoy using this book and good luck with your course.

UNIT 1

The travel and tourism industry

Introduction

The travel and tourism industry is one of the biggest and fastest growing industries in the UK. This unit will give you an introduction to the industry, providing a sound basis for further study. You will find out about the nature of the industry, its size and scale, and you will be introduced to the types of organisations that form its structure.

In addition you will investigate the development of the industry and the factors which have affected the growth of travel and tourism.

How you will be assessed

This unit is assessed through an external assessment set by Edexcel. A variety of exercises and activities is provided in this unit to help you develop your understanding of the industry and prepare for the external assessment.

After completing the unit you will achieve the following outcomes:

* Understand the nature and characteristics of travel and tourism and the travel and tourism industry
* Understand the development of the travel and tourism industry
* Explain the structure of the travel and tourism industry
* Explain the scale of the travel and tourism industry.

1.1 The nature and characteristics of travel and tourism and the travel and tourism industry

Key term

Tourism The World Tourism Organisation provides the most commonly used definition of tourism:

'Tourism comprises the activities of persons travelling to and staying in places outside their usual environment for not more than one consecutive year for leisure, business and other purposes.'

What is tourism?

Defining tourism is not a simple matter, as it is a complex industry made up of many different businesses, the common theme being that they provide products and services to tourists. The most usually accepted definition of tourism is that provided by the World Tourism Organisation:

'Tourism comprises the activities of persons travelling to and staying in places outside their usual environment for not more than one consecutive year for leisure, business and other purposes.'

This definition includes the word 'staying' and suggests that tourists stay at least one night. However, we must acknowledge that day visitors make a huge contribution to the tourist industry and some regions and organisations choose to include day visitors in statistics. Most UK statistics separate spending and volume of day visitors from overnight tourists.

According to the Department of Culture, Media and Sport, the total value of the tourism and travel sectors in 2002–2003 in the UK was £91.8 billion, most of which comes from domestic rather than overseas visitors.

It is acknowledged by the World Tourism Organisation that tourism is the fastest growing economic sector, bringing foreign exchange earnings to countries and creating jobs. Jobs are not only created directly in tourism but in related industries, for example in construction. Much tourism development occurs in developing countries, bringing economic opportunities to local communities.

Different types of tourism

For the purposes of statistics tourists are categorised as leisure, business or visiting friends and relatives (VFR) travellers. Thus, they are categorised by the purpose of their visit.

Leisure tourists (usually described as leisure travellers in statistics) are travelling for the purpose of leisure so they are likely to be on holiday or taking a short break.

Business tourists are travelling to go to a meeting, conference or event associated with their business. This is an important and growing market in the UK as more resorts and hotels provide conference facilities.

Visiting friends and relatives (*VFR*) *tourists* are visiting family or relatives and therefore they are unlikely to spend as much on tourism as they are not using accommodation facilities.

There are some other types of tourism that you should know about.

Incoming tourists or *inbound tourists* are those who visit a country which is not their country of residence for the purposes of tourism. If the tourist comes from France to the UK then they are outbound from France and incoming to the UK. Overseas visitors or incoming tourists to the UK spent about £11.9 billion in 2003.

Domestic tourists are those people who are travelling within their own country for tourism purposes.

We have already noted in the tourism definition that, strictly, people are only tourists if they stay in a place outside their usual environment. This means that people on day trips are not officially tourists, which statistics count as those who stay at least one night in a place. A day-tripper is also known as an excursionist.

Day-trippers spend money in the tourism sector and boost the economy, so it is important to measure the value of their spending. In the UK, this is measured in the Day Visits Survey. Day visits are defined as trips which last three hours or more and which are not taken on a regular basis. Day visitors spent almost £30 billion in 2003, even more than those on overnight stays, so they must be taken note of.

Outgoing tourists are those who leave their own country, in this case the UK, to visit another country. Thus, if you go on summer holiday to France or Spain, you are an outgoing tourist.

Adventure tourists are those who are participating in sports or adventurous activities whilst on holiday, for example whitewater rafting. It is difficult to measure them statistically as there is no agreement on what actually constitutes 'adventure'. Many tour operators use the term loosely to attract certain types of customer.

Package holiday tourists are those who have booked a 'package' from a tour operator. This will include their holiday accommodation, transport and transfer to resort.

Independent tourists are those people who have arranged all their own transport and accommodation without using travel professionals. This group is increasing as the Internet becomes more widely used.

Skills practice

Study each of the examples below. What kind of tourists are they? Note that the examples might fit into more than one category.

Example	Type of tourist
Janine is taking a holiday in the UK. She lives in France.	
Salim is going on holiday to Brighton. He lives in Loughborough.	
Miguel and Jose are visiting Wales on holiday from Spain. They are going on a hang-gliding course. They booked the course, accommodation and flight with a Spanish tour operator.	
Maria and Ken are going to Spain for a weekend break. They live in Glasgow.	
Marguerite is a doctor. She has to attend a conference in Tenerife.	
The Patel family are going on holiday to Disney in Florida. They booked directly with Thomson in their home town of Swansea.	
Suzie is going to New York for two days and has booked a flight on the British Airways website. She also booked a hotel on the Novotel website.	
Peter goes to visit his sister in Ireland every Christmas.	
Miguel is visiting the UK to attend a language course for two weeks.	

Characteristics of the tourism industry

Types of business

Many of the businesses in tourism are very small. Government figures show that the tourism industry consists of 127,000 businesses and 80 per cent of these have a turnover of less than £250,000 per year. In spite of this, the industry is dominated by a few large companies. They have the greatest market shares and the most influence in shaping the industry. These are companies you will have heard of, such as Thomson, First Choice and Thomas Cook. They are tour operators but also have retail travel businesses with hundreds of outlets. In each sector the same situation occurs. There are thousands of small hotels and bed and breakfasts, but the major hotel groups, such as Holiday Inn and Accor, dominate. In the airline sector, British Airways is still a major player, although it is challenged by some low-cost operators like Ryanair.

Most organisations in the travel and tourism industry are privately owned. These organisations may be huge companies, such as British Airways, or small businesses. They usually aim to make a profit and are commercial companies. When they fail to make a profit over a period of time they are likely to cease trading. All theme parks, restaurants, tour operators and travel agents in the UK are privately owned. There are different types of private ownership, ranging from sole traders to public limited companies. Sole traders are small and run by one person, as the name suggests. A public limited company is listed on the stock market and is owned by its shareholders, who may buy and sell shares as they see fit.

Key term

Public limited company This is a business which is owned by shareholders. Its shares are bought and sold on the London Stock Exchange.

Do not confuse this type of business with one which is 'in the public sector'. It is not the same thing. A business in the public sector is owned and usually financed and run by national or local government.

Use of new technology

Early forms of technology in the travel and tourism industry were systems which linked tour operators to travel agencies via terminals and allowed travel agents to make bookings through the system. These were 'Viewdata' systems. By today's standards, Viewdata is unsophisticated and out-of-date technology, although it is still used.

Meanwhile, airlines developed computer reservation systems (CRS). Airlines started to use computers in the 1950s to store and change the huge amount of information they needed to access. The CRS was used internally by airlines, and agents would use the OAG publication to look up flight times etc., and then telephone the airline to make a booking. Today, travel agencies have direct access to the CRS systems.

Global distribution systems (GDS) were introduced to link up several CRS systems to make them accessible to the travel agent. With the latest of these products, the travel agent can make late availability searches and view brochures and destination information online. The product allows multi-operator searches, a feature which saves considerable time for the travel agent. Information is also available on coach, rail, air and sea travel, and currency conversion. Some global distribution services include fully integrated back office systems. This means that a travel agency's booking and accounting procedures can be automated.

The Internet is growing rapidly as a means of booking our holidays and flights. It is estimated that the British book between 5 per cent and 10 per cent of their holidays and trips on the Internet. In America, this figure is about 30 per cent. The growth in Internet booking for flights can be attributed to the low-cost airlines, which have educated passengers in how to book quickly and easily via the Internet, and offered discounts for doing so. Travel agents and tour operators are also using the Internet to present their products and services and many, but not all, accept bookings online.

Here are some other examples of the use of new technology.

Self check-in at airports Where this service is available, passengers can save time by checking in at a kiosk where they can choose their seat and print their own boarding pass. From there they can go to a 'fast bag drop' and leave their hold baggage. Passengers without baggage can go straight to the boarding gate.

Online check-in for airlines This is an alternative where passengers can check in without even being at the airport. From home or the office they go online and follow instructions to check in, choosing their seat and printing their boarding pass. It is not offered by all airlines.

Online brochures Kuoni (a tour operator) has been one of the first to present online brochures, as well as providing traditional ones. The customer can browse the brochure at home online and Kuoni saves money on printing and distributing brochures.

CASE STUDY

Air France

'To enhance customer comfort and security and to assess the impact of new technologies on the fluidity of airport border crossings, Air France is trialling an experimental automated security screening system dubbed PEGASE (Programme d'Expérimentation d'une Gestion Automatisée et Securisée). It is based on a **biometric fingerprint identification technology** developed by Sagem and is to be tested on volunteer customers for a six-month period at Paris-Charles de Gaulle airport's Terminal 2F.

Click on our website **www.airfrance.fr**, section **e-services**, for the exact dates.'

The extract shows information about a border control system trialled by Air France. Participants, who are volunteers at the moment, have prints taken of their index fingers which are filed along with their personal data. When going through immigration control at Charles de Gaulle airport in Paris, a passenger is authenticated by placing their fingers on a scanner.

1 **What do you think are the benefits of the system?**

2 **Are there any drawbacks?**

3 **Find out more at www.airfrance.fr in the e-services section.**

External pressures

Currency fluctuation

Tourism is an invisible export. This means that if tourists spend their money in the UK it brings the same benefit to our economy as if they buy goods in their own country that have been exported from the UK. By the same token, when we travel abroad we spend our money in another country and this equates to buying imported goods of that country in the UK. The government would prefer us to spend our money in our own country and take our holidays here rather than go abroad, so it promotes domestic tourism. It also wishes to encourage more overseas visitors to come to the UK.

The value of one currency against another currency is known as the exchange rate. The value of the pound, or sterling, against another currency affects the cost of coming here for inbound tourists. Our appeal to them will increase when sterling is weak, as they will get more pounds for their money. Conversely, if sterling is strong, overseas visitors get less pounds in exchange for their money and are less likely to want to come here. In recent years sterling has been very strong against the dollar, or the dollar has been weak against sterling – which amounts to the same thing. This has meant that it has been relatively cheap for UK-outbound tourists to visit the United States and more expensive for Americans to come to the UK.

The fluctuation in currency rates can affect tourism in other ways. Tour operators will find that the fees they have agreed with hoteliers and transporters in other countries will increase or decrease in line with currency movements. Fuel prices are similarly affected. These problems can be mitigated by tourism businesses if they 'hedge', that is, agree a price at a fixed rate of exchange for hotels or fuel in advance. This would be done through their banks.

Skills practice

Track sterling against the euro for a month. Imagine you are changing £1000. Draw a graph showing how many euros you would get on each day.

Legislation

The following are some of the legislation which has specifically impacted on travel and tourism.

Development of Tourism Act 1969

This established a British Tourist Authority and tourist boards for England, Scotland and Wales. The British Tourist Authority (BTA) and the English Tourism Council (ETC) have now been merged to form VisitBritain. The Act's aim was to co-ordinate all the organisations that make up the tourism industry and provide it with a single voice.

Transport Acts 1980 and 1985

The 1980 Act ended licensing regulations affecting express coach routes and tours of over 30 miles. It led to competition between National Bus (then a public company) and private companies. The 1985 Act brought about wholesale de-regulation. This meant private companies could operate on any route.

Package Travel, Package Holidays and Package Tours Regulations 1992

As a result of an EC Directive, since 1992 all UK tour operators offering package holidays have been subject to the Package Travel Regulations. The regulations set out the tour operators' responsibilities to their customers and what those customers can do if the regulations are breached. If there is a breach, the customer has a case against the tour operator not each individual supplier.

More recent legislation will impact on the tourism industry in the UK, including changes to licensing laws and bans on smoking in public places.

Think it over ...

What impact will the changes in licensing laws have on tourism?

Climate

Climatic disasters have a devastating impact on destinations and on their tourist industry. Recent examples include the hurricane which hit Grenada badly in 2003 and the tsunami which devastated South East Asia in late 2004. The tsunami resulted in the deaths of hundreds of thousands of people across twelve countries. Apart from the appalling human toll, the livelihood of the survivors is threatened because of the devastation of the infrastructure and the reluctance of many tourists to return to the area.

Even minor climate change affects tourism. If there is a particularly hot summer in the UK there is usually an increase in domestic tourism and a corresponding decrease in outbound tourism the next year.

Terrorist attacks

The devastating terrorist attacks on New York's World Trade Centre on 11 September 2001 also had an impact on the UK and the worldwide tourism industry, as people were afraid to fly, particularly American tourists. The result was a decline in visitors to Britain and a decline in worldwide travel for leisure and for business.

In October 2002 terrorists bombed a resort in Bali, killing over 200 people. The tourism industry in Bali was ruined at the time and only began to pick up again two years later.

There have also been terrorist bombings in Istanbul, in Kenya and in Madrid in the past few years. Each of these events results in loss of tourism for the area affected, until travellers begin to feel safe to travel to these areas again.

Economic climate

The economic health of a country has an impact on the travel and tourism industry. A country that has a strong economy can afford to invest in tourism, in terms of new infrastructure, supporting the industry through the public sector, and mounting promotional campaigns such as those organised by VisitBritain. However, the strength of the economy will result in a strong currency and therefore, as we saw earlier, impact on the affordability of a destination for visitors.

Impact on host environment

The impacts of travel and tourism on a host environment can be both positive and negative. It is vital to the future of the travel and tourism industry that positive impacts are maximised and negative impacts are minimised. The impacts can be economic, environmental, social and cultural.

Positive economic impacts include:

* Tourists bring increased income with their spending on travel, accommodation, etc. The government also benefits from increased revenue as it receives taxes from businesses earning revenue from tourism and in VAT from goods and services bought by tourists.

* Tourism creates jobs both directly and indirectly in related industries.

* Development may also bring about improved infrastructure which can be used by tourists and local people alike.

The *negative economic impacts* can include:

* Leakage. This is when economic benefits are lost due to high imports of goods and services used in tourism, for example if food and drink for hotels are imported rather than bought locally. Similarly, if materials and workers for construction projects are imported, then the local economy does not benefit as it would if local materials and workers were used.

Key term

Leakage This is the term used for the amounts of taxes, the money spent on imports, wages paid outside the region and company profits, subtracted from direct tourism expenditure in an area.

* Economic distortion can occur when one region of a country is highly developed for tourism while other areas have no development.

The *positive environmental impacts* include:

* The conservation and preservation of historic sites and properties.

* National parks and other conservation bodies providing information and education for tourists to increase their environmental awareness.

* The regeneration of the environment. Both the built and natural environment benefit from upgrading and regeneration when a tourist opportunity is uncovered by local and national government.

The *negative environmental impacts* include:

* Traffic congestion where there is a high concentration of popular tourist attractions, for example the Lake District.

* Pollution from noise and petrol fumes, for example jet skis and motor boats in coastal resorts. Pollution may disturb or destroy the normal activities or habitats of wildlife, as in the case of marine life in coastal areas.

* The influx of tourists pressuring scarce resources. An example is the use of water, which is a scarce resource in many places, which is made worse where there are tourists, who tend to use more water than local people. In locations with golf courses and gardens even more water is used.

The *positive social impacts* include:

* The introduction of community facilities and services, primarily to cater for tourists, but which are also of benefit to locals, in time. For example, where sport and leisure facilities are introduced to cater for tourists, the standard of living for the host community may generally improve.

* The education and training of local people to enable them to take up jobs in tourism.

The *negative social impacts* include:

* Conflict between tourists and the host community may occur. Tourists sometimes cause irritation and offence by failing to respect the customs and traditions of the host country. Also, the host population may resent the perceived wealth of the incoming tourists.

* When tourism is regionalised in a country people may leave their homes and communities to take up jobs in tourism. This is known as displacement.

The *positive cultural impacts* include:

* Reinforcement of cultural identity if visitors are interested in the host culture.

* Traditional customs and crafts can be sustained by tourist interest and purchase of local goods.

The *negative cultural impacts* include:

* Changes in cultural tradition when traditional events and dances are degraded through use as entertainment for tourists.

* Destinations can lose some of their cultural identity as tourists demand products and services they are accustomed to at home, for example the insistence on having a English breakfast every morning and drinking in 'British pubs'.

Skills practice

Choose three organisations, one from each of the following categories:

* Tour operator or travel agency
* Transport principal or accommodation provider
* Public sector organisation such as Visit Britain.

Carry out research into your chosen organisations and find out the following:

* Ownership of the organisation
* Use of new technology by the organisation
* External pressures currently affecting the organisation
* Impact of the organisation on the environment.

Present your findings in a comparative report.

1.2 The development of the travel and tourism industry

Key stages in the development of the travel and tourism industry

Early tourism

In ancient times people travelled for the purpose of war, religious pilgrimage and trading. From the third century the ancient Greeks, for example, travelled to visit the sites of their gods and to visit the temples and the Parthenon in Athens.

During the Roman Empire, citizens of Rome travelled freely to those countries their armies had conquered, using their own currency and not having to worry about border restrictions. The Romans built long straight roads along which their armies could march and goods could be transported. In countries they conquered, the Romans established trade and created leisure facilities such as spas – the most famous example in this country is the Roman spa in Bath. Those who could afford to travelled to newly conquered countries and to visit their friends and relatives. With the fall of the Roman Empire around 400AD, and for a period after, only the most adventurous or those involved in international trade travelled abroad. In the Middle Ages people seldom travelled, apart from going on pilgrimage, however there were holidays, or rather 'holy' days. These were days on which a religious festival was celebrated. Many of the UK's traditional fairs can be traced to this period.

CASE STUDY

Nottingham Goose Fair

The Goose Fair was first mentioned in the Nottingham Borough Records of 1541. There, in the Chamberlain's accounts, is a reference to an allowance of 1s 10d for 22 stalls taken by the city's two sheriffs on Goose Fair Day. No one knows for how many centuries the fair existed before these references were made. The Charter of King Edward I, the first charter to refer to the city fairs, makes it clear that a fair on the Feast of St Matthew was already established in Nottingham in 1284. It is possible this occasion has come down through the ages to be today's Goose Fair, particularly as, until 1752, it was always held on St Matthew's Day (21 September). On that day there was worship at what was then the tiny church of St Mary.

1 Use the Internet to find out when the Nottingham Goose Fair is held. Find out what happens at the Fair.
2 Research the history of local fairs in your own area. Do they have religious origins? Present your findings visually with explanatory notes. You could produce a poster or a leaflet.

During the Middle Ages most transport was by foot or on horseback, though some people could afford a wagon. In the early 1600s the sprung coach was introduced. This was more comfortable but could only be afforded by the very rich. In the early seventeenth century wealthy young men were travelling across Europe on the Grand Tour, spending as long as a year visiting the capitals of Europe, as part of their education. Another development in travel at this time was the taking of 'a cure' by the wealthy, who visited the various spa towns to take the waters, which were reputed to provide a cure for a range of ailments. These resorts became very popular, and there are still spas today at Buxton, Bath and Harrogate. By 1815, tarmac had been developed for use as a road surface, which led to further developments in the road system in the UK and to an increase in the movement of people and vehicles.

The development of the railways increased the opportunity for travel. With the opening of the first rail services in 1825, people could travel longer distances for excursions to the seaside, for example. Steamships increased sea travel, particularly between England and France on the Dover–Calais route. People had a strong desire for travel to escape the dreary working and living conditions of the factories and towns that emerged during the industrial revolution of the nineteenth century. The development of transport made this possible. However, whatever holidays factory workers took, they were not paid during them. Paid holidays were not introduced until 1938.

Twentieth and twenty-first century developments	
1908	Ford introduced the motor car
1919	Commercial air services began
1936	First Butlins holiday camp opened
1938	Holidays with Pay Act
1939–45	Second World War
1949	First package tour was organised by Vladimir Raitz – to Corsica with 32 passengers on a DC3 aeroplane
1949	First British fully jet-powered passenger aircraft – the de Havilland Comet

1954	de Havilland air service suspended after two early models crashed
1954	Boeing 707 passenger aircraft introduced
1959	Boeing 707 goes into commercial service
1963	Boeing 727 introduced
1969	Boeing 747 Jumbo jet introduced, capable of seating 500 passengers
1969	Development of Tourism Act established tourist boards in the UK
1976	Collaboration between Air France and British Airways produced Concorde
1979	Exchange control restrictions lifted, allowing holidaymakers to take more money out of the country
1986	Anglo-French Channel Tunnel Treaty signed
1993	Deregulation of European skies allowed low-cost airlines to develop
1994	Channel Tunnel opened
2001	First non-stop flight around the world without refuelling
2003	Concorde taken out of service
2004	EU accession – now 25 states
2005	Introduction of the Airbus A380, capable of carrying up to 800 passengers

Think it over ...

After the Second World War the commercial aviation industry in the UK quickly expanded. Wartime pilots were available to fly commercial airlines and the technological advances made during the war were being applied to commercial services. What effect do you think these developments in the aviation industry had on the travel and tourism industry after the Second World War?

Key term

Deregulation of European skies With deregulation of the air travel industry, the airlines of the European Union could establish themselves in any member state and obtain an operating licence. All routes within the EU are available to all EU carriers.

Think it over ...

The Channel Tunnel opened in 1994. Its original budget was £4.8 billion, but its final cost exceeded £10 billion. Do you think the cost was worth it in terms of the impact the Channel Tunnel has had on travel and tourism between the UK and Europe?

Skills practice

Choose three of the developments illustrated in the timeline. Research them in more depth. Then produce a set of notes explaining the development and impact on travel and tourism at the time, and the residual effect today.

Factors leading to the growth of the UK tourism industry

Motivating factors

Why do people travel? One view is that there are two basic reasons for travel: 'wanderlust' and 'sunlust'. Many young people have the desire to travel and see other cultures and experience how other people live; this is wanderlust. Other people want to go somewhere warm and escape from our climate for a while; this is sunlust.

There are other motivating factors. These include:

* Relaxation
* Escape from a boring job/family/home
* Socialisation with friends – e.g. hen/stag parties
* Rest
* Prestige.

These motivating factors have not really changed over the years. However, the ways we are able to indulge them have changed, as *enabling* factors have changed.

Think it over ...

What were your motivating factors last time you went on holiday? Discuss them with a colleague.

Enabling factors

You might have motivators for wanting to go on holiday, but there are reasons why you cannot go. The obvious ones are time and money. If you can't afford it you can't go. Having enough money and time are examples of *enabling* factors.

Other enabling factors include:

* Availability of travel – e.g. flights to different locations, the Channel Tunnel, low-cost flights

* Suitable products – e.g. a range of different holidays

* Owning a car – to travel more easily

* Marketing of a destination – bringing it to your attention

* Ease of booking.

These enabling factors allow us to act on our motivators. You will find more examples of enabling factors throughout this section as we investigate changes in consumer needs and in society.

Socio-economic changes

Car ownership and use

Figure 1.1 shows the car use figures in the UK from 1992/1994 to 2003.

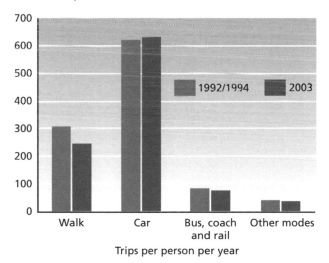

Figure 1.1 Car use in the UK, 1992/1994–2003

Car ownership in the UK has increased considerably in recent decades: today it is not uncommon for a household to own two or more cars. Only 27 per cent of households in the UK did not have access to a car in 2003, compared with 33 per cent 10 years previously.

Car ownership has a strong impact on travel and tourism. The car is used to drive to domestic destinations and to drive to airports to pick up flights abroad. The Channel Tunnel and car ferries allow outbound tourists to use their cars for travelling to destinations in Europe.

Income

The UK economy is one of the strongest in Europe, levels of disposable income and consumer credit are rising and expenditure on leisure is growing at around 6 per cent.

> **Key term**
>
> **Disposable income** This is the income you have left after tax, national insurance and pension contributions are deducted from pay.

As a nation we are wealthier now than we have ever been, and have higher expectations of travel and tourism. Most people today will have travelled abroad and expect to take at least one holiday a year. We are also better educated than ever before, leading to increased personal income. The more educated we are the more we are aware of the world and its possibilities; we are curious about different cultures and languages and keen to experience them. As we live in a multicultural society and are more familiar with different religions, foods and cultures, we are less anxious about travelling to new places.

The grey market

One of the most important markets in travel and tourism is the 'grey' market. This is made up of older people who are fit and healthy, have plenty of time and available funds, and want to travel. Having contributed to private pension schemes over their working years has given many older people a good income in retirement.

Technological factors

We have already discussed the use of technology in the travel and tourism industry (see pages 4–5). The main impact of new technology on consumers has been the Internet, which has given people the opportunity to be more independent and make their own travel and holiday plans and arrangements. The long-term effects of these developments on the industry are yet to be seen.

Technological developments have also led to new transport products, some examples of which are given in the next section.

Product development and innovation

Holiday products are developed to meet changing consumer needs and expectations. The demand for shorter, more frequent holidays, for example, has led to city-break products. The more aware consumers become about the dangers of sunbathing on a beach holiday, the greater the demand for activity or adventure holidays. Those seeking safety and reasonable cost, can choose an all-inclusive holiday.

The 'spa' holiday is another area of growth. Activities such as yoga are included and guests have massage and treatments included in the price of the holiday. Many hotels are now described as 'spa hotels'.

The increase in car ownership led to more people choosing to drive to their destination rather than take a train or a coach. It also led to a demand for car use on holidays, given that people are accustomed to the convenience of using cars in their daily lives, so why not on holiday. This led to huge growth in the car-hire industry, which became international. In response, tour operators developed 'fly-drive' holidays to give customers flexibility.

Developments in the commercial aviation industry have led to larger planes carrying more passengers to destinations around the world. The latest is the Airbus A380, which was introduced in 2005, though at present it has still to make its first commercial flight. It can seat between 555 and 800 passengers and will provide a range of facilities, including jacuzzis!

High-speed train routes, such as France's extensive TGV network, have helped maintain the

The Airbus A380

success of the railways in some countries. The TGV is operated by SNCF, the French nationally-owned and subsidised rail company, and travels at speeds of over 300 km/hour (186 mph).

The European high-speed rail network has been extended, with TGV services now running direct from Paris, the Channel Tunnel and Brussels to German destinations. The Belgian high-speed trains are known as Thalys. Remember, enabling trains to travel at these high speeds involves substantial investment in suitable new tracks.

Changing consumer needs and expectations

Changes in consumer needs and the developments in travel and tourism are inextricably intertwined. The more products consumers demand the more pressure there is on tourism professionals to make them available. The more products and destinations on offer, the more consumers expect, and the quicker they tire of the old and search for the new.

Technological advances in transport and communication have made the world more accessible to more people, and aroused the desire to experience more of it. Greater incomes in the western world and increased leisure time contribute to demand. As other countries develop, the desire for travel and tourism grows among their people. China and Eastern Europe are examples of the development of the freedom and means to travel not available even ten years ago.

1 Try to remember the holidays you have been on. List them. Then, note the types of activities you did while on those holidays.

2 Now, talk to two older people, one much older, such as a grandparent, and one of middle age, such as a parent.

Interview these two people and make notes on their holiday experiences up until they were the same age as you are now.

Some of the questions you may ask are:

- Did you have holidays and day trips?
- Where to?
- How did you travel?
- Who did you go with?
- Where did you stay?
- How many holidays a year did you have?
- What did you do on holiday?

3 Make a chart or poster comparing the three sets of experience.

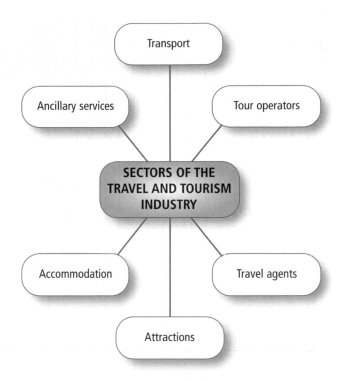

Figure 1.2 Sectors of the travel and tourism industry

1.3 The structure of the UK travel and tourism industry

In this section we will examine the different sectors that make up the travel and tourism industry. You will carry out research to find out about key organisations in each sector, what their products and services are, and you will describe their objectives and values.

We will examine the function of each sector and its roles and responsibilities. You will develop an understanding of the interrelationships and interdependencies within the industry and how horizontal and vertical integration apply in the industry.

Transport

The function of the transport sector is summarised in this quote from Sir Michael Bishop, chairman of bmi: 'Transport is the backbone of a sustainable economy; it brings people together, facilitates trade and sustains tourism.'

Principals in the transport sector include airlines and airports, ferry and cruise companies, car-hire businesses, coach operators, Network Rail and train-operating companies. Each of them has a role to play in the travel and tourism industry.

Air travel
Airports
The British Airports Authority (BAA) is the major organisation in airport ownership in the UK. It owns:

* London Heathrow
* London Gatwick
* London Stansted
* Glasgow
* Edinburgh
* Aberdeen
* Southampton.

BAA also has management contracts or stakes in ten other airports outside the UK, plus retail management contracts at two airports in the USA. Nearly 200 million passengers travel through BAA airports every year. Other major UK airports are Birmingham, Manchester and London Luton, all owned by different consortia.

Manchester airport is in public ownership, whereas BAA is a public limited company and therefore in the private sector. Manchester airport is part of the Manchester Airports Group Plc (MAG), which is the second largest airport operator in the UK and comprises the airports of Manchester, Nottingham East Midlands, Bournemouth and Humberside.

MAG is wholly owned by the ten local authorities of Greater Manchester:

* The Council of the City of Manchester – 55%

* The Borough Council of Bolton – 5%

* The Borough Council of Bury – 5%

* The Oldham Borough Council – 5%

* The Rochdale Borough Council – 5%

* The Council of the City of Salford – 5%

* The Metropolitan Borough Council of Stockport – 5%

* The Tameside Metropolitan Borough Council – 5%

* The Trafford Borough Council – 5%

* The Wigan Borough Council – 5%

Think it over …

What difference do you think public or private sector ownership makes to the running of an airport? Think about the impact on airlines, passengers and the local community.

Running an airport is a complex, lucrative operation. An airport provides products and services to various groups of people and businesses:

* Airlines are provided with the infrastructure and services to operate their flights

* Customers are provided with facilities, such as restaurants, toilets and shops

* Other businesses get a location in which to operate their business, for example car hire, retailing, ground handling.

An airport receives revenue from all these sources but also has to work at keeping all its groups of customers happy.

CASE STUDY

Ambitious Kent airport expansion outlined

Plans have been unveiled to expand a little used UK airport to handle two million passengers a year by 2014.

Lydd airport in Kent (renamed London Ashford airport) – part of a Middle East-based company, FAL Holdings – plans a new terminal and extended runway to handle flights to European and North African holiday destinations.

The owner of Lydd airport expects to create up to 4000 jobs on its Romney Marsh location in nine years time if the plans receive official approval. A 75-room hotel is part of the planned expansion.

More than £7 million has been spent on improving the existing runway and infrastructure, including a 13-acre aircraft parking apron and a VIP terminal for executive jet users.

The airport owners believe Lydd would provide an 'environmentally friendly' solution to runway and airspace congestion in the south-east of England.

The company claims that air travellers in Kent, Surrey and Sussex are being forced to drive north to Luton or Stansted due to constraints at Heathrow and Gatwick, resulting in added vehicle emissions and environmental pollution.

Chief consultant Jonathan Gordon said: 'The problem is that Gatwick is now at the limit of its runway capacity and with the dominance of scheduled services, it no longer offers room to grow for the leisure sector.

'Lydd is the closest UK airport to the popular European and North African holiday destinations and we are currently developing excellent facilities for the leisure sector.'

Source: Report by Phil Davies www.travelmole.com
30 June 2005

1 **What is the relationship between FAL Holdings and Lydd (London Ashford) airport?**
2 **Do research and find out more about FAL Holdings.**
3 **What kind of arguments could be made against the expansion?**

Airlines

British Airways, one of the world's most famous airlines, is the largest airline in the UK and the second-largest international airline. It flies to more than 200 destinations around the world. In the year to March 2004, more than 36 million people chose to fly with the airline. British Airways' main bases are at the London airports of Heathrow and Gatwick. The airline's products include four different types of cabin service, ranging from economy to Club World. It is owned entirely by private investors. It also fully owns subsidiaries such as British Airways CitiExpress.

Skills practice

Find out what products and services are available to British Airways customers. Compare the economy service with Club World and make a table charting your comparison. This information is available at www.ba.com

All UK airlines are privately owned. Other major UK airlines include British Midland and Virgin Atlantic, which are scheduled airlines. The UK also has many charter airlines, such as Monarch and Britannia Airways. Hundreds of other airlines from all over the world fly in and out of UK airports, paying for the services they use.

Key terms

Scheduled airline service These run to a regular timetable that is changed only for the winter and summer season. They must depart on schedule even if not all the seats are booked.

Charter airline service These are usually contracted for a specific holiday season and run to a timetable set by the operator. For example, each major tour operator will need seats for its summer passengers flying to the Mediterranean. They fill every seat on the contracted aircraft and each seat forms part of the holiday package.

The distinction between scheduled and charter services is becoming less clear as airlines move into different markets. For example, major tour operators often own their own charter airlines and some have ventured into the low-cost (scheduled) market. An example is My Travel, a tour operator which has two airlines, My Travel and My Travelite. Similarly, Monarch, also a charter operator, has begun scheduled services.

Low-cost airlines The principle behind the operation of a low-cost airline is to keep costs as low as possible with few or no 'extras' offered to the customer without extra charge. In this way the low-cost operators are able to offer very cheap fares. They practise a system known as 'yield management', which means that bookings are constantly monitored and prices adjusted accordingly. This means that in periods of high demand, such as school holidays or weekends, prices will be higher, and can be more expensive than traditional airlines.

One of the most successful low-cost airlines is Irish-based Ryanair, which reported net profits of 268 million euros in 2005. The low-cost airlines are scheduled airlines. They follow a business model where costs are kept as low as possible and any 'extra' services are charged to the passenger.

Airport charges These charges are paid per passenger and vary depending on who owns the airport and the deal negotiated by the airline. Low-cost airlines often fly to regional airports because of lower charges.

Aircraft Low-cost airlines usually have a fleet of aircraft, all of the same type, often Boeing 737s. This gives flexibility as the planes can be moved to any route as needed; it also means that maintenance is simpler.

There is no business class on a low-cost flight, which means more seats can be added to the plane. Ryanair's new planes do not have reclining seats or pockets for magazines, which enable it to make further savings.

Advertising The airlines rely on heavy newspaper advertising, which is costly, however they do carry advertising for other companies on their websites and on their seatback covers, giving an extra source of revenue.

Ancillary services The airlines charge the customer – and steeply – for food, drink, paying by credit card, and even lottery tickets on board some flights. The airlines also sell hotel rooms, car hire and insurance for commission.

Skills practice

Visit the website of a low-cost airline and find out what products and services are on offer at an extra charge. Try to determine which products bring direct revenue to the airline and which pay a commission.

Support services for the airline sector

The Civil Aviation Authority (CAA) regulates the UK aviation sector. The CAA is an independent statutory body; its responsibilities are outlined below:

* It ensures that UK civil aviation standards are set and achieved
* It regulates airlines, airports and national air traffic services economic activities and encourages a diverse and competitive industry
* It manages the UK's principal travel protection scheme, the Air Travel Organisers' Licensing (ATOL) scheme, licenses UK airlines and manages consumer issues
* It brings civil and military interests together to ensure that the airspace needs of all users are met as equitably as possible.

The CAA also advises the government on aviation issues. It receives no government funding but is funded by the charges it makes for its services.

The Air Transport Users Council (AUC) is the UK's consumer council for air travellers and receives its funding from the CAA. It acts as the independent representative of air passengers and aims to complement and assist the CAA in its duties to further the reasonable interests of passengers.

National Air Traffic Services (NATS) is the organisation responsible for air traffic control. It is a public/private partnership owned by the government, a consortium of seven airlines, and NATS staff. It looks after UK airspace and the eastern part of the North Atlantic. NATS handles more than two million flights a year, carrying over 180 million passengers.

The major air traffic control centres are at Swanwick in Hampshire, West Drayton in Middlesex and Prestwick in Scotland. There are also air traffic control services at the country's major airports.

Sea travel

Ferry travel

The main mode of transport to the continent is traditionally by sea travel across the English Channel. When the Channel Tunnel opened in 1993 it was expected that ferry services across the Channel would be threatened. The tunnel did take about 50 per cent of the market, but passenger ferries have also been severely hit by low-cost airlines offering cheap fares to Europe. It is often cheaper to fly and drive rather than take your own car. In 1997, 21 million passengers passed through Dover, which is the busiest port in Britain. By 2003 numbers had declined to less than 15 million. However, the ferry companies work hard to remain competitive on price and many passengers prefer the sea trip to the tunnel.

DOVER FERRY PASSENGERS	
1990	15,532,585
1991	15,989,318
1992	17,941,400
1993	18,458,557
1994	19,123,743
1995	17,872,712
1996	18,979,719
1997	21,463,570
1998	19,441,608
1999	18,276,988
2000	16,232,191
2001	16,002,464
2002	16,442,680
2003	14,681,003
2004	14,333,633

Source: Dover Harbour Board

Figure 1.3 Dover ferry passenger numbers, 2004

Here you will participate in a class discussion. The topic is whether the Channel Tunnel encourages more tourists to come to the UK or more UK tourists to go abroad.

Points to consider:

- Statistics for use of the tunnel (Eurostar and the Shuttle)
- Whether the tunnel creates new business
- Competition with air and sea routes
- Services and facilities built up around the terminals.

The Channel Tunnel and low-cost flights are not the only competition faced by the ferry operators, there are also high-speed catamarans operated by newcomer SpeedFerries, which is offering low fares to attract customers.

Other operators in the Channel include Hoverspeed, Norfolk Line and Trans Europa, which sails from Ramsgate to Ostend. Brittany ferries operate on longer routes to France and Spain, for example Poole to Cherbourg, Plymouth to Santander and Portsmouth to Caen, St Malo or Cherbourg.

CASE STUDY

Ferry travel

Not all ferry travel is across the Channel. Here are some examples of other important routes:

- Stranraer to Belfast
- Fleetwood to Larne
- Fishguard to Rosslare ⎫ Stena Line
- Holyhead to Dublin Port
- Holyhead to Dun Laoghaire

- Hull to Zeebrugge ⎫ P&O Ferries
- Hull to Rotterdam

- Holyhead to Dublin ⎫ Irish Ferries
- Pembroke to Rosslare

1 Check all these ports on a map and make sure you know the location and the country.
2 Choose one route and produce an information sheet detailing the services provided and extra products available on that route. A ferry brochure will help you.

In the event of business failure, the Passenger Shipping Association provides financial protection to the customers of some tour operators who offer cruise and ferry-based holidays.

The cruise market

The cruise sector has enjoyed steady growth over the past decade or more. The growth is accounted for by greater demand for cruises, but also by increase in capacity. Many new ships, including the *Queen Mary 2*, were launched in 2003–2004, five are set for delivery in 2005, and many more are scheduled for delivery in 2006. There were 1.14 million people from this country who went on a cruise in 2004, an increase of 8 per cent on 2003. Cruise companies are doing their utmost to reach new markets, such as families and younger people, rather than just the older groups who traditionally take cruises.

Most cruises take place on the sea and most passengers from the UK take fly-cruises. This means they fly to their cruising starting point rather than start at the UK coast. The Mediterranean and the Caribbean are very popular cruise destinations. Those looking for a difference might take a cruise to a colder place, such as the Arctic, to experience the beautiful scenery and the wildlife.

Not all cruises take place in the sea. River cruises are also growing in popularity and the destinations include rivers such as the Rhine, Moselle, Danube and the Nile.

Major cruise companies are P & O, Cunard, Royal Caribbean and Princess Cruises.

Got to a local travel agent and choose a cruise brochure. Go though the brochure and outline all the facilities and services included in the price of the cruise.

Road travel

The private car dominates road travel, and most domestic holidays and day trips in the UK are taken by car. In addition, many people choose to hire a car when abroad, which has led to the growth of the car-hire sector.

Car hire

Major car-hire groups in the UK include Hertz, Avis and Europcar. All have international operations. Their products and services have become very sophisticated, making car hire very easy and convenient for customers. They offer the following:

* Online or telephone pre-booking

* Airport pick-up or drop-off

* Wide range of choice of vehicles

* All insurances included in fixed prices

* One-way rentals – i.e. you don't have to return the car to the same pick-up point.

One of the largest companies in car hire is Holiday Autos, which claims to be the world's largest car rental service with access to over 750,000 cars worldwide. Holiday Autos is part of the Lastminute.com group.

Coaches

Coach operators have adapted their products to meet consumers' changing needs and coaches today are very luxurious. Fly/coach holidays are offered so that customers do not have a lengthy initial journey, but have the benefits of coach travel for touring, as on tours in California, for example.

Rail travel

Network Rail owns and operates the national rail network in the UK. Its role is to maintain the infrastructure and renew tracks as necessary. In addition, there are train operating companies (TOCs) who lease trains from rolling stock companies. There are 25 train operating companies in the UK and they compete for franchises to run each service.

The Strategic Rail Authority issues the franchises. This body also monitors the train operating companies to make sure the interests of rail passengers are protected. They are able to fine the TOCs if they fail to meet agreed standards. The TOCs are commercial companies and aim to make a profit but they do receive government grants. Examples of TOCs are Virgin Trains and Central Trains. The National Express Group, a British-owned transport group, owns Central Trains.

Other important aspects of the rail system are the London Underground, Docklands Light Rail and Eurostar.

Eurostar is the passenger train service for the Channel Tunnel. It operates from London Waterloo and Ashford in Kent to Paris, Lille and Brussels. Eurostar is owned by London and Continental Railways and run by a management company.

Skills practice

1   Visit the website of Network Rail at www.networkrail.co.uk Make notes on the following. Ensure that the notes are in your own words.
    * Company objectives
    * Company ownership
    * Summary of services.

2   Choose a train operating company and research:
    * Its role and responsibilities
    * Its products and services
    * Its relationship with Network Rail.

3   Analyse the interrelationship between the two companies.

4   Produce your findings as a short report or information sheet.

Tour operators

The role of tour operators is to put together all the different components that make up a holiday and sell them as packages to the consumer. They make contracts with hoteliers, airlines and other transport companies to put the package together. All the holiday details are incorporated into a brochure which is distributed either to travel agents or directly to customers. There are three main types of tour operators catering for the different types of tourism:

* Outbound

* Inbound

* Domestic.

Four major tour operators dominate the outbound market. These are often referred to as the 'Big Four': TUI, My Travel, First Choice and Thomas

Cook. TUI UK is the UK's largest holiday company and includes the leading UK brands of Thomson Holidays. Thomson Holidays has its head office in London and about 3000 people are employed, although most of them work overseas in resorts. The parent company, World of TUI, is the largest travel group in the world.

MyTravel is a major player in the market for air-inclusive holidays and other leisure travel services. It also has travel agents, hotels and airlines in its group.

First Choice has a major travel agent in its portfolio and an airline. It offers destinations such as Majorca, Menorca, the Canaries, Spain, Turkey, Greece and the Caribbean. Snow destinations include France, Austria, Italy, Andorra, Bulgaria and Switzerland.

German-owned Thomas Cook also has travel agencies, airlines and hotels, as well as tour operator brands, including JMC, Thomas Cook Holidays, and Club 18 30.

These companies produce an astonishing range of different holidays, packaged in brochures according to type of holiday or type of customer. As the tour operators use many different brands it is not always evident to the customer which tour operator group they are booking with.

There are many other tour operators in the market, some specialising in particular destinations, for example Simply Spain, or in a product, for example diving holidays.

Cosmos is the UK's largest independent tour operator and part of the Globus group of companies, a family-run organisation established in 1928, which encompasses Cosmos Tourama, Avro, Monarch Airlines and Archers Direct, along with Cosmos.

Key term

Air Travel Organisers' Licensing (ATOL) The ATOL protects air travellers and package holidaymakers from losing money or being stranded abroad if air travel firms go out of business. When a tourist books a holiday the cost of the financial protection is included in the price. Any package firm that includes a flight should by law hold a licence. ATOL is managed by the Civil Aviation Authority.

Inbound tour operators

Inbound tour operators cater for the needs of overseas visitors to the UK. An example is British Tours Ltd, which claims to be the longest established inbound operator. It offers tours for different sizes of groups and has a wide variety of products, including a Harry Potter tour. The tours are available in many languages.

Domestic tour operators

Domestic tour operators package holidays in the UK for UK residents. Some of them are coach companies who place advertisements in the local newspapers. Like outbound operators, they offer beach, city, touring and special interest holidays.

Support services for tour operators

UK Inbound is the trade body which represents tour operators and tourism suppliers to the UK. It was founded in 1977 to represent the commercial and political interests of incoming tour operators and suppliers to the British inbound tourism industry. It is a non-profit-making body governed by an elected council and funded by subscriptions from its members and from revenue-generating activities.

The Association of Independent Tour Operators (AITO) is an organisation which represents about 160 of Britain's specialist tour operators. AITO members are independent companies, most of them owner-managed, specialising in particular destinations or types of holiday.

The Federation of Tour Operators (FTO) is an organisation for outbound tour operators. It aims to ensure the long-term success of the air-inclusive holiday by influencing governments and opinion formers on the benefits to consumers of air-inclusive holidays compared to other types of holiday. Members pay an annual subscription based on the size of their organisation. All current members are also members of the Association of British Travel Agents (ABTA) and the two organisations work very closely together. In fact, it is likely that the two organisations will merge eventually.

Travel agents

The role of travel agents is to give advice and information and sell and administer bookings for a number of tour operators. They also sell flights, ferry bookings, car hire, insurance and accommodation as separate products. Thus, they are distributors of products. Many have a bureau de change. Increasingly, travel agents also do a little tour operating, for example putting together a holiday for a group. This is known as 'tailor-making' holidays. Some industry professionals believe that the role of the travel agent is in decline as many people are booking their own holidays and travel on the Internet or by telephone directly to tour operators.

> **Think it over ...**
>
> Last time you or your family went away on holiday, did you use a travel agent? Did you go on a package holiday? If so, why? If not, why not? Discuss the advantages and disadvantages of package holidays and making independent arrangements. Draw on your own experience where possible.

Types of travel agent

It is estimated that there are about 6500 travel agency shops, ranging in size from the multiples, with several hundred outlets each, to the individual shop. Most travel agents are part of a *multiple* chain. Examples you will be familiar with are Thomas Cook, Thomson and Going Places. These particular chains are linked to tour operators and may try to prioritise their own company's products. There has been a slight reduction in the number of branches of multiple chains in the last few years as customers choose to buy travel and tourism products through other means.

Miniples are small chains of travel agents, covering a region of the country.

Independent travel agents are usually run by their owner and a small team. There may be only one or two outlets. There are also independent chains. An example is Travelcare, which is the UK's largest independent travel chain with branches nationwide and sales in excess of £430 million per year. This company is part of the Co-operative group.

Implants are located within another business. They set up office within a company so that they are on hand to deal with the travel requirements of the company personnel.

Business travel agents specialise in the business market.

The Association of British Travel Agents is the body representing this sector. It also has tour operators as members.

> **CASE STUDY**
>
> ### ABTA in annual decline
>
> The number of ABTA agencies has decreased by 100 every year since 1991 and this year will be no exception, according to ABTA chief executive Ian Reynolds.
>
> He told delegates at the Abtech conference in London that there were 2800 agency members in 1991, compared with only 1500 this year. Reynolds attributed part of this fall to the consolidation within the industry as the Big Four bought up chains in the mid-1990s, and again more recently when the miniples followed suit.
>
> 'But aside from this, we are seeing an overall decline in retail outlets,' he said. 'It peaked in 1999 at more than 7000, but this has fallen by around 700 since then.
>
> 'This is natural rebalancing by the big vertically integrated groups as they drive new distribution channels such as the Internet and call centres.'
>
> 1 Explain the following terms:
>   * **The Big Four**
>   * **Distribution channel**
>   * **Miniples**
>   * **Call centres.**
> 2 Explain in your own words the reasons for the decline in numbers of retail travel agents.

Call centres

Call centres are widely used by banks and insurance companies as well as in the travel and tourism industry. It seems that customers increasingly prefer to book travel by telephone or the Internet rather than by visiting a travel agent.

Call centres are often located in out-of-town locations where rents, rates and labour are cheaper. TUI UK, a tour operator, has a call centre operating out of Newcastle under its Team Lincoln brand. Team Lincoln sells holidays. Some call centres are operator or airline owned and sell on behalf of that company exclusively, others are specialist call centres and handle calls and bookings for many companies.

Call centres rely on high staff productivity to be successful. They motivate staff through incentives such as bonuses on sales targets reached. Call answering time, call durations, sales and complaints ratios are carefully monitored.

Websites

Websites are the most recent means of distributing travel and tourism products and services.

Attractions

A survey of visits to visitor attractions is conducted annually by the national tourist boards of England, Northern Ireland, Scotland and Wales to monitor visitor and other trends. According to the survey, there are an estimated 6400 visitor attractions in the United Kingdom.

Attractions appeal to the domestic tourism market and the inbound tourism market. There are, of course, hundreds of different types of attractions but we can broadly divide them as follows:

* *Natural attractions* These include beautiful beaches, lakes and landscapes. In order to protect them, some are designated areas of outstanding beauty, national parks or heritage coasts.

* *Man-made attractions* Man-made attractions may still be historic; in the UK we have a wealth of historic houses, often cared for by the National Trust or English Heritage. We also have museums and galleries such as the Tate and the Tate Modern, the Victoria and Albert Museum and the Museum of Moving Image. These examples are in London, however there

The Colossus ride at Thorpe Park theme park

are museums throughout the country. Favourite man-made attractions are theme parks, for example Thorpe Park.

Events

Events such as the Edinburgh Festival or the Notting Hill Carnival attract many visitors. There are many events in the business tourism sector too, such as the World Travel Market.

Another way of categorising attractions is as paying and non-paying atractions. Museums, for example, are usually free, on the principle that we should all be able to view the nation's heritage. It is usually difficult to charge visitors to natural attractions as it means creating barriers to access. Non-paying attractions are still important for tourism as they attract visitors to an area and they will spend money on food, accommodation and shopping. Blackpool Pleasure Beach is the most popular free attraction, with an estimated 6.5 million visits each year. However, this is misleading, as although it is free to enter the Pleasure Beach, you have to pay to go on a ride.

CASE STUDY

Top attractions

The charts below show the top ten paid admission and free admission attractions in the UK.

Table 1.1 Top 10 paid admission attractions

ATTRACTION	REGION	2000	2001	2002	2003	% 02/03
British Airways London Eye	LON	3,300,000*	3,850,000*	4,100,000	3,700,000	–9.8
Tower of London	LON	2,303,167	2,019,183	1,940,856	1,972,263	1.6
Eden Project	SW	498,000	1,700,000	1,832,482*	1,404,372	–23.4
Flamingo Land Theme Park & Zoo	Y&H	1,301,000*	1,322,000*	1,393,300*	1,398,800*	0.4
Windermere Lake Cruises	NW	1,172,219	1,241,918	1,266,027	1,337,879	5.7
Legoland Windsor	SE	1,490,000	1,632,000	1,453,000	1,321,128	–9.1
New MetroLand	NE	650,000*	650,000*	810,000*	1,200,000*	48.2
Chester Zoo	NW	1,118,000	1,060,433	1,134,949	1,160,234	2.2
Kew Gardens	LON	860,340	989,352	987,266	1,079,424	9.3
Canterbury Cathedral	SE	1,263,140*	1,151,099*	1,110,529*	1,060,166*	–4.5

Table 1.2 Top 10 free admission attractions

ATTRACTION	REGION	2000	2001	2002	2003	% 02/03
Blackpool Pleasure Beach	NW	6,800,000	6,500,000	6,200,000	6,200,000	0.0
British Museum	LON	5,466,246*	4,800,938	4,607,311	4,584,000	–0.5
National Gallery	LON	4,897,690*	4,918,985*	4,130,973*	4,360,461*	5.6
Tate Modern	LON	3,873,887	3,551,885	4,661,449	3,895,746*	–16.4
Natural History Museum	LON	1,576,048	1,696,176	2,957,501	2,894,005	–2.2
Science Museum	LON	1,337,432	1,352,649	2,722,154	2,886,850	6.1
Victoria & Albert Museum	LON	933,150	1,060,235	2,210,302	2,257,325	2.1
Pleasure Theme Park	NW	2,100,000*	2,000,000*	2,000,000*	2,100,000*	5.0
Eastbourne Pier	SE	NK	2,000,000	1,900,000*	1,600,000*	–15.8
Pleasure Beach	EAST	1,500,000*	1,500,000*	1,500,000*	1,500,000*	0.0

* = estimate

1 **Study the tables and pick out the attractions with the biggest percentage change between 2002 and 2003.**

2 **How do you account for the increases or decreases?**
  You might need to research the individual websites of the attractions to find the relevant information.

3 **Discuss your findings with your group.**

To improve your knowledge of the UK visitor attractions sector, fill in the table below. Use your local TIC and the VisitBritain website to help you. Check your answers with your tutor.

Name of attraction	Two national examples	A local example
Historic house		
Garden		
Museum		
Art gallery		
Wildlife attraction		
Theme park		
Historic monument		
Religious building		

Whatever the visitor attraction, the main reason for the visit is the primary product or service. If you visit a gallery it is to see an exhibition of art, if you go to a stately home it is to admire the beauty of the architecture and learn about our history. When we go to theme parks it is to have fun on the various rides.

The primary product or service can change from time to time but rarely changes completely. If it were always exactly the same then there would be little reason for visitors to come back again. So, museums hold temporary exhibitions to attract people back again and theme parks introduce new rides regularly to entice us back. The primary product and service serves to attract visitors but is not always the main source of revenue.

Support services for the attractions sector

The *British Association of Leisure Parks, Piers and Attractions (BALPPA)* was founded in 1936. It is non-profit making and its role is to represent the interests of owners, managers, suppliers and developers in the UK's commercial leisure parks, piers, zoos and static attractions sector. It has about 300 members.

The *International Association of Amusement Parks and Attractions (IAAPA)* is a similar organisation to BALPPA, but is an international association and has members all over the world. The mission of the association is to promote safe operations, global development, professional growth and commercial success in the amusement industry.

Accommodation

Types of accommodation

There are many different types of accommodation available in the travel and tourism industry. They include:

* Hotels
* Guest accommodation
* Holiday parks and campsites
* Self-catering
* Youth hostels
* Campus.

According to the British Hospitality Association, there are approximately 22,000 hotels and guesthouses registered with the tourist boards, with an additional 16,000 bed-and-breakfasts. In addition there are thousands of unregistered establishments.

Hotels are in private ownership, with a large number of them having owner-operators, the average size being about 20 rooms. As with tour operations, the major groups have most influence in the industry.

An example of a major hotel group in the UK is the Moat House Group. There are over 30 Moat House hotels across the UK, from Glasgow in Scotland to Plymouth in the West Country. Moat House hotels are of three- or four-star standard and offer a range of good quality conference, meeting and business facilities to the corporate traveller. All hotels also offer a range of leisure breaks, which are featured on the website and within the Escapes brochure.

The major chains tend to be more impersonal, however they do provide consistency of quality throughout the world. For example, if you were to stay in a Mercure hotel in London or in Paris, the room would offer exactly the same facilities, and even the layout is often the same.

Many hotels are owned by international groups who encompass several chains within them, aiming at different types of customers. Examples are:

* Hilton
* Radisson
* Holiday Inn
* Accor.

Skills practice

1 Choose one of the above groups and conduct Internet research to find out the following:

- How they operate – fully owned or franchise
- How many hotels there are in the group
- Examples of country locations
- Products and services offered for the business market
- Examples of costs.

2 Compile your findings into an information sheet.

Hotels offer many products and services catering for different customers, and the prestigious and more expensive hotels like the Sofitel brand offer greater luxury. In addition, hotels cater for both business and leisure customers, so they need to have a range of products to suit each type. Conference customers may just come for the day and will need different services to residents.

Guest accommodation includes bed-and-breakfasts, guesthouses and farmhouses. Homeowners who wish to capitalise on any extra space they have available in their homes often run this type of accommodation. Many tourists find staying in a home environment charming and an opportunity to experience local culture. This type of accommodation is very popular in France where gîtes are rented out for holidays.

Holiday parks and campsites are popular with British tourists holidaying in France and Spain, although camping is probably less popular in the UK due to our inclement weather. Holiday parks, however, offer chalets and mobile homes so that tourists do not have to worry as much about the weather.

Self-catering accommodation may be on holiday parks or in rented apartments or houses. Cooking facilities are provided.

The Youth Hostel Association (YHA), which is a charity serving the needs of young people, runs *youth hostels* in the UK. However, you do not have to be a young person to be a member. It is very cheap to join the YHA and some of the hostels are of a very high standard, almost as good as hotels. There are 226 youth hostels in both city and rural locations. The original aim of the YHA was to promote love, care and understanding of the countryside in principle and in practice. There is also an International Youth Hostel federation with 5000 hostels in 60 countries. The YHA does not only provide accommodation but also a range of activity holidays.

Universities are keen to rent out their halls of residence outside term time. They encourage conference trade as they can also offer meeting rooms and catering facilities. This is an excellent means of using empty rooms and increasing revenue during students' holidays.

Grading standards

VisitBritain has created quality standards for a wide sector of accommodation in England. Scotland, Wales and Northern Ireland have their own schemes. Trained assessors determine the gradings.

Hotels are given a rating from one to five stars. The more stars the higher the quality and the greater the range of facilities and level of service provided.

Guest accommodation is rated from one to five diamonds. The more diamonds the higher the overall quality in areas such as cleanliness, service and hospitality, bedrooms, bathrooms and food.

Self-catering accommodation is also star rated from one to five. The more stars awarded to an establishment, the higher the level of quality. Establishments at higher rating levels also have to meet some additional requirement for facilities.

Holiday parks and campsites are also assessed using stars. One star denotes acceptable quality, five stars denotes exceptional quality.

The aim of the grading system is to make it easier for tourists to compare the quality of visitor accommodation offered around the country. However, as the Scottish and Welsh tourist boards use different systems and the English system uses a diamond system and a star system, it is still confusing.

When you travel abroad, you will find that there is no standard system. The star grading system is more or less accepted in Europe but cannot wholly be relied on. Tour operators tend to use their own grading standards so that they can indicate a level of quality to their customers. An example is the 'T' system adopted by Thomson.

Ancillary services

Most of the support or ancillary services for tourism are in the public sector. We have already discussed some of the public support and some of the voluntary support bodies in each sector.

The Department for Culture, Media and Sport (DCMS) is responsible for supporting the tourism industry at national level. In 1999 the government's overall strategy for the development of tourism was published in 'Tomorrow's Tourism'. This policy was reviewed and updated in 2004 and a new statement of the roles and responsibilities in tourism of the DCMS, VisitBritain, regional development agencies, local government and the Tourism Alliance was issued, covering the following areas for action:

* Marketing and e-tourism
* Product quality – introducing common standards for accommodation grading schemes

* Workforce skills, supporting People1st, the sector skills council
* Improved data and statistics.

Tourism Review and Implementation Group (TRIG)

This group was established in 2004. It has members from industry, the public sector and from education. Its role is to consider the wider issues affecting tourism and to monitor progress in the areas outlined above.

Tourism Alliance

This body was established in 2001 to represent the tourism sector. Its members are leading trade associations. It is a Confederation of British Industry (CBI) supported initiative. The CBI provides the secretariat and research capacity for the Alliance. Its purpose is to present the industry's views and concerns more effectively to the government and to the EU.

Other government departments have responsibilities for areas of tourism. The Department for Transport looks after aviation, railways, roads, and the London Underground. The Department for Education and Skills has responsibility for sector skills councils and training organisations. The Department for the Environment, Food and Rural Affairs (DEFRA) is responsible for issues affecting the countryside, wildlife and waterways, among others.

Another government department of importance to tourism is the Foreign and Commonwealth Office (FCO). The FCO provides a consular service around the world whose function is to help British nationals in trouble, and of course to promote Britain.

National tourist boards

The United Kingdom has four tourist boards: VisitBritain, VisitScotland, the Northern Ireland Tourist Board and the Wales Tourist Board.

VisitBritain reports to the Department for Culture, Media and Sport (DCMS). The Wales Tourist Board reports to the National Assembly for Wales and VisitScotland reports to the Scottish Executive.

VisitBritain

The role of VisitBritain is to market Britain to the rest of the world and England to the British. Formed by the merger of the British Tourist Authority and the English Tourism Council, its mission is to build the value of tourism by creating world-class destination brands and marketing campaigns. It also aims to build partnerships with other organisations which have a stake in British and English tourism. These organisations include the British Council, UK Inbound, the British Hospitality Association and the UK Immigration Service.

Skills practice

You will use the VisitBritain website many times during your studies as it is an invaluable tourism resource. For this activity access the website www.visitbritain.com to find out the objectives of the organisation. Make a note of them and ensure you understand the terminology used. You should be able to answer the following questions:

- What is a domestic tourist?
- What are the national tourist boards?
- What is meant by impartial tourist information?
- Who funds VisitBritain?
- What is the current grant given to VisitBritain?
- What are regional development agencies?
- Where are VisitBritain's overseas offices?

Part of VisitBritain's role is to advise the government and other bodies on issues that might affect the British tourism industry. The aim is to provide advice that reflects the needs of both the tourism industry and the tourist, and to recommend courses of action to the government.

The overseas offices work closely with British diplomatic and cultural staff, the local travel trade and media to stimulate interest in Britain.

Another example of the role of VisitBritain is its campaign to persuade high-spending tourists to come to the UK. There is no point in having lots of inbound tourists if they don't spend their money and boost our economy. VisitBritain launched a magazine called *So British* aimed chiefly at high-spending US tourists but also at emerging markets like Russia. The magazine features luxury British brands like Harrods, Barbour and Wedgewood, and carries articles on destinations in Britain.

VisitBritain owns the VB-grading scheme, which is administered by the regional tourist boards. This was covered earlier (pages 24–25).

Regional development agencies and regional tourist boards

Regional development agencies (RDAs) have responsibility for tourism in their regions and usually work closely with regional tourist boards.

Between 2003 and 2006, the RDAs are to receive £3.6 million per annum from the DCMS, specifically for tourism. This money is to be passed on to the regional tourist boards until the end of 2005. The RDAs will determine what objectives and targets the RTBs should meet in return for the funds. After this the money will still be earmarked for tourism but not necessarily through the tourist boards. This is because there has been overlap between the role of RDAs in tourism and the tourist boards.

Therefore, in some regions the regional tourist boards have disappeared as separate bodies and have been subsumed under the RDAs. In other regions the role of the tourist board has been altered to that of 'Destination Management Organisation' set up and monitored by the RDAs.

Below are some examples of the regional organisations:

* Tourism South East (www.seeda.org.uk)
* VisitLondon (www.londontouristboard.com)
* North West Tourist Board (www.northwesttourism.net)
* The Mersey Partnership (www.visitliverpool.com)
* Marketing Manchester (www.destinationmanchester.com)

The organisations are not totally dependent on government funding. Funds can be raised from business membership fees and from the provision of training courses to tourism organisations and employees.

Skills practice

Choose one of the example organisations listed and visit its website. Find out:
- Who runs the organisation?
- Who are the partner organisations?
- How does it raise funds?
- What is the primary role of the organisation?

and represent them, particularly to the government. In addition, the role of the public sector is one of supporting and guiding different businesses so that everyone – tourists, employees and management – can benefit from tourism, whilst minimising problems and issues.

Local authority tourism departments

Local authorities have an important role in supporting the tourism industry because of their statutory duties and because they recognise that tourism is a major contributor towards the economy, so they have tourism departments and plans. Most towns also have a tourist information centre (TIC). These are run independently, and most are subsidised by the local council. They all rely heavily on generating income to ensure their financial viability.

Tourist information centres provide a full information service for both residents and visitors. They give information on visitor attractions and on accommodation. They usually provide a booking service for accommodation. The TIC often incorporates a shop selling locally made crafts and gifts as well as books on local interests. The shop is more than a service for visitors; it is an important means of generating funds.

Skills practice

Visit your local tourist information centre. Your tutor may wish to organise a group visit. Find out what services it offers. Try to determine how many of its services generate revenue for the TIC. Discuss your findings with the group when you return.

Support networks

The travel and tourism industry is made up of diverse businesses of all different sizes and locations. It is essential that there are means by which these disparate organisations work together. In each sector of the industry the regulatory and trade bodies advise their members

Skills practice

Match up the following businesses with the relevant support organisations.

Business	Support organisation
Travel agent starting up	AUC
Passenger wishing to complain about an airline	ABTA
Tour operator needing an operating licence	TIC
Guest accommodation wishing to be graded	ATOL
A traveller wanting information about crime in Turkey	FCO
A tour operator targeting US tourists	DCMS
A regional development agency needing more funding for tourism development	UK Inbound

If you cannot remember what all these initials mean, look at the information earlier, in each section.

Interrelationships and interdependencies

Horizontal and vertical integration

Having looked at all the different sectors of the travel and tourism industry, it is apparent that the various businesses cannot work in isolation. Each of them relies on others for its success. In this section we will examine how businesses work together and who needs whom.

The chain of distribution and integration

The chain of distribution is the means of getting the product to the consumer. It applies in any industry and traditionally takes this form.

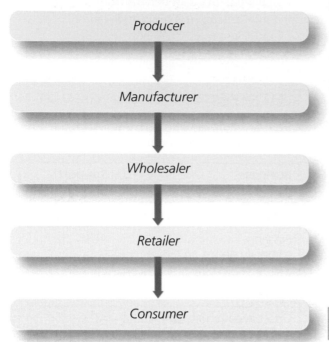

Figure 1.4 The traditional chain of distribution

In the travel and tourism industry there is also a traditional chain of distribution:

Figure 1.5 The traditional chain of distribution in the travel and tourism industry

In this traditional chain of distribution, businesses fit neatly into a category, for example travel agent, and perform the role of that business. However, the industry is much more complex than that, and in many cases the traditional chain has been shortened. Figure 1.6 gives some examples.

In addition to these permutations, companies do not stick rigidly to one line of business. They tend to buy or merge with other businesses, always striving for greater commercial success and market dominance. When companies do this it is known as vertical and horizontal integration. Tour operators have bought or created airlines, hotels and travel agencies. This means they own all the different components in the chain of distribution and are able to control the whole operation. They claim that this gives them economies of scale and allows them to offer better prices to customers. It can also mean that smaller operators are forced out of business.

Key term

Economies of scale These occur when a company is able to spread its costs over mass-produced goods or services. The economies can be achieved through discounts of bulk purchasing, rationalisation of administration systems and management, and lower production costs.

Integration takes two forms: vertical and horizontal. If a tour operator buys another tour operator at the same level in the chain of distribution, this is known as *horizontal integration*. In 2004, First Choice made 11 acquisitions at a cost of £28.3 million. The acquisitions included the Adventure Company, Let's Trek Australia, Trips Worldwide, StudentCity.com and the Adventure Center.

Skills practice

Take a closer look at First Choice. Go to the history page on its website. Find out which companies have been acquired and sold from 2000 onwards. What do you think are the reasons for these sales and acquisitions? Make notes and compare them with your group.

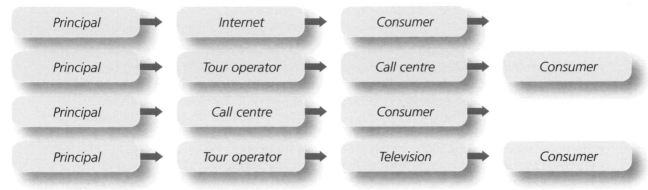

Figure 1.6 Shortened version of traditional chain of distribution

Vertical integration occurs when two companies at different levels in the chain of distribution merge or are bought. This may be backwards integration, for example a tour operator buys a hotel, or forward integration, for example a tour operator buys a travel agency.

All of the major tour operators in the UK are vertically and horizontally integrated, owning their own travel agencies, airlines and hotels, besides different tour operating businesses. In fact their operations are not limited to the UK; all are global operations.

There are those who think that vertical integration is no longer suitable for today's market. Capital is tied up in assets and is subject to risk.

Also, if customers do not want to buy from the high street agencies, then many of the chain stores will close as tour operators invest in other types of distribution.

Key term

Horizontal integration This occurs when companies are bought out or merged at the same level in the chain of distribution. Relevant examples are one travel agency buying out another one or a tour operator buying another one. Often original brand names are retained, so the general public are unaware of the takeover.

CASE STUDY

Holidaybreak

Overview

Holidaybreak is **the UK's leading operator of specialist holiday businesses**, all with high standards of service and product quality and market leading positions in the UK and other major European markets. In 2004 the Group provided 2.3m holidays in over 100 countries worldwide.

The business generates substantial cash, delivers double-digit margins and has proven resilient in the face of changing market conditions. The Group has the financial strength to respond to changing market trends and exploit opportunities for both organic and acquisition based growth whilst paying an attractive dividend.

History

1973: Eurocamp Travel founded

1988: Management Buy Out

1991: Eurocamp floated on the LSE

1995: Acquisition of Superbreak

1998: Acquisition of Keycamp

1998: Holding company renamed Holidaybreak

2000: Acquisition of Explore

2004: Acquisition of Dutch on-line leisure business BRC

2005: Acquisition of Dutch adventure business Djoser

Hotel Breaks

The Hotel Breaks division's core business specialises in UK and overseas leisure breaks. It is the principal provider of domestic short breaks to UK travel agents and has also been rapidly developing direct and internet distribution. The division continues to introduce new products and distribution channels to build on an outstanding record of success in recent years.

- 2004 Turnover: £120.9m
- 1.7m holidays sold in year to 30/9/04
- Strong relationship with 3000+ hotels, 250+ hotel suppliers
- Flexible cost base – no commitment to hotel room allocations
- Fixed selling margin
- Strongly cash generative – negative working capital
- Operates in a growth sector
- Acquired Dutch market leader in on-line leisure breaks Bookit (BRC) for £23.1m on 22 December, 2004

Adventure Holidays

Three businesses, Explore (UK), Djoser (Netherlands) and Regal Dive; market leaders in 'soft' adventure and scuba diving holidays. Explore offers a range of cycling, walking and trekking adventure short breaks and family adventures as well as the core worldwide, escorted tours programme. Explore adds genuine value to the customer experience, creating holidays which would be difficult or impossible for the DIY customer to replicate.

- 2004 Turnover: £37.4m
- 41,800 holidays sold in year to 30/9/04
- Increasing demand for active, special interest and unusual holidays
- Over 400 different tours to 107 countries
- Tight control of tour load factors underpins profitability
- Flexible cost base – Low commitment to flight seats
- Acquired Dutch market leader Djoser for £15.7m on 19 January 2005

Camping

The original part of the Holidaybreak group. Provides pre-sited mobile-home and canvas holidays on high-grade, third-party owned campsites throughout Europe. Customers are mainly families who book direct, attracted by good quality self-catering accommodation in desirable locations, with excellent leisure amenities. Flexibility, informality, independence and added value services all add to the appeal.

- 2004 Turnover: £123.2m
- 570,000 holidays sold in year to 30/9/04
- Market leading brands – Eurocamp and Keycamp
- Customers from nine different countries, mainly UK, Holland and Germany
- 9700 mobile-homes and 4500 tents on 212 campsites in France, Italy and seven other countries
- High levels of customer satisfaction and repeats

1 What is a management buy out?
2 Give examples of horizontal and vertical integration within Holidaybreak.
3 Why do you think Holidaybreak operates in the Dutch market?
4 Which was the most profitable division in 2004?
5 Which division is expected to achieve most growth in the near future? Why?
6 Find out what kind of adventure holidays are offered by Explore.

1.4 The scale of the UK travel and tourism industry

International tourism

Visitor numbers and spending

International tourist arrivals reached an all-time record of 760 million in 2004, according to data produced by the World Tourism Organisation. This is an amazing increase when you consider the setbacks international tourism has had to contend with over the last few years, including disasters such as the 9/11 terrorism attack, Sars and the Iraq war. However, 2004 figures do not reflect the impact of the tsunami disaster as it occurred in the last week of the year. The figures show an increase in international arrivals of 69 million.

Key terms

Arrivals The number of visitors to a destination.
International arrivals The total number of tourists visiting all destinations.
Receipts The amount of money spent by tourists in a destination.
International receipts The total amount spent on tourism throughout the world.

Skills practice

Source: World Tourism Organisation (WTO)

Figure 1.7 Origin of international arrivals

Study Figure 1.7, showing the origin of the 'new' tourists, that is where the increases in international arrivals have originated.

Consider Europe and analyse the reasons for the increase in numbers of tourists. You should consider:
- Exchange rate fluctuations
- The increase in members of the EU (to 25 states)
- Emerging destinations
- Economic factors.

The world's top destination is France, as you can see in Table 1.3. However, when you study Table 1.4 you will note that although France receives the most visitors, it is the United States that makes the most in terms of receipts.

Table 1.3 World's top 10 tourist destinations

Rank	Series	International Tourist Arrivals (million)		
		2000	2001	2002
World		687	684	703
1 France	TF	77.2	75.2	77.0
2 Spain	TF	47.9	50.1	51.7
3 United States	TF	50.9	44.9	41.9
4 Italy	TF	41.2	39.6	39.8
5 China	TF	31.2	33.2	36.8
6 United Kingdom	VF	25.2	22.8	24.2
7 Canada	TF	19.6	19.7	20.1
8 Mexico	TF	20.6	19.8	19.7
9 Austria	TCE	18.0	18.2	18.6
10 Germany	TCE	19.0	17.9	18.0

Table 1.4 World's top 10 tourist earners

Rank	International Tourism Receipts (US$ billion)		
	2000	2001	2002
World	473	459	474
1 United States	82.4	71.9	66.5
2 Spain	31.5	32.9	33.6
3 France	30.8	30.0	32.3
4 Italy	27.5	25.8	26.9
5 China	16.2	17.8	20.4
6 Germany	18.5	18.4	19.2
7 United Kingdom	19.5	16.3	17.6
8 Austria	9.9	10.1	11.2
9 Hong Kong (China)	7.9	8.3	10.1
10 Greece	9.2	9.4	9.7

Source: World Tourism Organisation (WTO)©
(Data as collected by WTO September 2003)

Skills practice

Study Tables 1.3 and 1.4 showing top destinations (receivers) and top earners.

- Why are these two charts not exactly the same?

- Give reasons for the appeal of the top three destinations to international tourists.

- Determine which destinations are undergoing a decline or increase in arrivals and analyse the reasons for the increase or decline. Present your findings in a brief report.

Visit www.world-tourism.org for further research. You will need to find the facts and figures page.

Levels of employment

According to the World Travel and Tourism Council, the travel and tourism industry worldwide will directly provide 74 million jobs in 2005. This represents 2.8 per cent of total employment. However, travel and tourism impacts on other industries and indirectly creates jobs in those industries. Examples include construction, which employs people to build roads and hotels, and agriculture, where farmers grow produce for tourists. When these jobs are added into the equation, the scale of employment is even greater, representing 221 million jobs or 8.3 per cent of total employment, worldwide.

UK tourism

Visitor spending

Tourism was worth £74.2 billion to the UK economy in 2003. Most of this expenditure is from domestic tourism, not from overseas visitors.

Table 1.5 Expenditure of overseas and domestic tourists

SPENDING BY OVERSEAS RESIDENTS	£ BILLION
Visits to the UK	11.9
Fares to the UK carriers	3.2

SPENDING BY DOMESTIC RESIDENTS	£ BILLION
Trips of 1+ nights	26.5
Day trips	31.8
Rent for second ownership	0.94

The figures are calculated using the new tourism satellite accounting (TSA) methodology, which measures all tourism-related expenditure. Tourism satellite accounting has been developed by the World Tourism Organisation, so that there is a common system which can be used internationally. It is described by WTO as

> *'a statistical instrument, a "satellite" revolving around the concepts, definitions and aggregates of the system of national accounts, that makes it possible to make valid comparisons with other industries, as well as between countries or groups of countries'.*

The impact on the economy of incoming and outbound tourism is recorded in the Balance of Payments. Each sector of the economy is measured in terms of its imports and exports. Travel services have their own balance, which contributes to the overall Balance of Payments. Unfortunately, the travel services balance shows a deficit (£15.8 billion in 2003) and has done so for some years. This means that more money is spent by UK residents travelling overseas than by inbound tourists and domestic tourists. Transport is shown separately to travel services.

Key term

Balance of Payments This is one of the UK's key economic statistics. It measures the economic transactions between the UK and the rest of the world. It tells us the difference between spending on imports and exports.

Skills practice

Find out what the current travel balance is. You can find this in *The Pink Book*, a government publication, in your library or online. Look at the transport balance also. Is there a deficit or a surplus? Discuss your findings with your tutor.

Think it over ...

How do you think the travel services deficit could be overturned?

Visitor numbers

Incoming and outgoing tourists

In 2004 there was a record high of 27.7 million incoming tourism visits, an increase of 12 per cent on 2003. The value of this business to the economy was £13 billion. This represented a 10 per cent increase in spending from 2003 (from 11.9 billion).

Figure 1.8 shows overseas residents' visits to the UK and UK residents' visits abroad.

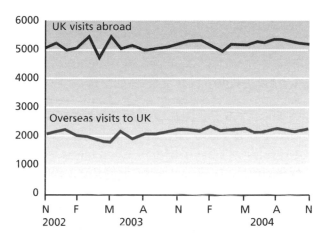

Figure 1.8 Overseas residents' visits to the UK and UK residents' visits abroad

In the same period, UK outgoing tourist visits also rose, to 63.5 million visits. The number of visits to Western Europe hardly changed, but visits to North America rose by 15 per cent, possibly reflecting the strength of the pound against the dollar.

Think it over ...

How do you think we know how many visitors come to the UK? The data is collected in the International Passenger Survey for the Office of National Statistics. Inbound visitors are questioned at airports and seaports, as are people travelling outbound. Around 250,000 interviews are carried out per year, representing 0.2 per cent of all travellers.

Visitor flow within the UK

Day visits represent the largest segment of domestic tourism with 60 per cent of expenditure.

Remember that these figures are recorded separately in the Day Visitors Survey.

Domestic tourism expenditure includes expenditure as a result of resident visitors travelling within their country and occurs en route, at the place visited, and in advance on spending for the trip.

In 2003 UK residents took:

* 70.5 million holidays of one night or more, spending £13.7 billion

* 22.3 million overnight business trips, spending £6.1 billion

* 34.3 million overnight trips to friends and relatives, spending £3.4 billion.

The UK Tourism Survey is very detailed and shows information including number of tourist trips, number of tourist nights, spending, breakdown between England, Scotland and Wales, and purpose of trip. You can find the survey data at Star UK.

Skills practice

1 Are inbound tourists or domestic tourists more important to the UK economy? Find current statistics to support your argument.

2 What can be done to
   • encourage more domestic tourists
   • encourage more inbound tourists?

Levels of employment

There are an estimated 2.2 million jobs in tourism in Great Britain, some 7.7 per cent of all people in employment in the UK. There are more jobs in tourism than in construction or transport. Approximately 156,000 of these jobs are in self-employment.

Table 1.6 Employment in travel and tourism

	TOTAL (MILLIONS)	TOURISM-RELATED (MILLIONS)
Total employment	28.1	2.17
Employee jobs	24.4	2.01
Self-employment	3.6	0.16

Key UK destination regions

The distribution of domestic tourism is measured by tourist board region, with the South West of England attracting most tourists, closely followed by the South East. The North East attracts the least number of domestic tourists.

Table 1.7 shows the top cities/towns visited by inbound tourists in 2003. Table 1.8 shows the top cities/towns visited by inbound tourists in 2002.

Table 1.7 Top 10 cities/towns visited by inbound tourists in 2003

10 CITIES/TOWNS VISITED BY OVERSEAS RESIDENTS, 2003	
City/Town	Visits (000s)
London	11,700
Edinburgh	770
Manchester	740
Birmingham	720
Glasgow	420
Oxford	360
Cambridge	310
Bristol	290
Brighton/Hove	270
Liverpool	270

Table 1.8 Top 10 cities/towns visited by inbound tourists in 2002

10 CITIES/TOWNS VISITED BY OVERSEAS RESIDENTS, 2002	
City/Town	Visits (000s)
London	11,600
Edinburgh	850
Birmingham	670
Manchester	590
Glasgow	400
Oxford	390
Bristol	310
Cambridge	280
Cardiff	280
Newcastle-upon-Tyne	240

Skills practice

Visit the website for your own tourist board region. Find out how many visitors came to your region last year. Is there an increase or decrease in the number of tourists? How do you explain the increase or decrease?

Think it over ...

Why do you think the towns in the tables opposite are the most popular with inbound tourists? Are domestic tourists likely to visit the same towns?

Local tourism

CASE STUDY

Tourism in Cambridge – the overall picture

Approximately 4.1 million visitors visited Cambridge in 1999. This was higher than previously estimated, largely due to a revised definition of day visitors.

Fifteen per cent of the visitors stayed. Half of staying visitors were from overseas. In addition to the 4.1 million visitors to Cambridge City, 3.2 million visitors visited South Cambridgeshire; 10 per cent of these were staying visitors.

The number of visitors to Cambridge more than doubled from the mid-1970s to the late 1980s. Since then growth has levelled off, and the late 1990s saw a decline.

In 2000 there was a drop by 10 per cent in visitors to the tourist information centre (TIC), and a drop of 7 per cent in 2001.

The majority of visitors come during the peak season: 38 per cent came in June, July and August in 2001. However, this is not as true as it used to be. In 1975, 54 per cent of visitors came in the summer.

It is estimated that the overall value of tourism to Cambridge is over £260 million. It supports 5500 full-time jobs, about 8 per cent of the total, and an additional 2000 part-time and seasonal jobs.

1 Research tourism in your own area and try to find similar information to that above. You should research your town council website, your regional tourist board website and your local tourist information centre.
Try to find out:

- The amount of spending on tourism in your area
- The numbers of inbound tourists
- The numbers of domestic tourists
- The number of jobs provided in tourism.

2 Compile a short report comparing your town with Cambridge.

Knowledge check

1 Give examples of three types of tourism.

2 What is the impact of the Internet on travel and tourism?

3 Explain what is meant by the exchange rate.

4 Give two examples of the positive economic impact of tourism.

5 Give two examples of the negative environmental impact of tourism.

6 How do low-cost airlines keep costs down?

7 Give three examples of motivating factors for tourism.

8 What is a scheduled airline?

9 What does ABTA do?

10 Who regulates airlines in the UK?

11 Name three types of accommodation.

12 Describe the traditional chain of distribution in travel and tourism.

13 An independent travel agent is bought out by a major travel agency chain. Is this an example of vertical integration or horizontal integration?

14 Give three examples of distribution methods that a tour operator could use.

15 Explain backwards integration.

16 Give examples of two tour operators who also own airlines.

The travel and tourism customer

Introduction

Customer service in travel and tourism is a core unit for the qualification and an important skill for everyone working within the industry. It is essential that travel and tourism organisations focus on their customers. They need to provide products and services that meet their customers' needs and expectations. Furthermore, their staff must provide excellent customer service. Many organisations provide similar products and services and the level of customer service provided could well determine with whom potential customers book. It will also influence the organisation's profitability and their competitive edge!

This unit will develop your understanding of why customers are the focus of travel and tourism organisations and the methods used by travel and tourism organisations to monitor and measure whether their customer service levels meet expectations. It will also give you the opportunity to develop skills so that you can deliver excellent customer service.

How you will be assessed

Throughout the unit, activities and tasks will help you to develop your knowledge and understanding. Some of these could be used as material for the final assessment. Case studies are included to add industry relevance and demonstrate how aspects of customer service are carried out in particular travel and tourism organisations.

After completing the unit you will achieve the following outcomes:

* Understand the organisation and its customers
* Provide effective customer service
* Measure and monitor the customer service of an organisation.

2.1 The organisation and its customers

The importance of customer focus

The travel and tourism industry is highly competitive. Many organisations are offering similar products and services, often within the same price range. How will customers decide with whom to travel? There are many contributing factors – any of which could result in a loyal customer or alternatively a lost sale. Customers' purchasing decisions are usually made on the basis of the following:

* The level of customer service offered – e.g. the friendliness of the hotel receptionist and her professional appearance; the fact that a phone call was returned within the hour, the prompt response to a letter, the cleanliness of an aircraft or an excellent website

* The product on offer – e.g. the daytime flights, the location of the hotel, a local departure airport, the size of the cruise ship or the entertainment on offer.

The product can be enhanced by:

* Additional (purchasable) services provided – e.g. kids clubs in beach resorts, ski lessons with an English-speaking instructor, airport transfers in a taxi, upgrades on an airline

* Free services included – e.g. a meet and greet service provided by the airport parking company, complementary meals, extra legroom and wider seats provided by the airline, free water sports on a summer sun holiday.

Travel and tourism organisations need to get all of these factors right. It is recognised that the provision of appropriate products and services, together with excellent customer service, is essential to a travel and tourism organisation. Not only does the travel and tourism organisation benefit, but its staff and customers do too.

Needs and expectations

When providing excellent customer service, organisations are aiming to meet their customers' *needs* and exceed their *expectations*. Customers buy products or services because they believe they need them, for example a drink, a car, a holiday. Expectations refer to what the customer expects from the product or service. A car may satisfy a need (i.e. for transport) but not meet expectations if it does not run quite as smoothly as expected, hasn't got a CD player or a sunroof! So, if a customer enters a travel agency needing a summer holiday for a family of four, he/she may also have certain expectations about the costs, ideal locations and activities available. You could meet his/her needs (by selling a holiday for this family), but to exceed his/her expectations you will need to also provide details of excursion possibilities, airport transfers, free child places and car hire.

Customer benefits

If an organisation is customer focused, satisfied customers will be the result – that is, they will have been greeted warmly, been dealt with by friendly and efficient staff, have received the goods or services they want. They will go away stress-free, having had their needs met and an enjoyable experience!

Over the long-term customer loyalty will develop, that is a customer would not dream of going elsewhere! They will tell their friends about your products and services too.

Think it over ...

Recall a situation when you received excellent customer service and/or purchased a product that exceeded expectations. Describe the incident to a partner. What aspects made it an excellent experience? How did it make you feel?

Providing customers with the products and services they want and as a result dealing with satisfied customers is very satisfying for employees. It is rewarding to be thanked for finding the perfect destination for a family holiday, your kindness, efficiency, solving a potential problem or providing advice. Positive feedback from customers provides job satisfaction and a feeling of well-being. This can contribute towards a good working environment in which

Benefits of Customer Focus

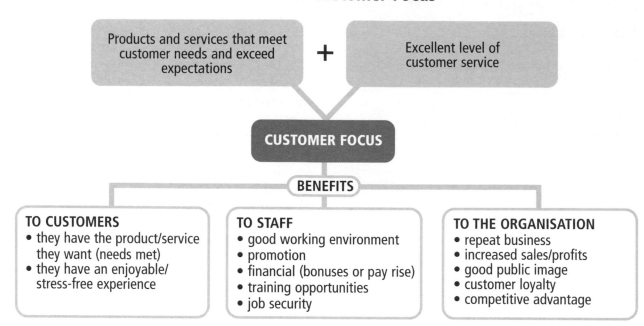

Figure 2.1 Benefits of customer focus

everyone is working as a team and supporting each other. For some individuals this may lead to promotion – maybe with a pay increase! The end result of excellent service and satisfied customers is a staff team who are productive and positive.

A further benefit to staff may include job security – after all with a good sales record, returning customers and positive feedback your position in the organisation will be secure. This may enhance your prospects for training and promotion – and may give you a sense of personal satisfaction as well as financial security.

Benefits to the organisation

All organisations are dependent upon their customers. Whether public, private or voluntary, all aim to provide a high level of customer satisfaction, so that the customers return (repeat business), and ensure the continuation of business. Increased sales may result from repeat business or the very fact that the satisfied customers tell other people – who then wish to purchase the same product or service. All result in increased profit for the organisation.

The public image of a company refers to the view held of that company by the general public.

This will be influenced by what you read in the press or hear about the organisation from your friends. It will also be influenced by the service you receive from sales consultants, your experience of the product and after-sales service.

For example, imagine you book a flight on the Internet. You may already have an image of the airline from previous experiences or word of mouth. However, this will also be influenced by the design of the website, its ease of use, the destinations available. Once on the flight your image will be further amended by the appearance and customer service levels of the cabin crew and whether or not you and your luggage arrive at the same destination on time! The image you had of the airline before the flight could be very different to the one you have when you arrive at your destination.

Competitive advantage may also result from excellent customer service. Customers will choose to travel with those companies that offer a reliable and consistent service. This image, as well as the increased bookings, means that those companies who offer a good service literally have an advantage over their competitors.

Key terms

Customer loyalty If a customer receives consistently good service from an organisation they will want to continue to travel with it. They become loyal to that particular organisation because they can rely on their products and services.

Competitive advantage An organisation strives to be better than (have an advantage over) its competitors. This could be through better pricing or a more attractive product. It could also be due to a higher level of customer service!

Public image This is the impression that we (the general public) may have of an organisation. This may be good or bad and could be formed by the press, TV, brochures or 'word of mouth'.

CASE STUDY

A high street hero

Kristina Hulme, managing partner at Travel By Design in Cheshire, explains how she gives her customers a service they'll never forget.

'A travel agent's job is to match the right holiday to the right client and then bank their commission, right? Wrong. If you want to keep customers coming back, it's no longer enough just to press the 'book' button: you have to go the extra mile.

'Let me give you some examples. We once had a couple who wanted to drive down California's Pacific Highway in their red Pontiac Sunbird, but we'd heard about major roadworks along the way. So we telephoned the Californian equivalent of the Highways Agency, which told us where the detour was, so we managed to plan the couple's route accordingly. Needless to say, the clients were amazed.

'Another time, we were booking a couple on a cruise, and they told us: "We want a cabin where you can walk around three sides of the bed." We didn't ask why, but we did phone the ship to find out whether it would be possible, and which cabin would be suitable.

'Our latest request was from a lady on her honeymoon. The weather had turned bad, she was unhappy and she wanted to be moved to a warmer place. We contacted the regional weather centre, found the weather was more settled on another island and moved her and her husband to a place where they sunbathed under clear skies for the rest of their stay. We had the BBC Weather Centre and a very helpful tour operator to thank for that.

'You need the cooperation of the tour operator when going the extra mile; you also need a good relationship with hotel groups and other companies. Being a member of AITO has helped us with this.

'Also, being a Canadian specialist has allowed us to increase our knowledge and get to know the people that matter at the operator companies and elsewhere – once, when a railway enthusiast was having trouble getting a "footplate pass" while travelling by rail through the Rocky Mountains, we contacted our friends at the Canadian High Commission who pointed him in the right direction. Another dream come true.

'Yet we're just an ordinary travel agency with clients who have extraordinary requests. I know we will never be rich and all this extra work eats into our commission, but we do have a high level of customer satisfaction and many repeat clients.

'The only trouble is, when they come back they ask us to do it all over again.'

Source: TIG Supplement Sept/Oct 2004

1 **What does Kristina mean by 'going the extra mile'? Give examples.**
2 **What helps her do this?**
3 **What are the benefits?**

CASE STUDY

Cruise cancelled due to blocked toilets

Thomson has been forced to scrap a cruise on its newly delivered ship, *Thomson Celebration*, due to 'plumbing problems'.

The majority of passengers were flown home from Lisbon on the sixth day of the two-week voyage from Southampton – only its third cruise.

The ship first encountered difficulties with blocked vacuum toilets on the third day of the cruise in Bilbao, when all 1180 passengers were put up in hotels as engineers worked all night to try and resolve the problem.

Thomson said the vessel was fixed and passengers returned to the vessel last Wednesday morning, but the problem recurred again on Thursday evening.

Three aircraft were deployed to fly passengers home to Gatwick and Bournemouth.

Passengers are being refunded the cost of the cruise and are being offered 25 per cent off a future cruise.

Thomson said in a statement: 'Due to ongoing problems with the plumbing system onboard the *Thomson Celebration*, regrettably Thomson has taken the decision to cancel its current cruise.

'Because a large number of cabins and bathrooms in public areas have been affected the decision was made to cancel the cruise when the ship arrives in Lisbon today, on day six of its cruise.

'Thomson is sincerely sorry for the disappointment and inconvenience it has caused to its cruise customers.'

About 500 people opted to stay on board the ship due to arrive back in Southampton today.

1 **Outline the problems encountered by the Thomson cruise**
2 **What actions were taken?**
3 **Name similar incidents that have occurred to other travel and tourism organisations. You may need to research these in the travel press.**
4 **What is the impact of such an incident on the organisation?**

Skills practice

Use the Internet to investigate the aims and objectives of three travel and tourism organisations. You may also wish to look at their mission statements. Do these organisations have a customer focus? Support your answers with evidence.

Skills practice

1 It makes financial sense for organisations to be customer focused. After all it costs five times as much to attract a new customer as to retain an existing one. List the costs involved in attracting new customers and those involved in retaining existing ones.

2 It is estimated that dissatisfied customers tell between six and eight other people while satisfied customers tell one. What implication does this have for organisations?

Think it over ...

The only people from an airline that customers meet are the cabin crew and check-in staff, while the resort representatives will be the only person the customers meet from a tour operator. These staff are referred to as 'frontline staff'. They are, quite literally, the face of the company! They play a key role in determining customer satisfaction levels. It is therefore essential that travel organisations train frontline staff well – the costs of doing so far outweigh the costs of poor service.

Can you give other examples of frontline staff?

We have established that to be customer focused, travel organisations must offer products and services to meet customers' needs. To do this they must firstly establish who their customers are.

Who are the customers?

We have already established that the objective of customer service is to meet customer needs and exceed their expectations. In order to do this we must first understand our customers' needs – but this is easier said that done. After all, customers are not one homogenous group. There are many different types of customers, all of whom have different needs. To be able to provide excellent customer service, organisations must understand their customers, recognise their differing needs and provide products and services that meet their requirements. For example, a tour operator will provide a different holiday and range of excursions for a single person, a group of young people wanting to go clubbing and a couple wanting to escape the British winter. Similarly, if on a day trip to a theme park, a young couple will have different needs to a family with two young children.

Before we examine the different customer types we must first differentiate between internal and external customers.

Internal and external customers

Colleagues and suppliers are known as *internal customers*, while people outside the organisation – that is, those who buy the products and services – are known as *external customers*.

We have already discussed why it is so important to provide excellent customer care, but it is perhaps more obvious why caring for external customers is so important. After all an organisation is dependent upon those who buy its products and services. Without external customers organisations don't exist – they need sales to make profits to pay wages.

But we sometimes need reminding that internal customer service is also important to an organisation. At a simple level, how you deal with colleagues, behave in the office and your level of efficiency will all affect your working relationships. This can impact upon how well a team works together, relationships with managers and overall productivity. All of these can also have an impact on job satisfaction and staff morale – which in turn can impact on the customer service provided.

The following are internal customers.

✱ Colleagues who work together. This may be on a daily basis, for example in a travel agency, or on an *ad hoc* basis, for example cabin crew.

✱ People in different departments who support the customer-facing staff: accounts departments are a good example of support staff whose levels of service can have a high impact. (How quickly they send out refunds or are able to answer invoice queries will have a direct impact on the level of customer service front office staff can provide.) Similarly, if the IT team tell you they are too busy to sort out your technical problem today, it will really affect your sales!

✱ Managers and supervisors. How quickly, efficiently and accurately you deliver

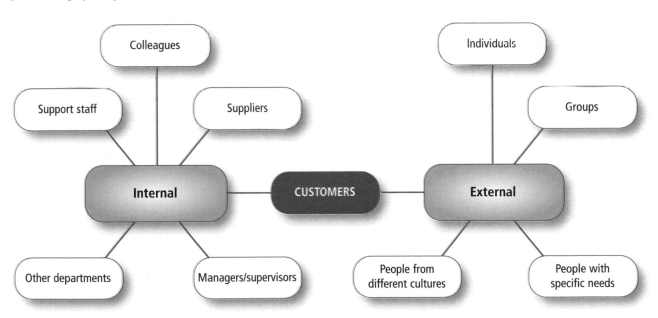

Figure 2.2 Customer types

information to your boss will also determine his/her level of efficiency. Leaving tasks to the last minute, delivering sloppy work or not meeting deadlines will have an impact of how well your boss can work – and his/her attitude towards you!

✱ Suppliers are people or organisations that contribute towards the product or service that you provide. They have an important impact on overall service. Examples include food companies which provide airlines with in-flight meals; cleaning organisations which clean the offices each morning; a coach company that provides airport transfers for the tour operator; a company that prints leaflets for the tourist information centre. In the travel and tourism industry suppliers can have a considerable impact on the end product!

Key terms

Internal customers These are colleagues and other members of staff who work within the same organisation to provide products and services. Internal customers can also include suppliers who contribute towards the products/service.

External customers These are people from outside the organisation, that is, those who buy the products and services.

Table 2.1 gives examples of the important role of suppliers in providing excellent service.

Table 2.1 The role of suppliers

An airline's suppliers may include	• The catering company which provides the in-flight meals • The cleaning company which cleans the aircraft during 'turnaround' • The air traffic control which provides information about conditions and advice for landing • The airport for the provision of runways, security checks, air traffic control • The agent who provides check-in staff
A tour operator's suppliers may include	• Hotels • Coach companies which provide airport transfers • Local guides for their services on excursions • Local visitor attractions • Local restaurants
A travel agent's suppliers may include	• Tour operators • Airlines • Hotels • Ferry companies • The computer reservation system, e.g. Galileo • The office cleaners

The case study below demonstrates the impact of good internal customer service.

CASE STUDY

Agents' comments

Kirker Travel recently won an award for the service they provide to their customers, travel agents. The following are comments about Kirker by some of the agents.

Carolyn Lodge Travel, Cranleigh, Surrey

Owner Carolyn Lodge praises Kirker's 'slick' service. She says the operator is 'extremely speedy', even when responding to things that have gone wrong, even if out of its control.

'You can ring them up at 5 pm on a Friday and have faith that they will have the tickets to you on the Saturday morning', she says.

Lodge says Kirker is also very fair about paying compensation and commission. 'If they get a direct booking from someone who got the brochure from us they will always kickback the commission', she says.

Marco Polo Travel, Bristol

Owner Polly Davies voted for Kirker at the AITO awards.

'Their service is marvellous – they always answer their phones in three rings.'

She says Kirker's knowledgeable staff are also honest.

'They will say if a hotel has small rooms or if a room has a building view. That is the kind of honesty you need in this industry.'

Davies says Kirker is also great for taking last-minute bookings 'even if you have someone who wants to travel that night'.

Liphook Travel, Liphook, Hampshire

Partner Andrew Meech says he would often sell a Kirker holiday to customers looking 'for that little bit more' for a special occasion.

'There are still people around who want to be looked after and that is where Kirker really comes into its own.'

Meech says Kirker staff 'obviously know their own hotels very well, are always helpful and are easy to get hold of on the phone.'

World of Wymayay, Warminster, Wiltshire

Director Billi Eaves says Kirker is 'the very best without a shadow of a doubt'.

She praises the operator's staff. 'They are more like a large office than a normal call centre,' she says.

'We roughly get the same person every time we call. But it doesn't matter, all the staff are well-trained and they all know their hotels – they have all been in them.'

She said the award for service was well-deserved.

'With my hand on heart, I can tell you we have never had a problem in 15 years – which in the travel industry is a rare thing, isn't it?'

Source: Travel Trade Gazette July 2004

1 **Identify six ways in which Kirker offers excellent customer service to the travel agents.**
2 **How do you think Kirker ensures such a high level of service?**

Skills practice

Work in pairs and identify the internal and external customers of airports and tourist attractions.

The needs and wants of different external customers

It is clear that all customers are not one homogenous group – they all have different needs and wants. The aim of all travel and tourism organisations is to meet these needs and wants by providing appropriate products and services.

Think it over ...

Think of your ideal holiday. Think of your parents'/guardians' ideal holiday. Also, what would your grandparents' ideal holiday be? (Thank goodness tour operators provide different products and services and do not send us all on the same holiday!)

We will now examine some of the different types of (external) customers and how their needs may differ.

Individuals

People travel alone for many different reasons. They may be travelling on business, wanting to participate in a specialist activity or hoping to meet a partner! Some may choose to travel alone, while others may do so reluctantly. Some single travellers are young (18–30), while many are 50-plus and some 70-plus. All such individuals will have differing needs. These must be provided for by airlines, tour operators, airports, hotels and their staff.

CASE STUDY

Friendship adds Prague breaks

Prague Castle

Singles specialists Friendship Travel has added city breaks to Prague and Istanbul, as well as holidays in the Caribbean, to its brochure for this winter and next summer.

The operator, which claims to be the only singles company to sell through the trade, has reported an increase in demand for city breaks.

Two-night breaks in Prague start at £298 for departures on 26 November. The price includes flights, transfers and half-board accommodation at the four-star Hotel Movenpick.

Seven-night Caribbean holidays start at £849, including flights from Gatwick, transfers and all-inclusive accommodation in the Dominican Republic.

Managing director Colum McLornan said: 'All-inclusive options in the Caribbean are an ideal choice for the single holiday maker.

'Guests can relax and take in the free on-site activities during the day, then enjoy the companionship of other members of the group in the evening.'

Friendship Travel caters for the over-25s and pays 10 per cent commission to agents.

Source: Travel Trade Gazette 6 August 2004

1 **Friendship Travel is a specialist tour operator catering for single customers. List all the products and services it could provide to meet the needs of these customers (e.g. room share, dinners at set times so that everyone eats together).**
2 **Check its website for more information and to see if you have missed anything.**

CASE STUDY

Room for the future?

The challenge for the hotel of the future is to supply the technology without baffling the guests. Nobody will want their room stuffed with so many gadgets and electronics that they need a 15-minute lecture before they can close the curtains and switch on the TV.

Business travellers want to operate at full efficiency away from the office and to be able to keep in close contact with their head offices, but they also want an easy and comfortable stay.

The Edwardian era is the inspiration for some hotels. They want to update what grand hotels of the past did supremely well.

Mark Selawry, Hilton Vice President of Management Services, says that a century ago the concierge at the Ritz in Paris was renowned for being able to greet every guest by name. 'The workforce is too transient for that to happen now, but technology allows us to do the same thing – to profile guests on a chain-wide basis,' he says.

'I can see our loyalty card doubling as a pass card and room key operated by radio frequency so the key opens the door without swiping it. Perhaps the same card would also enable guests to access the leisure facilities.'

Selawry's ideas are close to fruition. Transactions will be recorded on a database so that when a guest telephones or arrives at any Hilton, his preferences are known. If he likes dim lighting and Mozart, his room will be programmed to supply just that. If he likes tea and toast and a copy of *The Times*, they will be delivered.

The advent of the laptop and the Blackberry is already making business centres with a bank of personal computers and fax machines seem passé.

Hilton is starting to introduce 'relaxation rooms', divided into three zones, in hotels around the world. The relaxation zone, with an oversized bed and home entertainment centre, faces away from the work zone, which has a large desk, comfortable chair and Internet access. The bathroom zone features a hydro spa bath, powerful shower, second TV and natural daylight.

Joanna Wood, an interior designer, says hotels should adopt a commonsense approach to business and comfort. 'An uncluttered desk is essential so that I can get my laptop sorted out in a few minutes,' she says.

'I want access to a phone and fax and to be able to get online quickly. Air-conditioning, silence and a comfortable bed are also important.

'Business travellers also want good room service. If I'm about to dash out to a meeting, I don't want to ring for a club sandwich and coffee to be told it will take an hour. I could bake the bread in that time.'

Wood's hotel of the future will have improved lighting – soothing, dim lighting converted to a light that is bright enough to read every word of the small print on a contract. Bathrooms will be better lit so that women executives can confidently touch up their make-up rather than peering at a steamed-up mirror in the gloom.

'Lighting at the moment is moody to the point where it ceases to function,' she says.

Many top hotels agree that sophisticated lighting is vital. They believe that guests will also want to control their own environment, adjusting lighting, heating and air flow so that executives preparing to go to work can opt for the brightest light, while jet-lagged travellers desperate to go to sleep can arrange a blackout.

Holiday Inn asked Laurence Llewelyn-Bowen, the TV personality and interior designer, to create the hotel bedroom of 50 years' time.

Llewelyn-Bowen's vision included a fibre-optic-lit carpet, star lights that twinkle above the bed on the ceiling, textured glass walls that can be transformed with adjustable coloured lighting and the ability to create wall art from images of tropical beaches to famous monuments.

Source: The Times June 2005

1 **List all the products and services that hotels of the future could provide for their business customers.**
2 **Why is a personal greeting so important?**
3 **Why is so much provided for business customers?**

Groups

Some groups may all know each other and have similar needs (e.g. a group of young men wishing to go on a day trip whitewater rafting). They may be happy to be treated as a single entity for the purpose of their day trip. However, a coach party of Americans who have booked a Blue Badge guide for their tour of Cambridge may all have differing needs – some will want to visit King's College, others may wish to go shopping and others may want to enjoy an afternoon punting on the river.

For those dealing with groups, it is important to remember that the group is actually many individuals – and to consider their individual needs. This can be very demanding.

Groups include school groups, special interest groups, and friendship groups.

Specific needs

Some customers may have specific needs, which may require additional and sensitive customer service. This may be a result of:

* loss of hearing
* visual impairment
* speech difficulties
* non-English speaking
* a different culture (e.g. ethnic minorities)
* mobility problems (e.g. wheelchair users)
* special dietary needs
* minors travelling alone
* travelling with young children.

It is clear that all customers with specific needs must be treated individually. Many people are unsure how to deal with specific needs and this can result in customers feeling insulted or patronised.

The Disability Discrimination Act 1995 introduced new laws aimed at ending the discrimination some customers faced. The law requires service providers to make 'reasonable adjustments' to ensure their premises are accessible to those with sensory, physical or mental disability which seriously affect their day-to day activities. Around 8.6 million people, or 1 in 7 members of the UK population, fall into this category.

The Disability Discrimination Act covers building design and construction, building approach and exit, as well as public places such as footpaths and parks. Printed material, such as brochures or menus, may also need to be available in Braille or audio formats, and websites should be suitable for disabled users.

CASE STUDY

Thomas Cook

Thomas Cook aims to recruit more mature staff in a bid to match its customer profile.

The company says shop staff do not reflect the ageing of the UK population – 67 per cent of sales consultants are aged 16–34 while just 3 per cent are aged 55 or over.

But consumers aged over 55 represent a quarter of all sales made through Thomas Cook stores.

Cook's Head of Human Resources Development, Colin Dalby, admitted the 'low pay environment' made recruiting older people more difficult.

A more diverse age range is just one element of Thomas Cook's aim for its retail sales workforce.

It is also chasing a rise in male recruits – at present 89 out of every 100 sales staff are women; a wider ethnic mix; and staff who are able to work more flexible hours.

'At the moment, our peak store trading hours are between 11.00 and 15.00 – but this is when staff are out for lunch. This is a real problem for shops,' said Dalby.

To combat this problem, Thomas Cook aims to recruit more flexible staff, such as 'key time workers' over the lunch period, staff on nil-hour contracts who can be called up at short notice, long-term temps and graduates.

Source: Travel Trade Gazette 25 June 2004

1 **Why is Thomas Cook recruiting more mature staff?**
2 **What does 'customer profile' mean?**
3 **List the other changes that Thomas Cook intends to make to its staffing profile.**
4 **Do you think these will help provide excellent service?**

1 Research the Virgin Atlantic website and identify the products and services provided for the following customers:

- Business passengers
- Children and infants
- Passengers with restricted mobility.

Note: You will find a useful 'press kit' in the 'All about us' section on the website.

2 List the additional products and services provided by Alton Towers to ensure the specific needs of customers are met.

WELCOME

ALTON TOWERS make every effort to ensure that the
Park is accessible to all of our guests and this guide has been produced to assist visitors with disabilities to ensure that you have a magical day with us. All our rides/attractions display information on general ride/attraction restrictions at the entrance point and it is the responsibility of all visitors to check these prior to entry.

Not all rides/attractions are suitable for all visitors and each has strict operating requirements which our staff have to follow for health and safety reasons. Please do not ask our staff to break these rules; they are there for your safety and the safety of others.

When travelling by car or minibus, please follow the signs to the disabled parking areas. Disabled parking is free to disabled badge holders only.

In order to fairly accommodate all our visitors, those who are able to provide documentary proof of disability (i.e. blue/orange badge or

you may be asked to come back later should the access point be particularly busy. Guests should use their discretion when deciding whether or not to go on a ride and we suggest that you watch the ride before making a decision. Where appropriate, a visitor with disabilities should ensure that they have a suitable helper with them to assist with loading/unloading, observance of safety restrictions/messages and any emergency/evacuation procedures. Our staff will give full loading instructions and assistance to both visitors with disabilities and their helpers. However, in the interests of everyone's safety, our staff will leave all lifting of any disabled person in the capable hands of their helpers.

For safety reasons, the number of disabled people permitted on certain rides/attractions at any one time may be limited.

If you are using an electric scooter or very large wheelchair, please ask a member of the ride/attraction staff whether or not the ride/attraction is suitable.

Throughout the Park, toilets with disabled access are available and we have a First-Aid Centre on site (located between Towers Family Restaurant and the Skyride station on Towers Street) where special needs can be catered for e.g. cold storage of medicines.

Large groups of disabled people visiting the Park are advised to contact our Guest Services Team ideally prior to their visit or otherwise on arrival for further advice on access and facilities.

BALPPA STATEMENT ON PUBLIC SAFETY FOR DISABLED PEOPLE

similar) will be eligible for discounted admission to the Park for themselves and up to two helpers. At least one helper must be aged 18 or over. On application, persons admitted at the discounted rate may also be eligible to special access wristbands. These wristbands are available from our Guest Services Office (at the top of Towers Street) where our staff will also be available to provide advice on facilities and access issues. The wristbands allow visitors with disabilities who, due to the nature of their disability are unable to use the normal queue line, preferential access to rides/attractions via points highlighted overleaf which are designed for ease of access (e.g. ride/attraction exits). Please note that helpers will not be permitted to use these preferential access points unless they are accompanying a disabled visitor onto the ride/attraction. The provision of admission discounts and special access wristbands is entirely at the discretion of Alton Towers.

Wheelchairs are available for visitors with disabilities from our Guest Services Office (conditions apply). Please note that these are available on a first come, first served basis and visitors are asked to use their own wheelchairs wherever possible.

On arrival at the designated access point to a ride/attraction, please contact a member of the ride/attraction staff for assistance. It may be necessary to wait for a short while before boarding a ride/attraction or

Members of the British Association of Leisure Parks, Piers and Attractions (BALPPA) welcome visits by disabled people and will do all that is possible to ensure a safe and pleasurable stay. However, certain rides/attractions in our parks can be physically demanding and vigorous. We therefore reserve the right to refuse admission to certain rides/attractions should we feel there is a danger to a particular individual or individuals for whatever reason.

We have been advised by the Health and Safety Executive that refusal on the grounds of health and safety does not constitute discrimination. We hope that you understand and accept the decisions made in the interest of your safety.

CALL 08705 20 40 60
www.altontowers.com

Investigate a large hotel, an airport, an airline or a mass-market tour operator. What particular products or services do they provide to meet the needs of different customers. You may wish to consider the needs of single women travellers, business customers, children travelling alone (airlines only), people of different ethnic origins, group bookings, people of different religions, disabled travellers.

CASE STUDY

Prizes for pets

Virgin Atlantic has launched a 'Flying Paws' scheme that rewards frequent-flying pets. All pets travelling on the 'Passport for Pets' scheme will be given a passport allowing them to collect 'paw prints' that can be redeemed for gifts. These range from blow-drys and pedicures to Burberry, Prada and Gucci pet clothing and a personal 'Pawtrait' by the artist Cindy Lass. Contact Virgin on 08450 701701 for more details.

Source: Travel Telegraph 28 May 2005

1 Do you consider pets to be customers?
2 Why have Virgin launched this scheme?

CASE STUDY

Eurostar launches three-class service

Eurostar is to scrap its first and premium classes and replace them with a new three-class service from 1 September.

The train operator will introduce business class, leisure select and standard to better tailor the product to different markets.

The move follows extensive research among passengers which revealed that business travellers want to be as productive as possible on the journey while leisure passengers want greater indulgence.

Commercial director Nick Mercer said:

'Business customers want choice, not the restrictions of a single class of service offered on many airlines. While some airlines are losing their share of the business flyers, our significant investment reiterates our long-term commitment to this market.'

The business class service will offer a 10-minute check-in, lounge access, at-seat meal service and power sockets. A chauffeur service will also be offered at additional cost.

Leisure select will include a 30-minute check-in, larger seat pitch, at-seat meal service and power sockets, while standard service will provide a 30-minute check-in and a buffet.

Report by Steve Jones
www.travelmole.com 31 May 2005

1 Identify the products and services available to all three types of Eurostar passengers.
2 Why has Eurostar changed from a two-class to a three-class system?
3 Do you think airlines will follow?

CASE STUDY

BAA Stansted

Hi, I am Paula Heffron, Head of Customer Services at BAA Stansted. I am delighted that you are studying customer service. It is an issue we take very seriously within BAA and at Stansted airport, and we are very proud of the service we offer.

You will appreciate that handling over 20 million passengers a year, up to 75,000 in one day, can be a challenging operation with the variety of scenarios it presents. Added to that, the general public are, rightly, more and more demanding of excellent service (even if they are travelling on one of the low-cost airlines), which brings in itself a host of customer service challenges. Life is never dull for my customer service duty team (CSDT) and our frontline staff.

It takes a small army of front-of-house staff and behind-the-scenes staff to ensure an airport operates efficiently and effectively and that all our customers receive the best possible service. All of our passenger-facing staff receive customer training on induction and in their refresher training, and all are trained in dealing with special needs passengers, and how to handle and diffuse difficult situations; many speak foreign languages and all of the CSDT are first-aid trained and many additional staff are defibrillator-trained to assist with life-threatening collapses.

We take part in the government's Defibrillators in Public Places campaign and currently have 23 defibs at Stansted, with staff from many organisations trained to use them. They have saved several lives to date at the airport, and the team have received lovely letters and thanks from the families of those who have been saved.

We are also fortunate to have an on-site paramedic supplied by the Essex Ambulance Trust and co-funded by Stansted airport for 18 hours a day. This is to ensure a rapid response to passengers who require first aid or emergency treatment, and they attend many calls daily, from simple first-aid requests to life-threatening conditions. Our airport information desk is open 20 hours per day to provide face-to-face information and services to passengers, and all our information staff are multilingual and very knowledgeable about anything and everything passengers want to know!

We have a team of passenger service assistants who ensure that 3500 free trolleys are available to passengers on arrival and departure, and who also provide free assistance to special needs passengers and anyone requiring assistance, such as parents with children, the elderly, etc. We have help points located in the short-stay car parks and on the terminal forecourt from where assistance can be summoned.

Our security team comprises over 500 staff who ensure the safety and security of all passengers and staff at Stansted, and who regularly search up to 35,000 departing passengers in a day. You will appreciate it is not always possible to delight passengers in a security environment, but our passenger scores (see QSM below) for security staff helpfulness are consistently high.

The customer service duty team are a team of enthusiastic, proactive people who are experienced in dealing with almost any situation that may arise from unattended bags, lost children, delay situations, accidents/incidents, distressed passengers, missed flights, VIP movements, in fact any situation you can imagine! No two days are ever the same and they have to be prepared to deal with whatever may impact on the airport and our operation. During inclement weather we have found ourselves looking after 10,000 passengers who were stranded here overnight and ensuring their comfort and welfare as best we could, providing information, reassurance and trying to make the best of a difficult situation. Strikes, ATC problems, surface access problems, bad weather anywhere in Europe, etc., all bring issues for us to manage, even if we play no part in the original problem.

We encourage customer feedback through an online feedback system and a feedback leaflet on site, as well as via letters, email and telephone calls, and each contact is thoroughly investigated and replied to. We are targeted on reducing the number of complaints and track areas of concern and trends, and ensure we address these promptly. Should any aspect of our operation attract five complaints or more in any month (not a lot when you consider we handle over 1.5 million pax a month!) we are obliged to report these in our monthly customer services report to BAA's main board and explain our actions to remedy these.

We are also pleased to receive many compliments about services or facilities, often naming members of staff who have gone out of their way to help passengers and provided excellent service, and Stansted is proud to boast an excellent ratio of compliments to complaints, currently 1 to 5.

BAA has a market research team who carry out interviews with passengers at all of our airports as part of our quality of service monitor (QSM) with arriving and departing passengers. At Stansted some 7500 passengers are interviewed a year about many of the services and facilities provided and this helps us to track passengers' perceptions about the service we provide and focus our attention where most needed. All managers are targeted through these results and lower-than-acceptable scores have to be improved.

I hope this information helps you understand the complexity of customer services provision and some of the issues involved. I wish you all the best in your study of travel and tourism and future careers in the industry.

With very best wishes

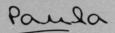

1 Identify the products and services provided by BAA Stansted for the travelling public.
2 What other products and services do airports need to provide for their other customers (service partners), for example airlines, handling agents, and tour operators?
3 Research the websites of another major airport and compare the products and services offered.

Key points

- The travel and tourism industry is highly competitive. Many organisations are offering similar products and services, often within the same price range.
- Therefore it is essential that travel and tourism organisations focus on their customers. They need to provide products and services that meet their customers' needs and expectations. Furthermore, their staff *must* provide excellent customer service.

- They need to provide products and services that not only meet the customers' needs but also exceed their expectations. The impacts of having a customer focus, that is meeting customers needs and exceeding expectations, are many.
- Suppliers (internal customers) are very important to most travel and tourism organisations.
- There are many different types of external customers – all of whom have differing needs.

Portfolio practice

For your assessment you need to investigate one sector of the travel and tourism industry in depth. Examples of sectors include travel agents, tour operators, visitor attractions, airlines, airports, ferry companies or similar. For the sector you have selected, you need to:

* Identify the types of customers who use the sector and describe their needs. You should give examples.

* Explain how the customers' needs are met within your selected sector. You should give examples.

Remember, for higher grades detailed descriptions will be needed. Explanations will need to be comprehensive and a wide range of appropriate examples given.

2.2 Providing effective customer service

We have established why it is essential that travel and tourism organisations have a customer focus and that there are two aspects to this focus:

* Developing products and services to meet customer needs

* Providing excellent customer service.

The aim of this section is to develop your skills in providing excellent customer service. When applying for travel and tourism jobs customer service skills will certainly be looked for and you will need to demonstrate that you are able to provide service to an industry standard.

Personal skills and qualities

Personal appearance

Personal appearance is an important element of customer service. It indicates how you feel about yourself, your customers and your level of professionalism. Travel and tourism is such a 'people' business that you should be aware of the importance of your own presentation and the impact it will have on customers and their confidence in your ability to provide a good service. Customers will judge you (and the organisation you work for) on the following:

* Your appearance – what you are wearing, whether it is neat and tidy or in need of ironing!

* How you care for yourself – is hair neat, jewellery discrete and are nails clean?

* Your body language – how you express yourself (see page 53)

* How you greet your customer – are you enthusiastic and smiling?

Personal appearance is part of customer service

* How organised you are – is your desk neat and the filing system organised, enabling you to find information quickly and easily?

In order to encourage good personal appearance, some organisations provide staff with a uniform. This is usual for staff in roles dealing directly with customers such as in a travel agency or tourist information centre, working in an overseas resort or as a local guide. There are many benefits of staff being in uniform:

British Airways stewardess serving in-flight meals to passengers

* Customers immediately know who the staff are – this is particularly important in some roles, e.g. as an overseas resort representative or ride attendant at a theme park

* A corporate image is developed

* Staff feel they are part of the company – and the team

* The organisation has direct control over what its staff wear.

Guidelines regarding the wearing of the uniform, caring for it and other aspects of personal presentation are usually provided. For example, Virgin Atlantic requires its female cabin crew to manicure and varnish their nails.

It takes customers just 10 seconds to form their first impression. These first impressions could be formed by:

* Scruffy staff who are chewing gum – or well-dressed staff with a professional appearance

* Staff slouching over desks – or positive behaviour (and body language)

* Eating in the office – or clear, tidy desks

* The un-ironed uniform – or the professional 'look'!

* Long hair covering the face – or a neat ponytail

* A queue of customers – or being served immediately

* Staff talking to each other and ignoring their customers – or being greeted with a smile.

Once a negative first impression is formed, it is very difficult to change.

Think it over …

Uniforms are not usually provided for staff who do not deal with customers. Examples include tour operators' head office staff, airline administration staff and back office staff at tourist attractions. However, many do provide a dress code. Why do they consider this necessary? What impact does this have?

Think it over …

Have you ever walked into a shop and walked out within a very short space of time? What was it that made you leave? What aspects created the (first!) impression that it was not worth waiting?

Positive attitude

Your personal appearance will reflect your attitude to yourself, your work and your level of professionalism. Customers need to know that you are positive, professional and will pay attention to detail with their travel requirements. People with a positive attitude have a 'can do' approach to situations. They are more likely to say yes, than no, accept challenges and have an enthusiastic approach to their work.

Your attitude will be conveyed not only by your personal appearance but also by your body language and your greeting (including tone of voice).

Think it over ...

Can you name someone with a positive attitude? What are their other personal characteristics? Are they fun to be around?

It is estimated that we convey more by our body language – the way we stand, use eye contact, hold our head, gesticulate and use facial expressions – than we do with our words. Similarly, our **tone of voice** can indicate how we are really feeling. We can use the same words in two different situations but our tone of voice may make the words have the opposite meaning. It's not what we say but how we say it that makes the difference. Your body language and tone of voice will determine whether the word 'hello' is meant as a cheery sign that you recognise someone, a threat, a put down or an ecstatic greeting! Similarly, does 'How can I help you?' mean ' I would really like to help you' or 'Please go away and stop interrupting my work'.

A good actor will be able to convey at least a dozen different meanings with the word 'no'. And we also perhaps have a dozen different ways of saying no – it's just that we do not think about it!

Key point

An important aspect of providing good customer service is recognising customers' feelings. Watching their body language and listening to their tone of voice are the best ways of working out what your customer is really feeling!

Skills practice

Carry out this activity in small groups. Write the following words (or others) onto individual cards:

- Impatient
- Annoyed
- Frustrated
- Angry
- Happy
- Stressed
- In a hurry
- Anxious
- Confused.

Turn each card face down. Pick a card and use body language to demonstrate the word to your class. The person who guesses how you are feeling has the next go.

Key point

How we communicate Research shows that the tone of voice we use and our body language convey much more than the words we use.

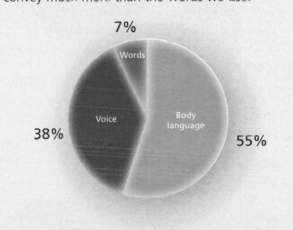

7%

38%

55%

Figure 2.3 The ways in which we communicate

Skills practice

1   This activity is about demonstrating how we use body language to communicate. Work with a partner. Take it in turns to act out different emotions. (Use facial expressions, gesticulate etc. but don't talk!) How successful is your partner at interpreting your body language?

2   This activity demonstrates that we use tone of voice to mean different things. Work with a partner. Imagine you have just been asked to a

party. Say 'Thanks, I would love to come' (or a similar positive phrase indicating you wish to go). Say the phrase in as many different ways as you can. Your partner must interpret what you are really meaning. (Some of these may indicate that you do not want to go at all!) You must use the same words each time and only change your tone of voice to indicate a different meaning!

3　How are these people feeling?

CASE STUDY

Your role as a crew member for Virgin Atlantic

The primary reason for having cabin crew on board an aircraft is for passenger safety. It is, however, no good being a role model in safety aspects if levels of customer service are inadequate. The ongoing success of Virgin Atlantic depends on the service we offer and the care and concern we extend to our customers. They will judge us in the first 10 seconds of boarding the aircraft. Have they been acknowledged? Have they received a genuine smile? Are the crew giving out positive body language? Has sufficient eye contact been used? Has a friendly and approachable stance been intimated? Is the appearance and grooming of the crew perfect? All these things from you, in addition to the appearance of the aircraft and cabin!

It is imperative that a good impression is created from the outset. You will not get a second chance to make a first impression. You are 'the company' from the customers' viewpoint.

After the first impression has been created, it is important that consistency is maintained throughout the flight.

Our objective must be that our customer service always exceeds passenger expectations and that there is no doubt that they will travel with Virgin Atlantic Airways on their next trip.

1　**What does Virgin mean by a 'genuine' smile?**
2　**Why is eye contact so important?**
3　**What does a 'friendly and approachable stance' mean?**
4　**How can you be 'the company' for the customers?**
5　**Give three examples of how cabin crew can give consistent service.**

Required resources available

To be able to provide excellent service you need to have required resources to hand. For example, travel agency staff need as a minimum, access to a computer reservations system and an adequate supply of brochures. The software on their terminal will need to be constantly updated, their Internet access reliable and the IT support prompt. This will allow them to provide a fast, efficient and reliable service to customers who are sitting in front of them or are at the end of a phone asking for specific information.

Resources required will clearly vary from job to job. It will include physical resources as well as information. For example, the transfer representative at Corfu airport will not be able to offer excellent service to the outbound passengers if she has not been told of the flight delay because no one at the resort office has picked up the fax.

Skills practice

Interview a local travel agent. What are their most used resources? You should include a list of websites and specific software.

CASE STUDY

The resources requirements of cabin crew

Anja loves her job. She works from a local airport and only does short-haul flights, but she likes the fact that she is working with so many different people and is often travelling to three or four different countries in a week. The airline she works for pushes her hard – the shifts are long, the turnaround fast and she never gets to see the destinations (although of course she does get the opportunity to travel at greatly reduced costs!)

She was actually offered two jobs but chose this one because she thought this airline really cared for their customers. The customer service training she was given was long – but she does feel prepared to deal with any situation. She gets regular training updates (e.g. safety updates, customer service refreshers, diversity training). But the thing that she finds helps the most is that she has access to lots of resources so that she can provide a good service.

Of course, all safety requirements are always met for all passengers (e.g. there are always sufficient life jackets and oxygen masks for all passengers). These are legal requirements. However, the airline provides other resources.

- A wheelchair is carried on board all aircraft
- Nebuliser masks are available
- The fleet is equipped with external automatic defibrillators
- Special children's meals are available
- There is a dedicated children's TV/film channel
- A children's activity 'backpack' is offered to all children
- Nappies, bottles and baby food are available on all flights.

All of these mean that she is able to provide an excellent level of service.

In addition, she always has with her whatever resources she needs to ensure she is immaculately presented and can cope with emergencies herself! Her own checklist includes:
- Passport
- Torch and spare batteries
- Cabin crew shoes
- Manuals
- Alarm clock
- Travel adapter
- Spare uniform
- Emery board
- Toiletries
- Makeup
- Nail varnish and remover
- Sewing kit.

1 **Why does the airline that Anja works for provide resources that are not legal requirements?**
2 **Do you think this makes a difference?**
3 **Research another airline. What other resources do they provide?**

Skills practice

Give examples of the resources needed by people in the following roles:

- Local guide
- Resort representative
- Hotel receptionist
- Housekeeper
- Check-in agent
- Travel consultant in a call centre.

Use of initiative

In many roles within the travel and tourism industry, there is no such thing as a 'normal' day. Different situations arise every day. In many of these cases, the use of your 'initiative' will get round the situations. In others you will need to seek help from your manager. While you will receive customer service training you cannot receive training to deal with the unexpected.

Key term

To use initiative To take decisions, act resourcefully, to take an action without being prompted.

Skills practice

What would you do in the following situations?

- You are working as a resort representative in Ayia Napa. It appears that one of the couples in the hotel is on their honeymoon. They have tried to keep it quiet – and you have only got to know because they have tried (unsuccessfully!) to change their twin room to a double.

- While working in the same resort you overhear a conversation about a proposed volleyball match in front of the hotel. Ball games are 'banned' on certain parts of the beach.

- You are on work experience in a local travel agency. An elderly man is hovering at the brochure rack. You have been advised not to serve customers – but everyone is busy and you can see he is becoming agitated.

Problem solving

Your initiative and positive attitude will certainly contribute towards your problem-solving ability.

A 'can do' approach is required within the industry. You will be asked for many seemingly impossible things – and it is your job to provide! With initiative and a positive approach many simple problems can be solved before they become major issues.

Problems are an inevitable part of life. When working in the travel and tourism industry you may have to deal with problems involving internal and external customers. All such problems will stretch your skills. You will need to listen, question and be calm. In addition, you will need to know how to deal with the situation effectively and be aware of your own responsibility limits.

Table 2.2 Potential problems

ROLE	PROBLEMS THAT MAY BE ENCOUNTERED
Check-in staff	Disabled passenger checks in but has not pre-booked an escort to the plane
Airline cabin crew	Sick child Air rage Drunkenness
Travel consultant	Hotel calls you to say it has overbooked; you must advise 10 of your clients A tour operator 'goes bust'; you have customers overseas and their relatives have come to see you as they are concerned
Hotel receptionist	An elderly lady passes out in the reception area A Japanese customer is on the phone trying to make a booking – he does not speak English

Skills practice

In groups discuss how you would handle the above problems. Remember, if you are able to effectively solve a problem, you will enhance customer loyalty. With poor handling, a problem could become a complaint.

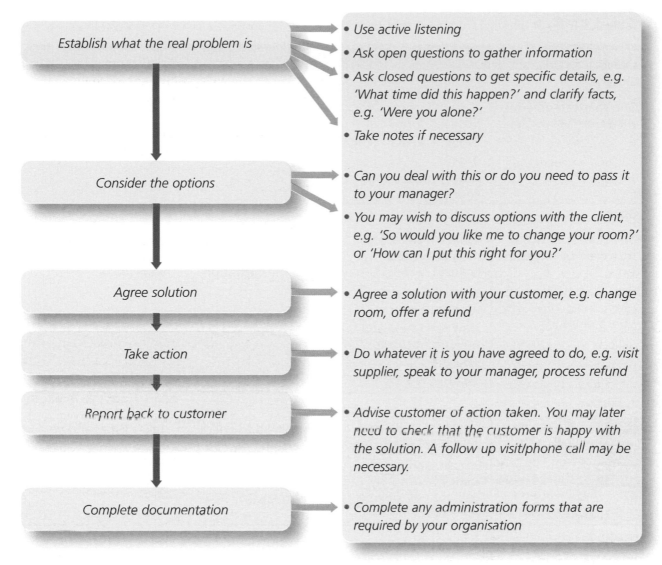

Figure 2.4 Dealing with a problem

Communication skills

This section will focus on those skills that ensure you communicate effectively with your customers and so ensure excellent service.

Questioning

Questions are an important aspect of good communication. Whatever your future role in travel you will be asking questions of colleagues and customers. In some situations the type of questions you use is as important as the words spoken. This is especially so when trying to sell or dealing with a difficult situation.

There are four types of questions: open, closed, leading and reflective. These are identified in Table 2.3 together with an example and the limitation of each type of question.

In most situations you will need to be asking open questions, for example when establishing a customer's needs. In some cases reflective questions may be useful, for example dealing with a complaint or making a sale.

Table 2.3 Types of questions, uses and limitations

TYPE OF QUESTION	EXAMPLE	USE	LIMITATION
Closed			
One that can only be answered 'yes' or 'no'	Have you sent in your booking form? Would you like a cup of tea? Have you received your tickets?	To clarify facts Should not be used if trying to gather details	Closed questions will not provide further information for discussion
Open			
One that cannot be answered by a 'yes' or 'no' They start with what, when, how, who, why, where or which	What did you enjoy most about your holiday? What is it that is upsetting you? How can I help you solve this problem? Where have you been on holiday before?	To start a discussion or conversation, to gather information	A talkative person may take up a lot of your time!
Reflective			
One that checks understanding and gives a person the chance to think about what they have said	So you feel the hotel staff were unfriendly? So you want somewhere sunny, but you are not looking for a beach holiday?	Allows you to check understanding and for the customer to add to what they have just said	Takes time, and you may lose the thread of the previous discussion
Leading			
One that suggests what the answer would be or leads the person into answering in a certain way	So you feel that if the flight had not been delayed you would have had a nice holiday?	Try to avoid using	Indicates what you are thinking and is unlikely to obtain a full or true answer

Key terms

Open questions They will help you to gather information.

Closed questions They may produce only a 'yes' or 'no' response.

The following are examples of open and closed questions:

CLOSED QUESTIONS	OPEN QUESTIONS
Did you enjoy your holiday?	How was your holiday? or What did you enjoy about your holiday?
Did you learn a lot at the welcome meeting?	What sort of things did the resort rep tell you about at the welcome meeting?
Do you want to go to Ibiza because of the nightlife?	What is it that makes you want to go to Ibiza?
You've been to Spain a lot haven't you?	What destinations have you been to before?

Skills practice

1 Change the following closed questions into open questions:
   • Can I help you?
   • Are you OK today?
   • Do you like the view from your balcony?
   • Would you like to go to Greece again this year?

2 Change the following closed questions into reflective questions:
   • Your budget is £400 per person?
   • You don't want to go to Spain?
   • You have not booked on the full-day excursion?

Listening

How good are you at listening? We all listen – and most of us think we are good at it. But do you interrupt when your friends are talking, look away or think about something else?

Key term

Active listening This is demonstrating through words and actions (body language) that you are understanding what is being said to you. For example, you can make appropriate expressions (wow!, huhhuh!) or ask questions (Did he really shout at you?) You can also use body language to demonstrate active listening. For example, nodding, maintaining eye contact, smiling or frowning.

Skills practice

Non-verbal behaviour is an important aspect of listening. Carry out this exercise to assess its impact.

Work in pairs. Each choose a topic to talk about (make sure it is something you know a lot about and can talk about for a few minutes).

Each speaker will speak on his or her topic twice. The first time the listener will practise active listening (e.g. nodding, smiling, maintaining eye contact). The second time the listener will demonstrate (through behaviour) that he or she is not listening, for example looking away or yawning. Remember, the listener is practising non-verbal behaviour and so must not speak.

1 What impact does active listening have on the speaker?

2 What impact does it have on the speaker when it is clear that he/she is not being listened to?

Responding to customers

We know that in order to provide excellent customer service you must first establish customers' needs. You will then be able to respond to them. You may think that simple open questions will establish customers needs, for example 'When do you want to travel, where would you like to go?' However, there may be

Skills practice

How good are you at listening?

1 Complete the following questionnaire to assess your listening skills:

When listening, do you ...	Almost always	Sometimes	Never
1 Face the speaker?			
2 Keep focused on the speaker, maintain eye contact?			
3 Nod and smile when appropriate?			
4 Think about other things?			
5 Look for body language and listen to the tone of voice (to give you more understanding)?			
6 Think about your answer while the speaker is still talking?			
7 Interrupt before the speaker has finished?			
8 'Tune out' or get bored?			

2 Consider points 1–8. Which ones indicate that you are listening? Use these (and any other points you can think of) to produce some guidelines called 'Improve your listening skills'.

some things that the client does not tell you, either because he or she does not think it's important or because he or she is embarrassed. For example, this may involve issues around money or special needs. These are referred to as 'underlying needs'. It is sometimes very difficult to establish underlying needs until late in a sale. It is therefore important to ask the right questions to try to understand what these are.

Skills practice

Imagine you are working as a sales consultant in a call centre. What questions would you need to ask to uncover the following underlying needs?

- Restricted mobility means that a wheelchair is needed at the airport
- One of the four passengers is over 80 and therefore needs additional insurance
- A baby is travelling
- A honeymoon couple don't want other hotel guests to know it is their honeymoon but do want a four-poster bed and champagne on arrival.

Key terms

Presented needs Those things the client tells you.

Underlying needs The needs that will affect the client's choice of product, but which he or she does not tell you about.

As a customer care professional you will need to respond to needs whether the client tells you them directly or not. Identifying a person's behaviour could help you to establish their needs and respond appropriately. You need to be aware when a customer is becoming stressed, anxious or angry. A good resort representative will notice the quiet person who is too shy to join in with things and offer words of encouragement. A good sales consultant will identify the signals that a customer is interested in buying. You may already be good at identifying behaviour – but simply unaware of your skills. So how will you do it? Through observing body language. If a person is speaking their tone of voice will also give you a clue if their mood is changing.

Providing information

Having questioned, listened and responded to the client you will have established their needs and you may now be in a position to provide your customer with information. You may do this in writing or orally (both of which are dealt with later in this section). When providing information you will need to consider:

✱ The method – e.g. phone, email, letter, interview, casual conversation

✱ The style and tone – e.g. a friendly telephone call may be better than a formal letter

✱ The need for accuracy – all information provided must be correct.

Style and tone

Style and tone refer to the way you communicate your information. The way in which you write or say words is as important as the words you use. We have already established that the tone of voice used to say something can alter its meaning. Similarly, the style, context and tone of a letter can be adapted to suit the purpose of the letter and the audience. Remember, a good business letter could be factual, formal, clear and concise, whereas a marketing letter is more likely to be friendly and persuasive.

Skills practice

1 Gather four pieces of written communication received within your household within the last month (make sure they are not confidential). Consider their style and tone. Describe them. Are they:
- Factual
- Formal
- Friendly
- Technical or conversational
- Clear/concise
- Persuasive.

2 Swap documents with a colleague and then compare descriptions.

Written communication

There is a vast amount of written communication used to provide information within the travel and tourism industry. How these are presented, how efficiently they are produced and their accuracy will contribute towards customer service levels and the image a customer will have of the organisation.

Examples of written communication include:

* Letter
* Email
* Memo
* Fax
* Brochure/Leaflet
* Web page/Internet
* Timetable
* Menu
* Window display
* Notice board
* Welcome pack
* Sign.

Skills practice

List the impact on customer service of a poorly presented window display, an incorrect timetable, a letter containing spelling errors or a grubby menu.

Written communication contributes towards the overall image the customer will have of a company. The design of the website may attract a customer to investigate it further or look elsewhere for a holiday. If an email has spelling errors, customers will certainly have an impression of poor service levels. Similarly, the style and tone used in letters could indicate whether a company is friendly and enthusiastic or more formal.

It is important that the correct form of written communication is used. For example, emails and faxes are an excellent method of communication if speed is important. However, they are informal and should not be used, for example, to deal with a complaint. Similarly, a memo would only be used for internal customers.

Skills practice

Complete the table below independently. Then compare your answers with other members of your group.

Which form of communication would be used for the following tasks?

Message	Method of communication to be used
The manager of a travel agency wants to advise a customer of a hotel change.	
A resort rep wants to let head office know that a customer has made a serious complaint about the hotel. She thinks other customers will also complain.	
Two hotel receptionists have agreed to swop shifts. They want to tell the manager.	
Head office has decided to make 20 airline staff redundant.	
A customer has had a great holiday and decides to tell the travel agent and tour operator.	
A visitor to a museum has been overcharged (he only realises when he gets home).	
After two weeks of reading about two destinations, Jo wants to confirm a holiday with the travel agent.	

Remember, written communication is more formal than face-to-face communication. It is therefore sometimes used to confirm decisions that have previously been discussed. In some of the choices above, you may decide that face-to-face communication or a telephone conversation is needed, as well as some form of written confirmation.

You work in a small travel agency in your local town. Your manager has asked you to write a letter to Mr J Ashwan of 36 Delver Drive, Hampton, Humbs GG3 9JL. Mr Ashwan is elderly. He has been into the agency several times asking about specific details of the hotel, the resort and his travel itinerary.

Your manager has asked you to send him a reassuring letter enclosing a copy of the brochure page, telling him a few details about the hotel facilities and the resort. You should confirm travel times. It would also be useful to advise him that there will be a representative in the resort who will be able to help him if he has any queries while he is on holiday.

Oral communication

Oral communication includes both face-to-face communication and telephone conversations.

Face-to-face communication

Whatever the situation, the following sequence is likely to happen in a face-to-face meeting with a customer:

We are all used to face-to-face communication. When shopping, getting on a bus, greeting friends and working in a team we all communicate directly with each other face to face. However, although you may be familiar with this form of communication it is important to know how to use it to its full advantage when dealing with a customer. For example, personal presentation is very important when facing a customer. It will give a first impression! You must also consider your tone of voice and be very aware of your body language – remember it will communicate more to your customer than the words you actually say (see page 53).

The advantage of face-to-face communication is that you can read your customer's body language; use brochures, leaflets, and other materials to help you get information across to your customers and answer any questions as they arise.

Face-to-face communication is often on a one-to-one basis. However, it can also involve groups of people, for example at a staff meeting or a welcome party in a resort.

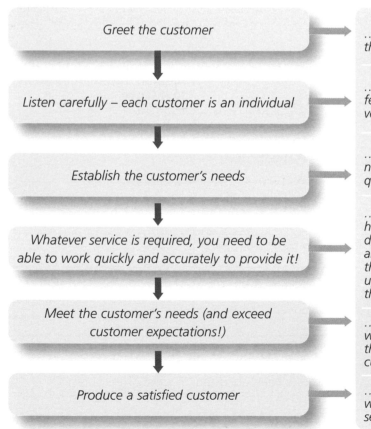

Remember...

... first impressions count! Smile as you greet the customer. Be warm, friendly and positive.

... all customers are individuals with differing feelings and different needs. Some will have very different opinions to you!

... the customer will tell you some of their needs but you may need to ask further questions.

... your product knowledge will determine how quickly and efficiently you can work, e.g. do you know where Bournemouth, Benidorm and Barcelona are – or do you have to look them up? Is your drawer organised, your diary up to date and can you find your way around the computer reservation system easily?

... your aim is to provide the customer with what he/she wants and in doing so to exceed their expectations. You will need good customer service skills to do this.

... the ultimate objective is a satisfied customer who has had an enjoyable experience being served!

Figure 2.5 Face-to-face communication

A tourist guide introducing tourists to the Ightham Mote manor house in Kent

Telephone communication

To be able to communicate well on the telephone you need good listening skills, and remember that you must listen to the tone of voice as well as the words being said! It is particularly important to talk clearly and check understanding when on the phone – as you cannot read the body language or any other non-verbal information (e.g. gestures and facial expressions) being passed from the other end of the phone!

Other techniques for good telephone communication include:

* Be clear – use short sentences and phrases

* Avoid jargon

* Be concise

* Pronounce your words clearly

* Speak slowly

* Make sure there is minimal background noise

* Smile.

Key point

You should smile when speaking to customers on the phone. It affects your tone of voice and the customer service you provide.

Many travel and tourism organisations require all their staff to answer the phone in the same way. For example, 'Good afternoon, Travel First, Harry speaking, How may I help you?' This is to ensure consistently good service and to present a corporate image.

Completion of appropriate documentation

Keeping appropriate records and documents is an important aspect of providing excellent customer service. You will need to record information in the following situations:

* Taking an enquiry for a holiday (establishing customers needs)

* Dealing with a complaint

* Taking payment

* Booking an excursion

* Taking a telephone message

* Dealing with a problem (with a colleague, customer or your manager).

In many situations pro-formas (a form to fill in) are provided. One example is an enquiry form which prompts the travel consultant to ask specific questions, such as dates of travel, number of adults and children, preferred resort, preferred departure airport, length of stay. Another example is a customer report form used in resorts. A resort representative will need to use this to write a report if a complaint is received in the resort. The representative will need to write a factual report to relay the necessary information to head office.

Customer report form

Tour operator: _____ Form no. _____

Resort (e.g. Palma Nova) _____ Area (e.g. Majorca) _____

Customer's name _____ Booking ref no. _____

Accommodation _____ UK departure date _____

Customer's UK address _____

Postcode _____ Telephone _____

Details of issues raised:

1 _____

_____

2 _____

_____

3 _____

_____

Actions taken to resolve the issues raised above:

1 _____

2 _____

3 _____

Customer signature _____Date _____

Copy received by _____ (on behalf of hotelier/supplier)

Additional comments _____

_____

Figure 2.6 Customer report form

Remember, when filling in any document, that it could potentially be used in court. Therefore, take your time over it, be professional and make sure the information is full, accurate and legible. Times and dates must be included. Give facts and not opinions!

General guidelines for all paperwork

✱ Write in block capitals in black ink

✱ Make sure all copies can be read CLEARLY

✱ Fill in all sections – if they are not applicable, write in N/A – do not leave any section blank

✱ Do not use jargon or foreign words (or your own abbreviations)

✱ Check the form once it is complete

✱ Make sure you are using the correct form. If unsure ask!

✱ State facts not opinions.

Use of ICT

Use of ICT is an integral part of most people's working life. This is no different in the travel and tourism industry. For most roles in the industry you will need generic ICT skills (such as word processing, use of databases, spreadsheets and email systems) as well as skills specific to a role. For example, people working in an airline reservation team will receive training on the use of a computer reservation system such as Galileo or Amadeus. In a tourist information centre you would need to be able to access the sites and use the software that provide timetables and local information.

Think it over ...

Many of the large travel agency chains always use standard letters. What are the advantages and disadvantages of this?

CASE STUDY

The impact of the Internet

The impact of the Internet on travel agents is clear. Customers have become more demanding. They expect greater flexibility and choice, Internet pricing in shops, as well as personal recommendations and experienced sales people with the insiders' touch. The Internet continues to improve and travel websites get better every month. Search engines can now integrate dynamic packaging products, major operators and independents (i.e. they can put the separate parts of a holiday together). Customer reviews are now often added to holidays and hotels – giving customers the confidence to make the right choice.

But agents can still add significant value. They must use their product knowledge to focus on high-value complex journeys. For short breaks they must ensure that their technology is at least as good as that on the Internet. Their expert knowledge must justify an extra fee from the customer.

The added challenge to agents is to ensure that they have access to an extensive product range, as well as the technology to meet customers' demands as quickly as possible.

Can you satisfy the customer who wants to book a break within three hours to a sunny destination for under £200 per person, somewhere with great beaches, suitable for kids and with a bit of culture thrown in? Can you show them agent and customer reviews of the hotel? And beyond the basics, can you add to the package by saving them money on car hire and transfers, as well as offering them deals on the restaurants, attractions or concerts that are on during their stay?

It is service that is the key – it enables the agent to add value in many different ways. This will lead to true customer loyalty.

Source: Brent Hoberman, *Travel Trade Gazette* 10 June 2005

1 What has been the impact of the Internet on travel agents? Do you think travel agents will survive?
2 How is the Internet changing?
3 What must travel agents do to compete with the Internet? (Name at least five things.)
4 What can travel consultants and their managers do to improve product knowledge within a travel agency?

Key term

Dynamic packaging Tailor-making a package holiday for a customer.

Product knowledge

It is essential that anyone working with customers has an extensive knowledge of those products they are trying to sell. After all, you cannot impress a customer and inspire them with confidence unless you are able to answer their questions about the holiday you are trying to sell or the destination you are recommending. This is why companies spend huge amounts of time and money on staff training. As a new member of the travel industry you cannot be expected to know everything – however you will be expected to know where to find information. Although the Internet provides an increasing amount of information, and many publications are also available on the Internet, traditional information sources are also used in the travel industry. Examples include:

✱ Brochures

✱ Manuals

✱ Travel guides

✱ Timetables and airline schedules

✱ Tourist information centres

✱ Reference books

✱ Yellow pages

✱ Promotional leaflets.

Skills practice

You work in the tourist information centre in your local town and the Internet is 'down' for the day. Can you answer the following customer questions? What sources of information would you use to find out the answers?

- I am here for a day. What do your recommend I see?
- I want to get to Manchester. How do you suggest I travel?
- Is there a late-night chemist?
- What's on at the local cinema tonight?
- Could you book me into a 4- or 5-star hotel in Manchester for tomorrow evening?

Skills practice

Because the travel industry is so diverse, you can be asked a vast range of questions. With training and experience you will have the answer to a lot of these in your head. For other questions you will know where to find information. The more knowledge you have, the better service you are able to provide.

Can you find the answers to the following questions? Name your sources of information

(name of publications or web addresses).

- When will the clocks change this year?
- When does Easter fall next year?
- When do local schools break up for the summer?
- How long is the crossing to Calais from Dover? Is it quicker to go on the shuttle service?
- Do we need visas to go to Cuba? – I am British and my partner is an American citizen.

Skills practice

Work in pairs. Use sources of information to devise 20 questions? Test your colleague's abilities to find the answers.

Key term

Product knowledge The knowledge you have about an organisation and its products and services.

Tour operators recognise the importance of product knowledge. How else can their staff or staff working in a travel agency sell their holidays if they do not know the destination or the hotel used? Hence, they regularly run familiarisation trips, or 'fam' trips as they are known in the trade. These are considered by many travel agency staff to be a perk of the job. After all it is a free trip, time away from the office having a good time. However, as far as the tour operator is concerned this is a serious exercise in customer care – they are looking after their internal customers (the travel agents) and making sure they know all about the tour operators' destinations so that they can go back to their agency with excellent knowledge of the destination, its hotels and attractions. Their excellent product knowledge will help them sell the tour operators' holidays.

Other methods used to increase travel agents' product knowledge include training packs, NVQs and staff training sessions. Many travel agencies do not open until 9.30 am or 10.00 am one day a week to allow for staff training. Sometimes the agency training mangers will run these sessions. At other sessions, tour operators visit to tell them about new products and destinations.

CASE STUDY

Gold Medal Holidays

We spoke to Joanne Raftery, sales consultant for the Middle East/Indian Ocean, about Dubai. This travel professional works alongside 450 colleagues in Gold Medal Holidays' modern call-centre in Preston's rather trendy Docklands area.

They are there to help travel agents advise their clients about Dubai, the Middle East and other possible twin-centre destinations such as the Indian Ocean.

How long have you worked for Gold Medal Holidays?

Joanne: Ten years.

What do you consider Gold Medal Holidays strengths to be?

Joanne: We all have specialist knowledge of our products and there is always someone here who has visited each of the destinations we feature – so we can always offer our clients first-hand experience.

Tell us more about the department's specialist knowledge?

Joanne: Most of our team have visited Dubai and seen most of our properties. We also have familiarisation trips planned this year for those who have not visited recently. We have lots of training sessions arranged in house for staff, but the best way to learn about a product is to experience it. From your experience you can form your own judgement and sell the product much more confidently to your clients. I was lucky enough to visit Dubai, South Africa and Mauritius last year and can now confidently talk about all three destinations.

How many times have you travelled to Dubai and when did you last visit?

Joanne: Four times. My last visit was in April this year.

What is your favourite time of year to travel to Dubai?

Joanne: November to April – it's much cooler!

What is your favourite attraction?

Joanne: The shopping is great, but I also enjoy the dune excursions (sand skiing and dune dinners).

You have a good reputation for offering clients flexibility; can you tell us how you achieve this?

Joanne: We deal with lots of hotels in Dubai, so if a particular hotel is unavailable we are always able to offer a good alternative. Again with airlines, we have good relationships and hold allocation with some carriers, which means we can offer low-cost seats even when GDS systems show no availability.

How does a successful company like Gold Medal Holidays offer a consistent level of service?

Joanne: By always putting the customer first.

How would you explain Dubai's appeal?

Joanne: Dubai caters for everyone. It is a cosmopolitan city and offers everything for a memorable holiday. There has been and still is so much development taking place over there at the minute, and tourism is a major factor contributing to Dubai's continuing success and universal appeal. All hotels offer fantastic levels of service and hospitality. So much money has been invested in leisure facilities that they rank among the best in the world, including championship golf courses, fantastic venues for tennis, horse racing, yachting and so on. Dubai is also a fantastic place to shop, and two shopping festivals are held here each year.

Source: Travel Trade Gazette 2005

1 **What does Joanne think is the best way to learn about a product? Do you agree?**

2 **What does 'holding allocation' mean?**

3 **Name a GDS.**

4 **List three features of Dubai.**

Customer service situations

You should now possess an understanding of the range of skills and knowledge required to provide excellent service to your customers. You must now practise these skills when dealing with different customers. Although you will always use the same set of skills, you may have to adapt aspects of the service you provide to meet different customer types. Remember each customer is an individual with different needs and wants!

Dealing with different customer types

We have already looked at the different customer types and how their needs vary. Figure 2.7 illustrates a range of different customer types and Table 2.4 summarises some key points.

Figure 2.7 Customer types

Table 2.4 Hints at dealing with different customer types

Groups	• A group is a collection of individuals, each with differing needs. Make sure you treat people as individuals. • Try to ascertain who is the group leader/organiser before you commence. If speaking to a group, gather them into an enclosed space. • Make sure everyone can hear you.
People of different ages	• People's needs vary with age – a couple in their 20s will have different needs from those in their 50s, and again in their 70s. • Don't be ageist. • Do not presume! Not all older people want culture and not all younger people want beaches. Ask open questions to establish their needs!

Business customers	• Business customers are usually under pressure, want an excellent service and are prepared to pay for it. • Time is important and they may need to work on their journeys, so consider offering additional products and services, for example express check-in, quiet coach on a train journey. • Business travel is not considered by many to be a perk of the job – many people would prefer to be at home than spending three days sorting out problems in an industrial city where no one speaks English. • Think how you can make life easier for them, for example an early morning flight rather than travelling the night before.

Those with specific needs	• Specific needs can cover a range of people. Examples of specific needs include:
	  ○ dietary, e.g. vegan passenger on a plane
	  ○ physical, e.g. child in a wheelchair visiting a theme park
	  ○ sensory, e.g. a hearing or visual impairment
	  ○ anyone needing assistance, e.g. minors travelling alone, adults travelling with children, elderly passengers.
	• Ask open questions to establish needs.
	• Be sensitive but do not fear giving offence – many complaints arise simply because the right questions are not asked.

Language differences	• Don't shout! • Be patient – how many languages do you speak?
Cultural differences	• Be sensitive. • Educate yourself – make sure you have a basic awareness of the beliefs of key religions, and also what causes offence.

CASE STUDY

Doing business in China

- When doing business in China, punctuality is considered extremely important. Your Chinese counterparts will not keep you waiting; being on time is essential.

- People will enter the meeting room in hierarchical order, as the Chinese are very status conscious. Senior members generally lead the negotiations and will direct the discussion.

- The exchanging of business cards is customary in Chinese business culture. One side should be printed in English and one in Chinese. You should present your card with both hands and the Chinese side facing up. When accepting your colleague's card study it carefully before placing it on the table, never in the back pocket, as this is extremely disrespectful.

- During negotiations, humbleness and patience is the key to success. The Chinese sense of time means that they use it knowingly and there is always enough.

- An important element before commencing a business meeting in China is to engage in small talk. Be prepared, as this may include quite personal questions.

Chinese business etiquette (Do's and Don'ts)

- Do maintain eye contact; avoiding eye contact is considered untrustworthy.

- Do address your Chinese counterparts with a title and their last name. If the person does not have a title, use 'Mr' or 'Madam'.

- Do wait for your Chinese counterpart to initiate formal greetings. Handshakes are the most popular gesture.

- Don't assume that a nod is a sign of agreement. More often than not, it signifies that the person is simply listening.
- Don't show excessive emotion whilst conducting business, as it may seem unfriendly.
- Don't use direct negative replies, as they are considered impolite. Instead of saying 'no', answer 'maybe' or 'I'll think about it.'

Chinese culture quiz – True or False

1 When a Chinese friend says to you 'Have you eaten yet?' he wants to invite you out for dinner.
2 When eating a Chinese meal it is customary to place your chopsticks standing up in the rice before starting.
3 In China white is the colour associated with death.
4 The word for clock in Chinese sounds similar to the expression 'the end of life', so a clock should never be given as a gift.
5 At the end of a meeting, you are expected to leave after your Chinese counterparts.

Answers

1 False. He is simply asking how you are and enquiring after your health.
2 False. This is a symbol of death used at funerals and should never be done.
3 True.
4 True.
5 False. You are expected to leave before them.

Key term

Culture This refers to people's beliefs and values.

Dealing with different situations

The travel industry is so diverse and customers needs so varied that you need to develop your customer service skills so that you are able to deal with a variety of situations. You will soon have the skills required to deal with *straightforward and routine situations*. Examples might include dealing with straightforward enquiries, giving timetable information or taking simple bookings to destinations with which you are familiar. You will also need to develop your skills to be able to deal with *complex and non-routine situations* as well. Examples for a travel consultant could include dynamic packaging (tailor-making a holiday for a client) or dealing with problems and complaints. In a resort, representatives occasionally have to deal with serious illnesses (requiring hospitalisation or repatriation) and occasionally deaths.

We will now focus on the most common situations that arise within the travel industry.

Providing information

The ability to provide correct information in a customer-friendly manner is vital to excellent customer service. Customers require some information in almost all encounters with travel and tourism organisations.

Some staff are employed simply to provide information, for example at the customer information desk at an airport or at a visitor attraction. Similarly, it is the primary role of all staff within a tourist information centre to provide accurate information on such issues as car parking, visitor attractions, transportation and accommodation. Simple queries that may be asked of almost anyone within the industry could include:

✱ When does your office close?

✱ May I have a refund?

✱ How can I make a complaint?

✱ May I speak with your manager?

Information provided must always be accurate. If you are unsure about anything, you must check – this may mean looking something up. Alternatively, it could simply mean asking a colleague. After all, telling a customer that a beach is ideal for small children, when in fact it has excellent surf, could have disastrous consequences, and is sure to result in complaint!

Excellent product knowledge will help you provide accurate information. You will develop this over time. However, one thing you can do now to ensure accuracy and efficiency when passing on information is to learn both the phonetic alphabet and the 24-hour clock.

Key terms

Phonetic alphabet The phonetic alphabet is used in the travel industry when communicating orally. By using a word instead of a letter, no mistakes can be made. It is most commonly used by pilots, air traffic control and tour operators.

24-hour clock The 24-hour clock is used worldwide to avoid mistakes and confusion between am and pm. Most timetables use the 24-hour clock.

Everyone working in travel needs to know the phonetic alphabet and the 24-hour clock. They will help you provide an error-free service. Make sure you learn them!

Giving advice

While information is factual, when asked for advice you are expected to give your personal opinion. Examples of advice requested from a travel agent could include: 'Do you think we should go a week later?' 'Would Benidorm be a better destination?', 'Do you think that would suit us?' If you have good product knowledge and have established your customers' needs, you should be able to make appropriate recommendations.

Often when asking advice people simply want you to confirm their own thoughts, for example 'We were thinking of camping in France this year instead of Spain as the campsites are better and usually have pools. This will be better for the kids. What do you think?'

Dealing with problems and complaints

Working in an environment with such a high level of person-to-person contact means that problems and complaints are inevitable. Complaints are dealt with later in this section. Problems such as lost luggage, delays or stolen goods, do not initially reflect badly on the company. Indeed, some of the problems may in fact be the customer's own fault. It is important to be aware that if a problem is not handled quickly and efficiently, it can often result in a complaint.

Skills practice

1 Spell your name using the phonetic alphabet.

2 Work in pairs. Give timetable information to each other, using the 24-hour clock to give departure and arrival times and the phonetic alphabet for departure and arrival points.

Table 2.5 Phonetic alphabet

A	Alpha	**B**	Bravo	**C**	Charlie	**D**	Delta
E	Echo	**F**	Foxtrot	**G**	Golf	**H**	Hotel
I	India	**J**	Juliet	**K**	Kilo	**L**	Lima
M	Mike	**N**	November	**O**	Oscar	**P**	Papa
Q	Quebec	**R**	Romeo	**S**	Sierra	**T**	Tango
U	Uniform	**V**	Victor	**W**	Whiskey	**X**	X-ray
Y	Yankee	**Z**	Zulu					

The 24-hour clock

You will deal with a problem in the same way as a complaint (see Table 2.6). However, the customer is less likely to be angry and therefore the situation may be easier for you to handle.

Examples of problems include the customer who has:

* lost their passport
* forgotten their ticket
* left a case at the airport
* broken their leg
* had a heart attack.

Even the most successful travel companies receive complaints. Sometimes these may be justified and sometimes not. Whichever the case, knowledge of procedures will help you to deal with the situation calmly without taking the complaint personally. It is important to remember that seven out of ten customers will do business with you again if you resolve the complaint in their favour. Therefore, it is important to view a complaint as an opportunity to 'turn a customer around', that is to change a complaining customer into a satisfied customer. This is challenging, but it will ensure repeat business and customer loyalty, as well as giving you job satisfaction. Examples of complaints a tour operator might receive include:

* Flight delays
* Accuracy of information on the website
* Call centres not answering phones quickly enough
* Poor excursions
* Resort rep who was late for an excursion
* Cleanliness of hotel
* Excursion prices.

Table 2.6 A flow chart of dealing with complaints

DEALING WITH COMPLAINTS	
Listen! ↓	Use active listening so that the customer knows you are taking his or her complaint seriously. Ask probing questions, but don't interrupt. Look interested.
Apologise ↓	Apologise for the inconvenience and that the customer is upset. Do not accept liability – i.e. do not say 'I'm sorry, our organisation has clearly made a mistake', but do say 'I'm really sorry this has occurred.'
Tell the customer that you will investigate the matter ↓	This may be a simple check to see if tickets are in the file, or it may be more complex. You may need to write to an airline, hotelier or other supplier. In this case tell the customer when you will have a response for him or her.
Empathise ↓	Try to see the situation from the customer's point of view.
Be calm ↓	Remember that even if the customer is angry, you must stay calm. The complaint is not about you, so don't take it personally.
Know your responsibility limits – agree a solution or refer to your manager ↓	If you are able to offer a solution, do so. But make sure you know your responsibility limits. If the complaint is outside your area of responsibility, you may need to refer the customer to your manager. Always discuss the solution with the customer.
Do what you have agreed to do ↓	Whatever the agreed solution, do it! Make it a priority. This is your chance to turn a bad situation into a good one by being efficient.
Record details	Make sure you follow company procedures about dealing with complaints. Fill in appropriate forms and send them to the right people.

Work in pairs. One of you is a customer and the other a resort rep. Role-play three complaints that you might encounter.

Key points

- It takes 10 seconds to form a first impression.
- You never get a second chance to make a first impression.
- It's not what you say, it's how you say it. The tone of voice you use and your body language is much more important than the words you use.
- You cannot know everything – but you must know where to find out about everything.
- You can show that you are listening.
- Smiling when on the phone can make a difference to how friendly you sound.
- Accuracy of information is vital to excellent customer service.
- A good product knowledge will help you provide a fast and efficient service.

ASSESSMENT

Portfolio practice

You need to practise your customer service skills prior to your assessment.

Work in pairs. Write out four customer service scenarios and role-play them. Alternatively, you can practise using the scenario's below.

1   You work in the local TIC. An elderly German couple come in. They are travelling the UK by car and have just arrived in the town. They intend to stay for two nights and would like information about possible places to stay and things to do. They would like a good standard of accommodation with some leisure facilities. Their interests include culture, good food and golf. Provide information to this couple.

2   You work in a local travel agency. Your manager has asked you to do some research for her. One of your regular clients, Jim Shobia, has telephoned. He would like to take his fiancé away for a week in the sun at Christmas. Ideally he would like to go to the Caribbean. However, he only has a budget of £1500 for both of them. Do some research prior to telephoning Jim to provide information and offer advice about possible destinations for a Christmas holiday in the sun.

3   You work as a resort representative in Santa Ponsa, Mallorca. One of your customers, Tamsin, has come to see you and is extremely upset. She has had a massive row with her boyfriend. She desperately wants to go home immediately. The return flight is tomorrow and although there is a scheduled flight this afternoon, you know that the fares are very expensive. If she stays, she wants another room in the hotel so that she does not have to see her boyfriend again. You know the hotel is full. You have never dealt with a problem like this one before!

4   You work as a hotel receptionist and received the following letter. Your manager has asked you to draft an initial response.

HOLDINGS
DOGSWOOD CLIFTON DV45 8JH

The City Hotel
Kingsmead Rd
Pavanna
Portmoth
PY67 8JH

Dear

Ref: AJB Holdings Conference 16–20 March

Further to my telephone conversation with Mr J Pearson this afternoon, I now wish to formally complain about the standard of care this company received on its annual conference at the City Hotel.

We have travelled from France for this conference as the venue had been recommended to us. Your website states: 'Situated in the heart of the city, this superb hotel has been awarded 3 AA Rosettes for fine food. The hotel has a leisure club, with heated indoor swimming pool, spa bath, steam room, fitness room and dermalogics spa for men and women.' Your conference organiser confirmed a conference room for 120 people with 10 breakout rooms, all of which would be equipped with the required AV equipment.

Our group experienced the following problems:

- 40 people suffered from food poisoning on the second day of the conference.
- The AC in the conference room was out of action for 2 hours each day.
- 5 of the breakout rooms did not have AV equipment and my colleagues had to use flipcharts.
- The steam room was undergoing repair work and the pool was simply too small to cater for the customers at such a large venue.

I look forward to hearing from you with an appropriate suggestion for compensation.

Yours faithfully

J K Symonds

J K Symonds
Managing Director

2.3 Measuring and monitoring the customer service of an organisation

We established at the beginning of this unit that it is essential for travel and tourism organisations to have a customer focus. The results of a customer focus include satisfied customers, repeat business, increased profits and a good working environment.

But customers change, new products develop, competitors emerge. It is therefore essential that organisations continuously monitor and evaluate the service they are providing in order to maintain high levels of customer satisfaction – how else will an organisation know whether their customers still like their products or that their levels of service remain excellent?

We will now examine some of the methods used by travel and tourism organisations to monitor and measure customer satisfaction levels.

Mystery shopper

Mystery shopping is used by many companies to assess the performance of their staff. Organisations are employed to visit shops or make telephone sales enquires, pretending to want to purchase the products and services. They assess the performance of staff and submit detailed evaluations of their experience using written reports or questionnaires. A mystery shopper can provide organisations with a fair, unbiased opinion regarding levels of customer service experienced. This method of evaluation is commonly used by call centres, travel agency chains and some tour operators.

Although there are now organisations that provide mystery shoppers to assess customer service levels, many large travel companies simply use staff from other parts of the organisation. For example, a ferry company may offer a member of staff from the call centre a free ferry crossing on the basis they complete a mystery shopping questionnaire. Or a travel agent from one part of the country may be asked to mystery shop in another town. Mystery shopping could involve face-to-face customer contact, for example visiting a travel agent, but a mystery shopper could also use the website of a tour operator or telephone an airline call centre to assess customer service levels.

Mystery shopping is used by VisitBritain when assessing accommodation standards for their star ratings. The case study shows how mystery shopping is part of the tourist board assessment for accommodation.

CASE STUDY
Mystery shopper (pre-accommodation visit)

Our assessors will research the accommodation from a customer's perspective prior to visiting. We are looking for effective communication and service to customers, response times of call answering and that responses to requests (e.g. for brochures) are dealt with promptly and professionally. We will be looking for staff knowledge of the properties and their location, for help, friendliness and advice, together with an explanation of any restrictions and terms and conditions that may apply.

This exercise will involve looking at the website for ease of use (how easy to navigate, find items and understand), making an enquiry online (if applicable), booking online (if applicable) and the overall aesthetics of the website (accuracy of property descriptions and photos will be assessed). We may also make enquiries by email, phone, post and out-of-office hours to assess staff knowledge, response times and customer service. We could be asking about procedures for booking, confirming and searching for a property, testing an offer to send a brochure, provide details of local amenities and area of a property, and general enquiries about the accommodation.

Source: Quality Accredited Agency Standard Information, published by VisitBritain

1 List the methods used to assess customer service levels at the accommodation providers.
2 Identify six quality criteria used to assess service levels, for example staff knowledge, friendliness of staff.
3 Design two questionnaires for mystery shoppers who are surveying accommodation – one for use when telephoning, one for assessing the website.

Skills practice

Every week a mystery shopper visits four travel agencies in a town in the UK. His or her findings are reported in the *Travel Trade Gazette*. Research several of these mystery shopping articles. Devise a checklist that the mystery shopper could use to gather his or her information and 'score' the travel agencies.

Observation

Observing customers and their behaviour may provide information about their levels of satisfaction. At a theme park managers will want to observe queues for rides to establish waiting times at different times in the day. A travel agency manager will be able to tell by a customer's body language whether he or she is satisfied with the level of service they are getting.

Observation of staff, as well as customers, can provide valuable information about customer service levels. A good manager will be continuously observing staff on an informal basis. They will note their appearance, attitude to clients and whether their desk is suitably neat and tidy. Some managers may also carry out formal observations as part of an ongoing assessment of customer service levels. For example, a resort manager may be required to observe occasional welcome meetings to ensure all staff are carrying our procedures and maximising their opportunities for sales.

Skills practice

Observe people's behaviour outside a local travel agency and note whether they

- look at the window display and then go in
- go straight in
- look at the window display and then walk away.

1 Design a form to monitor people's actions. (Your information could indicate the attractiveness of the window display to customers.) You could also measure other information, e.g. number of customers at specific times and whether they are alone or with others.

2 How could this information be used?

Skills practice

The resort representative observation form on page 77 is used by a small tour operator which specialises in the Greek Islands. The reps are all managed from the resort office in Athens and the area manager knows all representatives personally. This form would be unsuitable for a large operator with hundreds of reps whose annual bonus depended on the results from observations and customer comments. They would need to collect specific information, against which they could award points that could be statistically analysed. For example, all quality criteria could be given excellent, good, satisfactory or poor, each of which could be awarded a number of points. All reps could then be awarded an overall score at the end of the season.

1 Produce an observation form that an area manager for a large tour operator could use.

2 Swap observation forms with one of your colleagues. Evaluate their observation form.

Surveys

Surveys are the most common method used for monitoring and evaluating costumer service levels. They are a formal method of gathering information and provide organisations with data which they can analyse. While some questionnaires ask open questions and make general comments (see BAA questionnaire on page 78), most ask for specific information and require only a tick response. This has two advantages. Firstly, the customer can quickly and easily complete it – and therefore they are more likely to do so! Secondly, the data becomes quantitative and so is easier to analyse.

Key terms

Questionnaire A form used to carry out surveys.

Qualitative data This will tell you about people's feelings and perceptions. It is usually gathered by asking open questions (in a questionnaire) or through other research methods (e.g. interviews). It can be difficult to analyse.

Quantitative data This will give specific information. Closed questions in customer service questionnaires will provide qualitative information. For example, 'Did you enjoy your holiday?' (answer Yes or No). It is easy to measure (e.g. 86 per cent of people asked stated that they enjoyed their holiday).

Observation Record Form

Welcome meeting

Representative name _____   Resort _____

Observer name_____ Designation_____ Date of observation _____

SECTION 1: PREPARATION

Did the Representative:	Y/N	Please comment on any action seen and any action needed
1.1 Prepare the venue?		
1.2 Arrive in good time?		
1.3 Provide refreshments?		
1.4 Welcome guests on arrival?		

SECTION 2: INTRODUCTION

Did the Representative provide accurate and clear information about:	Y/N	Please comment on any action seen and any action needed
2.1 Himself/herself and the resort office?		
2.2 Times of hotel visits?		
2.3 The resort?		
2.4 The hotel?		

SECTION 3: SALES

Did the Representative:	Y/N	Please comment on any action seen and any action needed
3.1 Have visual material to help sell excursions?		
3.2 Present each excursion in an exciting and interesting manner?		
3.3 Focus on the benefits of the excursions?		
3.4 Tell guests how they could book the excursions?		

SECTION 4: GUESTS RELATIONSHIPS

Did the Representative:	Y/N	Please comment on any action seen and any action needed
4.1 Establish a good rapport with guests?		
4.2 Speak clearly?		
4.3 Provide prompt and accurate responses to all questions?		
4.4 Look and behave professionally?		
4.5 Provide plenty of time for guests to book excursions?		
4.6 Have all appropriate documentation with them?		

Feedback to the Representative and any agreed action points:

Observer signature _____   Date _____

Representative signature_____   Date _____

Representative comments:

Figure 2.8 Observation form

Please tick the location to which your feedback refers:

Departures ✈

- ☐ Forecourt drop-off
- ☐ Check-in
- ☐ Landside concourse
- ☐ Bureau de change
- ☐ Shopping before security
- ☐ Food and drink before security
- ☐ Security search
- ☐ Shopping after security
- ☐ Food and drink after security
- ☐ Departure lounge
- ☐ Gate area 1-19 ☐ Gate area 20-39
- ☐ Gate area 40-59 ☐ Gate area 80-88
- ☐ Getting on aircraft

Arrivals ✈

- ☐ Getting off the aircraft
- ☐ Immigration/Passport control
- ☐ Domestic Baggage reclaim
- ☐ International Baggage reclaim
  (including Channel Islands and Republic of Ireland)
- ☐ BAA Information desk
- ☐ Pick-up area (Zone D car park)
- ☐ Concourse

Car parks Ⓟ

- ☐ Short stay car park
- ☐ Mid stay car park (eparking.uk.com)
- ☐ Long stay (Pink Elephant parking)

Other 🚆 🚐 🚌 🚗 🚏 ✈

- ☐ Flight connections
- ☐ Left luggage/Lost property counter
- ☐ Transit train to/from Gates
- ☐ Coach station
- ☐ Forecourt bus service to/from car parks
- ☐ Road system
- ☐ Train station
- ☐ Taxis
- ☐ Rental car

BAA questionnaire

1 Compare the Holiday Inn and BAA customer service questionnaires.

2 Consider
- The type of data being collected (qualitative or quantitative)
- Ease of use by customer
- Ease of analysis by organisation
- Why the customer service managers of each organisation have decided on this format.

Please give your written feedback below:

DURING YOUR VISIT

Was your room clean and well maintained?
Was the overall hotel clean and well maintained?

Yes No
☐ ☐
☐ ☐

Please compare this hotel and room cleanliness to your best experience in a full service hotel.

Was everything in your room in working order?
Was the lighting in your room sufficient?
Did we make you feel safe and secure?
Did we handle your requests efficiently?
Would you like to see anything added to your room?

Yes No
☐ ☐
☐ ☐
☐ ☐
☐ ☐
☐ ☐

How would you rate the quality and state of your hotel facilities compared to other full service hotels?

OUR EMPLOYEES

Whenever our staff interacted with you, did they …

Prove to be knowledgeable about the hotel and its services?
Perform their duties promptly and efficiently?
Present themselves in a pleasant and welcome manner?

Yes No
☐ ☐
☐ ☐

Fulfil your requests and show commitment to your complete satisfaction?
Make you want to come back and to recommend the hotel to others?
Was there a particular employee who stood out during your stay?
If so, could you give us her/his name(s)?

☐ ☐
☐ ☐
☐ ☐
☐ ☐

Holiday Inn questionnaire

CASE STUDY

Assessing the service provided on a European tour

Genine works as a tour manager for Cusmar Tours, taking coach parties around Europe. She usually does two tours. Her favourite is 'Europe in 8 days'. This tour has an extremely busy itinerary – they stay in a different hotel every night and are usually 'on the road' by 8 am each morning. However, the clients are always Americans – and that means they will buy all the excursions and give excellent tips!! The other tour she does is a 13-day tour of Europe, which includes 6 nights in St Anton. It's much more relaxed – but the clients are always English and the tips appalling! As she only works from March to October, this is an important factor.

Cusmar offers a bonus at the end of the season. To get it the tour managers need good tour reports! The operations manager at Cusmar knows that tour managers often throw away reports if they get a bad one. So the bonus is calculated on the amount of reports returned to him, as well as what they say about the tour managers! These reports are simple tick box questionnaires. They are designed so that the customers can quickly and easily fill them in and head office can easily analyse them. There is space for brief comments too, so that customers can complain or compliment – useful information for Cusmar.

Genine has found that the way to get most reports back is to hand them out on the last morning of the tour – as they leave Paris. (She has found that if she hands them out any earlier customers lose the reports!) She tells clients that she will collect them as they get off the coach on the ferry crossing. She stands by the coach helping passengers disembark and collects the tour reports from them. If someone has forgotten she simply gives him or her a second tour report and asks that it be filled in while on the ferry (and then she collects it when they get back on the coach). She usually gets 100 per cent returns.

As soon as all the clients have left the coach in London, Genine flicks through the reports. She usually gets excellent grades for her customer service skills, but there is often someone who only ticks 'satisfactory' about her guiding skills. She knows she needs to give more information but it is difficult to know about so many places.

It is part of her job to informally feedback to the suppliers. Comments about the coach drivers are usually excellent and she is able to tell the driver there and then what the passengers have said. Customers often comment on the driver's excellent driving skills – which amuses Genine as the driver would of course be sacked if his skills were anything but excellent. For each hotel she will pass on the comments on the next tour. If there are any serious complaints she has to call her manager.

Genine completes a tick sheet for the tour reports (i.e. a simple analysis) and completes her own tour report before sending them to head office (with all her excursion details and accounts).

At head office the operations manager completes statistical analyses of all the aspects of the reports. If there are any immediate problems with a hotel or coach company, he will change them immediately. However, the analyses are used at the end of the season when each tour is evaluated by the product managers. Examples of the sort of information that the reports provide include:

- Hotels: levels of service, quality of food, service in restaurants, facilities
- Excursions: levels of enjoyment, guides, routes, timing
- Tour managers: service given, information provided, friendliness and approachability, appearance
- Coach: facilities, driver, helpfulness, knowledge, did he get lost?
- Overall enjoyment of tour.

The operations manager has a benchmark for each quality criteria assessed. Anything falling below the benchmark is reviewed and action taken before the next season. In some cases this means changing hotels, sacking tour managers and changing coach companies.

It is only by continually evaluating and improving their products that Cusmar Tours is able to remain the market leader.

1 What are the advantages of simple tick-box questionnaires?
2 Why does Genine give information to the suppliers about the customers' responses ?
3 Why are the reports analysed at head office?
4 What are quality criteria? Give six examples.

Skills practice

Produce a questionnaire (tour report) that Genine could use on these European coach tours.

Mystery shopping, observation and surveys will all provide organisations with information to evaluate. Thus they can measure and monitor service delivery. However, feedback from customers will also be received by email, by letter and informally though conversations. Increasingly, websites provide online forms to allow customers to give feedback easily.

Skills practice

Select two travel organisations. Compare their online feedback forms. What are the advantages and disadvantages of this system?

Skills practice

Carry out this activity in small groups.

1 Research a travel and tourism organisation. Establish how they measure and monitor their customer service.

2 Why do you think the organisation has selected those methods? Consider cost, level of formality, amount of information received, whether it is qualitative or quantitative.

3 Feedback your findings to the rest of the class.

4 Compare the advantages and disadvantages of each method of evaluating customer service levels.

CASE STUDY

Effectiveness of customer service delivery
Key customer service criteria

BAA owns and operates seven airports throughout the UK: Heathrow, Gatwick, Stansted, Southampton, Glasgow, Edinburgh and Aberdeen. In the context of customer service it should be borne in mind that BAA is responsible for the safety and security of the airport operation. Our aim is primarily to provide clean, working and friendly airports for airport users.

Essential to this is the provision of functioning equipment and facilities, not only for travellers using, for example, Stansted but for our business partners, that is, airlines and their handling agents. Airlines and their local agents have responsibilities for passengers, from check-in through to boarding the aircraft, and on arrival from disembarkation until passengers have reclaimed their baggage. Therefore, we need to provide reliable and efficient equipment for staff to use, for example the airport flight information and baggage belt systems. Other equipment, such as air bridges, lifts, escalators, transit trains, are also subject to service levels of availability. Targets are in place for faults on such equipment to be rectified within a four-hour period.

Procedures and practices used by managers and staff to achieve customer service quality criteria

Part of the role of our duty team is to carry out daily checks throughout the terminal. These cover safety (fire alarm checks) and standards of security and cleanliness. Particular attention is paid to the toilet areas, which are scored accordingly and the results then passed to the cleaning contractors. The security control area is audited for equipment and staff performance. We also monitor throughput and put in place contingency plans when queues start to build up.

Methods for measuring and monitoring the effectiveness of customer service

Since 1990 we have measured customer satisfaction through our quality of service monitor (QSM), scoring out of a maximum of 5. Every month a specialist survey team spends random periods at Stansted, compiling detailed questionnaires which ask departing and arriving, domestic and international travellers, a number of questions about their experiences as they travel through the airport. The results from these samples are compiled to provide a 'Quality of Service' report. This scores the results from a number of areas together with an overall score of the traveller's perception of his or her airport experience. The areas that we look at are:

- Flight information, which includes questions on ease of finding, reading and understanding
- Ease of finding way
- Walking distances
- Smoking arrangements – for both non-smokers and smokers
- Trolleys – availability and handling
- Toilets – cleanliness, waiting to use and ease of finding
- Departure lounge – crowding, cleanliness and ease of finding a seat
- Landside (pre-security) seating – ease of finding

- Check-in – ease of finding, crowding, cleanliness and waiting time
- Security – waiting time, effectiveness of check and staff helpfulness.

In addition, *ad hoc* surveys are carried out for areas of the business such as retail and planning. Retail in particular use such information compiled from travellers' responses when planning shops and catering outlets.

We also report on customer feedback each month to the BAA plc board and highlight areas where there are seven or more complaints, quoting what the complaint is and what we are doing to reduce comments concerning aspects of service or to improve a facility. Feedback is received via letter, feedback card, email and telephone. Feedback cards are available throughout the terminal building and we are shortly launching our newly designed BAA website, whereby passengers can provide us with feedback in a more structured manner. This will then automatically feed through to be recorded on our database used by all BAA airports. All feedback is replied to where requested. A proportion of feedback is airline or third party related, which will be forwarded appropriately or travellers advised of the best course of action to take.

1 Who are BAA's customers? What equipment does BAA have to provide for these customers?
2 What method is used to measure service levels for safety, security and cleanliness? Is this an appropriate method?
3 What method is used to measure customers' experiences of the airport environment?
4 Why do you think retail was only surveyed on an *ad hoc* basis?
5 By what other means do customers give feedback?
6 What will be the advantages of the newly designed BAA website?
7 What does 'third party related' mean? How is this feedback dealt with?

Quality criteria

All organisations need to determine which quality criteria they are going to assess. Although the context will differ for each organisation, most will need to assess customer satisfaction levels against health and safety standards, speed and availability of service, products and services offered, and whether their information and other needs were met.

Health and safety

It is imperative that all customer areas are spotlessly clean and a safe environment is available for all customers. However, health and safety is not only a matter that will affect customer satisfaction, it is a legal requirement that all places of work meet health and safety legislation. The main piece of legislation is the Health and Safety at Work Act 1974, which requires all employers and employees to have 'a duty of care'. Other legislation exists to ensure the safety of employees and members of the public. Examples of legal requirements that ensure the safety of the travelling public include:

* The provision of safety equipment (e.g. life jackets, oxygen masks and emergency chutes) for all air passengers

* Restrictions to prevent passengers getting too close to the jets (engines) when boarding

* Removal of all sharp instruments from hand luggage prior to boarding aircraft

* Tachographs in all coaches – to measure drivers' hours and ensure adequate rest periods are taken

* Emergency exits and first-aid equipment in all coaches

* The use of signs when floor surfaces are wet

* Adequate fire escapes in all accommodation

* Use of signs to indicate exits

* Signs to indicate swimming pool depth (and no-diving signs if it is too shallow).

To provide excellent service organisations will go beyond the legal requirements. For example, it is not a legal requirement that the cleanliness of toilet facilities are checked regularly – but many visitor attractions will do so to ensure they are hygienic for their customers. Many will not allow dogs – this prevents dog fouling and ensures a clean and safe environment for all. All aircraft are cleaned during 'turnaround' – such high standards of cleanliness and hygiene are simply expected by customers.

CASE STUDY

Illness on *Aurora*

Norovirus

P & O Cruises hit the headlines in November 2004 when one of its ships, *Aurora*, was turned away by port authorities in Athens due to an outbreak of Norovirus on board.

Norovirus is a stomach bug that usually lasts between 24 and 48 hours, but passes quickly from person to person.

It is a bug that is brought on board by passengers and spread from person to person. The largest factor in its virulence is people not washing their hands.

Many cruise lines – like most offices, schools, hotels and hospitals – have had to deal with Norovirus outbreaks in recent years, but as long as normal hygiene precautions are taken, there is no reason for passengers to be concerned.

After last year's incident on the *Aurora*, cruise lines now advise passengers to wash their hands frequently and thoroughly with soap for at least 20 seconds each time they use the toilet, after coughing or sneezing, and before eating, drinking or smoking.

On board many ships now, an alcohol-based hand gel is available on entering restaurants or buffets areas, to minimise the chance of the bug reappearing.

General welfare

If passengers do get sick, it is crucial they take advice from crew. In a contained environment like a ship, a bug passed from person-to-person can spread quickly.

The Passenger Shipping Association has set up the SHEW committee (Safety, Health, Environmental and Welfare) to monitor operational issues and give cruise lines the opportunity to share experiences and best practice in all these areas.

P & O Cruises writes to passengers with health tips before they embark and asks them to contact the company if they suffer adverse health symptoms in the week before they are due to join the ship.

P & O also displays notices in public bathrooms on board and leaves a letter in each passenger's cabin reminding them of the importance of basic hygiene protocols.

1 **Why is a virus such as Norovirus potentially damaging to P&O?**
2 **What does P&O do to avoid outbreaks?**
3 **Make recommendations to P&O's management regarding what more they could do to avoid a further outbreak.**

Speed of service

In order to be able to provide a fast and efficient service, several skills are needed. Firstly, you must be organised. You will not be able to know everything – but you must know where to find out! So if a customer walks into a travel agency wanting to book a long-haul holiday bird watching in Madagascar, you should know which resources to use to establish which tour operators sell such specialist holidays and where to find them. If you are organised, the hard copies of resources you need will be to hand and your computer filing system will be easy to use! Furthermore, your desk will be tidy – you will not be fishing through piles of paper for your enquiry form.

Secondly, you need product knowledge, that is, ideally you will know where Madagascar is! However, if you don't know it is important that you can quickly look it up on the Internet, Bespoke software or in the World Travel Guide, and establish that it is an island in the Indian Ocean, off the coast of Mozambique. Product knowledge also includes information about your organisation, for example what they sell, who to

refer complaints to and opening times.

Thirdly, your expertise in using the available technology will determine whether you provide an efficient service. If you lose people when transferring them on the phone, use the incorrect airport code on the computer reservation system, or 'lose' an unsaved document you have just produced, you will not be able to give a good service to your internal or external customers.

Availability of service

Customers increasingly demand that services are available as and when they feel they need them. We now have 24-hour Internet banking, 24-hour supermarket shopping and can entertain ourselves in front of the TV 24 hours a day. Few organisations now work the traditional 9–5 hours, recognising the need to be open when customers are free. The impact on the travel and tourism industry is significant. Many agencies open on Sundays, call centres are available long hours, 7 days a week, and of course web services are available 24 hours every day.

> ### UK distribution
> Our multi-channel distribution approach comprehensively covers our holidaymakers' needs, offering them the facility to 'click, call or come in'. Our distribution channels are the leaders in their fields, from the high street to the Internet, and teletext to call centre.
>
> Whether our customers find their perfect holiday through holiday brochures, our teletext specialists such as Team Lincoln, television or radio advertising, or our own Thomson TV on Sky Channel 637 they can....
>
> **Click** through to our websites where they can research destinations, tour many of our properties with an interactive high-speeded video library and build their own brochure, as well as book and pay for their holidays online.
>
> **Call** our direct sales call centres; our state-of-the-art centre in Glasgow, Skydeals in Bury, and reservations teams for some of our specialist products primarily in the South East.
>
> Or **Come in** to our retail stores. The UK's leading leisure travel retailer is Thomson (formerly Lunn Poly, Sibbald Travel, Callers Pegasus and Travel House) with over 750 retail stores, including award-winning flagship Superstores.
>
> *Source*: TUI website

Excellent customer service also implies additional services – such as the international language service offered by ThomsonFly.

International language services

Opening hours of our international language services are 08.00–16.30 UK time (09.00–17.30 European time) Monday to Friday. Outside these hours, and on public holidays, normally only English language speaking operators will be available.

Source: ThomsonFly website

Availability of services to all customers (including those with sensory, physical or mental disability) is an important consideration for all travel and tourism organisations. The Disability Discrimination Act (see below) covers building design and construction, building approach and exit, as well as public places such as footpaths and parks. Printed material, such as brochures or menus, may also need to be available in Braille or audio formats, and websites should be suitable for disabled users.

Key term

Disability Discrimination Act 1995 This introduced new laws aimed at ending discrimination some customers faced. The law requires service providers to make 'reasonable adjustments' to ensure their premises are accessible to those with sensory, physical or mental disability which seriously affect their day-to-day activities. Around 8.6 million people, or 1 in 7 members of the UK population, fall into this category.

Skills practice

Compare the 'availability' of services offered by two of the major tour operators. Don't forget to include their accessibility for people with special requirements.

A final point when considering availability of service: a trip to Alton Towers when the latest white-knuckle ride is being serviced, a trip to the London Eye when it is not working, or a holiday at a villa where the heated pool is not heated, would all result in dissatisfied customers. Providing excellent service means that those products and services expected by the customer must be available to them.

Key term

Availability of a service When considering the availability of a service the following are some of the issues you need to think about:

• Being able to get in touch with the organisation – is the service available or is the organisation not open for service yet?

• Being able to take a disabled relative on the holiday – is this service accessible (available) to all customers?

• Whether the rides at a theme park are working – is the service available or is it broken/out of order/sold out?

CASE STUDY

Success lies in store

Who's slotting in with other retail brands?

• **First Choice**: More than 40 branches in Asda. Truprint and Druckers coffee shops within its own branches. More partnerships on the cards.

• **Thomas Cook**: 16 branches in Sainsbury's, and some in other supermarkets.

• **Travelcare**: Branches in Tesco, Sainsbury's, Morrisons and the Co-op.

• **STA Travel**: It has Nomad outdoor equipment shop franchises in three of its branches.

• **Lets Go Travel**: Truprint outlets in its larger shops, and is about to sign a deal with a national coffee house.

• **Millington Travel**: Operates Millington Travel Lounge within Costa Coffee, which is located in a Waterstone's bookshop in Leicester – a triple implant.

Source: Travel Trade Gazette March 2005

Sharing shop space with non-travel brands as a means of paying for soaring overheads is becoming a key way for retail travel agents to ensure profitability. Multiples, miniples and independents are increasingly opening outlets within stores or inviting brands to take space within their shops to help pay the rent.

Thomas Cook has recently opened 11 shops within Sainsbury's supermarkets, while a First Choice outlet in Birmingham will welcome the first of many coffee shops to the chain next month thanks to a deal with Druckers.

First Choice already has more than 40 implants in Asda, as well as a deal with photo processor Truprint to operate within some of its stores.

First Choice retail trading director Cheryl Powell revealed the group was in talks with 'a number of other retailers about taking space in their stores and them taking space of ours'.

'Some of our hypermarkets are not as profitable as they used to be, so we are downsizing where we can and trying concessions to help pay the rent,' she said.

'We're picking products that make sense to travel, such as Truprint for holiday snaps. The coffee shop will also be fantastic for business.'

Powell said that implants in supermarkets were valuable as the market 'goes down the 24/7 route'.

'Customers increasingly want to book out of hours – supermarkets have already responded to this so the relationship suits us,' she added.

As well as reducing costs, Lets Go Travel managing director Simon Maunder said that concessions helped generate extra sales.

'The key for us is seeing the customers on their return. People process their photos in our shops, and it gives us a chance to speak to them about their next trip,' he said.

Source: Travel Trade Gazette March 2005

1 **Give reasons why travel agencies are sharing office space in other retail outlets.**
2 **Describe the characteristics of partner organisations.**
3 **How will these partnerships help travel agencies' customer service levels?**

Products and services provided

Organisations need to continuously assess whether their products and services are meeting customers' needs. The new website may look fantastic but can the customers navigate it easily?

A new catering provider may offer a reduced price to an airline, but do the customers like the meals? And what do they think about the new resort reps uniform?

Staffing levels may also determine whether services are being adequately provided. Staff cutbacks at a tourist information centre may result in longer queues, or reductions in staff training at a call centre may result in less ancillary services, such as car hire being offered to customers.

Our new trains
WHAT'S ONBOARD?

Pendolino First Class & Voyager Club Class// On most weekday services, enjoy the complimentary drinks, snacks and newspaper, or perhaps relax in a more spacious seat while listening to the audio entertainment system with your complimentary headphones.

For everyone// All seats have adjustable armrests and either a drop-down or fixed table. Powerpoints for charging mobiles and laptops and audio entertainment (see opposite) are available at or near every seat.

The Shop// Stretch your legs and treat yourself to some delicious refreshments from the onboard shop – there are plenty of snacks and a great range of drinks to choose from. **See pages 48 and 49.**

Mobility// Advance priority seating can be reserved for customers who have difficulties with mobility. There are also wheelchair areas with low-level tables and an emergency call button, while some lavatories are designed for the mobility-impaired and customers with young children.

Luggage// The overhead racks can hold a medium-sized bag, while additional luggage space can be found underneath seats. Please do not leave luggage in the aisles or doorways.

Safety// Instructions are displayed throughout the train with clear signs highlighting routes to the nearest exits and emergency equipment. For your safety, we have also installed Closed-Circuit cameras on all our trains. Smile!

AUDIO
AUDIO LISTINGS// PAGE 53

Your Voyager guide
Virgin FM offers Red Hot, Over Easy, Kidz and Radio 4.

Your Pendolino guide
There's a choice of 14 channels, including BBC Radio 1, 2, 3 and 4.

Everybody on our new trains has access to the at-seat audio entertainment system. If you're on a Voyager train, our exclusive Virgin music system offers Red Hot, Over Easy and Kidz channels, or you can tune into live BBC Radio 4. Customers travelling on a Pendolino have 14 channels of great sounds offering everything from club classics to classical gems, as well as BBC Radio 1, 2, 3 and 4.

The headphone socket, channel finder and volume control are on the panel between each seat. Headphones are sold in The Shop (for just £2) or you can use your own. To adjust volume or channel, press + or – on the panel. Please consider other passengers when adjusting your headphone volume.

Examples of additional products and services provided by Virgin trains

Information and other needs met

Customer complaints are often caused by a lack of information or mis-information. Travel and tourism organisations therefore need to ensure that appropriate information is provided for all their customers. All information provided must be accurate, up to date and appropriately presented. A typical package holiday customer would gather information about their holiday from many sources. These may include:

✽ Holiday description on the website

✽ Holiday details provided by the travel consultant

✽ Written information provided by the tour operator in the brochure

✽ A helpful hints leaflet provided in the document wallet

✽ Resort details provided by the transfer representative

✽ Excursion information provided by the resort representative

✽ Resort details provided in the resort file and on the notice board

✽ Historic details provided by guides on excursions.

Top Tips

● Our **Guest Services** team are here to help. You'll find them in Towers Street.

● Don't leave bags on ride platforms. It's easier and safer to use the **lockers** at Guest Services.

● Look out for the free **Fastrack** service on Air, Nemesis and The Flume Unplugged by Imperial Leather (selected days only)

● If you have young children, take advantage of a **free Child ID wristband** available from Guest Services - this will help us to help you should you and your children become separated. Plus, don't miss out on the extreme rides - **parent queue share passes** also available from Guest Services.

● Not bothered about who you sit next to? Then our **Single Rider queues** on Air, Nemesis, Rita - Queen of Speed, Oblivion and Spinball Whizzer will reduce your waiting time. Further details at ride entrances. Subject to availability.

Additional information provided by Alton Towers

The accuracy of information, how much was given and its presentation could certainly affect customer satisfaction levels. A tour operator would therefore need to monitor whether customers were accessing the information (i.e. were the methods used appropriate) as well as its accuracy.

Additional information can often pre-empt problems. It is often the case that if customers know about things in advance they are not a problem. For example, a tour operator knows there are minor renovation works at a hotel next month. Guests are forewarned by letter and told it will not affect them. However, a free excursion is being offered to compensate for minor levels of disruption. An alternative hotel is offered. The fact that customers are forewarned and have a choice will usually avoid problems.

The above additional information about products and services available will help guests enjoy their stay at Alton Towers.

Documentation

Now that you know some of the methods used to measure and monitor customer service and the quality criteria you could be assessing, you need documentation on which to record your findings. You should be aware that the success of data collection will often depend on the quality of the documentation used. Questionnaires, observation forms and mystery shopper reports need to be carefully worded, the questions carefully structured and the layout of the document appropriately presented.

Gather customer service questionnaires from three organisations. Compare them and note the following:

- Number of questions used
- Layout
- Order of questions.

1 Can the questions be answered quickly?
2 Are the questions easy to understand?
3 Will the data collected be useful to the organisation?
4 Are they collecting qualitative or quantitative information?
5 Can the qualitative information be easily analysed?
6 What method is used to record answers?

Recording answers on questionnaires

The BAA questionnaire featured on page 78 asks for detailed written explanations. This form will collect qualitative data.

Quantitative data collection, however, can use a variety of measures. At the simplest level, Yes/No answers (see Holiday Inn questionnaire on page 78) will provide data that can be easily analysed. However, limited information will be obtained. The most common method used within the travel and tourism industry includes systems whereby respondents use tick boxes (see extract from Fleece Hotel) or a scale to rate services received (see table below).

Extract from the Fleece Hotel questionnaire

Room Service

	Good	Acceptable	Poor
Accuracy of taking your order	☐	☐	☐
Quality of food	☐	☐	☐
Quality of service	☐	☐	☐
Staff friendly and helpful	☐	☐	☐

Any comments:

Hotel Breakfast

	Good	Acceptable	Poor
Quality of food	☐	☐	☐
Quality of service	☐	☐	☐
Staff friendly and helpful	☐	☐	☐

Any comments:

Hotel Dinner

	Good	Acceptable	Poor
Quality of food	☐	☐	☐
Quality of service	☐	☐	☐
Staff friendly and helpful	☐	☐	☐

Any comments:

Choose a holiday you have been on where you stayed at a hotel. Rate the hotel by filling in the table below using a scale of 1–7:

	1	2	3	4	5	6	7	
Comfortable bedroom								Uncomfortable bedroom
Extremely clean room								Dirty room
Excellent quality of food								Poor quality of food
Pleasant hotel staff								Rude hotel staff
Excellent hotel facilities								Poor hotel facilities
Very suitable for families								Totally unsuitable for families

It would be easy for a tour operator to compare the scores received for this hotel with other hotels used. They would be able to advise their supplier which attributes of the hotel were well received and which needed improving. They would also be able to analyse to what extent customers thought the hotel suitable for family holidays – i.e. to what extent the product they were offering met expectations. If required they could then make changes for future years.

Rules for designing customer service questionnaires

1. Before you start designing questions, make a list of what you want to find out.
2. Decide whether you want qualitative information, quantitative information, or both.
3. Discard anything on your list that is not essential.
4. Order the information so that it is logical to your customer.
5. Write out your questions.
6. Never ask more than one thing in a question.
7. Avoid bias in a question.
8. Try to use closed questions, i.e. those with a limited range of answers. They will be easier to analyse.
9. Use open questions only if you need qualitative data.
10. Use filter questions if the respondent does not need to answer every question, e.g. if you answered Yes to question 5, please go straight to question 9.

Skills practice

You are on work experience at a small regional airport. The customer service team is concerned about a recent rise in complaints and wants to implement more measuring and monitoring procedures to establish why this is happening. At a recent team meeting they decided that once a month all members on the customer service team would work in the airport compiling questionnaires from passengers. The results from these questionnaires would be used to compile a monthly report on customer service levels at the airport. Each area will be given an overall score. Once a benchmark has been established, any area scoring below the benchmark will be scrutinised.

You have been asked to design a questionnaire that can be used to gather information from passengers about the customer service. The team would like the following areas to be assessed:

- Flight information
- Ease of finding way
- Walking distances
- Trolleys – availability and handling
- Toilets – cleanliness and ease of finding
- Departure lounge – crowding, cleanliness and ease of finding a seat
- Landside seating – ease of finding
- Check-in – ease of finding, crowding, cleanliness and waiting time
- Security – waiting time and staff helpfulness.

Key term

Benchmark This is anything that can be used as a standard or point of reference. (For example, a tour operator might consider that a hotel must be scored good or excellent by 75% of customers in order to be used in subsequent years.)

- Although most commonly used to assess customer service levels in face-to-face situations, mystery shopping can also be used to assess telephone and written customer service situations. VisitBritain also uses mystery shoppers to assess websites.

- Surveys are used by many travel and tourism organisations to assess customers' experience of service levels. Although most of the data collected is quantitative, the surveys can also be used to collect qualitative information.

- Organisations need to assess to what extent their products and services are meeting customers' needs, as well as assess the customer service provided.

- Questionnaires need to be designed carefully in order to ensure the survey gathers the information required.

- A benchmark is a point of reference. In customer service terms it could be the point at which a bonus is offered to staff for performance or at which a service is considered unacceptable and, for example, suppliers must be changed.

Knowledge check

1. Explain what is meant by a customer focus.
2. Give six examples of an external customer for a travel agent.
3. Outline the benefits to employees of providing excellent service.
4. What is meant by 'frontline staff' and why are they so important?
5. Do you have a positive attitude? Justify your answer.
6. Why is your tone of voice important?
7. What does active listening mean?
8. Give an example of a closed and a leading question.
9. Why do most travel and tourism organisations welcome business customers?
10. Give examples of specific products and services provided for business customers.
11. Say your name out loud using the phonetic alphabet.
12. Why do organisations measure customer service levels?
13. What is qualitative data?
14. Why do many organisations collect qualitative data through customer service questionnaires?
15. What methods could be used to collect quantitative data?

ASSESSMENT

Portfolio practice

For your assessment you need to select a travel and tourism organisation with which you are familiar and carry out the following tasks.

1. You must develop systems to evaluate customer service within the organisation. You must carry out the following tasks:
   - Suggest how customer service should be evaluated within the organisation.
   - Produce appropriate documentation to capture information (e.g. questionnaires, observation sheets). Make sure you use appropriate quality criteria.
   - Explain why the methodology you have chosen is appropriate for your organisation.

2. You must carry out an evaluation of customer service. To what extent do customer service levels meet benchmark standards? For higher grades you will need to include a reasoned conclusion and recommendations.

Resources

The key resource that you need to complete this unit is access to travel and tourism organisations. Where possible you should visit local and national organisations to see how they deal with their customers and measure their own performance.

You will also need access to the Internet to carry out research.

Useful websites are indicated within the text.

Access to the *Travel Trade Gazette* will be required for some activities.

UNIT 3

Destination Europe

Introduction

This unit is about the main destinations in Europe that both leisure and business travellers visit. By the end of the unit you will be able to identify where they are located, the features that give them popularity and appeal and the transport routes that link the destinations to the traveller. You will have the opportunity to learn about a range of destinations in Europe, some in detail.

How you will be assessed

This is an internally assessed unit and you will be required to submit a portfolio of work to be assessed. Your tutor will provide details as to what assessment evidence should be contained within your portfolio.

Assessment evidence could be in many different forms. You will be asked to include a series of maps, but other tasks could be in the form of written reports, production of promotional material or witness testimonials of oral presentations or customer service role-plays with supporting notes.

You are also required to investigate three destinations for this unit. Each destination will be related to a specific focus:

* One destination focusing on features
* One destination focusing on accessibility
* One destination focusing on the factors that have affected popularity and appeal.

After completing this unit you will achieve the following outcomes:

* Know how to categorise the location and types of tourist destinations
* Identify and describe the features and appeal of destinations to different types of tourists
* Know the modes of transport and routes available to European travel destinations
* Know the factors affecting the popularity and appeal of European travel destinations.

3.1 Location and types of tourist destinations

In this section you will learn how to categorise destinations in *Europe* and locate examples of each category on a map. Europe is defined by the countries in continental Europe (west of the Ural Mountains) including Iceland, Cyprus, Madeira, the Canary Islands and the Azores. For the purpose of the assessment of this unit, Europe does not include the United Kingdom (including the Channel Islands and the Isle of Man) or the Republic of Ireland, as these are covered in Unit 4 Destination Britain.

A *travel destination* is the end point of a journey. People travel to a destination for a variety of different reasons, including holiday, business or visiting friends and relatives. A *tourist destination* combines travel with facilities and attractions that appeal to tourists. A tourist destination can include towns, cities, purpose-built resorts, seaside resorts and even whole regions. For the purpose of this unit tourist destinations do not include whole countries (e.g. Spain or Portugal) or individual tourist attractions (e.g. Port Aventura theme park in Spain).

Tourist destinations in Europe are described as *short-haul* destinations as they require a relatively short flight of less than five hours from the UK. The major short-haul tourist destinations in Europe are Spain and France. In comparison, *long-haul* destinations involve a flight of more than five hours, which tend to be outside of Europe, the most popular destinations being the USA and Canada.

Skills practice

1 Using an atlas and a blank map of Europe (see page 198), identify each of the countries represented by geographical Europe.

2 Using Table 3.1, add the information to your map of Europe. You may wish to use a colour code key.

3 Suggest reasons why Spain and France are popular destinations with tourists from the UK.

Table 3.1 Top 10 short-haul destinations from the UK in 2004

RANK ORDER	COUNTRY	NUMBER OF VISITS ABROAD BY UK RESIDENTS (000s)
1	Spain	13,807
2	France	11,603
3	Irish Republic	4,112
4	Italy	2,968
5	Greece	2,701
6	Germany	2,332
7	Netherlands	2,161
8	Belgium	1,799
9	Portugal	1,797
10	Cyprus	1,280

Source: Office for National Statistics (2005)

The different types of tourist destination are:

* Coastal areas
* Tourist towns and cities
* Business and conference destinations
* Countryside areas
* Heritage and cultural destinations
* Purpose built – built specifically to meet the needs of tourists.

Coastal areas

According to the European Union *coastal areas* are the favourite destination for 63 per cent of European holidaymakers. Coastal areas can include seaside resorts and other areas of the coastline that have become popular with tourists. A coastal area destination is an expanse of coastline that is specifically defined as one area (e.g. Costa Blanca in Spain or the Venetian Riviera in Italy). It can also include specific coastal resorts (e.g. Benidorm in Spain or Taormina in Sicily). Islands that are popular specifically for their coastlines can also be included (e.g. Tenerife and Corfu). However, for the purpose of assessment whole groups of islands are not considered as destinations for this unit (e.g. the Canary Islands and the Greek Islands), nor are general areas such as the 'South of France'. Individual island destinations and specific coastal resorts are acceptable.

Europe has long coastlines which are popular with tourists looking for holidays by the sea. On the south western coast is the Atlantic Ocean; on the northern coast is the North Sea; and on the southern coast is the Mediterranean Sea. The Atlantic coastline is characterised by beaches and resorts that attract family holidaymakers and powerful waves that attract water sport enthusiasts such as windsurfers, particularly along the coast of France, Portugal and south-west Spain. The North Sea is much cooler and less turbulent than the Atlantic, but still attracts visitors to destinations along the coastlines of the Netherlands and northern Germany.

The Mediterranean Sea is much calmer, without extreme tidal movements, though strong winds can occur unexpectedly and cause problems for inexperienced water sports enthusiasts. Without strong tidal movements the discharge of pollutants into the waters from the towns and resorts around the coastline means that these pollutants are not so quickly washed away and tend to build up close to the shores. Considerable efforts have been made in recent years to clean up the Mediterranean Sea, including the Blue Flag scheme that categorises beaches according to their cleanliness based on European quality standards.

A Blue Flag is awarded to a coastal area when the beach and water quality meets the standard of the European Union Bathing Water Directive. The eco-label is administered by the Foundation for Environmental Education in Europe (FEEE) and beaches are assessed on an annual basis. If a beach does not meet the required standards the award can be withdrawn. The award has been given to nearly 3000 beaches and marinas in 24 countries across Europe and South Africa.

European coastal areas offer a variety of coastal features, such as sandy beaches, like those found in the popular tourist destinations of Benidorm and Magaluf in Spain, and dramatic cliffs and harbours, like those found along the Amalfi coastline in Italy.

The most popular coastal areas for UK tourists buying package holidays with the tour operator TUI during the summer are:

1 Majorca
2 Ibiza
3 Costa Blanca
4 Costa del Sol
5 Tenerife
6 Minorca
7 Corfu
8 Paphos, Cyprus
9 Gran Canaria
10 Lanzarote.

The most popular coastal areas for UK tourists buying package holidays with the tour operator TUI during the winter are:

1 Tenerife
2 Costa Blanca
3 Gran Canaria
4 Lanzarote
5 Costa del Sol
6 Majorca
7 Paphos, Cyprus
8 Fuerteventura
9 Tunisia
10 Sharm el Sheikh.

Source: TUI (2004)

Skills practice

1 Which of the top 10 summer and winter destinations are located outside of Europe?

2 Label these destinations on a map of Europe, using a suitable key.

3 Suggest why different coastal resorts are popular during the winter and summer months.

4 Would the list of popular tourist destinations be different for another tour operator? Give reasons for your answer.

5 Using a selection of summer sun holiday brochures or travel guides, identify resorts that do not appear in the top ten but are popular with tourists from the UK. Using an atlas, mark these destinations on your map of coastal resorts in Europe.

CASE STUDY

Benidorm, Spain

Benidorm is the most popular resort on the Costa Blanca. The resort attracts approximately 5 million visitors each year, with over 600,000 visitors from the UK. The resort is also popular with visitors from Scandinavia and Germany. Benidorm has two Blue Flag beaches that stretch for 5 kilometres (3 miles). Visitors are attracted by its wide sandy beaches and warm climate with average summer temperatures around 30 ℃, compared to 20 ℃ in London. To maintain the level of sand and quality of the beaches, sand is imported from Morocco. The beaches are gently sloping and the water is warm and clear, making the sea relatively safe for adults and children.

Levante Beach in Benidorm

Behind the sandy beaches high-rise hotels dominate the skyline. There is plenty of nightlife, with English and Spanish bars, nightclubs, casinos and restaurants.

Skills practice

1 Using a summer sun holiday brochure, describe the reasons why Benidorm is a popular tourist destination.

2 Using the holiday brochure, identify different groups of tourists that would be attracted by a holiday in Benidorm.

Skills practice

1 Using an atlas, locate each of the ten most popular cities in Europe visited by UK tourists on a blank map of Europe (see page 198).

2 Which of the top ten most popular cities in Europe is not included in this unit?

3 For each of the most popular cities visited by UK tourists, identify one major visitor attraction in each destination.

4 Using a selection of city break holiday brochures or travel guides, identify destinations that do not appear in the top ten but are popular with tourists from the UK. Using an atlas, mark these destinations on your map of Europe.

Tourist towns and cities

Major *towns* and *cities* provide destinations for short-break holidays, which is the fastest growing sector of international travel. Europeans tend to take two or more city breaks a year in addition to their main annual holiday. Low-cost airlines have expanded the choice of destinations even further. Examples of tourist destinations are capital cities, such as Paris (France), Rome (Italy) or Tallinn (Estonia), and other cities such as Venice (Italy), Oporto (Portugal), Nice (France), Barcelona (Spain) and Milan (Italy).

The most popular cities visited by UK tourists are:

1	Paris	6	Brussels
2	Amsterdam	7	Bruges
3	Dublin	8	Barcelona
4	Rome	9	Venice
5	Prague	10	Vienna.

Source: ABTA (2004)

The following are some of the reasons why towns and cities are popular with tourists:

* They provide a range of cultural attractions, from art galleries, theatres and entertainment to sports and leisure facilities.

* They provide a wide range of shops and boutiques, as well as theatres, restaurants, nightclubs, and entertainment venues hosting events exhibitions and concerts.

* They provide a wide range of accommodation, both in terms of price and level of comfort.

CASE STUDY

Oporto, Portugal

Oporto is the second largest city in Portugal and is located in the north of the country. It is a good location from which to explore the wine-producing Douro region and the Costa Verde coastal resort.

The city is also known as Porto. The name has been made famous by the locally produced port wine. Oporto has a historic centre dating back over 1000 years and is classified by UNESCO as a World Heritage Site. Popular historic attractions include the Ribeira waterside and its busy downtown district, including the Stock Exchange, cathedral, and the Clérigos tower. The city has a wide range of hotels, bars, restaurants and nightlife. It was awarded the title of European City of Culture in 2001, which it shared with the city of Rotterdam in the Netherlands.

Oporto has one of three international airports in Portugal with frequent flights to and from the UK. Porto International airport handles 3 million passengers each year, although there are plans to develop the airport, doubling its capacity to 6 million passengers.

For more information visit http://www.portugal.org

The Ribeira district on the waterfront of the Doura River, with the white facade of the Bishop's Palace above in the centre of the city Oporto, Portugal

* They are attractive to tourists who have friends or relatives who live in them, making them more appealing as places to visit.

* They are often the hub of transport networks. People use road, rail, sea or air transport which ends at a terminus near or in a large town or city.

* They have large concentrations of commercial, financial and industrial services that act as a focus encouraging people to visit for conferences and business travel.

Think it over ...

Why are European towns and cities popular short-break destinations with visitors from the UK?

Business and conference destinations

Business travel includes travelling for the purpose of meetings, conferences, trade fairs and exhibitions. Meetings and conferences can be held at the headquarters of international organisations, 65 per cent of which are based in Europe. Most are held in purpose-built conference and exhibition centres and in dedicated spaces within hotels. Companies and organisations that provide services to support business and conference meetings are sometimes referred to as MICE industries – Meetings, Incentives, Conferences and Exhibitions.

Business and conference destinations are defined as towns and cities with facilities to cope with business tourists, such as large conference and/or exhibition centres, a range of business tourist facilities (e.g. a large number of four- and five-star hotels and good transport links) and usually close proximity to an international airport. Some may lack large conference and exhibition centres but be a significant commercial centre and therefore still attract significant numbers of business travellers. Examples include Berlin (Germany), Barcelona (Spain) and The Hague (Netherlands).

Business and conference destinations are an important source of income for city destinations. This comes from the hire of conference and meeting rooms, accommodation and travel, and visits to local restaurants, bars and evening entertainment.

Other European business and conference destinations that are growing in importance, based on the number of people who visit, include: Helsinki, Florence, Munich, Stockholm and Rome.

Table 3.2 Estimated total number of delegates at international meetings held in European destinations, 2003

RANK	CITY	NUMBER OF DELEGATES
1	Berlin	89,713
2	Paris	79,477
3	Vienna	78,303
4	Lisbon	73,406
5	Barcelona	60,942
6	Prague	56,065
7	Madrid	52,002
8	Copenhagen	36,436
9	Amsterdam	32,461
10	Milan	30,700

Source: ICCA (2003)

CASE STUDY

Berlin the conference city

Berlin has Europe's largest convention centre and is Germany's number one conference location. The German capital is home to the ICC, Europe's largest conference centre, as well as an unusually large selection of conference facilities and venues, Europe's most modern hotels and an overall capacity of 69,000 beds.

A total of 72,400 events were held in Berlin in 2003, attracting 5.7 million participants. Together, conference delegates generated turnover of €754 million.

The International Congress Centre (ICC) has 80 halls and rooms with seating for between 20 and 9070 people, with a total capacity of 20,300. The ICC has 5000 metres of exhibition space and has one of the world's largest theatre stages.

The Estrel Hotel and Convention Centre has 70 conference rooms and halls, with a capacity for up to 5000 people and 15,000 metres of exhibition space.

Source: Berlin Business Location Centre

For further information visit http://www.blc.berlin.de

Countryside areas

Countryside areas are rural areas away from towns and cities and not necessarily specifically named resorts. They are areas that incorporate a number of features, such as mountains, lakes, forests and hills. Examples include the Black Forest (Germany), Provence (France) and Tuscany (Italy). For the purpose of assessment, whole mountain ranges (e.g. the Alps) would not be considered a countryside area; however a specific area within a mountain range would be acceptable (e.g. Berner Oberland in the Swiss Alps).

Countryside tourism takes place in rural areas and includes farm-based holidays, rural hotels and restaurants, special interest nature holidays, activity holidays and walking holidays.

Skills practice

1 Using an atlas, locate the top ten European business and conference destinations on an outline map of Europe (see page 198).

2 Add to your map of European business and conference destinations five business and conference destinations that are growing in importance.

3 How does a city benefit from hosting an international conference or exhibition?

4 Produce an example of an international conference or business venue in Europe. You may need to use the Internet to help you research this question.

Each country within Europe has identified areas of countryside that are considered to be unique or contain rare species of plants or animals. These areas are often protected as national parks or nature reserves. People are attracted to these areas for walking, sightseeing, mountain biking, horse riding and water sports.

Many visitors are attracted by the relaxed pace of life, compared to the pressures of busy towns and cities. Rural areas in France, particularly in Normandy, are popular with visitors from the UK who can drive a relatively short distance and stay in a *gîte*, a French farmhouse. The Italian region of Tuscany is also popular with UK holidaymakers who are attracted by the rolling countryside, local foods and vineyards. The lakes and mountains of Austria are represented in many holiday brochures as providing walking and sightseeing holidays during the summer and skiing holidays during the winter.

Table 3.3 Popular activity holidays in Europe

COUNTRY	France	France	France	Austria	Austria	Austria	Austria	Italy	Switzerland	Slovenia
Resort	Messanges	Les Gets	Chamonix	Kaprun	Mayhofen	Zell am See	Kitzbuhel	Val di Fassa	Interlaken	Bovec
Biking	●	▲	▲	▲	●	●	▲	▲	●	●
Rafting	✔	●	●	●	✔	✔	●	●	✔	✔
Canyoning		●	●	●	✔	✔	●	●	✔	✔
Climbing		●	●	✔	✔	✔	✔	✔	✔	✔
Hiking	●	●	●	●	●	●	●	●	●	●
Paragliding		✔	✔	●	✔	✔	✔	✔	✔	✔
Windsurfing	✔									
Waterskiing	✔					✔			✔	
Golf	✔	✔	✔	✔	✔	✔	✔	✔	✔	
Horse Trekking	✔	✔	✔	●	✔	✔	✔	●	✔	✔
Summer Skiing				✔	✔	✔				
Tennis	✔	✔	✔	✔	✔	✔	✔	✔	✔	✔
Surfing	✔									

● = included option   ✔ = available in resort   ▲ = specialised fleet
Source. Crystal Holidays (2005)

Rural activity resorts in Europe

For further information see 'Natural attractions', pages 105–107.

For further information see 'Natural attractions', pages 105–107.

Skills practice

1 Using an atlas, locate the rural activity holidays from the Crystal Holidays brochure and the examples given in this section on an outline map of Europe (see page 198).

2 Describe the main attractions and activities that are available in each of the areas located on your map.

3 Using a variety of tourist brochures, identify 10 winter ski resorts that are popular with visitors from the UK and locate these on your map of countryside areas.

4 All of these areas on your map are categorised as countryside. Can these areas also be placed in other categories, and if so which other categories can they be placed in?

Heritage and cultural destinations

Heritage and cultural destinations are specific towns, cities, villages and resorts that are known for having maintained the history and heritage of the destination and/or the culture of the region or country. Examples include many cultural capital cities, such as Paris (France), Budapest (Hungary) or Rome (Italy), and smaller destinations such as Seville (Spain), Reims (France), Bruges (Belgium) or Carcassone (France). Examples can also be linked to UNESCO cultural heritage sites such as Dubrovnik (Croatia) or Warsaw (Poland).

Heritage destinations provide visitors with a link to the past. These destinations include historic buildings, castles, sites where important events took place and places associated with famous people. *Cultural destinations* provide visitors with a link to the identity, values and creativity of the people who live in a particular country. These include music, dance, art, architecture, literature, language and food, as well as crafts and festivals. The tourist industry encourages souvenir shops and places of interpretation, such as visitor centres, exhibitions, trails and tours, to educate and entertain visitors.

Many major cities are heritage and cultural destinations in their own right as they provide a range of historic attractions and represent the cultures of the people who live there.

CASE STUDY
Bruges, Belgium

The medieval canal city of Bruges has been recognised by many names: City of Romance, Venice of the North, the City That Time Forgot, and Cultural Capital of Europe in 2002.

The city centre is pedestrianised, so the beauty and culture of this city can be easily explored on foot or by horse-drawn carriage along cobblestoned streets; there are also boat rides along quiet canals. Bruges is a small city but it takes more than one day to explore all the architectural and artistic treasures, folklore, chocolate shops, lace boutiques, and restaurants.

The historic centre of Bruges is on the list of UNESCO World Heritage Sites and has many places of interest, including the Belfry, the Groeninge Museum and the Straffe Hendrik Brewery.

For further information on Belgium visit http://www.visitbelgium.com
For further information on Bruges visit http://www.brugge.be
For further information see 'Built Attractions', pages 107–110.

Skills practice

1 Why is Bruges described as a heritage and cultural destination?
2 Describe the main tourist attractions in Bruges.
3 Compare Bruges to another heritage and cultural destination in Europe.

Skills practice

1 Using the UNESCO website, select ten World Heritage Sites and mark them on an outline map of Europe (see page 198).
2 For each of your ten sites identify the reasons why they are considered to be of world importance. You may need to research both the UNESCO website and the websites of each World Heritage Site to answer this question.

CASE STUDY
UNESCO World Heritage Sites

The United Nations Educational Scientific and Cultural Organisation (UNESCO) has identified cultural and heritage sites of world importance. Cultural sites can be:

- Monuments – including sculptures, memorial stones, cave paintings or inscriptions
- Groups of buildings – these can be separated or connected but are usually set in a unique landscape
- Sites of human or historical importance.

For further information visit http://www.unesco.org

Purpose-built tourist destinations

Purpose-built tourist destinations are specifically built to meet the needs of tourists. These are destinations developed specifically for tourists to provide all the facilities needed in one place. The destinations can provide a range of services, including entertainment, leisure and accommodation, in one resort. As the weather in northern Europe is often unpredictable, some purpose-built resorts have included all-weather facilities to encourage visitors.

Think it over ...

What are the benefits of a purpose-built tourist destination?

For assessment purposes theme parks are not generally acceptable as they are regarded as purpose-built attractions rather than purpose-built resorts. However, theme park resorts such as Disneyland Paris or large holiday centres such as Center Parcs are acceptable. Purpose-built destinations can also include some entire resorts in their own right, such as La Manga Club resort in Spain.

For more information see 'Built attractions', pages 107–110.

CASE STUDY

La Manga Club resort

The La Manga Club resort is a purpose-built luxury resort set in 1400 acres. It includes a five-star Hyatt Regency hotel and self-catering apartments, three golf courses, 28 tennis courts, a luxury spa and wellness centre, a Professional Football Centre, cricket pitches, golf and tennis academies, over 20 restaurants and bars, a mini-club for the children, conference and banqueting facilities, as well as mountain biking, horse riding and water sports.

For further information visit http://www.lamangaclub.com

CASE STUDY

Center Parcs

Center Parcs has 20 villages spread throughout Europe: 8 in the Netherlands, 2 in Belgium, 4 in Germany, 2 in France and 4 in the UK. They are designed as purpose-built complexes with villa accommodation based around an undercover pool, bars, restaurants, indoor sports facilities and shops. Outdoor sporting activities include sailing, canoeing, cycling, walking, skating and tennis. The Parcs are designed to blend in with their natural surroundings by using local building materials. Activities for children have also been considered, including the Kids Klub which provides children's entertainment, pony riding and play areas.

For further information visit http://www.centerparcs.com

CASE STUDY

Club Med

Club Med operates in 40 countries around the world. It provides purpose-built all-inclusive accommodation specifically designed around a series of themes, from family resorts, sports and entertainment, relaxation and spa therapy to resorts that are for adults only with an emphasis on dance, partying and sport.

For further information visit http://www.clubmed.co.uk

Club Med resort in the south of France

1 Using an atlas and an outline map of Europe (see page 198), identify ten purpose-built destinations. You may need to use the Internet to research this question.

2 What attracts visitors to purpose-built destinations like Club Med and Center Parcs?

3 Suggest why Club Med has selected different villages to appeal to different types of tourist.

As we have discovered, not all destinations can be easily categorised. By using a range of examples you will be able to explain the features that differentiate each category and how there are often overlaps between them. For example, a purpose-built tourist destination can exist in a coastal area and tourist towns and cities often attract business and conference delegates. It is important to be aware that a tourist destination can serve more than one purpose and appeal to more than one type of tourist. For example, Center Parcs offers purpose-built village resorts in countryside locations and therefore does not fit into just one category. A city destination may also appear in three or four different categories.

CASE STUDY

Naples, Italy

Naples is the third largest city in Italy and receives over two million visitors each year. It is located along the southern coastline of Italy on the Bay of Naples. Its historic centre is recognised as a UNESCO World Heritage Site with many traditional buildings, museums and churches. The city also hosts a variety of national and international conferences each year. As a result, Naples can be categorised as a coastal area, a tourist city, a heritage and cultural destination, and a business and conference destination.

Think it over ...

Name five tourist destinations in Europe that can be placed in more than one category and identify which categories they can be placed in.

Key terms

Coastal area An expanse of coastline, a coastal resort or an island popular specifically for its coastline.

Tourist towns and cities A specific town or city which is known as a tourist destination.

Business and conference destination Towns or cities with facilities to cope with business tourists, such as large conference and exhibition centres.

Countryside areas Rural areas away from towns and cities and not necessarily specific named resorts.

Heritage and cultural destinations Specific towns, cities, villages and resorts that are known for having maintained their history, heritage or culture.

Purpose built A destination developed specifically for tourists to provide all the facilities needed in one place

ASSESSMENT

Portfolio practice

This is an internally assessed unit and you will be required to submit a portfolio of work to be assessed.

1 For this task you are asked to produce six maps, one for each type of destination. Each map should locate European travel destinations popular with UK tourists. You may have already done this by following the skills practice. Make sure that your maps show the accurate location of your European travel destinations.

These maps will require a lot of detail, so you may wish to consider using a larger sheet of paper such as A3 rather than standard A4 size.

2 Using a colour key on your six maps, identify destinations which are emerging as popular travel destinations. You may wish to do some more research using holiday brochures, travel guidebooks and the Internet.

3 On each of your six maps highlight the relevant European gateways and road and rail routes for each of these destinations from the UK. See section 3.3 'Modes of transport and routes available to European travel destinations', pages 117–124.

Your six maps need to show the main road and rail routes from the UK, as well as airports and seaports. You are not expected to mark on every road, but show the main ways of getting to the destination. You will need an atlas to do this. Consider using a key to represent different modes of transport on your map, for example

 Airport   Seaport   Railway   ——— Road

You may also wish to select some of the less important airports and seaports as part of your map, but make sure that they do provide a route from the UK.

4 For each of the six types of destination, you will need to provide an explanation of their main features, using a range of examples. You may wish to start with defining each of the six categories.

5 Using a range of examples, explain the difficulties in categorising some destinations. Some European travel destinations can be placed in more than one category.

3.2 The features and appeal of destinations to different types of tourist

In this section you will learn about the features that attract tourists to destinations, so that you can identify and describe the key features that give them appeal. You will be able to differentiate between those features that give a destination appeal and those that exist but are not relevant. You will also be able to find information about features of destinations and use these sources to research a range of destinations and their features. Features you should consider include:

* Climate
* Landscape
* Transport and communication links
* Accommodation

* Facilities provided for activities, for business and general facilities for tourists
* Natural and built attractions
* Events and entertainment
* Cost of visiting and living
* Local culture, including food and drink.

Climate

Climate affects the appeal of destinations. It is the second most important reason for choosing a holiday destination. Climate is important because warmer climates are often more attractive to tourists from the UK.

Climate is a measure of atmospheric conditions, such as temperature, sunshine and rainfall, that are based on yearly or monthly averages over a period of not less than thirty years. These figures are usually displayed in holiday brochures, holiday guides and atlases.

Weather conditions are events that occur daily and form part of the climate for the destination. People prefer warm, bright sunny conditions rather than cold, damp and overcast ones.

Major destinations tend to be in warmer climates. Colder climates also have an appeal but receive smaller numbers of visitors. One exception is the popular ski resorts that rely on an abundance of snow.

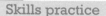

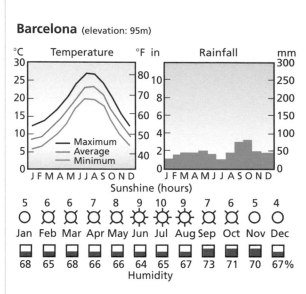

Figure 3.1 The climate of Barcelona, Spain

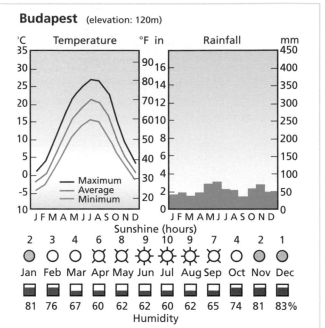

Figure 3.2 The climate of Budapest, Hungary

1 For each destination, identify the hottest month and the coldest month of the year in °C.

2 For each destination, compare the annual temperature range (hottest to coldest monthly average) in °C.

3 For each destination, what is the annual average temperature?

4 For each destination, identify the wettest and the driest months.

5 For each destination, identify the month that receives the most sunshine.

6 Suggest which is the most popular holiday destination. Give reasons for your answer.

Landscape

Landscape represents inland scenery that includes mountains, valleys, woodland, rivers, and towns and cities. There are considerable variations in landscapes and visitors' preferences and responses to them. Some tourists are impressed with tourist picnic areas and car parks combined with interesting views. Some prefer rural or countryside landscapes, others are more attracted to the architecture or skyline of towns and cities.

Think it over ...

What type of landscapes appeal to you? Suggest reasons why you find these landscapes appealing.

Transport and communication links

Destinations that have good transport and communication links will appeal more to tourists than those that are difficult to access. To travel to a destination tourists have to face getting from their house to a departure point, and when they arrive at the destination, to get from the airport to their accommodation. Direct routes are preferred as less time is spent travelling, leaving more time to spend at the destination. Direct routes may also be less expensive.

Communication links are important for tourists to keep in contact with families at home. Most hotels and tourist facilities have telephones, but many visitors may prefer to use their own mobile phone. Access to the Internet may be necessary for business travellers, with telephone, broadband or Wi-Fi being made available.

Accommodation

The *range of accommodation* available at a tourist destination varies according to the quality and level of service on offer and also the price of staying there. Some visitors prefer the independence of self-catering accommodation, whereas others prefer serviced accommodation with various levels of service provided. Levels of service can be classified into bed and breakfast; half board, where an evening meal is provided in the cost; full board, which includes lunch and evening meal; and all-inclusive, which adds bar snacks and drinks to the full board option.

The main *types of accommodation* on offer includes: hotels, guesthouses, inns, holiday centres, hostels, villas, apartments, chalets, caravans, camping, and farm accommodation. Each appeals to different types of tourist, so many destinations seek to provide a range of accommodation types to attract a wide cross-section of holidaymakers. Disabled groups and the elderly need accommodation that has good access. Young families will seek family accommodation with children's rooms adjacent to the main bedroom. Backpackers and students tend to seek cheaper accommodation with fewer facilities.

A hotel tends to have five or more guest bedrooms. A guesthouse is a modern name for a boarding house, a private house where the owner rents out rooms and may also provide meals. An inn or public house may have a small number of guest bedrooms used as bed-and-breakfast accommodation.

Farm accommodation is a popular option for rural holidays, with farmers offering rooms and farm cottages to let. Tourists can experience rural life first hand while living in authentic rural accommodation.

The range of sites for caravans and camping includes a field on a farm to purpose-built sites with restaurants, bars, shops, children's activities and other on-site services.

Think it over ...

What are the advantages of a tourist destination offering a wide range of different types of accommodation?

Holiday centres for large numbers of tourists have become resorts in their own right. They include an all-inclusive package of accommodation, food and entertainment.

CASE STUDY

Haven Europe

The UK company Haven Europe operates 30 holiday parcs in France, Italy and Spain. In 22 locations they rent spaces in locally managed parcs to provide luxury mobile homes and camping facilities. In addition, they own 8 French Siblu holiday parcs in the popular tourist regions of Aquitaine, Brittany, Charente Maritime, Languedoc and Vendee.

For further information on Haven Europe visit http://www.siblu.com

Facilities provided for activities, for business and general facilities for tourists

Tourists expect facilities to be fit for their purpose and to meet, if not exceed, their expectations. Many tourist destinations have a diverse range of facilities to appeal to a wide range of tourists and also encourage them to return. Facilities include accommodation, restaurant or local shops if self-catering, transport, relevant equipment, events or services.

Accommodation providers may offer a wide range of facilities, from satellite television, tea- and coffee-making facilities, to laundry and room service. In warm or hot climates air-conditioned rooms may be provided in hotel accommodation.

Hotels catering for families and children may provide activity clubs and supervised play areas, while other hotels may offer beauty treatments, spa and leisure facilities. The range of facilities on offer are displayed in holiday brochures.

Think it over ...

What facilities do you expect to be provided with when you go on holiday?

Majorca

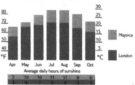

"Majorca offers excellent value for money and has something for everyone. Superb beaches, fantastic scenery and a great variety of resorts."

Basking in Mediterranean sunshine, it's easy to see why Majorca is so popular. It's an island with something to please everyone.

Beaches vary from wide sandy bays to charmingly secluded inlets. The landscape changes from dramatic mountains and the spectacular scenery of Cap de Formentor to gently terraced hillsides and fertile valleys. You'll soon discover the pace of life varies from the frantic to the sleepy. Wherever you go and whatever pace of life you choose, the warm friendly welcome doesn't change.

If you're looking for lively beaches with lots going on and a vibrant atmosphere after dark, head for Magaluf and Palma Nova. Whether you want great shops, English-style pubs and discos or a more local flavour, it's all here. Puerto Pollensa and Cala d'Or are much more relaxed with a typically Majorcan ambience. For a cosmopolitan choice of shops and restaurants and the chance to indulge in a spot of sightseeing, spend some time in Palma where you can admire the magnificent cathedral, Bellver Castle (beautifully floodlit after dark), and one of the biggest (and exclusive) marinas in the Mediterranean.

If you can't bear to lie still for long on the beach, you'll be spoilt for choice when it comes to watersports. Water-skiing, jet skiing or paragliding are all on offer and you'll find windsurfing available at most resorts. Should scuba-diving seem a bit too energetic, a trip on a glass bottomed boat is a pleasant and relaxing way to glimpse the underwater life.

Although long lazy days on the beach are extremely tempting, don't miss the chance to explore inland. The old-fashioned train through the mountains is an unforgettable day out, especially if you combine it with a leisurely lunch in Soller or visit some of Majorca's famous underground caves with their immense caverns and subterranean lakes. Majorca is one of our favourite destinations – ideal for families, couples or groups.

fact file Ask your travel agent for further information on accommodation in this resort. See A-Z guide.

Your **Local** Expert *"We're here to help you have the best holiday"*

Money Matters There are 1.39 euros to the £1.00 as at 4th October 2004. Banking hours are Monday-Friday 08.30-14.00. All our resorts have banks or exchange bureaux, while major credit cards are accepted at most places.

HolidayLine Getting ready for your holiday may prompt a few last minute questions. Call our HolidayLine on 0905 069 0169 for information and advice on in-resort services and activities from experts in our overseas offices. The lines are open 24 hours.

Holiday Tips In most hotels and aparthotels gentlemen are required to wear long trousers to dinner.

Please note Holiday Reps do not accompany you on your coach transfers so that we can provide you with a more dedicated service both in your accommodation and at the airport. Most hotels or apartments ask customers to vacate their rooms between 10am and 12 midday. For late afternoon or evening flights, late check out rooms may be available. Please see Your Holiday, Your Choice options on accommodation pages.

Local Specialities Vegetable soups, fish stews, rabbit, suckling pig and sausages are favourites, while some of the local red wine, made in Binissalem, is not unlike a mild Rioja. Artificial Pearls and leather are some of the best buys.

Facilities holidaymakers can expect to enjoy in Majorca

Source: Thomson

Specialist holidays, such as activity holidays, will provide specialist equipment as well as trained and qualified staff. There will be rooms set aside for training and instruction, as well as the storage and maintenance of equipment. At the destination tour operators may use local companies who specialise in outdoor pursuits and activities. Tourists may only need to bring personal belongings and some basic items of equipment, most of what they need will be provided at the destination.

Hotels catering for business meetings will provide the required facilities to cope with small or large groups. They may equip rooms with audiovisual equipment, such as projectors, computers, flip charts, whiteboards and Internet connections. Accommodation is available for those who need to stay overnight, and hotel bar and restaurant facilities provide business delegates with hospitality during their meetings.

Skills practice

Using a range of summer sun brochures, specialist activity holiday brochures and details of conference facilities on the Internet, list a range of facilities that you would expect to find if you were going on:

- an activity holiday, e.g. mountain biking or pony trekking
- on a business trip, e.g. to an international conference
- a general leisure holiday, e.g. to a beach resort.

Natural and built attractions

Major destinations provide either natural or built attractions, or both.

Natural attractions

Natural attractions are based on the *topography* or shape of the land. Each destination has its own unique topography, which tourists may find attractive.

Natural attractions include:

* Lakes
* Rivers
* Forests
* Mountains
* Caves
* Volcanoes
* Coastlines
* Waterfalls.

Think it over ...

Discuss a natural attraction that you have visited and give reasons why you found it interesting.

Lakes

Lakes are large inland areas of water. They attract tourists, including those seeking scenic beauty and water sports.

CASE STUDY

The Italian Lakes

The Italian Lakes are a popular destination for UK tourists. Based in the region of Trentino in the north of Italy, the lakes are surrounded by the Dolomite Mountain range to the north. The lakes are deep and have steep sides, producing a dramatic landscape. There are four main lakes:

- Lake Como
- Lake Garda
- Lake Lugano
- Lake Maggiore.

Lake Garda is the largest lake in Italy and is the most developed in terms of tourism, with many small towns and camping sites situated along the shore. A mild climate and rich fertile soils have encouraged olives, lemon trees and grape vines to flourish. The steep sides of Lake Garda rise to 1750 metres (5740 feet) at Monte Baldo. Views across the lake are possible from a panoramic rotating cable car.

The Trentino Tourist Board has encouraged the growth of tourism based on natural attractions. These include:

- Wine tourism
- Dairy and local food tourism
- Mountain bike holidays
- Horse-riding holidays through the mountains
- Windsurfing holidays.

nuova funivia panoramica
neue Panorama - Seilbahn
new panoramic cableway

MALCESINE · MONTE BALDO

Rivers

Rivers are a popular destination for tourists because of their scenic beauty, wildlife and fishing. Over 60 per cent of UK river cruise passengers travel to European destinations. The Rhine and the Danube, both major European rivers, are linked by the Main River and a series of canals. This makes it possible to conduct cruises from the North Sea to the Black Sea, along 3500 kilometres (2200 miles) of waterways. Popular cruises include those from Frankfurt to Munich and from Amsterdam to Vienna and Budapest.

The top five European destinations for UK river cruise passengers in 2002 were:

1   River Rhine and Moselle
2   River Danube
3   River Rhone and Seine
4   The Russian waterways
5   River Po.

Source: Mintel (2004)

Forests

Forests are unique habitats for wildlife and popular destinations for walking and activity holidays. The Black Forest in southern Germany is famous for its highland scenery, cuckoo clocks, fairy-tale castles and cherry schnapps, which is used to make the famous Black Forest Gateau. The forest is over 200 kilometres (125 miles) long and 60 kilometres (37 miles) wide, with mountain peaks of up to 1500 metres (4920 feet). The forest runs along a stretch of the River Rhine and borders other tourist regions that are famous for their natural attractions: these include Lake Constance in Switzerland and the Alsace region of France.

Mountains

Mountain areas offer dramatic landscapes, with high mountain peaks, often capped with snow, and deep valleys with lakes and rivers. Mountain resorts such as Kitzbühel and Zell am See in the Austrian Alps are popular for walking holidays during the summer months and skiing during the winter months. Zell am See is also a popular water-sport destination during the summer months.

CASE STUDY
Hohe Tauern National Park, Austria

The Hohe Tauern National Park in Austria is the largest protected natural area in Central Europe. The area is dominated by the Grossglockner (3798 metres/12,457 feet), the highest mountain in Austria. In the valley below the Grossglockner is the Pasterze glacier, the largest glacier in the European Alps. The glacier covers an area of 19 square kilometres (12 square miles) and is 9 kilometres (5.5 miles) long. The park is famous for its summer walks, sightseeing, hiking and mountain climbing. A series of 'teaching-routes' has been devised to help visitors understand the key features of the national park, with signposts and information points situated along circular walks.

Caves

A *cave* is a natural hole in a rock, most commonly found in areas of limestone. They can be spectacular features, with columns of stalagmites that rise from the floor and stalactites that hang from the ceiling.

CASE STUDY
Show caves at Nerja, Spain

The Nerja caves

The show caves at Nerja, on the Costa del Sol in Spain, are situated 3 kilometres (1.9 miles) from the coast on the slopes of the Sierra Almijara mountains. The caves are 4823 metres (15,820 feet) long, over 5 million years old, and have been carved out by the gradual erosion of water. The widest column of rock in the world is found here, the grand centre column in the *Sala del Cataclismo* (Cataclysm Hall), which is 32 metres (105 feet) high, and 13 by 7 metres (43 by 23 feet) wide. The caves were inhabited from 25,000 BC until the Bronze Age and there are ancient wall paintings. The centre of the caves has been transformed into a performance area where music concerts and ballets are accompanied by a light show that illuminates the large columns of rock.

Volcanoes

A *volcano* is an opening on the Earth's surface from where magma, molten rock or ash erupts, often violently. Most volcanoes tend to be conical in shape and are found where there is a weakness in the Earth's crust. They are popular with tourists but they are dangerous when they erupt. Mount Etna in Sicily is Europe's most active volcano; it last erupted in 2002.

Built attractions

Built attractions include a wide variety of purpose-built venues. Some of these have been adapted to meet the needs of tourists.

Built attractions include:

* Theme parks
* Indoor arenas
* Historic buildings
* Ancient monuments
* Museums and art galleries.

Theme parks

Theme parks are purpose-built visitor attractions offering a wide range of facilities, including shopping, restaurants and gardens. The parks are themed around historic events, fantasy, childhood or a futuristic world. Many contain 'white-knuckle rides', but have become increasingly more sophisticated in their use of fantasy and illusion.

Theme parks offer value for money in that they provide a full day's entertainment at a fixed price. Pricing structures often allow discounts for

groups and for families. Details of special offers are usually displayed on a theme park's website. Even when the weather is poor many theme parks have attractions which people can still enjoy no matter what the weather, as well as having a range of indoor attractions and facilities. Some theme parks are specifically targeted at families and younger children, whereas others have more exhilarating rides attracting teenagers and young adults. Although most visitors to theme parks are day visitors, many theme parks are encouraging visitors to stay overnight in purpose-built themed accommodation.

For more information, see 'Purpose-built tourist destinations', pages 99–100.

For more information, see 'Purpose-built tourist destinations', pages 99–100.

Skills practice

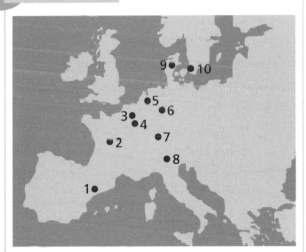

Popular theme parks of Europe

Complete the following table of popular theme parks in Europe:

Theme park	Location number	Main attractions and facilities
Disneyland Paris		
De Efteling		
Europa Park		
Futuroscope		
Gardaland		
Legoland		
Parc Asterix		
Phantasialand		
Port Aventura		
Tivoli		

Gladiators in the Spanish arena of the Europa Theme Park in Germany

Indoor arenas

Indoor arenas provide a variety of public exhibitions, entertainment, music events and sporting facilities, as well as business exhibitions (trade shows) and conventions. They are large enough to support exhibitions and events on a grand scale and usually include:

✳ Conference rooms and meeting rooms

✳ Registration and welcome areas

✳ Box office services for public events

✳ Good transport access – road, rail and air

✳ Car parking facilities

✳ Support services for exhibitors and event organisers

✳ Food and catering facilities

✳ Adequate toilet facilities

✳ Easy access for visitors with special needs

✳ Nearby hotel accommodation.

CASE STUDY

Color Line Arena, Hamburg

The Color Line Arena in Hamburg, Germany, is one of the newest purpose-built indoor arenas in Europe. It has the capacity to hold 17,000 spectators for a variety of events, including concerts by international celebrities and bands, sporting events and exhibitions. The arena can also be transformed into an ice rink for the Holiday On Ice show. Approximately 120 events occur in the arena each year. The Color Line Arena also has Europe's largest indoor restaurant, seating approximately 6000 people.

Historic buildings

Historic buildings include stately homes, castles, royal palaces, birthplaces and houses of famous people. They have been adapted for tourists to visit, have improved health and safety features and have incorporated additional tourist facilities such as guides, toilets and souvenir shops. Historic buildings help visitors understand the history and culture of the country they are visiting.

CASE STUDY

Palace of Versailles, France

The Palace of Versailles estate is one of the most famous historic buildings in Europe, with three chateaux and extensive gardens. It was originally built as a hunting lodge in 1624 and became the royal palace of King Louis XIV. Until 1789 it remained the seat of the monarchy in France and its design reflects its power and wealth. The buildings contain 700 rooms and 67 staircases, highly decorated and beautifully preserved. The most popular attraction in the estate is the Hall of Mirrors, a magnificent room that was the focus of grand celebrations and royal marriages. The parkland covers some 800 hectares and includes over 200,000 trees.

The royal palace is also historically significant as the place where Germany signed the Treaty of Versailles in 1919 to signify the end of the First World War and claim responsibility for the lives lost.

The Palace of Versailles in France

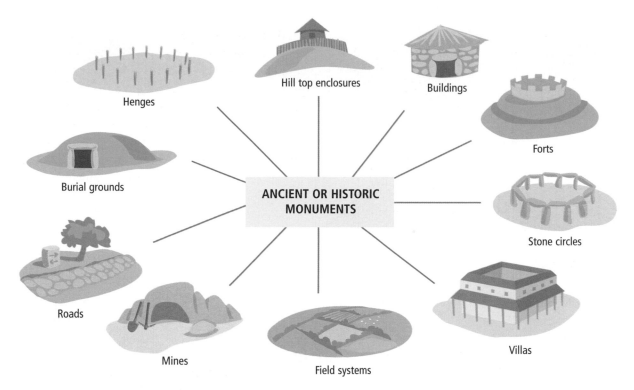

Figure 3.3 Ancient and historic monuments are popular tourist attractions

Ancient monuments and historic monuments

An ancient monument or historic monument is a site that was built before the end of the Roman Empire, in 476 AD, and represents evidence of what life was like in ancient times and before. Monuments can include a variety of features from the past (see Figure 3.3).

One of the most visited ancient or historic monuments in Europe is the Roman town of Pompeii in southern Italy. In AD 79 Mount Vesuvius erupted burying the town of Pompeii. The remains were discovered in 1750, including buildings, temples and the bodies of people who lived there. The early excavations are on display in the National Archaeological Museum in Naples, including colourful paintings and mosaics. The buildings in Pompeii are very well preserved and include the Forum – the centre of civic and religious functions – the gladiators' barracks, theatres and many fine houses.

Think it over ...

Over 2.5 million people visit Pompeii each year. Why do you think it is such a popular tourist attraction?

The Forum at Pompeii in southern Italy

The Louvre in Paris is one of the world's greatest museums and art galleries

Museums and art galleries

Millions of people visit *museums and art galleries* every year to view and interact with exhibits which give an insight into the culture and history of a destination.

The Louvre in central Paris houses, amongst the 29,000 pieces of art and artefacts, the world's most famous painting, the *Mona Lisa*, and the statue *Venus de Milo*. Approximately six million people visit the Louvre each year. The building was first used to exhibit artefacts in 1793, making it one of the earliest European museums. The Louvre is clearly recognised by its glass pyramid entrance.

Events and entertainment

Entertainment

Entertainment plays an important role in attracting people to visit a particular destination. Some tourists go to a particular place solely for the entertainment on offer; others seek amusement once they have arrived. The entertainment available can be of various forms and appeal to a range of ages and types of visitor. It can include: theatre, cinema, music, comedy, sport, street performers, nightclubs, pubs and bars. Each of these can also be divided into different aspects which will appeal to different visitors, for example music can mean experiencing live music such as classical, opera, musicals, pop and rock concerts, participating in music in karaoke sessions, as well as listening to recorded music in pubs and nightclubs.

Large cities will offer many types of entertainment for a range of tourists, some of which are found within particular areas, such as the theatre districts. Tourist resorts can also offer a range of entertainment to visitors or specialise in certain types of entertainment; hotels also play a role in providing a programme of activities to keep guests entertained.

CASE STUDY
Ibiza

The Mediterranean island of Ibiza has become increasingly popular as a holiday destination during the past ten years, due to its reputation as being the centre of the world's clubbing scene, which dominates three months of the year.

Many clubs and resorts on the island have gained international status for the DJs and music on offer. Famous clubs include Café del Mar, Pacha and Space. The island is advertised as the summer party capital of the world.

The island not only offers clubs and music, it also provides the traditional Mediterranean attractions of warm climate, sandy beaches, history and a wide range of holiday accommodation, food and entertainment. Ibiza tourism officials estimate that 65 per cent of visitors return for at least a second time, although it is difficult trying to attract new types of tourists to the island because of its reputation as a summer party capital.

Source: TUI

Ibiza's reputation as a thriving club scene attracts young people from all over Europe

Think it over ...

1 What entertainments and events interest you when you are on holiday?

2 Is this the same as your friends and family?

3 How does a tourist destination cater for tourists with different needs?

Events

Events can provide the main attraction to a particular destination and appeal to a wide range of audiences. They are organised and designed to attract large numbers of people. They include sporting events, music festivals, art festivals and carnivals, and range from international to local events. Some local events develop international appeal. The Venice Carnival in Italy, where participants wear traditional masks and jugglers, and mime acts, acrobats and fire-eaters crowd the narrow streets, attracts visitors from all over Europe.

Skills practice

1 Describe one major event in Europe.

2 Why does it attract large numbers of people?

3 What factors might affect the popularity of the event?

Cost of visiting and living

The price of a holiday is the most important factor in choosing a holiday destination. The price includes transport, accommodation, food and drink, and leisure and entertainment. Being short-haul, Europe's destinations are cheaper to get to than long-haul destinations. What it costs will be determined by the airline used, the destination and the standard of accommodation required. Costs can be reduced by choosing a package holiday, which are purchased in bulk so that tour operators can pass on the saving in the form of discounts to their customers.

Some countries in Europe have a higher cost of living than others, which can make a significant difference to the overall amount spent on a holiday. Table 3.4 compares average costs between a selection of countries inside and outside of Europe.

Table 3.4 Comparison of average prices (£)

	UK	FRANCE	UNITED STATES	AUSTRALIA	SPAIN	SOUTH AFRICA
Big Mac	1.99	1.77	1.50	1.40	1.40	1.20
Fuel per litre	0.85	0.66	0.42	0.36	0.50	0.40
Pint of beer	2.50	2.35	2.10	2.24	0.60	0.35
Loaf of bread	0.65	0.40	0.60	0.38	0.50	0.35
Pint of milk	0.45	0.35	0.35	0.30	0.30	0.20
Cinema ticket	6.50	5.50	5.00	4.00	4.00	1.20

Source: Daily Express 6 May 2005

Skills practice

1 Using Table 3.4, identify which is the cheapest country in Europe and which is the most expensive.

2 How does the cheapest country in Europe compare with the cheapest country outside of Europe?

3 Suggest reasons why prices may vary in different countries.

4 What impact would cost of living have on your decision to visit a particular holiday destination?

Local culture – food and drink

Food and drink is associated with specific countries, regions and places. When travelling abroad we expect to be offered traditional foods to eat as part of the tourist experience of visiting another country. People are attracted to a particular country because of the local food and drink. However, many destinations offer a range of international menus and local foods to meet the needs of a wide range of tourists.

Food and wine are fast-growing areas of tourism which offer insights into local culture and produce. Such tourism is popular in Italy and France, where you can visit wineries and local restaurants, join cookery classes and go grape picking.

Wine museums are one of the attractions in the growing food and wine tourism sector of Europe

Complete the following table, identifying the food and drink of different countries or regions. The first two have been done for you:

Food and drink	Country or region
Pizza	Italy
Champagne	France
Pasta	
Black Forest Gateau	
Sherry	
Paella	
Strudel	
Smorgasbord	
Goulash	
Tapas	
Souvlaki	
Schnitzel	

Different types of tourists

In this section you will learn about the different needs and expectations different types of tourists have of destinations. As part of the assessment for this unit your tutor will give you pen portraits of tourists. These are case studies giving details of customers and their wants, needs and interests. You will learn to apply your knowledge of the key features that make destinations appealing by recommending destinations for different types of tourists to meet their needs and circumstances, as described in the pen portraits. You should learn to recommend destinations that meet their straightforward needs. You will also learn to justify any recommendations you make. There are many different types of tourist:

* Families
* Young people
* Senior citizens
* Couples
* Visitors with specific needs
* Visitors with special interests
* Business travellers.

However, it is important to remember that although we can categorise different types of tourists and aim to meet their general needs, there is still a range of individual needs that each person requires to be satisfied.

Families

A family consists of two adults with children, or a single parent with children. Children at different ages have different needs: a young baby, for example, needs nappy-changing facilities and perhaps crèche facilities where they are looked after by qualified staff; older children, between the ages of 3 and 12 years, may require supervised activities to keep them entertained. Many family hotels and resorts offer a range of activities and clubs for children of various ages.

Young people

Young people between the ages of 11 and 16 years are more independent and choose to take part in family activities, but also join in organised events for their own age group. This provides them with their own space and gives them a chance to meet other young people.

Senior citizens

People aged 65 are regarded as senior citizens. These are an active group, more so than previous generations of senior citizens, given that they are generally healthier and live longer. However, with increasing age, mobility and health problems do arise, so individuals may need greater levels of assistance.

Couples

Couples tend to prefer to holiday in non-family resorts. Young couples in particular will have different needs and aspirations compared to older couples.

Visitors with specific needs

Visitors with specific needs, which can include medical or religious ones, require that those needs are met. For example, there may be serious consequences if medical needs are ignored.

Medical needs may be the taking of specific medication, keeping to a recommended diet or just knowing that there are local medical facilities that can deal with any illness they may have. Those with mobility needs may require wheelchair access and assistance.

In the case of those with special dietary needs, it is important to inform the hotel or wherever meals are taken that certain foods are to be avoided.

Visitors with special interests

Visitors with special interests will visit those places where their interests will be met. These may be sporting and leisure activities, such as windsurfing, live music, history and local food, or bird watching. Such interests may form the basis of the entire holiday or a small part of the visit.

Business travellers

Business travellers need easy access to where they will be conducting their business activities, and expect a high standard of accommodation that is value for money. They may also need secretarial or office services during their visit. See page 105 for further information.

Skills practice

Pen portrait 1

Pen portrait 2

Richard and Gabi wish to travel to a European destination with their two young children, Philip aged 7 and Simon aged 3.

The family like swimming and Philip is very keen on sport.

Richard likes visiting historic buildings and local places of interest.

Gabi would like time to relax.

Nikki and Amy wish to travel to Europe after they have finished studying at university.

Nikki likes sunny beaches and Amy likes to party.

Amy is an active person and gets bored with sitting on a beach all day.

They both want to be around people of a similar age group.

Nikki and Amy do not wish to spend a lot of money on holiday.

Amy is allergic to dairy products.

Pen portrait 3

Ruth and Harry wish to travel to Europe after recently retiring.

Harry is a keen gardener and enjoys making his own wine.

Ruth likes walking in the countryside and watching wildlife.

The holiday is a retirement present to each other and they would like to stay in luxury accommodation.

Pen portrait 4

Jasmine is a single person who uses a wheelchair.

She is determined to visit a European cultural destination as she has a love of art.

Jasmine would like to spend a few days on a city break but she is concerned that being in a wheelchair may stop her from going on holiday.

She would prefer not to fly.

Jasmine is a vegetarian.

1 For each of the four pen portraits, describe the type of holiday that the people are looking for.

2 Recommend a suitable European destination that meets their needs. You will need to carry out research to answer this question by including a range of activities or places to visit.

3 Identify any special requests that need to be made on behalf of those travelling.

4 Justify each of your recommendations by using a range of examples.

Skills practice

1 Working in pairs or small groups, each person writes a pen portrait for a type of tourist stating a range of needs.

2 Swap your pen portrait with another person.

3 Identify any special requests that need to be made.

4 Recommend a tourist destination based on the information that you have been given. You may need to research a number of destinations using holiday brochures and travel guides before reaching a decision.

5 Present your findings to the person who wrote the pen portrait by explaining how your choice of destination meets the needs of the person that you were given.

Portfolio practice

For this portfolio practice you will be required to identify the key features that give destinations appeal to different types of tourist.

You are required to investigate one European tourist destination. It must not be the same destination that you use for the portfolio practice on pages 125 and 139.

Travel agents are often asked to recommend tourist destinations to their clients. You need to recommend a European destination that meets the needs of a tourist or group of tourists. The precise needs and circumstances of the tourist will be given to you by your tutor in the form of a pen portrait. These might be complex.

The following is an example of a complex pen portrait:

William and Katrina have two sons, Edward who is 4 years old and Oliver who is 10 months old.

Edward does not like long flights, so they would like a destination that has a short transfer time from the gateway.

Katrina has an Australian passport.

William is planning to run the London Marathon after the holiday.

The family likes culture and wants to experience a traditional event or activity.

They would like to travel over Easter.

Based on your assessment of the family's needs contained in the pen portrait, recommend a suitable destination and describe the main features that give the recommended destination appeal. Make sure that you only include features that are relevant in meeting their needs.

Using examples, provide a detailed explanation of how the features you have identified in the destination meet the complex needs of the person or group described in the pen portrait.

3.3 Modes of transport and routes available to European travel destinations

In this section you will learn about key transport gateways in Europe so that you can locate them on a map. You will also learn to locate key rail and road routes linking European tourist receiving and generating areas on a map. You will learn about the suitability of different modes of transport available between tourist receiving and generating areas so that you can apply your understanding to the needs and circumstances of different types of tourists. The needs and circumstances will be given to you by your tutor in the form of pen portraits. You will learn to consider complex needs of tourists, although initially you will learn how to assess the suitability of different modes of transport to meet more straightforward needs. You will learn to analyse the suitability of different modes of transport in terms of the following:

✳ Overall length of journey time

✳ Cost of the entire journey

✳ Quality and convenience, e.g. departure times, transfer connections

✳ Service available, e.g. class of service, support for specific needs

✳ Safety and security.

You will also learn about access to a range of different European destinations, departing from different points in Europe.

A *gateway* is a place where a traveller can enter or leave a country or destination. Gateways include airports, seaports, border crossings, railway and bus stations.

Land border crossings offer gateways into other countries when travelling by road or rail. Since 1995 border controls between the member countries of the European Union who signed the Schengen Treaty have been relaxed, causing unrestricted movement of tourists between these countries. Routes into mainland Europe are still strictly controlled, which is why passports are required.

Travel routes

Travel routes include road, rail, air and sea. These are chosen depending on distance to travel, cost, convenience and availability, length of journey time and services available whilst travelling.

Road travel involves cars and coaches journeying along motorways, autobahns, freeways, trunk roads and through tunnels. (See Figure 3.4.) Road travel tends to mainly be for domestic tourism and short visits over

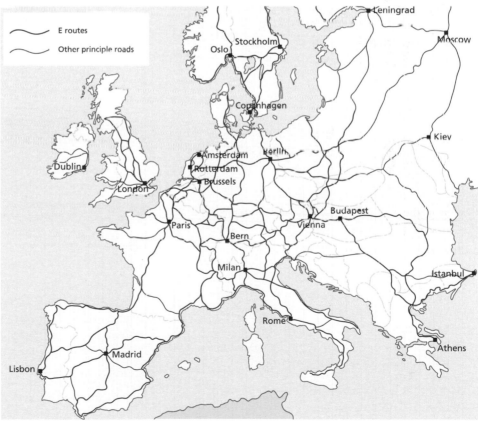

Figure 3.4 Key road routes of Europe

international borders. Using a car offers flexibility in terms of choosing route, time of departure and time of arrival. A driver can choose to break a journey with stops en-route or drive straight through to a destination. Tourists can also choose to combine modes of transport. For example, they can fly-drive by flying to a travel destination and then hiring a car at the airport.

Coach travel tends to be less flexible as pick-up and drop-off points need to be clearly identified. Coaches are often used to transfer large groups of people between European cities. Coaching holidays also offer value for money and are popular with visitors from the UK. Coaches and taxis can be used to transport passengers from airports to their holiday destination – this is known as a *transfer*.

Rail travel offers high-speed links between major destinations, as well as regional links and also some scenic railway routes. Rail companies may offer a range of services, including standard and first-class seating accommodation, buffet cars and refreshment services, and a range of ticket types depending on the time and type of journey. (See Figure 3.6.)

CASE STUDY
Eurolines

Eurolines is the brand name for more than 30 independent coach companies operating throughout Europe, creating Europe's largest coach network to over 500 destinations.

Eurolines coach travel includes these facilities to make travel as comfortable as possible:

- Advanced braking system
- Air conditioning
- Air suspension
- Double glazing
- Non-smoking on all services
- Regular rest stops
- Toilet/washroom
- Video.

Eurolines offers the choice of three passes of 15, 30 or 40 days' travel, offering unlimited luxury coach travel between 35 cities. To make travel as flexible as possible, the first journey can be pre-booked, then all other journeys can be booked whilst at the destination.

For further information and details of routes visit http://www.eurolines.com

CASE STUDY
Thalys International

Thalys International is a European railway company specialising in high-speed train services. It operates passenger services on the high-speed network in Belgium, Germany, France and the Netherlands.

Thalys transports over 6 million passengers each year: 47 per cent are leisure travellers, 48 per cent are business travellers and 5 per cent are regular commuters.

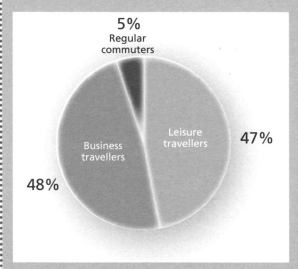

Figure 3.5 Thalys international passenger types

The Paris–Brussels route is the most popular route, carrying 47.3 per cent of Thalys passengers. The rail network has been so successful that Air France cancelled its flights from Paris to Brussels. It takes 1 hour 25 minutes to travel between Paris and Brussels and travellers have a choice of 27 high-speed trains each day.

For further information and details of routes visit http://www.thalys.com

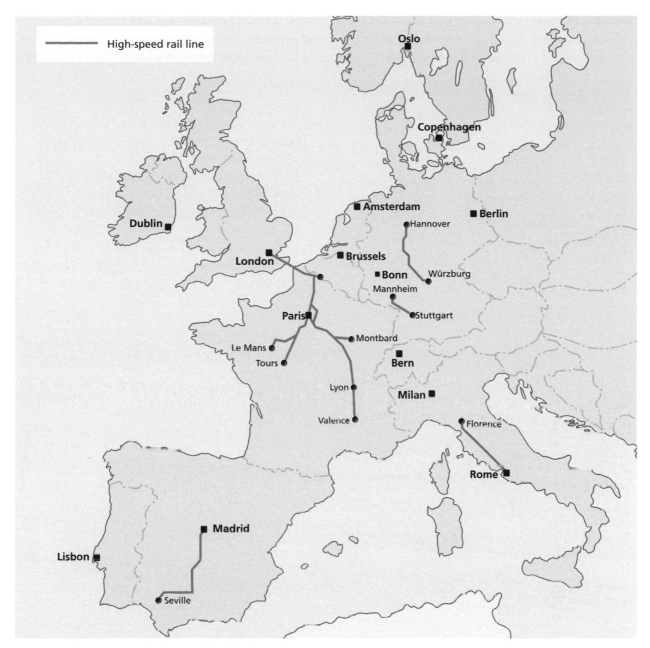

Figure 3.6 European high-speed rail routes

Air travel is the fastest method of travel available to a destination and can be used for domestic, short-haul and long-haul journeys. Air travel has increased in popularity over the past ten years with more airlines offering access to new destinations and more frequent flights. More airlines competing for passengers has resulted in lower prices. There are now more low-cost airlines offering cheaper seats, with a reduced level of in-flight service to ensure that they remain competitive.

There are two types of air travel: scheduled flights and charter flights. *Scheduled flights* follow a regular timetable and fly whether or not all the seats are occupied. *Charter flights* are associated with package holidays. Aircraft are booked by tour operators to fly to specific destinations on specific days as part of a tour operator's programme of activities. Flights do not follow a regular timetable.

Travelling by air allows a quicker journey time and the opportunity to travel over long distances with relative ease. In-flight services of food, drink and entertainment may be provided as well as duty-free sales. Passengers are restricted to specific times of travel and also have the disadvantage of having to check-in for their flight up to two hours before departure. (See Figure 3.7.)

CASE STUDY

easyJet

easyJet operates 100 aircraft across 203 routes and carries over 27 million passengers each year. Its success has been due to its approach to airfares and the level of service it offers to passengers such as:

- Use of the Internet to reduce costs. Approximately 95 per cent of all seats are sold over the Internet, making easyJet one of Europe's biggest Internet retailers.
- Ticketless travel. Passengers receive an email containing their travel details and booking reference when they book online.

- No free lunch. Eliminating free catering onboard reduces cost, however passengers can purchase food onboard.
- No pre-assigned seats, which reduces administration costs.
- Efficient use of airports. easyJet flies to main destination airports throughout Europe, but gains efficiencies by reducing the time it takes to turnaround an aircraft in order to be ready to fly again in under 30 minutes.

For further information and details of routes visit http://www.easyjet.com

Figure 3.7 European airports

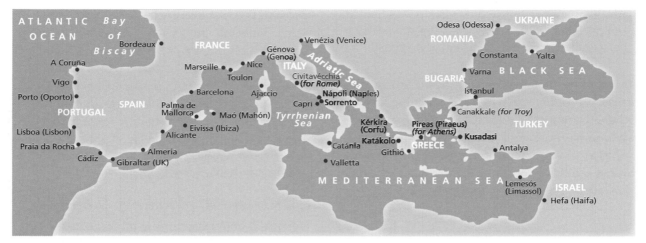

Figure 3.8 European cruise destinations

Sea travel includes ferries and cruises. *Ferry* services take travellers on foot, in cars, lorries and coaches across stretches of water and offer facilities such as shops, restaurants, cabins, lounges and play areas.

Cruises are conducted on large ships carrying over 200 passengers; these ships are described as floating hotels. A cruise involves travelling to a variety of ports whilst offering luxury, relaxation and entertainment onboard. The Mediterranean is the leading European cruise holiday destination, although Northern Europe and Scandinavia are increasing in popularity. Mediterranean ports that receive the most cruise ships include: Barcelona, Genoa, Venice and Naples. (See Figure 3.8.)

CASE STUDY

easyCruise.com

easyCruise began operating in May 2005. It is owned by Stelios, the founder of easyJet. His idea is to change the thinking behind cruise holidays to appeal to younger and more independently minded travellers. Seventy-five per cent of easyCruise passengers are aged between 18 and 40, with an average age of 35. Travellers can visit the playgrounds of the rich and famous. Unlike traditional cruising, the ship will stay in port in the afternoon and the evening so that people can have fun ashore, and then sail in the early hours each morning for the next destination. Its one-week itineraries include ports such as Nice, Cannes, St Tropez, Monaco, Genoa, Portofino, Imperia (for

An easyCruise ship at Nice on a European cruise

San Remo), before returning to Nice.

For further information and details of routes visit http://www.easycruise.com

Skills practice

Using a cruise holiday brochure, suggest why cruise holidays are growing in popularity and appeal.

Travel routes link major *tourist receiving areas* and *tourist generating areas*. Tourist generating areas are where the majority of tourists are coming from and tourist receiving areas are where they are going to. The following tables show the top five tourist receiving countries in Europe and the top five tourist generating countries in Europe.

Table 3.5 The top 5 tourist receiving countries in Europe

COUNTRY	INTERNATIONAL TOURIST ARRIVALS (MILLION)
1 France	75.0
2 Spain	51.8
3 Italy	39.6
4 United Kingdom	24.7
5 Austria	19.1

Source: World Tourism Organisation (2004)

Table 3.6 The top 5 tourist generating countries in Europe

COUNTRY	INTERNATIONAL TOURISM EXPENDITURE (US$ BILLION)
1 Germany	64.7
2 United Kingdom	48.5
3 France	23.6
4 Italy	20.5
5 Netherlands	14.6

Source: World Tourism Organisation (2004)

Skills practice

1 What is the difference between a tourist generating country and a tourist receiving country?
2 Which countries generate the most tourists and which countries receive the most visitors?
3 Suggest why it is important for airline companies and other transport operators to know which are the tourist generating countries and tourist receiving countries.

Different types of tourists have different travel needs. Some may prefer to fly, some may prefer to drive and others may prefer to travel by rail. Each mode of transport has its own level of suitability, for example a business traveller will expect to arrive at a destination in the shortest possible time and in relative comfort, whereas a family may choose to travel at a more relaxed pace at a reduced cost. We will now compare the suitability of different modes of transport.

Overall length of journey time

The length of journey time is important as tourists wish to maximise the amount of time they spend at their destination. Journey time is often calculated by the time spent on the primary mode of transport. However, total journey time should also take into account the amount of time spent getting to the airport or railway station, the time spent on the primary mode of transport, and the time taken to transfer to the destination.

Cost of entire journey

When calculating the cost of the entire journey it is not just the primary mode of transport that needs to be taken into consideration but also the other costs involved. For example, the cost of a bus or taxi to an airport, transfer costs at the resort, as well as the cost of a flight. Approximately 45 per cent of the cost of a typical package holiday is the cost of the flight. The cost of transfers and other costs at the destination accounts for approximately 3 per cent of the price.

Quality and convenience

Quality and convenience of the service is important for passengers as they require accurate departure times and reliable transfer connections. The time of travel is important; although an early flight may be cheaper, it may not be convenient if the time taken to travel to the airport and the check-in time is also taken into account. Transfer connections may be organised as part of a package holiday, but for independent travellers it is important to know how to reach their intended destination. A gateway may be at a distance to the intended destination and therefore thorough planning is essential. If arriving late at night or early morning, it is important to establish whether bus, rail or taxi services will be operating. Certain types of tickets can have restrictions in terms of the times or days of travel. Reduced ticket prices for travel outside of peak times may be cheaper but may not always be convenient.

Services available
Class of service
The level of services provided by the transport operator is important to consider. Those travelling for a special occasion may wish to travel first class and those on business may wish to pay extra for increased leg room and space in which to work or relax. Different standards of service and seating accommodation are available on most forms of transport, apart from budget airlines.

CASE STUDY

Eurostar

Eurostar passengers can choose from a range of options designed to suit their priorities and budget. Standard class includes a reserved seat in air-conditioned comfort with access to either of two bar-buffet carriages serving food and drink. First class offers the added advantages of more space and a reclining seat, plus a glass of champagne and a three-course meal. Premium combines the benefits of first class together with a four-course meal, dedicated check-in/ticket office facilities, lounge access and a pre-bookable taxi service to any city centre address on arrival.

For more information and details of routes visit http://www.eurostar.co.uk

Support for specific needs
Most European travel companies offer support to people with specific needs. It is advisable to inform the travel company or tour operator of any specific needs before departure. However, the level of support can vary depending on the needs of the individual.

When travelling with small children it is advisable to pre-book seats and to carry toys and activities to keep them occupied. If food is served onboard then it is advisable to request a suitable children's menu. If hiring a car in another country, then it should be correctly fitted with an appropriate car seat.

Travellers who are diabetic or those needing medication need to take adequate supplies of their medication with clear labels identifying their prescription. Medication should be kept in hand luggage for easy access.

Elderly travellers with a medical condition are usually advised to consult with their GP as to whether they are fit to travel. Any medication should be clearly labelled, kept in hand luggage, and there should be an adequate supply for the length of the visit.

Women who are pregnant can usually travel without difficulty, but most airlines will only allow women to fly up to between 32 and 36 weeks into their pregnancy. It is advisable for a pregnant woman to consult with a GP or midwife as to whether they are fit to travel and to request a letter of confirmation. The transport operator may ask for confirmation before making a booking, especially if the woman is further into her pregnancy. Pregnant travellers are advised to take care with their food and drink and should avoid partially cooked meat, unpasteurised milk products and soft cheeses.

Safety and security
Safety and security at international gateways has been improved since the terrorist attacks on the United States on 11 September 2001 and the attacks on the railway network in Spain on 11 March 2004. There has been an increase in the number of passenger searches and regular police patrols to tighten security.

Before 2001 most airport security teams screened a sample of baggage carried by passengers, now every item is searched by sniffer dogs, x-ray machines and by airport staff. To further improve security, many departure points require that a photograph of each passenger be taken; in time the use of biometric data, information on fingerprints, facial features or a photograph of the eye may be used to confirm a person's identity. The UK may soon be adopting the use of national identity cards as a security measure, a strategy also used in other European countries.

When travelling between different countries, personal identification, such as a passport, is often checked by security officials. If travelling from outside of the European Union, then a travel visa is required to give permission to enter.

Safety measures are linked to security. In addition, passengers are informed of safety procedures through information cards, signage, safety demonstrations and public announcements.

Personal safety is important in unfamiliar settings. Every town or city has some petty crime, and tourists are seen as easy targets as they often take expensive items such as cameras, mobile phones, personal entertainment systems and extra amounts of money when on holiday. Local police are aware of this and regularly patrol areas frequented by tourists.

Skills practice

We will now begin to analyse the suitability of different modes of transport by comparing a journey between Paris and Berlin for a single adult travelling standard class. Three methods of travel have been identified, by air, railway and road.

	Route (return ticket)	Time (each way)	Cost
Air	Alitalia – Paris Charles de Galle (CDG) to Berlin Tegel (TXL) via Milan	5 hours	£279.50
	Swiss International Airlines – Paris Charles de Galle (CDG) to Berlin Tegel (TXL) via Zurich	4 hours	£387.40
	Air France – Paris Charles de Galle (CDG) to Berlin Tegel (TXL) direct	1 hour 45 minutes	£391.50
Railway	Paris Gare du Nord to Berlin Spandau direct	11 hours 2 minutes	£143 standard class £168 first class
Road	Private motorcar – fastest route 1048 kilometres (650 miles) direct and one way	10 hours 54 minutes (12 hours 4 minutes)*	650 miles × 2 @ 40p per mile = £520**
	Eurolines coach operator – Paris to Berlin direct	13 hours	£169 low season £235 high season***

* The RAC recommends a 15-minute comfort stop every two hours. That would increase the time taken by road by 1 hour 15 minutes, creating a total time of 12 hours 4 minutes to travel one way.

** This figure can vary depending on the price of fuel, the size of the engine, price of tax, insurance and rate of depreciation of the vehicle. The Inland Revenue suggests a figure of 40p per mile when calculating the cost of motoring expenses in the UK.

*** Prices based on a 15-day pass. High season June to September and mid-December.

1 Which modes of transport provide the shortest and the longest journey time between Paris and Berlin?

2 Is the length of the journey identified in the table the actual time it takes to travel between these destinations? Explain your answer using examples.

3 Explain the variations in price between the different modes of transport.

4 Compare the different levels of service experienced on each of the different modes of transport.

5 Which mode of transport would you recommend for each of the following passengers travelling between Paris and Berlin?
- A single parent travelling with a young child to visit her best friend for a long weekend
- A student returning to study at university
- An elderly passenger visiting her son for a week
- A young woman who is 18 weeks pregnant attending her sister's wedding.

Fully explain your recommendations.

ASSESSMENT

Portfolio practice

For this assessment you will be required to identify the suitability of different modes of transport to a European travel destination.

You are required to investigate one European tourist destination. It must not be the same destination that you used for portfolio practice on pages 116 and 139.

You will assess the suitability of different modes of transport to a European destination for a type of tourist. Details of the type of tourist and their needs and circumstances will be given to you in the form of a pen portrait by your tutor. This will include details of their departure point and destination. The tourist might have complex needs and circumstances.

The following is an example pen portrait:

José and Maria are an elderly couple who wish to travel from Barcelona to Florence.

- José has mobility problems but does not use a wheelchair, although he does need to move around regularly.

- Both enjoy seeing landscapes different to their own and like to take in the images of the local environment.

- On the visit they will be taking some equipment as they are planning to paint during their stay.

- They have no time restrictions and no budget restrictions.

- Both have a current driving licence and own a car.

- They also have railcards that allow reduced train fares. Neither speaks a language other than Spanish.

You will need to take these factors into account and consider different modes of transport. Access to some parts of the destination may be difficult, so you will need to present suggestions to overcome this. Make sure that your recommendations meet the complex needs of the tourist, or tourists, identified in the pen portrait.

You may wish to support your recommendations by the use of maps showing appropriate travel routes.

You will be expected to use a variety of sources from atlases, guidebooks, and route planners available on the Internet.

3.4 Factors affecting the popularity and appeal of European travel destinations

In this section you will learn about the factors that have affected the popularity and appeal of tourist destinations to gain an understanding of why some destinations with comparable features are more popular than others. Some factors are controllable by the destination and some are uncontrollable. You will learn to research destinations in Europe and to evaluate how they have controlled factors to maximise their appeal and popularity. Factors affecting the popularity and appeal of European travel destinations include:

* Accessibility

* Image and promotion

* Availability of attractions and other tourist facilities

* Destination management

* Cost of visiting

* Political factors.

Accessibility

Destinations that are easily accessible tend to be more popular than those that are not. Accessibility is not just about an airport, seaport or a railway station being close to the destination, it is also the degree of access that someone has from the tourist generating region. For example, a European destination with an airport that receives flights from London and Bristol is not easily accessible to people living in Newcastle, Liverpool or Manchester.

The expansion of regional airports has helped to widen access to a greater variety of destinations. This has been made possible by the growth of budget and low-cost airlines in response to EU regulations in 1997 that allowed greater competition between destinations. Where cost used to be a factor in prohibiting many to travel by air on a regular basis, budget air travel has encouraged people to travel to new destinations and to travel more frequently.

Efficient transport networks are important in encouraging people to visit a destination. If there are many obstacles or delays then passengers will be attracted to destinations with easier access. A popular tourist destination will be able to offer its visitors different methods of access whether it is by road, rail, air or sea.

CASE STUDY

Paris, France

Paris is the most popular tourist destination from the UK. The French capital has a reputation as a romantic city with popular attractions, including the Eiffel Tower, the Louvre museum, Notre-Dame, the Arc de Triomphe and the Pompidou Centre.

In 2004, 25 million people visited Paris, an increase of around 500,000 visitors on the previous year. In 2004, 1.23 million American tourists visited Paris compared with 1.2 million from the UK and 649,000 from Italy. The number of visitors from the UK increased by 2 per cent on the previous year.

Transport networks and infrastructure provide a variety of ways to travel to the French capital: 3 hours from London on the Eurostar train, 1 hour and 25 minutes from Brussels on the Thalys train, and 90 minutes from Madrid by aeroplane. Paris has two international airports: Orly is 14 kilometres (8.5 miles) south of Paris and Roissy Charles De Gaulle is 25 kilometres (15.5 miles) to the north.

There are six train stations in Paris. The station used by the Eurostar is the Gare du Nord, with frequent services from London Waterloo and Ashford International. The TGV high-speed train service has brought Paris within reach of most European cities within a few hours. The French national railway company (SNCF) has a railway network that extends approximately 35,000 kilometres (21,700 miles) across the country, providing national and regional services.

Transfer to the centre of Paris is relatively easy, as 15,000 taxis operate in the capital and there are nearly 500 taxi ranks. The Métro is a reliable and inexpensive underground network with frequent trains operating between 5.30 am and 12.30 am. Gare du Nord station is served by three Métro lines and a taxi rank.

Paris is the most popular European destination for visitors from the UK

The RER train system has only five lines but extends into the suburbs. Buses also operate on a frequent basis and Métro tickets can be used on both buses and on the RER in the centre of Paris.

Travelling by road to Paris is relatively easy as all motorways join the Boulevard Périphérique, the outer ring road. However, parking spaces in Paris can be difficult to find depending on the day and time of travel. Coach services are available from the UK from the main operator, Eurolines. Coaches from the UK arrive at Gare Routière International in the east of the city.

Disabled access has been improved since the *Tourisme & Handicap* logo has been used to indicate the extent to which tourist attractions and facilities are accessible. The scheme takes into account four categories of disability: hearing, visual, mental and physical.

The scheme has helped to develop a range of tourist attractions and facilities that have been adapted and integrated into the general range of tourism services, in particular accommodation, restaurants, museums, monuments, art galleries and leisure facilities.

Since 1978, it has been the law in France that new facilities open to the public are accessible to people with limited mobility.

For more information about the Paris Convention and Visitors Bureau visit http://en.parisinfo.com

For more information about the Committee of Tourism Paris Ile-de-France visit http://english.pidf.com

Skills practice

1 Why is Paris the most popular tourist destination from the UK?

2 How easy is it to travel to Paris from the place where you live? Describe the most convenient route from where you live to the centre of Paris.

3 To what extent does transport and accessibility affect the popularity and appeal of travel destinations?

Image and promotion

How a destination is *promoted* can have a major impact on its popularity and appeal. National tourist boards spend thousands of pounds on marketing to attract inbound tourists. It is important that potential visitors know what destinations can offer in terms of accommodation, facilities and attractions.

Most of the national tourist boards have regional offices in major cities across the world.

They raise awareness of their country, promote a range of travel destinations, and offer advice and travel services. Promotional campaigns can use a wide range of media, including newspapers, magazines, posters, point-of-sale material, brochures, leaflets, television and radio.

Promotional campaigns are aimed at raising awareness of new travel destinations and creating new images and reputations of existing destinations. For example, the Spanish Tourist Board has been updating its reputation from a budget-priced summer sun package holiday destination to highlighting the country's culture, art, history and rural attractions. A recent campaign, 'Smile you are in Spain', focused on the pleasure people get from visiting Spain.

For more information visit http://www.spain.info

The 'Smile you are in Ibiza' is part of a campaign to promote Spanish destinations to European tourists

Spain: Highlighting its diversity

Valencia's regional tourist board has appointed its first tourism minister to help promote the diversity of attractions on offer.

In the hot seat is Milagrosa Martinez, who said:

'Our main aim is to position Valencia as a leading destination different from its competitors. Our new tourism policy will introduce some fresh approaches based on diversity, quality improvement, innovation, the use of new technology and an intense advertising and marketing campaign, as well as continuing with tried and tested initiatives.'

She said that while beach holidays continue to be the region's main source of tourism, Valencia is aiming to maximise the potential of rapidly developing visitor trends such as cultural city breaks, business tourism, health and golf, nautical and cruise tourism, and in particular rural and non-coastal tourism.

The Valencia Region Tourist Board recently created an office to focus on rural tourism and has stepped up its promotional activities, with a budget of £7 million set aside for participation in trade and consumer fairs and other events. Its total budget this year is £10 million.

It is also launching a dedicated information service for the UK travel trade and planning various roadshows in British cities, as well as familiarisation trips for travel agents.

The UK is the main source of foreign visitors to the region, with nearly 2.5 million tourists drawn each year to resorts on the Costa Blanca and Costa del Azahar – the Orange Blossom Coast along with its cities of Valencia, Alicante and Castellón.

Valencia has the biggest growth in tourism of any European city within the past 10 years, with a 169 per cent increase in visitors, five times greater than the European average, according to a study by the European Cities Tourism Association.

Last year, the city attracted more than one million tourists, a 3.5 per cent increase on the previous year, with a 2.9 per cent rise in overnight stays, according to figures from Spain's National Statistics Institute.

Opening later this year, the Palau de les Arts Opera House will add to the city's pull for culture vultures. Meanwhile, the city's seafront area is being redeveloped in time to stage the America's Cup in 2007.

Valencia is also hoping to become a more popular short-break destination with the increased number of direct flights from various UK airports, including the arrival of easyJet from Stansted and Bristol last November. This month sees easyJet operating from Gatwick and Jet2 from Manchester.

Source: Travel Weekly 17 March 2005

Skills practice

1 To what extent have Spanish tourist destinations been successful in promoting alternative forms of tourism?

2 To what extent have short-break city holidays increased in popularity and appeal in Valencia?

3 How has accessibility affected the potential to develop tourism in Valencia?

Skills practice

1 Using a range of newspapers, travel supplements and magazines, provide examples of advertisements of European travel destinations.

2 Which destinations are being promoted and what images are being used in the advertisements?

3 What types of tourists would be attracted to these travel destinations?

Availability of attractions and other tourist facilities

A travel destination needs to offer a wide range of attractions and facilities to meet the needs of a wide range of visitors. If a destination has a limited range of attractions, then there is less potential for attracting different types of tourists or encouraging them to visit a second time.

Attractions also need to be accessible so that visitors can spend time visiting the attraction rather than spending the majority of their time travelling. Public transport networks are important for allowing visitors to travel easily. New and emerging destinations may not always have a full range of attractions and tourist facilities. Initially, this may be part of the appeal as visitors can experience another country before it is fully developed as a travel destination.

CASE STUDY

Tallinn, Estonia

Tallinn Plaza in the Estonian city of Tallinn, which has become a popular short-break destination

Tallinn is the capital city of Estonia. It is a destination that has grown in popularity during the last fifteen years. In 1995 Tallin received 530,000 international visitors compared to an estimated 3 million inbound visitors in 2004. In 2004, 39,000 visitors from the UK travelled to Tallinn, an increase of 30 per cent on the previous year.

After Estonia gained independence from the Soviet Union in 1991, there was considerable investment in tourist infrastructure. The international airport has been upgraded and expanded with an additional runway and refurbishment of the terminal building, increasing retailing space and developing modern business lounges. Tallinn is also a sea cruise destination popular with visitors sailing from Finland. The seaport has been modernised, increasing its capacity. In 2002, 64 per cent of international visitors to Estonia travelled by cruise ship.

Recently many new hotels have been constructed, along with restaurants and bars.

In 2004, 99 new accommodation establishments opened, bringing the total in Tallinn to 247. In 2003 there were 34 hotels in the city compared to 43 in 2004. Many hotels have invested in health, spa and conference facilities to meet growing demand. The Radisson SAS, Reval Hotel Olumpia and Sokos Hotel Viru have the largest conference facilities in Tallinn.

Tallinn is the oldest capital city in northern Europe and has a reputation as one of the best-preserved medieval towns, some of the streets dating back to the 11th century. The city has the best-preserved Gothic Town Hall in Europe and in 2004 celebrated its 600th anniversary. The city also has the oldest continually functioning apothecary, or chemist, in the world, having been in business in Tallinn's Town Hall Square since 1422. For four days in the middle of the summer the Town Hall Square is turned into a medieval market, where local goods, food, crafts and art are sold, and street entertainers and musicians entertain the crowds. The city is host to the largest choir event in the world. The Estonian Song Festival is held every five years , featuring a mass choir of 20,000 voices singing to an audience of 100,000. The Old Town of Tallinn has been recognised as a site of significant importance and has been designated as a UNESCO World Heritage Site.

Tallinn is growing in popularity as a short-break destination. With Estonia joining the European Union in 2004, there is much potential for new attractions and tourist facilities to be developed. The city has a growing reputation as a party capital and is becoming popular with British stag and hen parties, taking advantage of cheap flights offered by budget airlines.

For further information on Tallinn visit http://www.tourism.tallinn.ee
For further information on Estonia visit http://www.visitestonia.com

Skills practice

1 What are the benefits and appeal of visiting a travel destination before it is fully developed as a tourist destination?

2 Using the example of Tallinn, describe how the availability of attractions and other tourist facilities can affect its popularity and appeal.

Destination management

The management of a destination is important in attracting visitors and in encouraging repeat visits. It is also essential to make sure that the needs of local people are met. Tourism can bring a great amount of financial and economic wealth to a destination, but can also bring many problems associated with rapid development. Tourists visit natural and built attractions. In order for these attractions to keep attracting people to visit a destination in the future, they need to be protected and preserved. *Sustainable tourism* is about protecting resources for the benefit of future generations. Therefore, destination management applies to towns and cities and beach resorts as well as national parks and rural areas.

Think it over ...

1 Why do travel destinations need to be managed?

2 Which groups of people are responsible for managing a travel destination?

In order to manage a destination successfully there needs to be a plan or strategy. This will enable a destination to know where it wants to be in the future. This may involve presenting a new image through marketing and promotion, widening access, and developing new attractions and facilities. Destination management also takes into account the needs of visitors. These can include keeping beaches and resorts clean and free of litter, clear signage to find their way around, good public transport, and training local people working in the tourism industry so that visitors receive a high standard of customer service.

CASE STUDY

Malta

The island of Malta has traditionally relied on tour operators selling sun and beach holidays. Malta attracts over 1 million inbound tourists each year. In 1985 there were 256,468 tourist arrivals from the UK compared to 459,565 in 2003. The island has seen a gradual increase in visitors during the last fifteen years, mainly due to its tourism management plan.

The island is the most densely populated country in Europe, with 375,000 people living in an area of only 316 square kilometres (196 square miles). The island does not have a huge range of natural resources to compete with other European summer sun resorts.

There was recognition by the Maltese government that they had to diversify into other forms of tourism away from sun and beach holidays. A Tourism Master Plan was produced in 1989. The plan identified forms of tourism that could provide a greater income for local communities and were potentially more sustainable. These forms of tourism include:

- Cultural holidays – watching religious festivals, military ceremonies, crafts and traditional music
- Heritage tourism – viewing architecture and archaeological sites
- Business tourism – conferences and meetings
- Special interest holidays – scuba diving, golf, sports and film tourism.

By adopting this plan the government has aimed at attracting fewer tourists but at the same time encouraging those who are likely to spend more money. This is made possible by constructing high-quality resorts and promoting Malta to potentially new markets, including Eastern Europe. During the last decade there has been a 75 per cent increase in the number of four- and five-star hotels that have been built on the island.

The Malta Tourism Authority (MTA) has the responsibility for planning, advising government, regulating and promoting tourism.

Mdina Cathedral in Malta, which has extended its appeal to a wider range of tourists

The MTA has needed to change the image of Malta through promotional activities and to repackage the way in which the tourism industry is managed. By offering an alternative experience in comparison to traditional summer sun resorts and by focusing on its key resources of a warm climate, history and culture, Malta has regained its popularity and appeal to a wider group of tourists. Malta is focusing on niche markets and appealing to those seeking second holidays and short breaks.

The change in management strategy has been met with some opposition from hotels and tour operators who support the summer sun market. However, a change of direction has been necessary to ensure that the benefits of tourism continue into the future. It is hoped that a balance can be achieved between traditional resort holidays and new tourism products.

For further information on Malta visit http://www.visitmalta.com
For information on Malta Tourism Authority visit http://www.mta.com.mt

Skills practice

1 How did the changes in destination management affect the tourism industry in Malta?

2 To what extent does the management of a destination affect its appeal and popularity?

Skills practice

1 Italy receives over 3.5 million inbound visitors each year, an increase of 3.8 per cent between 1997 and 2002. After reading the newspaper report on Italy (below), to what extent does price have an affect on the popularity and appeal of a travel destination?

2 Using examples, explain how the cost of living can vary within a country and what affect this might have on the popularity and appeal of tourist destinations.

Cost of visiting

The cost of visiting does have a major appeal in the popularity of a destination, as we have previously discussed on pages 111–112.
A visitor needs to be able to afford to visit a particular destination. Even when this is possible, a decision is made as to whether a destination offers value for money. If this is not the case then an alternative destination will be chosen. It is important for destinations to meet the needs of the tourists that they are trying to attract.

Popular tourist destinations within a country are often more expensive in terms of the cost of food and drink compared to less popular areas. Some areas of a country are considered to be wealthier than others, which can also create a difference in the cost of living.

Political factors

Government policy affects the popularity and appeal of a destination. Governments can decide whether to focus attention on attracting investment into the tourism industry by encouraging building and development programmes to provide new facilities. They can decide which areas of the country should be developed for tourism and which areas should be protected. A government can impose strict regulations or, alternatively, decide to have few regulations.

CASE STUDY

Italy is now bargain buy holiday hotspot

Italy is a now one of the cheapest countries in the Euro zone for a range of common holiday purchases, according to a new survey.

Once regarded as a pricey playground for the rich, Italy emerged as the least expensive destination for a typical 'holiday hamper' of 13 items, including sunscreen, a meal at a restaurant, a bottle of Coke, and a postcard.

The cost of the items in Italy fell by 9 per cent compared to last year – the only European country in the survey where prices dropped.

A cappuccino in Italy cost just 64p and a three-course meal for two with a local bottle of wine cost only £28.42.

In Greece, a favourite UK holiday destination, a coffee cost £2.84, while the meal and wine in Norway cost a massive £75.14.

In Italy a bottle of beer at a bar cost just £1.39 and a bottle of mineral water came to 71p, while in Norway beer cost £3.98 and water cost £1.54.

Source: The Scotsman 14 May 2005

Governments need to raise money in order to pay for public spending. This is made possible through a system of taxation. However, a country that pays higher taxes is usually more expensive to visit. This can affect the popularity and appeal of a destination.

National tourist boards are financed by national government. The extent of promotional campaigns and initiatives are confined to what they can achieve within their set budgets. Governments will help decide what the priorities are through national policy but it is up to the national tourist board to spend its budgets wisely.

Governments can also make agreements and political alliances with other countries. Countries within the European Union have agreements on trade and the movement of people, both of which involve travel and tourism. As the European Union encourages other countries to join, new tourist destinations begin to emerge.

The European Union is the main tourist-generating area and tourist-receiving area for international tourism flows. On 1 May 2004, ten new countries joined the EU: Cyprus, Czech Republic, Estonia, Hungary, Latvia, Lithuania, Malta, Poland, Slovakia, and Slovenia. This has increased the geographical size of the European Union by 23 per cent and added 75 million people to its population. This has created the biggest economic area in the world, with a market of some 370 million people. This will provide many new opportunities for tourism. Further countries are set to join the EU, including Bulgaria, Romania and Turkey.

Eastern Europe has seen a growth in the number of tourists from the UK and other countries in Western Europe. The Czech Republic, Poland, Croatia and Russia have become more accessible due to the increase in the number of flights and package holidays on offer.

Prague (Czech Republic) is the number one Eastern European destination for UK tourists, followed by Budapest (Hungary), Krakow (Poland) and St Petersburg (Russia). New destinations are emerging each year and a growing number of Eastern European destinations are being offered by tour operators.

The following case study applies the ideas discussed in this section by exploring the factors affecting the popularity and appeal of one European travel destination that has grown in popularity during the last 15 years. The destination has controlled some of the main factors to maximise the number of tourists who visit.

Skills practice

1 To what extent do political factors affect the popularity of travel destinations?

2 Some factors that affect popularity and appeal are controllable by organisations and government, however some are not. Complete the following table to show how the popularity and appeal can and cannot be controlled at a destination:

	Examples of factors that can be controlled	Examples of factors that cannot be controlled
Accessibility		
Image and promotion		
Availability of attractions and other tourist facilities		
Destination management		
Cost of visiting		
Political factors		

CASE STUDY

Budapest, Hungary

Budapest is the capital city of Hungary and attracts over 1.6 million international tourists each year, including 122,000 tourists from the UK. The number of international visitor arrivals is increasing by an average 3 per cent each year. Budapest also attracts large numbers of domestic tourists, with over 330,000 Hungarians visiting the capital.

Accessibility

There are regular flights from European capital cities and a growing number from regional airports. There are regular services to and from the UK on British Airways and Malév, the Hungarian national airline, as well as budget-airlines such as easyJet. Flights arrive at Ferihegy International airport, 16 kilometres (10 miles) to the east of Budapest. Terminal 1 at Ferihegy has been upgraded to accommodate the rise in the number of European budget airlines using the airport.

Visitors can also arrive by car or by railway. Most visitors who travel by these modes of transport travel via Vienna in Austria. Austria is a major tourist-generating country for the Hungarian tourist industry. Fewer numbers of visitors use the River Danube as a gateway to Budapest.

There is an efficient public transport system in Budapest with an underground railway, regular bus services, trolleybuses and a suburban railway. City authorities have integrated the cost of using public transport as travel cards can be purchased allowing easy access between different modes of transport.

Access to tourist information is also an important aspect in increasing popularity and appeal. A tourist is more likely to visit if they can receive information about the city in their own language. The official *Budapest Guide*, written by the Budapest Tourism Office, is published in 17 different languages.

Image and promotion

The Budapest Tourism Office works in conjunction with the Hungarian National Tourist Board, whose role is to promote the country to a global audience. The Hungarian Tourist Board recognises that Eastern Europeans are familiar with what Hungary has to offer, whereas Western Europeans know very little. The Tourist Board aims to change the perception of the country from an Eastern European country to one that is recognised as a fellow European country by other Europeans.

In the UK the Hungarian Tourist Board organised a series of promotions based on '2004 Year of Hungarian Culture'. City breaks to Budapest were promoted in Germany, the UK and Belgium. Current campaigns focus on health tourism, as Budapest is Europe's largest spa city, with 80 thermal springs and 20 spa baths. Promotional channels include billboards, posters in travel agents, advertisements in the press and on television, including CNN, CNBC, Eurosport, National Geographic and the Travel Channel.

Availability of attractions and other tourist facilities

Budapest has been described as the 'Queen of the Danube', with its walled castle, the embankments of the River Danube, cafés, restaurants and opera houses. The city has many historic and cultural attractions. Some date back to when the city was two separate cities of Buda and Pest that were on either side of the River Danube. The two cities joined together in 1873 to create Budapest.

The castle on the Buda side of the River Danube dominates the skyline and is one of six UNESCO World Heritage Sites in Hungary. Castle Hill Várhegy also contains the Museum of Contemporary Art, the National Gallery and Mátáys Church, a nineteenth century recreation of a medieval church.

On the east bank of the river is Pest, which is accessible from Castle Hill via the Chain Bridge. The eastern side of the river contains the Hungarian parliament. Guided tours of the building can be taken, including a chance to see the Hungarian crown jewels. The dome of St Stephen's Basilica can also be clearly seen; from

Castle Palace at Várhegy is one of the most popular tourist sites in Budapest

St Stephen's Basilica, showing pinnacled towers and dome

the Basilica there are excellent views of the city.

The Market Hall provides an opportunity to sample traditional food and purchase traditional souvenirs, to see local people haggling over prices and going about their daily business.

Budapest has had an interesting history, which is presented through a variety of museums that are popular with tourists. There are over 40 museums to visit. Two examples portray Budapest's recent history. The Statue Park contains memorials and large statues from the Communist era that ended in 1989. Rather than destroying these statues at the end of Communist rule, they were taken down and removed to this site where they are now a focus of curiosity.

The Terror Museum or House of Terror is located on the fashionable Andrássy Boulevard. It was the headquarters of the Hungarian Nazis during the Second World War and later became the headquarters of Communist terror organisations. The museum was built with the support of the Hungarian prime minister and is a national memorial to the victims of terror.

Statue Park and the Terror Museum provide fascinating insights into the Communist period in Hungary's history

TerrorHáza
ANDRÁSSY ÚT 60.
HOUSE OF TERROR

Budapest, 1062
Andrássy út 60.

STATUE PARK
B U D A P E S T

GIGANTIC MEMORIALS FROM THE COMMUNIST DICTATORSHIP

A glance behind the Iron Curtain. Lenin, Marx, Engels, Dimitrov, the Soviet Heroes, the Communist Martyrs (etc.) Statues were removed from the streets of Budapest. It's the most exciting outdoor museum in Eastern Europe from the period of communist cultural politics. Unique souvenirs in the museum shop.

SZOBORPARK • PARC AUX STATUES PARCO DELLE STATUE • STATUENPARK

To get to the Park: From Bp. city centre (Ferenciek tere, Metro Nº3) take a red-numbered bus Nº7 to Étele tér (terminus). From there take the yellow Volán bus leaving from stall Nº2-3 toward Diósd-Érd. The buses leave every 15 minutes; the ride is 35 minutes. Budapest XXII. district (South Buda) corner of Balatoni út and Szabadkai utca.

www.szoborpark.hu

Direct bus line to Statue Park from Downtown in June, July and August every day at 9, 10, 11 A.M. and 3, 4, 5 P.M. It starts from Deák tér (Metro Nº1,2,3), in front of the Hotel Le Meridien. Return tickets 1.250 HUF/pers. (with Bp.Card, it's only 950 HUF/pers.), the price includes the ticket for the Statue Park as well.

Open: Every day from 10 A.M. to dusk.

The city of Budapest is built on the site of hot springs that rise from deep beneath the ground. The spa waters have been fashionable in the past for bathing, relaxation and for medical treatment. The most famous spa is found at the Hotel Gellért – its thermal waters are kept at a constant 38 °C.

There is a wide range of accommodation in Budapest, with many three- and four-star hotels as well as a selection of five-star hotels. In total there are 35,000 bed spaces across 213 accommodation providers, that include hotels, guesthouses and youth hostels. Many hotels have developed business and conference facilities. Budapest is a major commercial centre and in 2003 11,322 visitors travelled to the city to attend international meetings (ICCA 2003). The city is ranked 14th in Europe in terms of the number of people attending international meetings. Part of the strategy for future growth is to attract more visitors through encouraging business and conference tourism by promoting existing facilities and developing new conference and exhibition venues.

Destination management

The Budapest Tourism Office is responsible for the management of tourism in the city. It works with the Hungarian National Tourist Board and with local and national government to produce a coordinated approach. It is responsible for producing official guidebooks and maps of the city. The Tourism Office operates several tourist information centres, giving advice and information to visitors.

The Budapest Tourism Office was concerned that visitors could easily get lost in the city or not find the tourist attractions they were looking for. To make the city easier to navigate, it installed 750 signposts in 124 locations to direct tourists to the main attractions. These signs help to manage the movement of tourists across the city by encouraging them to use certain routes and explore parts of the city that they would not normally visit.

Budapest is a member of European Cities Tourism, which is a network of more than 80 city tourist offices and destination managers.

It enables Budapest to share ideas on the management of city tourism with other destination managers in Europe. The city can measure its success against similar cities and compare its management plans with that of others. It also enables cities to cooperate on joint ventures to improve the overall quality of city tourism in Europe.

Cost of visiting

The Budapest Tourism Office introduced the Budapest Card in 1997, to offer access to the main sights of the city for travellers on a budget. The card provides free travel on public transport and free access into many tourist attractions. The Budapest Card encourages visitors to stay longer in the city as there is much to see and do. Cards can be purchased in advance of arrival. In 1997, 12,000 cards were sold compared to 83,000 in 2001. A three-day card costs 5900 Hungarian forints (£16.20) and a two-day card is also available. The cost of a single ticket on public transport is 160 Hungarian forints (£0.44).

The cost of living in Budapest is relatively low compared to other cities in Europe. This makes it appealing as a travel destination.

Table 3.7 Comparison in costs between Hungary and the UK

Type of product or service	Price in Hungarian forints	Price in UK sterling*
A three-course meal	1000–3000HUF	£4.14–£8.28
1 litre of milk	100HUF	£0.28
A loaf of bread	100HUF	£0.28
1 litre of wine in shops	350–2000HUF	£0.97–£5.53
1 bottle of beer in shops	100–350HUF	£0.28–£0.97
1 hamburger	200–700HUF	£0.55–£1.93
1 night in a youth hostel	2500–6000HUF	£6.91–£16.57
1 cinema ticket	700–1000HUF	£1.93–£2.76

* Exchange rate based on £1.00 = 362 Hungarian forints. The National Bank of Hungary sets the rate of exchange on a daily basis.

Hungary may adopt the single European currency, the euro, by 2010. This will make it easier for people in other countries who have adopted the euro to visit and spend money without worrying about exchanging currency. Local people are concerned that the adoption of a single currency may encourage shops and businesses to raise their prices. However, the government has decided not to rush into adopting the euro. Budapest continues to represent good value for money.

Political factors

Since Communism ended in 1989 Hungary has developed its economy and has one of the lowest rates of unemployment in Eastern Europe. Tourism is regarded as a major source of income for the country and for the city.

Hungary joined the European Union in 2004 and has benefited from economic support and increased trade with other member countries.

Most visitors to Hungary travel to Budapest. Part of the future role of local and national authorities is to increase the numbers of different types of tourists who visit Budapest and its surrounding region. Lake Balaton is a popular resort with Hungarian and Austrian tourists, but its appeal could be promoted to other European countries.

Another potential area of growth is its spa tourism. There has been an increase in special interest holidays centred on health and fitness throughout Europe. Budapest is in a unique position to promote its famous hot spas as a focus for relaxation, therapy and beauty treatments. The Hungarian government spent 300 million Hungarian forints (£800,000) in 2004 on upgrading accommodation and tourist facilities in spa hotels to encourage the further development of spa tourism.

The aim of the Hungarian National Tourism Office is to make Hungary one of the top ten most visited countries in Europe by 2010.

For further information from the Tourism Office of Budapest visit
http://www.budapestinfo.hu/en

For a guide to Budapest visit
http://www.budpocketguide.com

For further information on Hungary visit
http://www.hungarytourism.hu

Panoramic view of the Danube River and the Chain Bridge from Gellért Hill in Budapest

ASSESSMENT

Portfolio practice

For this assessment you will need to identify the factors affecting the popularity and appeal of European travel destinations.

You are required to investigate one European tourist destination. It must not be the same destination that you used for portfolio practice on pages 116 and 125. The destination must have grown in popularity during the last 15 years.

You will provide an analysis of the factors that have led to the growth in popularity and appeal of one European travel destination and how the destination has controlled factors to maximise its appeal and popularity.

The destination chosen must be one that has recently become popular, with current and relevant factors for its rising popularity identified and analysed.

You also need to provide clear and detailed analysis of how the destination has maximised the controllable factors to increase its popularity.

When producing this piece of assessment you need to clearly show that research has been undertaken using a range of different sources. These sources must have been obtained independently, rather than been given by your tutor. The evidence that you have researched should be referenced accordingly.

3.5 Research skills, referencing and useful sources

Throughout this unit you are expected to carry out research into European travel destinations. When using sources make sure that information is current and relevant to today's travel and tourism industry.

Research involves:

* Being clear about what you are trying to find out

* Knowing how to search for information

* Deciding what might be useful

* Collecting and presenting relevant information

* Drawing conclusions about your findings

* Acknowledging your sources.

There are many useful resources regarding European travel destinations.

The *Internet* is a popular source for a huge range of information and many national tourist boards and visitor attractions have dedicated websites to provide information to visitors. In addition, travel guides, brochures and route planners can also be found.

The Association of National Tourist Office Representatives (ANTOR) has a directory of its members and the European Travel Commission (ETC) has a directory of national tourist boards in Europe. The ETC also provides visitor information for the whole of Europe.

Most tourist board websites display sufficient information without the need to contact the tourist boards directly. (*Note*: Some national tourist boards are not open to members of the public and only deal with trade enquiries.)

The following are websites of organisations mentioned above:

* ANTOR http://www.antor.com

* European Travel Commission (Travel trade) http://www.etc-corporate.org

* European Travel Commission (Visitors) http://www.visiteurope.com

Brochures are produced by tour operators and

tourist attractions in order to promote a range of products and services, including holidays and accommodation. You can find these in travel agents and there is a growing selection available via the Internet:

* First Choice http://www.firstchoice.co.uk
* Kuoni http://www.kuoni.co.uk
* MyTravel http://www.mytravel.com
* Thomas Cook http://www.thomascook.com
* Thomson http://www.thomson.co.uk

Maps provide the location of geographical features and can include road maps and other travel routes:

* Automobile Association (AA)
  http://www.theaa.com
* Multimap http://www.multimap.com
* National Geographic
  http://www.nationalgeographic.com/maps
* Royal Automobile Club (RAC)
  http://www.rac.co.uk

Travel guides are produced to provide information about a particular country or travel destination and contain information on visitor attractions, history, places of interest, culture, sport and accommodation:

* Fodor's http://www.fodors.com
* Lonely Planet http://www.lonelyplanet.com
* Rough Guides http://travel.roughguides.com
* World Travel Guide
  http://www.columbusguides.com

Newspapers report information on destinations as items of news. Some national newspapers publish regular supplements that provide details about travel destinations. Searchable news items also appear on the Internet:

* The Guardian http://www.guardian.co.uk
* The Mail on Sunday
  http://www.mailonsunday.co.uk
* The Times http://www.timesonline.co.uk

Trade journals are publications devoted to news and features designed to inform members of the industry. Examples of trade journals for travel and tourism include *Travel Weekly* and the *Travel Trade Gazette*. These can also be found on the Internet:

* Travel Trade Gazette http://www.ttglive.com
* Travel Weekly http://www.travelweekly.co.uk

Referencing

It is good practice to reference the books and resources you have been using in your written work. This is useful if you want to come back to a source to add more detail or to let the reader know where to find further information. It is also important if you are copying information to quote the source. You would feel cheated if someone copied your work without permission; copying other people's work without referencing is called *plagiarism*.

After writing a quote in speech marks, place the author and date in brackets with the relevant page number separated by a comma:

'A travel destination is the end point of a journey' (Dale, Marvell and Oliver 2005, p.92).

At the end of your assignments you need to include a list of references. They should be arranged alphabetically. If the same author is used then the most recent date is used first.

The correct way of acknowledging and referencing sources is to use the Harvard style of referencing. In a book the reference is as follows:

Author, Author initials. (Date) Title. Place of publication: Publisher.

The title should be underlined or placed in *italics*, for example:

Dale, G., Marvell, A. and Oliver, H. (2005) *AS level for Edexcel Travel and Tourism.* Oxford: Heinemann Educational Publishers.

In a newspaper the reference is as follows:

Author, Author initials. (Date) Title of article. Title of newspaper, day of publication, page numbers.

For example:

Holden, W. (2005) Hidden gems of townhouse Paris. *The Mail on Sunday,* 1 May, pp.92–93.

When using Internet sites try to quote the author and date of publication if at all possible, and the date accessed, for example:

Little, M. (2004) Freelance Spain. A brief history of Spain, 17 November, http://www.spainview.com/history.html.

1 Name six different types of tourist destination.

2 For each type of destination, give at least two named examples.

3 Identify on a map of Europe examples for each type of destination that are popular with visitors from the UK.

4 Explain some of the problems in categorising travel destinations.

5 What are the features that attract tourists to destinations and give them appeal?

6 Name seven different types of tourists.

7 Describe how you would recommend a destination to meet the needs of different types of tourists.

8 Identify the resources you might use to research European travel destinations.

9 What are the modes of transport available to European travel destinations?

10 Name some of the main gateways in Europe from the UK.

11 What are the factors that affect the popularity and appeal of tourist destinations?

12 Which factors identified in question 11 can be controlled by the destination and which factors cannot?

Resources

Golden, F.W. and Brown, J. (2002) *Fromer's European Cruises and Ports of Call*. 2nd ed. New York: Hungry Minds Inc

Lonely Planet (2001) *Europe on a Shoestring*. 2nd ed. London: Lonely Planet Publications.

Lonely Planet (2001) *Mediterranean Europe*. London: Lonely Planet Publications.

McDonald, F. and Marsden, C. (2001) *EyeWitness Travel Guides: Europe*. London: Dorling Kindersley Ltd.

Ratcliffe, L. (2001) *The Rough Guide to Europe: 2002 Edition*. London: Rough Guides Ltd.

Williams, R. (2000) *Insight Guide: Continental Europe*. Singapore: APA Publications Pty.

Wood, K. (2002) *Europe by Train*. London: Robson Books.

Destination Britain

Introduction

This unit looks at the British Isles as a popular destination for visitors from overseas. By the end of the unit you will find out just how popular the locations are by investigating the scale of tourism in the British Isles. The unit will give you the opportunity to look at the organisations involved in maintaining that popularity and appeal. You will examine a range of popular tourist destinations across all of the British Isles and the features they have that give them popularity and appeal. You will have the opportunity to develop itineraries for tourists planning to visit one or more of these islands. You will also look at the factors that affect the future popularity and appeal of tourist destinations in these islands.

It is important to know which countries are part of the British Isles and to make sure that you use the correct term when describing groups of countries:

✱ The British Isles includes England, Scotland, Wales, Northern Ireland, the Republic of Ireland, the Channel Islands and the Isle of Man

✱ The United Kingdom includes Great Britain and Northern Ireland

✱ Great Britain includes England, Wales and Scotland.

> ### How you will be assessed

This is an internally assessed unit and you will be required to submit a portfolio of work to be assessed. Your tutor will provide details as to what assessment evidence should be contained within your portfolio.

Assessment evidence could be in many different forms. You will be asked to produce a travel itinerary but you could also be asked to produce written reports, newspaper articles, radio or television scripts, or witness testimonies of oral presentations accompanied by supporting evidence. You will be expected to have researched widely using relevant sources of information.

You will be asked to produce evidence that demonstrates:

✱ A study of travel and tourism organisations in one selected area of the British Isles

* An itinerary that includes a range of destinations for a group of incoming tourists

* Research and analysis on the scale and importance of tourism in the British Isles

* An evaluation of the factors that have affected the popularity and appeal of a selected tourist destination in the British Isles.

After completing the unit you will achieve the following outcomes by gaining an understanding of:

* Travel and tourism organisations that support tourism in the British Isles

* Features of destinations in the British Isles

* Constructing itineraries for tourists

* Scale of tourism to the British Isles

* The factors that affect popularity and appeal of destinations.

4.1 Travel and tourism organisations that support tourism in the British Isles

By the end of this section you will be able to identify the local, regional and national organisations involved in supporting tourism in a selected area of the British Isles and be able to explain their roles. A selected area can include a regional tourist board, a regional development agency area, one or more counties, or a themed area. You will also be able to explain how different organisations work with each other to support tourism in the British Isles.

There are many different travel and tourism organisations that support tourism in the British Isles. There are public, private and voluntary sector organisations.

* *Public sector* organisations provide a service to society rather than focusing on producing a profit. Examples include local and national government.

* *Private sector* organisations provide a service in order to maximise profits. The majority of travel and tourism organisations are private

sector organisations. Examples include tour operators, travel agents, transport companies and hotels.

* *Voluntary sector* organisations are not-for-profit organisations that provide a service to their members and to the general public. Many voluntary sector organisations receive funding from private or public sector organisations as well as raising funds through the cost of membership. Examples include the Youth Hostels Association (YHA) and the National Trust.

Different organisations support tourism in different ways and operate at different scales and levels of administration: at national, regional and local levels. These include:

* Government departments and agencies

* Regional tourist boards and national tourist offices

* Local authority tourism departments

* Regional development agencies

* Tourist information centres

* Membership organisations

* Transport operators, accommodation providers, incoming tour operators.

Figure 4.1 The structure of tourism in the UK

The structure of tourism in the UK is a complex web of organisations. Government decides tourism policy but a variety of different organisations apply these decisions at different levels of administration. We will now look at each of these in turn. (See Figure 4.1.)

Government departments and agencies

Department for Culture, Media and Sport

The UK government Department for Culture, Media and Sport (DCMS) has the responsibility for supporting the tourism industry at national level and for establishing regional and local support. The DCMS has many duties, including the arts, entertainment, broadcasting, architecture, creative industries, the film industry, libraries, museums, galleries, national heritage, the National Lottery, sport and tourism. A cabinet minister, the Secretary of State for Culture, Media and Sport, who works closely with the prime minister, oversees the Department. Other government departments that support tourism include the Department of Environment, Food and Rural Affairs (DEFRA) and the Department for Transport (DfT).

Skills practice

1 What is the name of the UK Minister for Tourism?

2 How does the Department·for Culture, Media and Sport support the growth of tourism in the UK?

As a result of devolution in the UK, Scotland has its own parliament and Wales and Northern Ireland both have their own assemblies. All three groups are responsible for tourism in their own countries.

The government strategy for tourism was published in 1999 and is called *Tomorrow's Tourism*. Its main aims are to:

* Encourage investment in the tourism industry

* Provide a new support structure for tourism

* Develop quality tourism experiences to meet customer expectations

* Provide better information for customers and businesses

* Improve career opportunities in the tourism industry

* Develop and promote a sustainable approach to tourism

* Increase access to tourism for those with low incomes, families, the elderly and disabled people.

As a result of *Tomorrow's Tourism*, the DCMS made a number of important changes to the way in which tourism is supported in the UK:

* VisitBritain was established in April 2003, bringing together the former English Tourism Council and the British Tourist Authority

* Regional development agencies were to have strategic responsibility for tourism in their regions and to work closely with the regional tourist boards

* Major surveys were to be carried out to assess the levels of accommodation quality and business information

* The Tourism Alliance was established in 2001 as the voice of the tourism industry, with an aim to represent the views of the industry more effectively to the government

* People 1st was launched in May 2004 as the new Sector Skills Council for the travel, tourism, hospitality and leisure sectors, to promote careers and training in the industry.

In July 2004 the government published *Tomorrow's Tourism Today*, a revised statement on tourism policy that establishes a revised set of priorities. The new statement focuses on the importance of marketing, quality, skills and data.

CASE STUDY

People 1st

People 1st is the Sector Skills Council for the hospitality, leisure, travel and tourism industries. It is an employer-led, UK-wide government-licensed organisation set up to coordinate skills issues within the hospitality, leisure, travel and tourism sector. People 1st is part of the government's Skills for Business network.

The aims of People 1st:

* It is the voice of industry on skills matters and encourages best practice

* It helps direct funds for skills where they are needed most

* It ensures qualifications are developed that are fit for purpose

* It produces the information employers need on skills training

* It helps people find the training and the provider that fits their training needs.

For further information visit http://www.people1st.co.uk

People 1st is part of the Skills for Business network

Regional tourist boards and national tourist offices

National tourist offices (NTOs)

VisitBritain is the government-sponsored national tourist office responsible for promoting Britain as a tourist destination to overseas markets, and promoting England as a tourist destination to the British. Its website holds an enormous amount of information about tourism in Britain. It was formed after a merger of the British Tourist Authority and the English Tourism Council, with a mission to build the value of tourism by creating world-class destination brands and marketing campaigns. It also creates partnerships with other organisations that have a stake in British and English tourism.

VisitBritain has a range of goals:

* To promote Britain overseas as a tourist destination, generating additional tourism revenue throughout Britain and throughout the year

* To grow the value of the domestic market by encouraging key audiences to take additional and/or longer breaks in England

* To provide advice to government on matters affecting tourism and contribute to wider government objectives

* To work in partnership with the devolved administrations and the national and regional tourist boards to build the British tourism industry.

VisitBritain works in partnership with the national tourist boards in England, Northern Ireland, Scotland and Wales to promote an attractive image of Britain. It provides impartial tourism information and gathers essential market intelligence for the UK tourism industry. VisitBritain is funded by the Department for Culture, Media and Sport to promote Britain overseas as a tourist destination and to lead and co-ordinate England's tourism marketing.

It received £35.5 million in 2004–2005 to promote Britain overseas. The total resource available for marketing England is £14 million (of which £3.6 million is deployed directly through regional development agencies). A further £1.5 million 'challenge fund' is available for domestic marketing subject to VisitBritain raising £3.5 million with other tourism organisations. VisitBritain also raises around £17 million from non-government funding through partnerships and other activities.

The VisitBritain logo

VisitBritain operates a network of 25 offices covering 31 key markets. It employs 450 staff, 60 per cent of whom are based overseas in Britain's key tourism markets.

For further information visit http://www.visitbritain.com

Regional tourist boards (RTBs)

Regional tourist boards (RTBs) assist the government in achieving the goals set out in *Tomorrow's Tourism*. Regional tourist boards are not government agencies and board members are not appointed by ministers. They are funded by membership fees from tourism businesses, local authorities, commercial income generated through consultancy and training courses, as well as some public funding from DCMS, VisitBritain and the regional development agencies (RDAs). There are 9 regional tourist boards in England and 4 in Wales. (See Figure 4.2.)

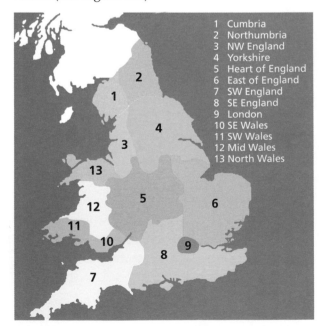

1 Cumbria
2 Northumbria
3 NW England
4 Yorkshire
5 Heart of England
6 East of England
7 SW England
8 SE England
9 London
10 SE Wales
11 SW Wales
12 Mid Wales
13 North Wales

Figure 4.2 Map of regional tourist boards in England and Wales

Under the regional tourism strategies being developed by the regional development agencies, the regional tourist boards will in some regions be the RDAs' principal partner in delivering tourism support. In other regions the regional tourist boards oversee the work of sub-regional destination management organisations (DMOs), or partnerships, which have been established by the RDAs to support tourism at a specific tourism destination. In most cases regional tourist boards are responsible for putting the tourism strategy into practice.

Regional development agencies

Regional development agencies are responsible for the development of tourism in the regions. There are eight regional development agencies (RDAs) in the English regions and one in London. Their role is to: co-ordinate regional economic development and regeneration, enable the regions to improve their competitiveness and reduce imbalances that exist within and between regions.

Under the Regional Development Agencies Act (1998), each agency has five statutory purposes, which are:

* To further economic development and regeneration

* To promote business efficiency, investment and competitiveness

* To promote employment

* To enhance development and application of skills relevant to employment

* To contribute to sustainable development.

Each RDA works with partner organisations within each region to create a regional economic strategy. This strategy establishes the goals for economic development across the region. Tourism is important in creating jobs, increasing the amount of money spent by tourists using local businesses, and developing attractions and facilities that can be enjoyed by people who live in the region as well as visitors.

For further information visit http://www.englandsrdas.com

CASE STUDY

One NorthEast

In March 2004, Northumbria Tourist Board was transferred to One NorthEast. This re-structure means that One NorthEast is now responsible for both the strategic direction and delivery of tourism across the region. As part of this new remit, the development agency, working with partners and businesses, has produced a new tourism strategy. The new strategy aims to improve co-ordination across the region and increase the contribution of tourism to the regional economy through enhanced investment and smarter delivery.

For further information, visit One NorthEast http://www.onenortheast.co.uk or visit Tourism NorthEast http://www.tourismnortheast.co.uk

Newcastle attracts many visitors to the North East

Local authority tourism departments

Local authorities and *local government* represent the needs of residents and businesses and bring the benefits of tourism to local areas at the same time as reducing any negative effects. Local authorities provide a range of services that include litterbins, toilets, signposts, car and coach parking, and planning regulations. Most of their services enhance and improve a local area and therefore contribute to the local tourism industry. Local authority tourism departments are also responsible for promoting the area that they represent.

Activities of local authority tourism departments can include:

* Media and public relations
* Supporting film production companies
* Producing brochures, leaflets and newsletters
* Tourist information centres (TICs)
* Websites aimed at visitors and tourism businesses
* Theatres
* Museums
* Art galleries
* Parks and gardens
* Accommodation booking services
* Conference and exhibition services
* Events and attractions ticketing
* Business surveys and market research
* Business development
* Designing tourist routes, cycling routes and walking trails
* Promoting sustainable forms of tourism.

The tourist information centre in Lavenham, Suffolk, provides information on a wide range of services for tourists

Skills practice

1 Identify where your nearest tourist information centre is located.
2 Describe the range of services that it provides.

Skills practice

1 Investigate the range of leisure and tourism services provided by your local authority tourism department.
2 Identify examples of businesses and organisations that your local authority tourism department works in partnership with.

Tourist information centres (TICs)

Tourist information centres (TICs) provide a service for visitors and local residents by giving information about visitor attractions, events, transport services, and provide a booking service for those seeking accommodation. Most are funded by local authorities and local government. TICs have widened the services that they offer by selling souvenirs, guide books and postcards, tickets to events and shows, and guided tours. They also provide information to the local community, for example details about local clubs and societies, bus timetables and changes to local services, for example refuse collection.

Membership organisations

Membership organisations represent various groups within the tourism industry. The organisations are responsible for supporting their members by lobbying government on their behalf and promoting best practice within the industry. Most membership organisations hold conferences and events to provide a forum to discuss new ideas and any concerns that are affecting the industry. Some membership organisations represent tourism companies and businesses such as the Tourism Alliance and UKinbound.

CASE STUDY

The Tourism Alliance

The Tourism Alliance seeks to establish and maintain a favourable operating environment for all businesses involved in the delivery of tourism, particularly in England.

Its main purpose is to lobby government both in England and Europe on important issues facing the industry. The Alliance aims to identify and develop policies and strategies to raise and promote quality within the industry and to liaise with the media on behalf of the industry.

For further information visit http://www.tourismalliance.com

CASE STUDY

UKinbound

UKinbound (formerly the British Incoming Tour Operators Association) is the official trade body representing the UK inbound tourism industry. It represents over 270 major companies and organisations in all sectors of the industry, operating 5000-plus outlets in the UK.

Members of UKinbound include tour operators, ground handlers and destination management companies who specialise in leisure and tourism in Britain. UKinbound organises events, conferences and exhibitions on behalf of its members.

Each month the organisation produces a business barometer, based on a confidential online survey of UKinbound members, comparing visitor numbers and booking forecasts with the previous year.

For further information visit
http://www.ukinbound.co.uk

Skills practice

Complete the following table that identifies the roles, activities and benefits of three membership organisations:

Name of organisation	Website	Roles and activities	Benefits to members
Institute of Travel and Tourism	http://www.itt.co.uk		
The Tourism Society	http://www.tourismsociety.org		
Tourism Management Institute	http://www.tmi.org.uk		

Transport operators, accommodation providers, incoming tour operators

Transport operators support tourism in the British Isles by providing a range of services to transport a tourist from the point of entry to their destination, and provide transport services whilst at their destination. Accommodation providers support tourism by offering a range of services and standards from serviced accommodation in hotels and guesthouses to self-catering, student hostels and caravan and camping sites.

Incoming tour operators provide tours and guiding services for inbound visitors as well as ground-handling services. *Ground handlers* are specialist companies that provide a range of local services for tourists such as transfers to and from the airport to the accommodation, day trips and excursions. These companies work on behalf of tour operators and airlines.

CASE STUDY

British Tours Ltd

British Tours Ltd is Britain's longest-established personal tour operator, having been founded in 1958.

It provides tours for all size groups – private groups of up to seven travel by car with their own driver-guide and larger groups by minibus and coach. Tours are available in most languages, including French, German, Spanish, Italian, Russian, Japanese and Chinese. British Tours Ltd employ over 50 guides with academic and professional backgrounds. It works with hundreds of travel agents worldwide, as well as with many of the UK's companies, to provide flexible sightseeing for their overseas visitors, ground-handling arrangements, interpreting and special events. The company is also a member of UKinbound and VisitLondon.

For further information visit
http://www.britishtours.com

Interdependence and interrelationships

The structure of tourism management in the British Isles appears at first to be complex, with many organisations seeming to have similar roles and responsibilities. What is important is how these organisations work together in supporting tourism. The interdependence and interrelationships of the organisations refers to how they fit into the structure of tourism management. Interdependence describes how different organisations depend on one another and interrelationships describe how different organisations communicate ideas and work together. As you can see from the examples in this unit, regional development agencies work together with regional tourist boards and VisitBritain as well as with the government, local authorities and tourism businesses.

CASE STUDY

EnglandNet

EnglandNet has brought together many organisations to support the development of tourism. VisitBritain works closely with regional tourist boards, regional development agencies, local authorities and commercial organisations to build a one-stop 'virtual high street' for English tourism. It is expected to increase visitors to www.visitbritain.com and www.visitengland.com from 11 million to 27 million visitors by 2006. EnglandNet is not a website but a powerful database. England's tourism will be represented in a national product database that is accessible to regional tourism partners and commercial operators. The database will enable customers to link to booking services by creating search engines for online real-time availability.

For further information visit http://www.englandnet.co.uk

Tourism in the Republic of Ireland

The structure of tourism in the Republic of Ireland is similar to that of the UK, but there are some differences.

Fáilte Ireland is the Irish government's National Tourism Development Authority. The organisation provides strategic and practical support to develop and sustain Ireland as a high-quality and competitive tourist destination.

Fáilte Ireland works in partnership with tourism businesses and organisations to support the industry in its efforts to be more competitive and more profitable. There is an emphasis on strategic partnership at national, local and regional levels, working together towards a common goal.

Fáilte Ireland provides a range of support and services to those involved, or considering becoming involved in Irish tourism, with a one-stop shop to meet their business or professional needs.

Key aspects of Fáilte Ireland include:

* Marketing
* Training
* Product development
* Research and statistics.

For more information on Fáilte Ireland visit http://www.failteireland.ie
For more information on tourism in Ireland visit http://www.ireland.ie

Skills practice

Investigate the main similarities and differences between the organisation of tourism in the UK and in the Republic of Ireland.

We will now describe the roles of key travel and tourism organisations that support tourism in one selected area, the county of Wiltshire.

CASE STUDY

Wiltshire

Wiltshire is a county in southern England. Its popular tourist attractions include Stonehenge, Longleat House and Safari Park, Stourhead House and Gardens, Salisbury Cathedral and the Steam Museum in Swindon.

Wiltshire receives 1.7 million visitors who stay 5 million nights, spending a yearly average of £266 million. Each visitor stays on average 2.9 nights and spends £156 per visit.

Wiltshire Tourism is a local authority organisation, part of the Economic Regeneration and Resources team at Wiltshire County Council. Part of its role is to encourage further investment into Wiltshire and to encourage the sustainable use of existing resources.

Wiltshire Tourism produces an annual visitor guide, *Welcome to Wiltshire*, as well as several walking and cycling publications. It works closely with VisitBritain and South West Tourism Regional Tourist Board on their marketing campaigns. It also liaises with tourist information centres throughout Wiltshire in order to distribute promotional materials and information.

It represents the county of Wiltshire at the South West Tourism EnglandNet meetings to discuss how tourism business in Wiltshire can benefit from the new database.

Wiltshire Tourism offers a range of training courses to suit local business needs. These are coordinated by the Tourism Skills Network, which is a South West of England Regional Development Agency initiative. It works with employers to identify training needs and deliver programmes in partnership with training agencies to improve the skills base and capacity of the workforce, as well as promoting tourism as a career.

It also offers business advice through its partnership with Business Link, a national network offering business support. Business Link Berkshire and Wiltshire offers training and advice, legal services and business development planning.

Wiltshire Tourism promotes tourist destinations and attractions throughout the region

Accommodation providers in Wiltshire are encouraged to join the VisitBritain's Quality Grading Scheme. Accommodation can be awarded stars for hotels or diamonds for guesthouses based on the standard of accommodation and the level of services. Accommodation providers in Wiltshire work with Quality in Tourism, which administers the Quality Grading Scheme.

Following the publication of the *Walking in Wiltshire* booklet, the South West Regional Development Agency has given Wiltshire Tourism funds to develop four new walks and five new cycle routes around Salisbury Plain. This is to encourage more visitors to explore areas that people would not normally visit. Other initiatives include the Wiltshire Breakfast and a series of Taste Trails, to tempt new visitors to local bakeries, delicatessens, breweries and tearooms, as well as many speciality producers of local produce around the county.

Wiltshire Tourism has been part of the consultation for the South West Tourism Regional Tourist Board's tourism strategy *Towards 2015*. South West Tourism has successfully bid for funding from the Regional

Development Agency to begin developing a series of marketing campaigns, starting with 'Sheer indulgence'. The 'Sheer indulgence' brand represents the finest that the South West region has to offer in terms of hotels and restaurants.

For further information on Wiltshire Tourism visit http://www.visitwiltshire.com

For further information on South West Tourism Regional Tourist Board visit http://www.swtourism.co.uk

For further information on South West Regional Development Agency visit http://www.southwestrda.org.uk

Skills practice

1 Identify the different organisations that Wiltshire Tourism works in partnership with.

2 Describe the benefits of working with other organisations.

ASSESSMENT

Portfolio practice

You will be asked to provide a description of the roles of key travel and tourism organisations that support tourism in a selected area of the British Isles.

A selected area can be a regional tourist board area such as One NorthEast, a county such as Wiltshire, a group of counties such as Wessex, or a themed area such as Heartbeat Country or Last of the Summer Wine Country.

You also need to identify organisations from outside the area that influence and support tourism in your selected area. Their roles need to be clearly described.

Once you have identified the key travel and tourism organisations, you will then need to provide an explanation of the interdependence and interrelationships of these organisations in supporting tourism to the selected area in the British Isles. It is important to use examples to show the way in which these organisations work together to attract tourists.

4.2 Features of destinations in the British Isles

In this section you will learn that there are different types of destination in the British Isles. These are categorised as:

* Coastal areas
* Tourist towns and cities
* Business and conference destinations
* Countryside areas
* Heritage and cultural destinations
* Purpose-built destinations.

You will be able to give examples of the main destinations within these categories that are popular with incoming tourists to the British Isles. You will learn to locate these destinations on a map.

Coastal areas

Coastal areas can include seaside resorts and other areas of the coastline that have become popular with tourists. A coastal area destination is an expanse of coastline that is specifically defined as one area. It can also include specific coastal resorts.

The *coastline* of the United Kingdom extends for over 14,580 kilometres (9040 miles), not including the many islands that lie offshore. Most people live no more than 125 kilometres (78 miles) from the sea. For the last 150 years the most popular form of holiday has been by the seaside. A beach can offer golden sands, a chance to sit in the sun or take part in activities such as water sports, beach sports, arcades, amusements and children's entertainment.

Not one area of the coastline is exactly the same as another. Some areas of coastline have beaches, some have cliffs and some have mud flats and salt marshes. Even where there is a beach some may be made of sand, others made of pebbles or shingle, and others a combination of both sand and pebbles.

Seaside resorts are urban in appearance, with entertainment, amusements, bars and restaurants. Further along the coastline at a distance from the seaside resorts, rural coastal areas can be found.

There are 552 official bathing sites in the UK that are monitored for water quality, including 374 beaches that have been given Seaside Awards in recognition of their cleanliness, water quality and provision of facilities. A Seaside Award is given to clean and safe beaches in the UK and a Blue Flag is a measure of beach and water quality across Europe and South Africa.

In 2003 a survey of 170 beaches across the country was carried out by the environmental charity ENCAMS and the Keep Britain Tidy group. The beaches were compared on safety, cleanliness, water quality, facilities and access, and scored out of one hundred.

Table 4.1 Top 10 beaches in the UK

| TOP 10 BEACHES IN THE UK ||
Beach	Score out of 100
Bournemouth Pier	99
Bridlington	96
Filey	96
Scarborough	96
Burnham-on-Sea	94
Dawlish Warren	94
Clacton	93
Weymouth	93
Eastbourne	93
Ramsgate	93

Source: ENCAMS

For more information on Seaside Awards, visit http://www.seasideawards.org.uk

Skills practice

1 Are visitors attracted more to beaches that are safe and clean than those that are not?

2 Suggest why Bournemouth received the highest score.

3 Using an atlas and an outline map of the British Isles (see page 199), identify the beaches named in Table 4.1 and in question 4 and mark these on your map.

4 Complete the following table. You may need to carry out research to answer this question.

Coastal resort	Main attractions
Blackpool	
Bournemouth	
Brighton	
Great Yarmouth	
Newquay	

Brighton seafront provides shops, activities and other facilities for tourists

Tourist towns and cities

Tourist towns and cities include a specific town or city which is known as a tourist destination. London receives the majority of overseas visitors to the UK. It accounts for half of all overnight visits to the UK, with 11.7 million overnight stays generating £5.9 billion in 2003. The number of overnight visits to London was over seven times

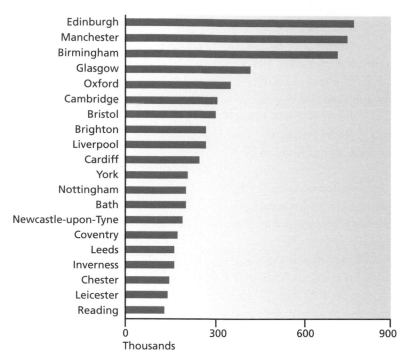

Figure 4.3 Top 20 UK towns visited (excluding London) by number of overnight visits

greater than those made to Scotland and thirteen times more than visits made to Wales. Second to London, the next most popular place of visit was Edinburgh, which hosted 0.8 million overnight visits, followed by Manchester and Birmingham.

The reasons why many people visit towns and cities are described in Unit 3: Destination Europe pages 94–95.

Think it over ...

1 What are the main reasons why tourists visit towns and cities?

2 Why does London receive the largest amount of overseas residents compared with other towns and cities in the UK and the rest of the British Isles?

CASE STUDY

Dublin, Republic of Ireland

Dublin is the third most popular city destination in Europe. The city is famous for its hospitality and offers a wide range of attractions and entertainment. Dublin has become a reputable venue for stag and hen nights in a city that has over 1000 pubs. The south side of the River Liffey has become popular with fashionable bars, restaurants and shops, especially along the cobbled streets of Temple Bar. There are also ancient and historic castles in the heart of the city along with cultural attractions, including the National Museum and the National Gallery. The streets have retained their Georgian charm and a central shopping area offers a range of traditional products and designer labels. The city is also famous for its Guinness beer. At St James Gate visitors can tour the largest brewery in Europe, see an audiovisual show and sample a glass of Guinness. Dublin has over 15,000 bed spaces in serviced accommodation (hotels, guesthouses and bed-and-breakfast accommodation), as well as 113 registered self-catering apartments and nearly 3000 bed spaces in student and backpacker hostels.

For further information visit http://www.visitdublin.com

Dublin is one of the most popular city destinations in Europe

Think it over ...

Why is Dublin a popular destination for visitors from overseas?

Business and conference destinations

Business and conference destinations are defined as towns or cities with facilities to cope with business tourists, such as large conference or exhibition centres; a range of business tourist facilities, including hotels; and good transport links and close proximity to an international airport.

Over seven million overseas visitors come to Britain on business each year. In the last ten years there has been more than 50 per cent growth in international business trips. Business tourism accounts for 28 per cent of all inbound visits to Britain. Although business visitors have shorter visits than most other travellers, they spend more than twice as much per day.

Business travel accounts for 12 per cent of all trips. Travelling on business includes travelling for the purpose of meetings, conferences, trade fairs and exhibitions. These are sometimes referred to as the MICE industries – Meetings, Incentives, Conferences and Exhibitions.

Conferences are worth an estimated £7.7 billion to the British economy. In addition, the total value of business and conference meetings is even higher when account is taken of how much delegates spend on items such as drinks in the bar, meals in local restaurants, entertainment and visits to attractions and transport costs.

Approximately 60 per cent of the conferences are held in hotels with dedicated meeting rooms and exhibition spaces. Some business travel destinations and conference venues use large purpose-built facilities such as indoor arenas, for example the National Exhibition Centre (NEC) in Birmingham, the Scottish Exhibition and Conference Centre (SECC) in Glasgow, the ExCeL exhibition and conference venue in London and the King's Hall Exhibition and Conference Centre in Belfast. The peak months for conferences are September and October, followed by June and November.

London, Birmingham and Manchester remain the most popular destinations. London is the leading business and conference destination and is regarded as Europe's best city for business. In 2003 the economic value of events to London was £3.2 billion, with over 500 business and conference venues. Table 4.2 shows the most popular conference destinations. Businesses that were surveyed in the UK Conference Market Survey included all destinations used and therefore the figure represents the percentage of all respondents having held an event in the destination in 2005.

Table 4.2 Most popular conference destinations in 2005

CONFERENCE DESTINATION	PERCENTAGE
London	51.3
Birmingham	30.6
Manchester	19.4
Edinburgh	11.2
Glasgow	10.2
Cardiff	8.2
Belfast	6.3
Brighton	5.6
Harrogate	5.6
Bournemouth	4.6
Torquay	4.3
Blackpool	3.6
Dublin	3.3
Eastbourne	2.3
Elsewhere in UK	52.3

Source: UK Conference Market Survey (2005)

Skills practice

1 Using Table 4.2, suggest why over 50 per cent of businesses prefer to choose London as a business and conference destination.

2 Using an atlas and an outline map of the British Isles (see page 199), locate the most popular business and conference destinations on your map.

3 Suggest why towns and cities wish to attract business and conference visitors.

Tourists enjoying the countryside in Ullswater in the Lake District

Countryside areas

Countryside areas are rural areas away from towns and cities and not necessarily named resorts. People visit the countryside for many reasons. Some want to relax, enjoy a picnic or admire the landscape. Some want to experience sporting activities such as hiking, mountain climbing, mountain biking or fishing. Others may simply wish to take their dog for a walk, visit friends and family or escape the hustle and bustle of major towns and cities.

Rural villages offer an alternative to urban life. Cottages, small local shops, village pubs and a community spirit often appeal to those who wish to leave the hustle and bustle of busy towns and cities behind.

Farm-based accommodation has become a familiar sight in the countryside, with farmers offering rooms and farm cottages to tourists. Such accommodation is attractive as it provides an authentic location in which visitors can witness rural life at first hand. Some farms remain working farms whilst others now dedicate themselves to serving a growing demand in tourism. Many popular rural pursuits are available to those wishing to stay in villages or in farm-based accommodation, including horse riding, fishing, cycling or golf.

CASE STUDY

UK national parks

There are twelve national parks in England and Wales. Ten were established as a result of the National Parks and Access to Countryside Act (1949) and the Norfolk Broads was established under a separate Act in 1981. The latest national park to be officially recognised in England is the New Forest, which became a national park in March 2005.

The purpose of a national park is to preserve wildlife, conserve areas of the countryside and provide for recreation. The most visited national park in the UK is the Lake District with 22 million day visits per year.

In Scotland the National Parks (Scotland) Act was passed in July 2000. The first Scottish national park, Loch Lomond and the Trossachs, was established in July 2002, and the Cairngorms National Park was established in March 2003.

Table 4.3 National park visitor numbers

NATIONAL PARK	NUMBER OF VISITOR DAYS (MILLIONS PER YEAR)
1 Lake District	22
2 Peak District	19
3 Snowdonia	10.5
4 Yorkshire Dales	9
5 North York Moors	8
6 Brecon Beacons	7
7 Norfolk Broads	5.4
8 Pembrokeshire Coast	4.7
9 Dartmoor	4
10 Northumberland	1.5
11 Exmoor	1.4
12 New Forest	n/a

Source: Council for National Parks (2005)

For further information visit the Council for National Parks http://www.cnp.org.uk

Figure 4.4 National parks of England and Wales

Skills practice

1 Where are the most popular areas of countryside in Britain?

2 Why do national parks attract large numbers of visitors?

3 Select one national park. Identify activities, attractions and facilities that make it popular with incoming tourists. You may have to research a number of sources to answer this question.

Heritage and cultural destinations

Heritage and cultural destinations are specific towns, cities, villages and resorts that are known for having maintained the history and heritage of the destination and/or the culture of the region or country. They also include destinations linked to UNESCO World Heritage Sites, including Bath and Edinburgh. Other examples include Oxford, Cambridge, York, Canterbury and Stratford-upon-Avon. Within each heritage and cultural destination is a range of different heritage and cultural attractions.

For information on UNESCO see Unit 3: Destination Europe, page 98.

CASE STUDY

Oxford

Oxford receives over 7 million visitors each year. Most of the visitors come to see the University and its colleges, some of which are open to the public. The city has been home to many authors, including Lewis Carroll, who wrote *Alice in Wonderland*, and JRR Tolkien, who wrote *Lord of the Rings*. The city has also become famous through television and film, particularly through the popular TV detective series *Inspector Morse*, which was filmed there. Several of the college buildings were also used in the filming of the Harry Potter series, the most famous being Christ Church College, which was used as Hogwarts dining hall. The city has many museums and cultural attractions, including the

Oxford is one of the most popular city destinations in the UK

Ashmolean Museum of Art and Archaeology, the oldest public museum in Britain.

For further information visit http://www.visitoxford.org

Skills practice

1 To what extent can Oxford be described as a heritage and cultural destination?

2 Using an atlas and a guidebook of the British Isles, identify ten heritage and cultural destinations and locate these on an outline map of the British Isles (see page 199).

3 Complete the following table:

Name of heritage or cultural destination	Examples of heritage attractions	Examples of cultural attractions
Bath		
Cambridge		
Canterbury		
Dublin		
Edinburgh		
Oxford		
Stratford-upon-Avon		
York		

CASE STUDY

Liverpool, European Capital City of Culture 2008

Liverpool has been chosen as the European Capital City of Culture for 2008. It is estimated that it will bring an extra 1.7 million visitors to Liverpool, generating extra spending of over £50 million a year. Leading up to 2008, the city is spending over £2 billion on cultural and tourism projects, including city centre regeneration and the building of a new arena and exhibition venue. Its 'three graces', three distinctive buildings – the Liver, the Cunard and the Port of Liverpool – dominate Liverpool's skyline. In 2008 a new building or 'fourth grace' will open; it is called 'The Cloud' and will be a futuristic design to house the World Discovery Centre.

Currently, the city has the largest collection of modern art outside of London and has eight national museums and galleries and four theatres. Liverpool has 2500 listed buildings, 250 public monuments and the largest collection of grade II listed buildings outside of London. It has well known links to sport, music, film, festivals and events, offering a wide variety of history, culture, retail and entertainment.

Adapted from BBC *Capital of Culture*

Liverpool will increase its number of visitors when it becomes the European Capital of Culture in 2008

Think it over ...

1 Why was Liverpool selected as the City of Culture 2008?

2 How does Liverpool benefit from being awarded the title, City of Culture 2008?

Purpose-built destinations

Purpose-built destinations are developed specifically for tourists, to provide all the facilities needed in one place. Theme parks are not generally included as they are purpose-built attractions rather than destinations (see pages 170–171). A good example of purpose-built destinations is Center Parcs. These provide high-quality purpose-built villages in rural locations. There are four Center Parcs in the UK: Longleat Forest, Sherwood Forest, Elveden Forest and Whinfell Forest.

Figure 4.5 The four Center Parcs villages in the UK

For an introduction to Center Parcs see Unit 3: Destination Europe, page 99.

Although holiday camp resorts, such as Butlins, are popular with domestic visitors from the UK, they are less popular with inbound tourists.

CASE STUDY

Center Parcs, Longleat Forest

Longleat Forest opened in July 1994 and has 638 villas and 60 apartments set in 400 acres, and caters for up to 3442 guests per break. Facilities include 11 restaurants and bars and 6 shops, spread throughout the three main centres of the Village. The dome of the Plaza is home to the Subtropical Swimming Paradise, along with several restaurants and bars and most of the shops. There is a separate Village Square where the French restaurant, La Sapinière and the Grand Café are located. The Jardin des Sports offers indoor and outdoor leisure activities as well as a lake for water sports.

Source: Center Parcs

Longleat Forest Center Parcs village

Skills practice

1 Identify the benefits of staying in a purpose-built destination.

2 How successful has Center Parcs been in combining the attractions of a purpose-built destination and a countryside destination?

Key terms

Coastal area An expanse of coastline, a coastal resort or an island popular specifically for its coastline.

Tourist towns and cities A specific town or city which is known as a tourist destination.

Business and conference destination Towns or cities with facilities to cope with business tourists, such as large conference and exhibition centres.

Countryside areas Rural areas away from towns and cities and not necessarily specific named resorts.

Heritage and cultural destinations Specific towns, cities, villages and resorts that are known for having maintained their history, heritage or culture.

Purpose-built destination A destination developed specifically for tourists which provides all the facilities needed in one place.

In the previous section we looked at the different types of destinations in the British Isles. We will now identify those features that are important to the appeal of a destination. These include:

* Climate
* Landscape
* Transport and communication links
* Accommodation
* Facilities provided
* Natural and built attractions
* Events and entertainment
* Local culture, including food and drink.

Climate

The British climate can be regarded as a natural asset to the tourism industry. It is temperate, characterised by warm wet summers and mild winters. This may not suit seaside resorts, but it complements rural locations. The prevailing west wind is responsible for much of the rainfall in the British Isles, which in turn produces green fields, dense woodland, lakes and waterways.

The south of Britain receives more sunshine than in the north. The south has the warmest, driest and sunniest climate and as a result receives 40 per cent of all British holidays.

The effects of global warming may influence the British climate as summers and winters are becoming warmer, however there is an increase in rainfall.

Climate conditions can influence a decision to stay at home or to travel abroad. Short-break holidays tend to be dependent on the weather. Activity holidays and seaside holidays depend on sunny and warm conditions. The British Isles may benefit if some popular overseas holiday resorts become too hot due to global warming. On certain days of the year the British Isles can experience temperatures higher than the Mediterranean beach resorts.

32°C IT'S HOTTER THAN MED

Britons will swelter today as the mercury hits 32°C (89.6°F) – hotter than many Mediterranean spots.

Yesterday was the hottest of the year so far – beating 31.9°C on May 27 – and left Spain and Italy in the shade.

Brits flocked to beaches like Brighton early to grab the best spots. And 60,000 hit Bournemouth beach with many eating barbecued bacon and sausages for breakfast. The mini-heatwave was a boon for racegoers at Royal Ascot in York, but heavy coastal traffic caused jams. At the Isle of Wight Zoo 25-stone lioness Nahla suffered a sunburnt nose.

Sunday Mirror 18 June 2005

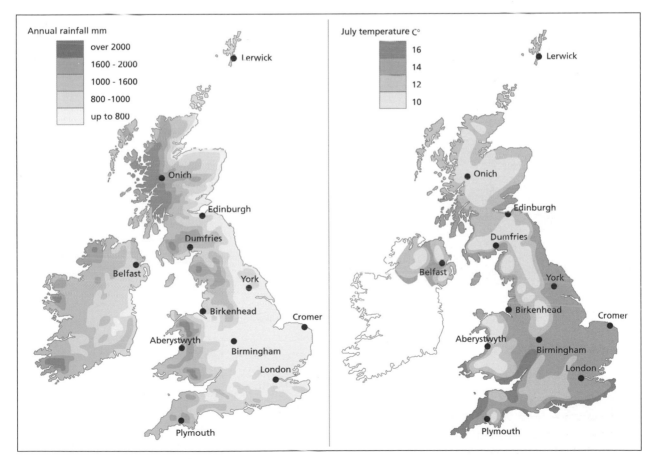

Figure 4.6 Variations in UK climate

Think it over ...

To what extent does climate affect the popularity of tourist destinations in the British Isles?

Landscape

Landscape describes inland scenery. Some people prefer the landscapes of cities and towns and other people prefer the landscape of countryside or mountainous areas. The UK has many different types of landscape. This is one reason why the UK is popular as a tourist destination, as many areas have their own unique characteristics that are appealing to visitors.

Location	Description of the landscape
Exmoor	
Lake District	
Norfolk Broads	
Peak District	
Snowdonia	
Cotswolds	
New Forest	
Scottish Highlands	
Lough Neagh	
Wicklow Mountains	

Figure 4.7 Physical map of the British Isles

Think it over ...

To what extent does the landscape of Britain appeal to visitors from overseas?

Transport and communication links

It is important for any visitor attraction to be accessible to visitors. Successful tourist destinations have good transport services that make travelling as easy and as comfortable as possible.

Transport and communication links can include:

* Air   * Road
* Rail   * Sea.

Figure 4.8 shows the most popular gateways or points of entry used by overseas residents visiting the UK. Altogether these airports and seaports received 19.2 million visits from overseas residents.

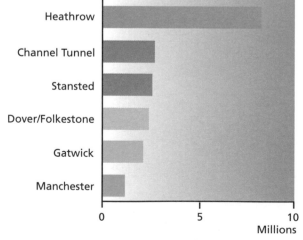

Source: International Passenger Survey (2003)

Figure 4.8 Number of visits by UK gateway

Skills practice

1 Using Figure 4.8, identify which gateways are airports and which are seaports.

2 Using Figure 4.8, suggest why these are the most popular points of entry for visitors from overseas to the UK.

Air

Air travel is the most popular form of travel for those visiting the UK. In 2003 overseas residents made 17.6 million visits to the UK by air. The most popular point of entry or *gateway* is Heathrow airport, which accounts for 34 per cent of all overseas residents that visit the UK.

There has been a growth in the use of regional airports, which has added to an overall growth in air travel. (See Figure 4.9.) New routes bring new opportunities to attract visitors from different countries. For example, a new route between Bristol International airport and New York by Continental Airlines opens up new possibilities for attracting visitors to destinations in the South West of England. At present most visitors from America fly into London Heathrow and Gatwick airports. New routes between England, Scotland and Northern Ireland also provide new opportunities, especially with the increase in the number of low-cost airlines.

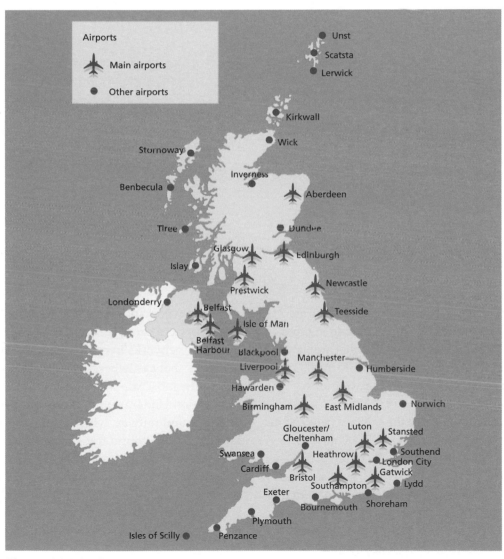

Figure 4.9 UK airports

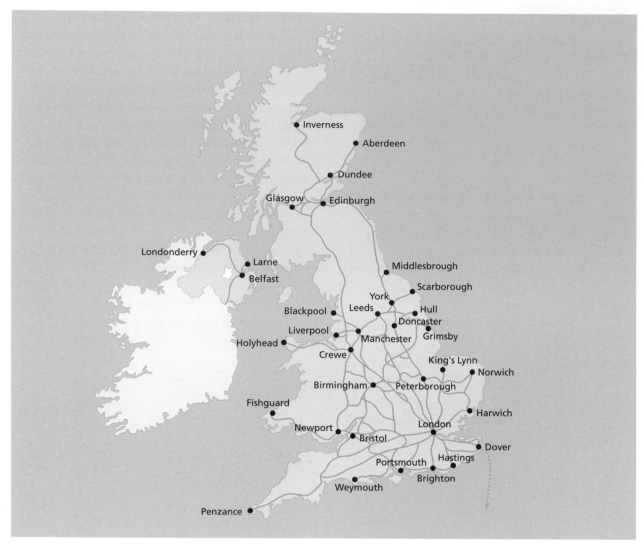

Figure 4.10 Intercity railway network of the UK

Rail

The Channel Tunnel brings 2.7 million visitors from overseas to the UK. Most inbound visitors travelling through the Channel Tunnel are French, who made 1.2 million visits to the UK in 2003. Visitors can travel by train on Eurostar or by coach or car on Le Shuttle.

Network Rail manages the railway network in the UK. It owns and maintains 21,000 miles of track and owns 2500 stations. Each day over 25,000 trains use the rail network. Train services are provided by private railway companies that operate in the UK. Examples include First Great Western, First Scot Rail, Virgin Trains, Wessex Trains, Great North Eastern Railway and Heathrow Express. (See Figure 4.10.)

Some major cities have underground railways. These services provide convenient and efficient transport networks in comparison to road networks that easily become congested at peak times. The most famous underground railway is the London Underground, the world's first underground railway, which opened in 1863. London Underground transports 3 million passengers a day and operates 275 stations. The busiest station is Victoria, handling 76.5 million passengers each year. The network is popular with visitors to the capital city who find it easy to navigate using the distinctive colour-code route map.

CASE STUDY

High-speed rail links confirmed

High-speed rail links are planned to be introduced between London and Kent to coincide with the London Olympics in 2012. New trains will run on the Channel Tunnel line to a new Eurostar terminus at St Pancras station in London. The new trains will be able to travel at a top speed of 140 miles per hour and will cost £200 million.

It is expected that the new service will reduce the journey times between London and Ashford International in Kent by 40 minutes. The new service will be able to transport spectators from Central London to the Olympic Park in Stratford in less than eight minutes. It is anticipated that the service will be available in 2009. It has been proposed that the high-speed service may include new routes to destinations such as Gravesend, Sittingbourne, Folkestone and Canterbury.

Source: BBC

Road

The motorway network is the main transport network for motorcars and buses in the UK. The M1 was the first official motorway in the UK; the first section between St Albans to Birmingham was opened in 1959. The motorway was originally designed to cope with 13,000 vehicles a day. Today the 187-mile route from London to Leeds carries an average of 88,000 vehicles a day. Congestion is becoming a major issue, especially in towns and cities during peak times. In 1959 there were only 2.8 million cars registered in the UK, today there are over 28 million. In total there are 321,000 miles of road in Britain, enough to circle the Equator 13 times.

The upkeep of local roads is the responsibility of local authorities and local councils, with national routes and motorways being looked after by the Highways Agency. This is an executive agency of the Department for Transport and is responsible for operating, maintaining and improving the road network in England on behalf of the government. The road network is important to UK tourism in allowing tourists to travel to a range of destinations across the country. (See Figure 4.11.)

Sea

The seaports that receive the most overseas visitors are Dover and Folkstone, which received 2.4 million inbound passengers in 2003. These ports are popular with visitors from France, Germany and Belgium.

Figure 4.11 UK road network

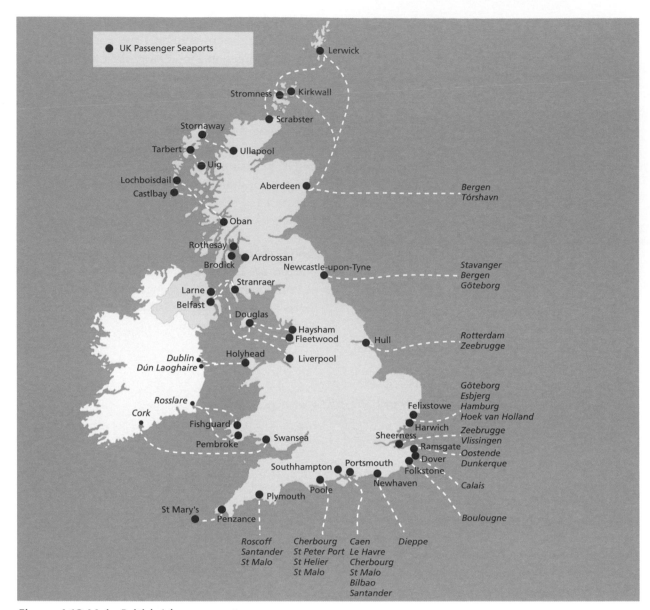

Figure 4.12 Main British Isles sea routes

Ferry services are facing tough competition from budget airlines and have seen a reduction in the amount of passengers during the last ten years. The Channel Tunnel also provides an alternative for those who wish to travel from France. Ferry services can no longer compete on price alone but have upgraded their services to passengers, offering shopping, restaurants, cinema and bars.

Sea travel is also possible within the British Isles with routes between the Republic of Ireland, the Channel Islands, the Isle of Man and the Scottish Islands. (See Figure 4.12.)

Skills practice

Compare the features of the following types of transport that would appeal to tourists visiting the British Isles: air, rail, road and sea.

Accommodation

The range, quality, availability and price of accommodation can affect the popularity of a destination. It is important that the range of accommodation reflects the needs of the visitor and reflects value for money.

There is a range of accommodation available to visitors to the UK, including corporate hotels with leisure facilities, guesthouses, family-run bed-and-breakfast accommodation, student hostels, camping and caravan sites. There are approximately 30,000 hotels and other businesses in the UK offering accommodation. The Office for National Statistics estimates that there are more than 10,000 registered hotels in the UK and these generate an annual turnover of £10 billion. Most of the hotels are situated in England, with the highest concentration being in London.

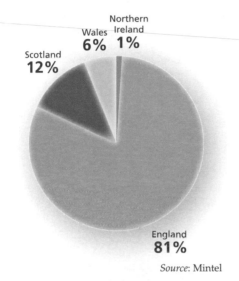

Northern
Wales Ireland
6% 1%
Scotland
12%

England
81%

Source: Mintel

Figure 4.13 Distribution of hotels in the UK

Tourist boards in the UK have developed classifications of grading accommodation standards. Inspected accommodation is graded based on the standard of accommodation it provides. In England over 20,000 hotels and 11,000 self-catering facilities are inspected each year. Stars are awarded for hotels, self-catering and caravan parks, and diamonds are awarded for guesthouses and university accommodation.

The higher the number of stars and diamonds the higher the level of quality a visitor can expect to find. However, accommodation at a lower star rating can also provide facilities found at a higher rating. During the last five years there has been a growth in the number of luxury four-star hotels and budget-priced travel lodges, with a reduction in the number of mid-range or three-star hotels.

Different types of tourist will demand different types and quality of accommodation. The type

and quality of accommodation may be restricted by availability, location and price. Some tourists may prefer different arrangements such as self-catering (kitchen area provided), room only, bed and breakfast, half board (bed and breakfast and evening dinner) or full board (bed and breakfast, lunch and evening dinner).

> **Skills practice**
>
> Select a popular travel destination in the British Isles and identify the range of accommodation that is available.

Facilities provided

Destinations that can offer a wide range of facilities to meet the needs of tourists are more popular than those that do not. Most visitors require accurate information on where tourist attractions are located and how to get there. They may require car parks, cafés, restaurants, retail outlets and toilet facilities. Facilities are provided within the tourist destination as well as in individual attractions. As visitor demand changes so must the facilities in order to meet expectations. If tourist facilities do not meet expectations then the destination or tourist attraction runs the risk of losing visitors.

Tourist destinations have increased their range of facilities so that they can appeal to a wider audience. New facilities can include indoor arenas, indoor retail and leisure facilities, parks and gardens, walks and trails, and outdoor sporting and leisure facilities, such as golf courses.

For visitors with specific needs, such as those with limited mobility, the availability of additional facilities can be important. The National Accessibility Scheme assesses the degree of accessibility for wheelchair users and those who have difficulty walking. The scheme forms part of the Tourism for All campaign that is promoted by national and regional tourist boards. However, only 2 per cent of accommodation in the UK has been assessed as being accessible for disabled users. As a result of the Disability Discrimination Act (1995), all accommodation providers, including small hotels and guesthouses, have to make reasonable adjustments so they do not discriminate against disabled people and are better able to meet people's requirements. By law, all service providers, including visitor attractions and accommodation and entertainment venues, must take reasonable measures to remove, alter or provide a reasonable means of avoiding any physical barriers to accessing and using their premises.

For further information, visit Tourism for All http://www.tourismforall.org.uk

Skills practice

1 Describe the facilities provided for visitors at Wookey Hole.

2 Select five popular tourist attractions in the UK. List the range of tourist facilities that are provided in each of the five attractions.

Wookey Hole is a popular South West tourist attraction

Natural and built attractions

Major destinations can provide either natural or built attractions, or both.

Natural attractions are based on the *topography* or shape of the land. Each destination has its own unique topography, which can be attractive to tourists.

Natural attractions can include:

* Lakes
* Rivers
* Forests
* Mountains
* Caves
* Coastlines.

Lakes

Lakes are popular with tourists, for example the Lake District in Cumbria. Lake Windermere is located in the centre of the Lake District and is 17 kilometres (10.5 miles) long. It attracts many visitors and the picturesque towns of Ambleside, Windermere and Bowness are located nearby. The lake has a long history of sailing, with boats available for hire. Power-boating and water-skiing are popular, but there are attempts to reduce the numbers of powerful craft on the lake to help maintain the safety of other water users and the quality of the environment. The largest lake in the British Isles is Lough Neagh in Northern Ireland, which covers approximately 383 square kilometres (237 square miles).

Hikers viewing the Lake District from the summit of Langdale Pikes

Rivers

Rivers can be a popular destination for their scenic beauty, wildlife and fishing. Other waterways in the UK include canals, which were originally built over 200 years ago to transport industrial goods before the existence of railways and motorcars. Over 25,000 boats use UK rivers and canals each year and many of these are pleasure cruises. Rivers also provide many tourist activities, including riverside walks, watching boats, ferry trips and fishing, and more physical activities like canoeing, rowing and boating.

Think it over ...

1 Why are lakes and rivers appealing for visitors?

2 What are some of the problems associated with large numbers of visitors in these environments?

Forests

Forests provide unique habitats for wildlife and are popular destinations for walking and activity holidays. Forests in the British Isles include Sherwood Forest in Nottingham, the New Forest in Hampshire and Castlewellan Forest Park in Northern Ireland.

Skills practice

What makes Sherwood Forest appealing to visitors?

Mountains

A *mountain* has steep sides rising to more than 300 metres (984 feet). Although mountainous regions are located away from large urban areas, most are accessible by road, with car parks and lay-bys to enable drivers to stop and admire scenic views. For those wishing to walk or climb, footpaths are usually signposted, although sensible precautions need to be taken as the weather can change suddenly at higher altitudes. Most of the mountain areas within the UK are located within national parks. Some of the most popular mountains are Ben Nevis (1343 metres/4400 feet) in Scotland, Snowdon (1085 metres/3560 feet) in Wales, Scafell Pike (987 metres/3237 feet) in England, Slieve Donard (852 metres/2800 feet) in Northern Ireland and Carrantuohill (1041 metres/3400 feet) in the Republic of Ireland. Mountains are popular amongst those who enjoy walking, sightseeing and mountain climbing.

Caves

A *cave* is a natural hole in a rock, and even though they can occur in any type of rock, they are most common in areas of limestone. Caves can be spectacular, with columns of stalagmites that rise from the floor and stalactites that hang from the ceiling. The two most famous show caves in the UK are Cheddar Gorge and Wookey Hole.

Coastlines

Coastlines are the most popular natural attractions. They can be dramatic, with steep cliffs and crashing waves. Other parts of the coast contain sand or pebble beaches. The coastline can offer many opportunities for pleasure, such as sitting in the sun, and taking part in water sports, beach sports or children's entertainment.

Skills practice

Using a blank outline map of the British Isles (see page 199) and an atlas, identify examples of each of the following types of natural attractions, representing them on your map with a suitable key.

- Lakes
- Rivers
- Forests
- Mountains
- Caves
- Coastlines.

Built attractions include a wide variety of purpose-built venues. Some have been adapted to meet the needs of tourists.

Built attractions include:

* Theme parks
* Indoor arenas
* Historic buildings and ancient monuments
* Museums and art galleries.

Theme parks

Theme parks are purpose-built visitor attractions, offering a wide range of facilities, including shopping, restaurants and gardens. The parks are themed around historic events, fantasy, childhood or a futuristic world. Many contain 'white-knuckle rides', but increasingly they are more sophisticated in their use of fantasy and illusion.

Popular theme parks in the UK include:

* Alton Towers, Staffordshire
* Blackpool Pleasure Beach
* Chessington World of Adventures, Surrey
* Flamingo Land Theme Park and Zoo, North Yorkshire
* Legoland, Windsor
* Pleasure Beach, Great Yarmouth
* Pleasureland Theme Park, Southport
* Thorpe Park, Surrey.

Rita – Queen of Speed ride at the Alton Towers theme park

Theme parks offer value for money in that they provide a full day's entertainment at a fixed price. Pricing structures often allow discounts for groups and for families. Even when the weather conditions are poor many theme parks have attractions which people can enjoy in the wet, as well as having a range of indoor attractions and facilities. Some theme parks are specifically designed for families and younger children, such as Legoland Windsor and Paultons Park near Southampton, whereas others have more exhilarating rides, which attract teenagers and young adults, as at Alton Towers. Although most visitors to theme parks are day visitors, many theme parks are encouraging visitors to stay overnight in purpose-built themed accommodation.

Indoor arenas

Indoor arenas provide a variety of public exhibitions, entertainment, music events and sporting facilities, as well as business exhibitions (trade shows) and conventions. They are large enough to support exhibitions and events on a grand scale, see 'Business and conference destinations', pages 155–156.

Historic buildings and ancient monuments

Historic buildings include stately homes, castles, royal palaces, birthplaces and houses of famous people. They have been adapted to appeal to tourists, have improved health and safety features, and incorporated additional tourist facilities such as guides, toilets and souvenir shops. Historic buildings help visitors understand the history and culture of the place they are visiting.

Table 4.4 Top 10 historic properties in England, 2003

HISTORIC PROPERTY	NUMBER OF VISITS
Tower of London	1,972,263
Windsor Castle	856,199
Roman Baths	837,457
Stonehenge	745,229
Tatton Park	700,000*
Chatsworth House	687,297
Hampton Court Palace	505,630
Blenheim Palace	475,945
Leeds Castle	433,707
Shakespeare's Birthplace	352,501

* = estimate
Source: VisitBritain (2004)

An *ancient monument* is a site that was built before the end of the Western Roman Empire, 476 AD, and represents an example of the past.

CASE STUDY

Stonehenge

The most famous ancient monument in the UK is Stonehenge. Built between 3000 and 5000 years ago this impressive circle of stones is recognised as a UNESCO World Heritage Site, not only receiving regional and national recognition but also international recognition as a site of special importance. The stones weigh between 4 and 50 tons each and are arranged in a series of circles. Their geometric pattern has baffled archaeologists as to whether Stonehenge is a temple or an astrological observatory.

Stonehenge receives nearly 750,000 paying visitors annually with approximately another 200,000 who stand on the roadside in order to look at and photograph the stones.

Stonehenge is a World Heritage Site that attracts thousands of visitors every year

Museums and art galleries

Millions of people visit *museums and art galleries* every year to view and interact with exhibits which give an insight into the culture and history of a destination. Museums and art galleries range from national museums that receive millions of visitors each year to local museums that are often run by volunteers.

Table 4.5 Top 5 museums and art galleries in England, 2003

MUSEUMS AND ART GALLERIES	NUMBER OF VISITS
British Museum	4,584,000
National Gallery	4,360,461*
Tate Modern	3,895,746*
Natural History Museum	2,894,005
Science Museum	2,886,850

* = estimate
Source: VisitBritain (2004)

Events and entertainment

Inbound visitors are attracted by the variety of events and entertainment hosted by venues in the British Isles. Special interest events can attract large numbers of visitors from outside of the British Isles. These events include:

* Major sporting events, e.g. international football matches, the FA Cup Final, British Grand Prix, Wimbledon Lawn Tennis Tournament, The London Marathon, Six Nations Rugby Union

* Concerts, musical and theatrical events, e.g. the Glastonbury Festival, Henry Wood Promenade Concerts (The Proms), Edinburgh Festival

* Events linked to heritage and tradition, e.g. Trooping the Colour (the Queen's official birthday parade), Lord Mayor's Procession, Hogmanay and New Year, Royal Highland Gathering, St Patrick's Day.

1 What major events are occurring in the British Isles during the next four weeks that may be of interest to visitors from overseas?

2 Using examples, suggest why some events and entertainment are important to the appeal of a destination.

Local culture including food and drink

The availability of locally produced *food and drink* is a growing factor in the popularity of tourist destinations. Many visitors expect to taste locally produced food and drink that they would not experience at home. Local produce is considered to be fresher, of high quality and part of the local culture of an area.

There are places within the UK that have become known through their association with locally produced food and drink. Tourism organisations across the UK promote a range of farmers' markets, food trails and schemes identifying the use of local food in hotels and restaurants in order to satisfy a growing number of visitors.

Local crafts are also part of an area's culture, as many gifts and souvenirs are made using local materials and traditional skills. Local culture also includes music, dance, poetry, art and language. Festivals and events can be based around the celebration of local culture.

Think it over ...

Describe five festivals or events in the British Isles that celebrate local culture.

Although the majority of inbound tourists may not specifically travel to destinations for local foods or crafts, local culture enhances the visitor experience and plays a significant part in providing an identity to an area or region of the British Isles.

CASE STUDY

The Real Bath Breakfast

The Real Bath Breakfast aims to provide visitors to the city of Bath with a taste of local produce when they eat their breakfasts in hotels, restaurants and guesthouses. Hotels can display the Real Bath Breakfast logo if they serve breakfast that has been prepared using produce from within 40 miles of Bath. Tea and coffee cannot be produced locally so Fair Trade products have been used instead.

The average ingredients needed for an English cooked breakfast, if purchased in a supermarket, may have travelled a total of 2050 miles. The ingredients for a Real Bath Breakfast that are sourced locally travel a total distance of only 95 miles.

Although The Real Bath Breakfast costs 5 per cent more than breakfast ingredients bought from a supermarket, the benefits to the visitor and to local businesses are seen to outweigh the increase in price.

The Real Bath Breakfast

1 What are the benefits for a hotel or restaurant that serves locally produced food and drink?

2 What are the benefits for the tourist in being able to enjoy locally prepared food and drink?

3 Complete the following table by identifying the following places, regions or countries of the British Isles by their food or drink:

Food or drink	Places, regions or countries of the British Isles
Cumberland sausage	
Haggis	
Shortbread	
Cider	
Pasty	
Brown ale	
Cheddar cheese	
Guinness	
Lava bread	
Black pudding	

It is important to differentiate between features that are crucial to the appeal of a destination and those that have little or no influence. When assessing the appeal of destinations you need to describe the key features that give popular destinations appeal and explain how they meet the needs of different types of incoming visitors.

Needs of different types of tourists

In this section you will learn to identify different needs from information provided by your tutor and recommend suitable destinations to meet those needs, justifying your choices. Information on the needs of visitors will be given to you by your tutor in the form of a pen portrait. A pen portrait is a short description of the tourists and their particular circumstances.

Different types of tourists will have a variety of different needs. These include:

* Groups
* People of different ages
* Business customers
* Those with specific needs, e.g. customers with disabilities, adults with young children, medical conditions such as pregnancy, diabetes, or age related
* Language differences
* Cultural differences.

Groups

Groups include families, students on a study tour, clubs and societies attending an event, or a group of people going on holiday together. Groups of visitors can often receive discounts and special rates when booking in advance with accommodation and transport providers. For a group of people who wish to stay together, the same accommodation will need to be large enough to meet with the demand.

Transport will need to be organised so that the group can travel together. Public transport may provide discounted rates for group travel, however a minibus or small coach may be preferred, depending on the number of visitors.

Groups can also have a different range of specific needs, for example a group of students travelling to the British Isles to improve their language skills will have different needs to a school orchestra on tour.

Think it over ...

Identify the different needs of a group of language students travelling to the British Isles compared to a school orchestra on tour.

People of different ages

People of different ages will have different needs. Some tourist attractions provide baby-changing facilities, a bottle-warming service and high chairs in restaurants. Tourist attractions and accommodation providers operate Kids Clubs and activities for older children. Senior citizens may require assistance with mobility and some tourist attractions have responded by installing ramps, handrails, easy-access parking facilities and wheelchairs that can be borrowed or hired.

Each age group may have similar needs, but often groups of different ages can be mixed, for example in a family group.

Business customers

Business customers require efficient and reliable services that are value for money. They seek relaxed environments in which to work. Very often business customers will work whilst commuting on public transport. Modern railway carriages can be equipped with charging facilities for mobile phones and laptop computers. Some tourist attractions meet the needs of business customers by offering a range of corporate services, including venues for business meetings, conferences and events.

Specific needs

There are many specific needs that tourists may have. Some examples include:

* Customers with disabilities
* Adults with young children
* Medical conditions, e.g. pregnancy, diabetes, age related.

There are a wide variety of specific needs that should be taken into consideration, so it's important to identify the needs of an individual rather than to make assumptions.

Guidebooks, brochures and company websites sometimes include details regarding the level and extent of facilities for those with specific needs.

Customers with disabilities

Disabilities can include a wide range of individual needs, such as being visually impaired, having impaired hearing or speech, mobility problems and learning difficulties.

At the major tourist attractions, tourists who are visually impaired may benefit from audio guides and clearly written information printed on different coloured backgrounds, depending on the level and type of visual impairment.

People with impaired hearing benefit greatly when tourist attractions and facilities have hearing loops, members of staff trained in sign language, the use of clearly written information or staff trained to talk clearly and appropriately.

Speech impairment may present difficulties in communication, however these can be overcome through written communication, sign language or employing staff who have been trained to listen carefully.

Wheelchair users, people who need walking sticks or crutches, and those with visual impairment may have mobility problems. Accessibility is increased by having extra handrails on stairs, wheelchair lifts and ramps, and wheelchairs that may be borrowed. Accessible toilet facilities and rooms modified to allow for wheelchair access are also a considerable help.

Tourists with learning difficulties will need to have information provided in a variety of formats, depending on their need.

Adults with young children

Tourists with young children may require facilities for nappy changing, a crèche and children's clubs depending on the child's age. Very young children may not be comfortable travelling long distances. Tourist attractions need to provide information and entertainment to meet children's needs in an appropriate way. Some are specifically designed to do this. For example, accommodation providers may have family rooms and facilities, including a cot and high chair for very young children and a children's menu in restaurants.

Medical conditions

The range of medical conditions may include pregnancy, diabetes or a condition may be age related. Those taking medication need to bring suitable supplies for the duration of the visit or to know how and where to call for assistance.

For more information see 'Different types of tourists', pages 113–114, and 'Support for specific needs', page 123.

Cultural differences

Different cultural groups have different needs in terms of language, diet and religion. Cultural background can influence people's preferences and opinions. It is useful to have an understanding of some of the main cultural differences but avoid making assumptions, as misunderstandings can be interpreted as offensive.

Language differences

Tourists visiting the UK who have a limited understanding of the English language may benefit from tourist attractions, accommodation providers and tour guides employing multi-lingual staff. Also, many organisations produce information such as brochures, leaflets and websites in a variety of languages.

A multilingual brochure of London's facilities for Japanese tourists

---

Identify the needs of the following tourists:

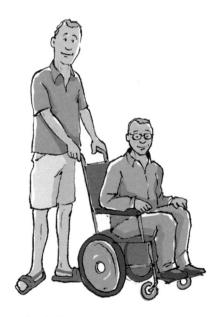

Pen portrait 1

Bob is travelling from New York to attend a sales meeting in London.

He will need to communicate with his office and finalise a presentation that he will give the following day to his clients.

He is also planning to meet a new client to discuss business and will need a convenient place to hold a meeting.

Bob will require accommodation for one night.

Pen portrait 2

Bruno and his brother Laurence are travelling from Paris for a one-week tour of England during September.

They wish to travel by Eurostar.

Laurence uses a wheelchair.

Bruno likes visiting places of historic interest and Laurence likes visiting the theatre and reading Shakespeare.

Pen portrait 3

A group of 15 university students from Munich are travelling to Manchester to attend a student conference for five days in July but wish to stay on in Manchester for two extra days.

They all wish to stay in the same accommodation.

They wish to see some of the local attractions and to have fun in the evening.

Two of the students are vegetarian and one student has a nut allergy.

Pen portrait 4

The Mok family are travelling from Beijing in China to visit friends and relatives in Edinburgh for two weeks during Easter.

The family comprises two adults and two children, aged 3 years and 7 years. Both parents do not speak English.

4.3 Constructing itineraries for tourists

An *itinerary* is a plan or schedule for tourists to follow. In this section you will learn how to construct an itinerary of complementary destinations to meet a visitor's specific needs. The visitor's specific needs will be given to you by your tutor in the form of a pen portrait. You will learn to include the following in an itinerary:

* Who the itinerary is prepared for

* Dates

* Timing

* What is included

* Contact details

* Details of the destination.

Who the itinerary is prepared for

It is important to identify the needs of the person or group of people that the itinerary is prepared for. A group of 40 elderly people travelling by coach on a one-week touring holiday will require a different itinerary to a young couple on a weekend break, even if it is to the same area. Before researching potential places of interest, accommodation and routes, you need to assess the needs of the group, in this case the detail contained in the pen portrait.

Dates

When producing an itinerary it is useful to find out preferred dates of travel. Tourists may not be aware of public holidays, religious celebrations or other important dates that may interfere with travel plans. Travelling to the British Isles outside of the peak holiday season may mean that there is a greater range of accommodation available, shorter queues at tourist attractions and cheaper prices.

Timing

Timing is important when constructing an itinerary of places and attractions to visit. The time it takes to travel from the accommodation may vary depending on the time of day and the type of transport used. The itinerary should take into account any comfort stops on the way to the tourist attraction, time to look around the tourist attraction, enough time to see other places of interest, plus time to have lunch or tea before returning to the accommodation.

What is included

Information needs to be provided in terms of what is included in the itinerary. Some companies provide itineraries that are a set of instructions to follow a given route, with details of what to see and do and where to stay. Other companies provide a complete package, for example transport costs including transfers, accommodation costs, food, drink and entrance fees. Some companies will organise special events for groups as part of an itinerary. It is important to know what is being included and any costs incurred.

Contact details

During the visit tourists should be aware of who to contact should they have any questions or if they have any problems.

Usually messages can be left 24 hours a day or a member of the company is on call to cover any eventualities.

Details of destination

The itinerary should give sufficient details, such as the attractions featured, accommodation provided and arrangements for food. Tourists not only need to be informed of what they are seeing when at the destination, they also need to be given a summary of information in advance. This is necessary as inbound tour operators can provide individual itineraries based on individual needs, and will need to provide sufficient detail to show thorough planning and also to encourage potential tourists to make a booking.

Skills practice

Using the pen portraits on pages 176–177, provide an itinerary based on each of their requirements. Include a suitable map showing the destinations that you have selected.

Skills practice

1 Working in pairs or small groups, each person writes a pen portrait for a type of tourist stating a range of needs for a five-day tour of part of the British Isles.

2 Swap your pen portrait with another person.

3 Identify any special requests that need to be made.

4 Produce an itinerary based on the information that you have been given. You may need to research a number of destinations using holiday brochures and travel guides before reaching a decision.

5 Include a map of the places mentioned in your itinerary.

6 Present your findings to the person who wrote the pen portrait by explaining how your choice of destination meets the needs of the person that you were given.

SAMPLE ITINERARY FOR A SHORT BREAK HOLIDAY BASED IN BATH

Prepared by Sulis Guides – specialists in car, coach and walking tours

This short break is based on a 3-day/2-night stay in Bath and would suit a couple or a larger group
(subject to suitable transport arrangements, e.g. coach hire).

DAY 1

10.30–11.00 am:	Arrive Bath and check in at a pre-booked city centre hotel.
11.30 am:	A Blue Badge guide will meet you at your hotel and take you on a guided walking tour of Bath. The tour will provide a history of the city and stories about the extraordinary range of people who visited. It will include a visit to Bath Abbey.
12.30 pm:	With your guide, you will visit the Roman Baths.
1.00 pm:	A table is booked for lunch in the Pump Room. Please select from their menus. You will also have the opportunity to taste Bath's famous spring water.
2.15 pm:	The walking tour continues to the Upper Town with visits to the Jane Austen Centre, the Museum of Costume and No. 1 Royal Crescent. During the tour the guide will point out interesting shops and places to eat.
5.30 pm:	The tour will conclude back at your hotel.
7.30 pm:	Dinner in the hotel.

DAY 2

9.30 am:	Depart hotel and drive through the pretty Limpley Stoke Valley to Longleat, the stately home of Lord Bath.
10.15 am:	Arrive Longleat and visit the Elizabethan mansion, full of spectacular treasures and artworks, set in grounds designed by Capability Brown.
1.30 pm:	Arrive Bishopstrow House Hotel for a 2-course lunch plus wine, water and coffee.
3.00 pm:	Depart for scenic drive to the delightful town of Bradford-upon-Avon, famous for its pretty stone, weavers' cottages, a magnificent tythe barn and an historic Saxon church.
5.00 pm:	Depart Bradford-upon-Avon and return to Bath.
7.30 pm:	Evening at leisure with option of a visit to the Theatre Royal or dinner in a city centre restaurant.

DAY 3

10.00 am:	Check out of the hotel and travel to Bristol.
11.00 am:	A Blue Badge guide will meet you at the entrance to Bristol Cathedral and take you on a guided walking tour which will include details of Bristol's fascinating maritime history. It will also include a visit to the Cathedral (service times permitting), a walk across Pero's Bridge, King Street, Queen Square and St Mary Redcliffe.
12.45 pm:	A table is booked for lunch at the River Station, a contemporary restaurant overlooking Bristol's docks. Please select from their menus.
2.00 pm:	Your guide will lead you from the River Station, via Queen Square to Prince Street bridge where you can pick up a ferry for a cruise around the docks.
3.30 pm:	With your guide, visit the SS *Great Britain*.
4.15 pm:	Re-join the ferry and cruise to the water feature in the city centre where you will disembark at 4.30 pm.

Tour ends and depart.

This itinerary has been prepared by and is copyright of Sulis Guides Ltd, Bath, UK
For further information visit http://www.sulisguides.co.uk

ASSESSMENT

Portfolio practice

You will be asked to produce an itinerary for a group of tourists to the UK.

The itinerary will include examples of different types of British destinations.

You will be given details of incoming tourists by your tutor in the form of a pen portrait and your itinerary should include destinations that meet the needs that are specified in the information that you are given.

Destinations should be located on a map and the features that give each destination in the itinerary appeal should be described.

Your itinerary should show evidence of planning in the choice and sequence of destinations that have been selected.

There should be an explanation of how your itinerary meets the needs of the incoming tourists. You should make clear links between their needs and the features available in the destinations within the itinerary. Your explanation is likely to go beyond the stated needs in the pen portrait; in order to meet those needs there may be certain associated additional requirements. The idea is to think carefully about the needs of tourists, not just in terms of their holiday requirements, but also in terms of any medical, dietary or special needs that they may have in order to maintain their well-being.

It should be clearly evident that you are aware of those features that give the destination appeal in relation to the tourists described in the pen portrait, as well as those attractions that exist but are not relevant to your particular group of tourists.

Make sure you include some of the less well-known attractions in order to show that you have researched a wide range of attractions and facilities to meet the needs of the tourists.

4.4 Scale of tourism to the British Isles

In this section you will learn to use different sources of information to research the scale of tourism to the British Isles. Through research, you will need to obtain statistical data and then interpret and analyse the data to draw reasoned conclusions. You will research the importance of visitors to the British Isles in terms of:

* Visitor numbers
* Type of visitor
* Visitor spending
* Bed nights used.

Visitor numbers

In 2004, 27.7 million overseas visitors visited the UK. The UK has many popular tourist destinations that attract visitors both from within the UK and from the rest of the world. Visitors from the USA represented 13 per cent of the total visits to the UK, France 12 per cent and Germany 11 per cent.

Table 4.6 Top 10 overseas visitors to the UK in 2004 by country

COUNTRY	VISITS (000)	PERCENTAGE OF TOTAL VISITS TO THE UK
USA	3,623	13
France	3,252	12
Germany	2,958	11
Irish Republic	2,559	9
Netherlands	1,619	6
Spain	1,462	5
Italy	1,346	5
Belgium	1,096	4
Australia	788	3
Canada	742	3

Source: International Passenger Survey, provisional data (2005)

The UK has many tourist attractions that require an entrance fee, whilst others are free of charge. Table 4.7 shows the most popular paid admission attractions in the UK and Table 4.8 shows the most popular free admission attractions in the UK. The figures represent total visitor numbers and include both domestic and inbound tourists.

Table 4.7 Top 10 paid admission attractions in the UK, 2003

ATTRACTION	REGION	2003
British Airways London Eye	London	3,700,000
Tower of London	London	1,972,263
Eden Project	South West	1,404,372
Flamingo Land Theme Park and Zoo	Yorkshire and Humberside	1,398,800*
Windermere Lake Cruises	North West	1,337,879
Legoland Windsor	South East	1,321,128
New Metroland	North East	1,200,000*
Chester Zoo	North West	1,160,234
Kew Gardens	London	1,079,424
Canterbury Cathedral	South East	1,060,166*

* = estimate
Source: VisitBritain (2004)

Table 4.8 Top 10 free admission attractions in the UK, 2003

ATTRACTION	REGION	2003
Blackpool Pleasure Beach	North West	6,200,000
British Museum	London	4,584,000
National Gallery	London	4,360,461*
Tate Modern	London	3,895,746*
Natural History Museum	London	2,894,005
Science Museum	London	2,886,850
Victoria and Albert Museum	London	2,257,325
Pleasureland Theme Park	North West	2,100,000
Eastbourne Pier	South East	1,600,000
Pleasure Beach	East	1,500,000*

* = estimate
Source: VisitBritain (2004)

Skills practice

1 Using Tables 4.7 and 4.8 and the Internet or guidebooks, describe what makes each of the top ten attractions popular with visitors.

2 Using Tables 4.7 and 4.8, suggest reasons why some attractions are more popular than others.

Visitor spending

In 2004 inbound tourists to the UK spent a total of £13 billion. Visitors from the USA represented 18 per cent of the total amount spent in the UK, Germany 6 per cent, France 6 per cent, and the Irish Republic 6 per cent.

Table 4.9 Top 10 overseas visits to the UK based on the total amount spent, 2004

COUNTRY	TOTAL SPEND (£MILLION)	PERCENTAGE SHARE OF TOTAL SPEND
USA	2405	18
Germany	822	6
France	770	6
Irish Republic	749	6
Spain	617	5
Australia	588	5
Italy	521	4
Canada	477	4
Netherlands	463	4
Switzerland	282	2

Source: International Passenger Survey, provisional data (2005)

Visitors from Saudi Arabia spend the most money per visit in the UK, an average of £1535 per visit. However, visitors from Saudi Arabia spent a total of £98 million in 2004, representing 1 per cent of total visitor spend.

Table 4.10 Top 10 overseas visits to the UK based on the amount spent per visit, 2004

COUNTRY	AVERAGE SPEND PER VISIT (£)
Saudi Arabia	1535
Mexico	1513
Thailand	1502
Iran	1465
China	1374
Nigeria	1301
United Arab Emirates	1215
Egypt	1163
Taiwan	1051
Pakistan	1026

Source: International Passenger Survey, provisional data (2005)

Type of visitor

The majority of visitors to the UK are on holiday, although those visiting friends or relatives (VFR) have seen a significant rise in numbers since 1999, an increase of 39 per cent. Although there are 6 per cent more visitors to the UK travelling on business, they spent 7 per cent less than they did in 1999.

The majority of inbound visitors to the UK are between the ages of 25 and 34, closely followed by those aged 35–44. Together they represent 45.7 per cent of all inbound visitors to the UK. However, the greatest growth has been in the 55–64 age group, 28 per cent, closely followed by the over-65 age group, 27 per cent. In terms of the amount spent the greatest increase has been in the over-55 category, and the only decrease in the amount spent compared to 1999 is amongst 45–54 year olds.

Table 4.11 Overseas visits to the UK based on the purpose of visit and amount spent, 2004

PURPOSE OF VISIT	1999 VISITS (000)	2004 VISITS (000)	PERCENTAGE CHANGE	1999 SPEND (£M)	2004 SPEND (£M)	PERCENTAGE CHANGE
Holiday	9,826	9,262	-6	4251	4212	-1
Business	7,044	7,458	+6	3967	3675	-7
VFR	5,640	7,852	+39	2133	3025	+42
Study	718	578	-19	1113	1044	-6
Miscellaneous	2,166	2,558	+18	996	1024	+3
Transit				39	45	+16
Total	25,394	27,708	+9	12,498	13,025	+4

Source: International Passenger Survey, provisional data (2005)

Table 4.12 Overseas visits to the UK based on the age of visitor and amount spent, 2004

AGE	1999 VISITS (000)	2004 VISITS (000)	PERCENTAGE CHANGE	1999 SPEND (£M)	2004 SPEND (£M)	PERCENTAGE CHANGE
0–15	1,808	1,828	+1	548	553	+1
16–24	3,263	3,377	+3	1734	1909	+10
25–34	5,860	6,408	+9	2820	2906	+3
35–44	5,678	6,262	+10	2699	2882	+7
45–54	4,966	5,009	+1	2604	2393	-8
55–64	2,435	3,127	+28	1334	1539	+15
65+	1,184	1,498	+27	602	692	+15
Not known	199	199	0	158	151	-5
Total	25,394	27,708	+9	12,498	13,025	+4

Source: International Passenger Survey, provisional data (2005)

Bed nights used

Visitors to the UK slept an equivalent of 227 million bed nights. Visitors from the USA slept the most bed nights in the UK and represent 13 per cent of the total. *Bed nights* are calculated by the number of visitors multiplied by number of nights that they stayed in the UK.

Table 4.13 Top 10 overseas visits to the UK based on the total number of nights per country, 2004

COUNTRY	NIGHTS (000)	PERCENTAGE SHARE OF THE TOTAL
USA	30,510	13
France	17,278	8
Germany	16,553	7
Spain	12,929	6
Australia	12,249	5
Poland	11,298	5
Italy	9,572	4
Irish Republic	9,210	4
Canada	9,051	4
India	6,831	3

Source: International Passenger Survey, provisional data (2005)

The average number of nights per visitor from overseas is 8 bed nights. However 41 per cent of visitors stayed between 1 and 3 nights. Between 1999 and 2004 the number of visitors staying on short-break holidays to the UK increased by 13 per cent. Day-trippers who do not stay overnight only represent 7 per cent of the total number of inbound visitors to the UK.

As the geographical area of this unit is the British Isles we will now look at the following case studies: the islands of Jersey, the Isle of Man and Guernsey.

Table 4.14 Overseas visits to the UK based on the number of nights, 2004

	1999 VISITS (000)	2004 VISITS (000)	PERCENTAGE CHANGE
Nil nights	2,053	2,073	+1
1–3 nights	10,046	11,380	+13
4–7 nights	6,782	7,548	+11
8–14 nights	3,478	3,607	+4
15+ nights	3,035	3,100	+2
Total	**25,394**	**27,708**	**+9**

Source: International Passenger Survey, provisional data (2005)

Skills practice

1 Describe the importance of tourism in Jersey, the Isle of Man and Guernsey.
2 What attracts visitors to these islands?

CASE STUDY

Isle of Man

The Isle of Man is a self-governing kingdom of the British Isles that has its own parliament, laws and traditions. It is located in the Irish Sea and is surrounded by Northern Ireland, Scotland, England and Wales. The Isle of Man Passenger Survey provides statistics and trends regarding the number of visitors, amount spent, type and number of bed nights.

Visitor numbers

There were 340,902 visitors to the Isle of Man in 2004.

Spend

In 2004 tourists on the Isle of Man spent a total of £113 million. The Isle of Man records slightly different categories of visitor compared to the UK: Period Visitors in Paid Accommodation (PVPAs) includes passengers visiting the Isle of Man staying in paid accommodation for at least one night, but excluding business travellers. For the purpose of comparison, this category can be referred to as holiday or leisure visitors.

The total average expenditure of PVPAs was £380 in 2004.

Type of visitor

The number of PVPAs was recorded as 120,270 in 2004. They accounted for 35.28 per cent of total visitors. The number of Period Visitors Visiting Friends and Relatives (PVVFR), the same category as VFR, was 120,688. The number of business visitors was 92,658. The number of day-trippers, who do not require overnight accommodation, was recorded as 7286.

Bednights

The average total number of bed nights spent by PVPAs was 5.3 nights in 2004. This compares to 4.8 nights in 2001.

Source: Isle of Man government

For further information visit the Isle of Man government website http://www.gov.im/tourism

Note: Tourism figures represent all visitors to the Isle of Man, including visitors from the UK.

CASE STUDY

Jersey

Jersey is the most southerly island of the British Isles. It is located 160 kilometres (100 miles) south of mainland Britain and only 14 miles (22 kilometres) from the coast of France.

Visitor numbers

In 2004, 731,000 tourists visited the island of Jersey.

Visitor spending

- Visitors to the island spent a total of £215 million in 2004
- Leisure visitors spent a total of £154 million
- Business visitors spent a total of £18 million
- Conference visitors spent a total of £4 million
- Day trippers spent a total of £8 million.

Types of visitor

The number of leisure visitors in 2004 was 377,900; they stayed an average of 4.9 nights. The number of business visitors in 2004 was 60,900; they stayed an average of 2.1 nights. The number of conference visitors in 2004 was 5500; they stayed an average of 4.3 nights. The number of day-trippers in 2004 was 147,500.

Bed nights used

The total number of tourists visiting Jersey generated 2.16 million bed nights.

Source: Jersey Tourism Board

For further information visit http://www.jersey.com

Note: Tourism figures represent all visitors to Jersey, including visitors from the UK.

CASE STUDY

Guernsey

Guernsey is located off the coast of France and includes the islands of Guernsey, Alderney, Sark and Herm.

Visitor numbers

In 2004, 412,000 tourists visited Guernsey.

Visitor spending

Visitors to Guernsey spent in excess of £100 million in 2004. The average expenditure per person in Guernsey, that is excluding travel to and from the island and the cost of the inclusive holiday, was £171 compared to £167 in 2003. For holiday visitors, this average figure increased to £197 per person compared to £193 in 2003.

Type of visitor

The types of visitors in 2004 were recorded as:

- Holiday visitors 227,000
- VFR visitors 76,000
- Business visitors 52,000
- Yacht crew 26,000
- Cruise ship passengers 31,000.

Between 80–90 per cent of visitors to Guernsey are in the 35–54 and 55 years and over age groups. However, amongst overseas visitors, there continues to be a younger age profile, with 20 per cent aged less than 35 years and 33 per cent aged over 55 years.

Bed nights used

Nine out of ten of all visitors to Guernsey in 2004 (90%) stayed at least one night on the island, compared to 88 per cent in 2003. This represents 318,000 staying visitors in 2004, of which 238,000 used commercial accommodation (75%), with a further 80,000 staying in non-commercial accommodation.

In terms of length of stay, the average for hotels was 4.1 nights compared to 5.1 nights in guest accommodation.

Source: VisitGuernsey

For further information visit http://www.guernseytouristboard.com

Note: Tourism figures represent all visitors to Guernsey, including visitors from the UK.

Portfolio practice

You will be asked to provide evidence of thorough research of statistical data to determine the scale of tourism to the British Isles from incoming tourists in terms of:

- Visitor numbers
- Visitor spending
- Type of visitor
- Bed nights used.

Make sure that you have used a wide range of sources of information and that these have been obtained independently of your tutor. Sources can include websites, textbooks, destination media, national and trade press articles. You need to include a bibliography of the sources that you have used. You also need to make sure that you have referenced these sources to show where they have come from throughout your analysis. For further information on referencing, see Unit 3: Destination Europe, page 140.

You will be asked to provide a detailed analysis of the scale of incoming tourism in the British Isles using statistical information and other data. Data and other information should be relevant and clearly interpreted. Make sure to draw conclusions from your research.

The most recent tourism statistics can be found on the following websites:

Statistics on Tourism and Research (Star UK)   http://www.staruk.org.uk
Department for Culture, Media and Sport (DCMS) http://www.culture.gov.uk
Office for National Statistics (ONS)   http://www.ons.gov.uk

4.5 The factors that affect popularity and appeal of destinations

In this section you will learn the factors that have led to the popularity and appeal of different British destinations. Factors include:

✳ Accessibility

✳ Availability of attractions and other tourist facilities

✳ Cost of visiting

✳ Change in customer needs and expectations

✳ Destination management

✳ Image and promotion

✳ Political factors.

You will learn that destinations are affected by different factors and identify and describe those that are relevant. You will learn how to evaluate the factors that are key to the popularity and appeal of different destinations and to assess the affect that these factors can have. You will also learn to recommend ways that destinations can increase their appeal to make them more popular with incoming tourists, justifying your recommendations. You will also examine a range of destinations and focus on one for assessment.

Accessibility

The more accessible a destination is the easier it is to get to. Accessibility involves travelling to and around the British Isles. As we have discussed on pages 162–166, there are many inbound routes and gateways. Inbound tourists will tend to travel by the most convenient route. In 2003, 71 per cent of visits to the UK were by air, 18 per cent by sea and 11 per cent by the Channel Tunnel. However, not every airport or seaport offers routes to every destination.

Inbound tourists can travel from the gateway to their destination by rail, coach, or hire a car or drive their own car if entering via Le Shuttle or by ferry. The motorcar offers freedom of choice, however with increased usage and congestion, alternatives for travel may need to be offered. Rail travel may be a popular alternative but carriages are often busy at peak times. Visitors may also connect with an internal flight to travel to their intended destination.

The five most popular counties for overnight visits by overseas residents to the UK after London are:

* West Midlands (Birmingham)

* Greater Manchester

* Lothian (Edinburgh)

* Kent

* Surrey.

Source: International Passenger Survey (2003)

Skills practice

1 Explain why London, Kent and Surrey are some of the most popular areas for overseas tourists.

2 Suggest reasons why West Midlands (Birmingham), Greater Manchester and Lothian (Edinburgh) also feature in this list.

Think it over ...

Are popular destinations always easily accessible?

Think it over ...

The motorway network in the UK does not extend to all areas of the country. For example, the motorway network does not extend into Cornwall, the western coastline of Wales or the Highlands of Scotland. To what extent does this have an impact in terms of accessibility?

If destinations or attractions are not easily accessible or services are seen as congested, unreliable or expensive, then potential visitors may choose to find alternative destinations.

Availability of attractions and other tourist facilities

The British Isles has a diverse range of tourist attractions and facilities that appeal to overseas visitors. However, not all destinations can offer the same attractions and facilities as one another. You would not expect to find a major theme park like Alton Towers in every part of the British Isles. Large towns and cities have the largest number of tourist attractions. London is the most visited destination in the British Isles and has the highest number of tourist attractions.

Think it over ...

Why does London have the highest number of visitor attractions in the British Isles?

Even within regions there is a difference in the availability of attractions and facilities. For example, the type and number of attractions within the South West varies between counties. There are historic reasons for where places of worship have been built, which include churches and cathedrals. Theme parks and leisure parks will tend to be located in places that are easily accessible or near to large towns and cities. Destinations that are already popular with visitors will attract other tourism businesses to the area. An attraction or tourism facility is not going to open in a place that has very few visitors or is not easily accessible.

Table 4.15 Tourist attractions in the South West region, 2003

	Devon	Cornwall	Gloucestershire	Somerset	Wiltshire	Dorset	Avon	Total
Museums/art galleries	53	38	37	31	25	35	23	242
Historic houses/castles	47	24	27	17	16	27	5	163
Other historical/archaeological sites	12	30	17	14	19	11	8	111
Gardens	20	43	10	10	11	15	5	114
Workplaces	24	13	13	18	0	13	3	84
Wildlife attractions/zoos	18	13	6	10	0	10	2	59
Natural heritage visitor attractions	14	5	8	4	5	3	5	44
Visitor/heritage centres	11	7	9	7	2	3	5	44
Farms	13	5	9	5	3	4	1	40
Places of worship	8	2	7	4	3	5	6	35
Leisure/theme parks and attractions	8	10	3	4	1	5	2	33
Steam/heritage railways	8	5	6	3	1	1	0	24
Boat trip	7	2	0	1	1	0	2	13
Total	**243**	**197**	**152**	**128**	**87**	**132**	**67**	**1006**

The number of tourist attractions is based on information held on the South West Tourism database. Some tourist attractions may not appear, as they are not members of the regional tourist board. For further information visit South West Tourism http://www.swtourism.co.uk

Source: South West Tourism (2004)

Skills practice

1 Using Table 4.15, describe the availability of attractions and other tourist facilities in the South West.

2 Which counties do you think receive the most visitors? Suggest reasons for your answer.

3 How do the different counties of the South West region compare in terms of their mix of visitor attractions?

4 Explain why there is such a variation in the availability of attractions and other tourist facilities between the different counties in the South West.

CASE STUDY

The Eden Project

The Eden Project in Cornwall attracts approximately 1.8 million visitors each year. It is unique not just in terms of its design but also its location, being built on the site of a disused quarry. There are over 100,000 plants representing 5000 species from across the world, set in two large domes or biomes. There are facilities for 1000 cars and 40 coaches as well as disabled access and a land train that operates between the visitor centre and the biomes. There is a direct rail link and an entrance ticket to Eden can be bought from any railway station.

The Eden Project

Source: The Eden Project

For further information visit the Eden Project http://www.edenproject.com

Cost of visiting

The cost of visiting a destination can affect visitor numbers. If a destination is too expensive or fails to deliver value for money, then tourists will tend to go to less expensive destinations. Costs vary depending on the time of year. It is cheaper to travel to the British Isles at off-peak times compared to the peak times of July and August.

The cost of visiting can also vary due to differences in the value of currency or rate of exchange. When people visit the UK they often exchange some of their national currency, for example the euro or American dollar, for British pounds, so they can spend money here. When the value of the British pound is lower than other currencies it makes travelling to the UK cheaper, as visitors are receiving more British pounds for their money. When the value of the British pound is higher compared to other currencies it makes travelling to the UK more expensive, as visitors are receiving fewer British pounds for their money. Values of foreign currency are displayed in travel agents, in a bureau de change, in banks and in newspapers. Each time money is exchanged a bureau de change or bank charges a small commission fee, adding to the cost. Although some offer commission-free exchanges, where no charge is made, the amount of commission is usually hidden in the rate of exchange.

Some countries within the European Union have replaced their traditional currency with the euro. The euro was launched in January 1999 and enables tourists and businesses to trade between countries using the same currency. There are twelve countries that have the single currency: Austria, Belgium, Finland, France, Germany, Greece, Republic of Ireland, Italy, Luxembourg, Netherlands, Portugal and Spain. For example, visitors from Spain taking a holiday in the Republic of Ireland do not lose money through exchange rates as both countries share the same currency.

Exchange rates are not the only consideration when calculating the cost of goods and services. The *rate of inflation* is an important factor as this shows how much prices have increased. The annual rate of inflation in the UK is approximately 2 per cent, which means that prices in the UK rise by an average of 2 per cent each year. Any rise or fall in the rate of inflation has a direct impact on cost.

Within the British Isles there are some areas that are more expensive than others. Large cities such as London can be more expensive when paying for accommodation, food, drink and admission to attractions compared to other destinations in the British Isles.

Think it over ...

Do variations in cost between destinations in different parts of the UK have an affect on popularity and appeal?

Some companies have devised a prepayment scheme to reduce the cost of visiting attractions and encourage visitors to stay longer in a destination.

CASE STUDY

London Pass

The London Pass is a pre-payment card that allows entry to 50 attractions in London. For an extra fee, transport on buses, London Underground and railway services in London can be included. The card costs from £12 a day and includes a 132-page guide book.

The London Pass allows families and groups to pay in advance and know how much they are spending towards their visit. People using the card can visit as many attractions as they wish. To visit every attraction listed in the guidebook would cost over £400 per person.

For further information visit The London Pass http://www.londonpass.com

Change in customer needs and expectations

Customer needs and expectations change frequently. High standards of living in Europe and greater experiences of other destinations through increased travel have raised customer expectations. The growth in short-break holidays throughout Europe has meant that people are travelling more frequently than before. Visitors demand efficient and high levels of service that they have experienced in other destinations.

Europe has an ageing population, as people are living longer and healthier lives. This has meant that there is a change in needs and expectations as the age profile of visitors change. As increasing numbers of older people travel to the UK, tourist attractions and accommodation providers have to make sure that the needs of such visitors are being met.

It is not just older people who are travelling more frequently; there has been an increase in the number of backpacker holidays. More students are taking gap years or travelling after completing university. Backpackers seek budget-priced accommodation, often in youth hostels, and visit attractions that do not charge a large entrance fee.

New technology also brings changes in expectation. Business travellers may expect to find high-speed Broadband connections or Wi-Fi points in hotels in order to access the Internet. Some hotels offer a digital television service where guests can play computer games, use the Internet, order room service, check their bill and see what's on in the local area. Other uses of technology include real-time booking services, where rooms and tickets to attractions can be purchased in advance using the Internet. Visitors may also wish to see virtual tours of attractions, hotel rooms and tourist destinations on the Internet before deciding whether to book.

Think it over …

What affect will an ageing population have on the appeal and popularity of tourist destinations in the British Isles?

Destination management

Destination management plays an important role in co-ordinating travel and tourism businesses and those that provide a service to visitors from overseas.

Destination managers are responsible for promoting a tourist destination, handling enquiries and carrying out market research. Other responsibilities include reducing the amount of litter, ensuring transport networks operate efficiently, providing adequate parking and leisure facilities, as well as encouraging tourism businesses and services to invest in the destination.

Destination managers work to a tourism plan or strategy that has been agreed with local businesses and organisations such as regional tourist boards and regional development agencies. The strategy sets out key objectives and targets that are to be achieved over several years.

Destination management companies (DMCs) are private companies that offer a range of services to those wishing to plan a meeting or event. They provide local knowledge and expertise in arranging transport, transfers, accommodation, catering and entertainment.

Skills practice

Using the Internet, investigate one destination management company and describe its range of services.

Image and promotion

Destination managers promote tourist destinations and regions through a variety of different publicity material, such as brochures, leaflets and websites. Their aim is to promote the area in a positive way, to describe the main attractions, events and accommodation that are available. National tourist boards can spend thousands of pounds on advertising and marketing campaigns to encourage potential tourists to consider visiting their country. National campaigns are supported by regional tourist boards which benefit from increasing numbers of visitors.

News stories and the media can also have an important affect on the popularity and appeal of a destination. Visitor attractions and destination managers can promote positive news stories and events by issuing press releases and encouraging newspaper and magazine articles. However, negative media coverage can have a devastating impact on the perception of a tourist destination. Negative stories can leave a lasting impression in the minds of potential visitors and may discourage people from visiting.

Creating the right image is vital to attracting tourists to a region

CASE STUDY

Foot and mouth disease

Foot and mouth disease affected not only the farming community in 2001 but also the tourism industry. The images of closed footpaths, signs proclaiming 'foot and mouth disease infected area' and the mass slaughter of cattle, produced an image of the British countryside that appeared to be full of disease and closed to the public. These negative images were broadcast around the world. Many overseas visitors stayed away from Britain fearing that many of the tourist attractions would be closed or that they could not travel outside of the major cities.

The foot and mouth disease outbreak in 2001 and the sight of animals being incinerated damaged the tourism industry in the UK countryside

The effects of foot and mouth disease on the tourism industry resulted in a loss of £2–3 billion in 2001, and the British Hospitality Association estimated that the number of overseas visitors fell by 10 per cent. One-third of hotels and other accommodation providers reported that their bookings had fallen by more than 25 per cent, as many inbound and domestic tourists chose alternative destinations.

Skills practice

1 To what extent does the media influence the popularity and appeal of destinations?

2 Using the example of foot and mouth disease, explain how negative images can reduce visitor numbers.

3 Using the Internet, newspapers or magazines, identify current stories and articles in the news that would:

- attract more visitors to the British Isles
- reduce the number of visitors to the British Isles.

Political factors

Political factors are the consequences of government action. This may be through government policy, for example the tourism policy *Tomorrow's Tourism* and its updated strategy *Tomorrow's Tourism Today*, see pages 144–145.

Some government actions are in direct response to events. The terrorist attack on the United States on 11 September 2001 reduced the confidence of many visitors to travel overseas. In October 2001, immediately after the event, the Office for National Statistics reported that overseas visitor numbers to the UK fell by 30 per cent. In response the UK government made efforts to reduce the threat of terrorism by improving security to win back confidence amongst overseas visitors.

Recent events, such as the London terrorist attack on 7 July 2005, which claimed over 50 lives, had a direct impact on the appeal of London as a tourist destination.

Think it over ...

How has the threat of terrorism affected the tourism industry in the British Isles and how has the government responded to these threats?

The government is also responsible for encouraging the future development and growth of tourism. This is made possible by supporting national marketing campaigns, making funds and grants available to encourage investment, and also organising large-scale events.

CASE STUDY

London Olympics 2012

The London Olympics in 2012 is expected to generate an additional 500,000 overseas visitors and generate an additional £9 billion. According to the British Hospitality Association, more than 17,000 new London hotel rooms are planned by 2012. The government appointed a new Olympic Minister to make sure that everything is ready in time for the opening of the games.

An 80,000-seat stadium will be the focal point for the Olympic Games. The stadium will be built in Stratford, in East London, and will be the venue for the main athletic events.

It is estimated that it will cost £3.8 billion to stage the 2012 games. There will be 9.6 million tickets on sale: 8 million for the Olympics and 1.6 million for the Paralympics. Most of the tickets are expected to cost less than £50 and include free travel on London transport.

In 2000 more than 3.7 billion people across the world watched the Sydney Olympics on television. In 2012 London will be the focus of one of the biggest media events in the world. As well as 20,000 journalists, the city will also host 17,000 athletes and officials, 56,000 volunteers and hundreds of thousands of spectators.

For further information visit http://www.london2012.org

A computerised image of the Olympic Stadium for the London Olympics in 2012

Think it over ...

What are the benefits of hosting an international event in the British Isles?

In the following case study we are going to look at an evaluation of the factors that have affected the popularity and appeal of a selected destination.

CASE STUDY

Bath

Bath is famous for its historic Roman Baths and Georgian architecture and was designated by UNESCO as a World Heritage Site in 1987 to reflect its international importance. The Romans originally began constructing the baths in AD 43 as a place of rest and relaxation. The site known as 'Aquae Sulis' became a religious shrine and a bathing complex, and was visited by wealthy Romans from all over Europe.

Tourism is a very important part of Bath's economy, with 1 million staying visitors, including 350,000 visitors from overseas, and 2.8 million day visitors, spending a total of £195 million each year.

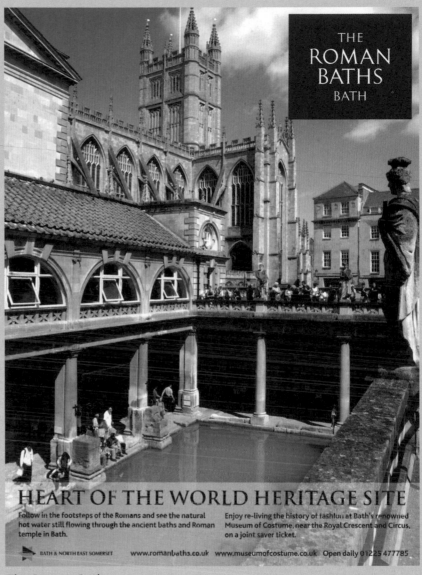

THE ROMAN BATHS BATH

HEART OF THE WORLD HERITAGE SITE

Follow in the footsteps of the Romans and see the natural hot water still flowing through the ancient baths and Roman temple in Bath.

Enjoy re-living the history of fashion at Bath's renowned Museum of Costume, near the Royal Crescent and Circus, on a joint saver ticket.

BATH & NORTH EAST SOMERSET   www.romanbaths.co.uk   www.museumofcostume.co.uk   Open daily 01225 477785

The Roman Baths

Accessibility

The city of Bath is easily accessible. It is located 120 miles west of London, and travel by road takes approximately 2 hours. The city is 10 miles from Junction 18 of the M4 motorway, which provides access from London and Wales. The M5 motorway, which joins the M4 at Junction 20, provides access from the South of England and the North.

There are regular train services direct from London Paddington and Waterloo to Bath, with a journey time of 90 minutes. National Express operates coach services from London Victoria, London Heathrow and London Gatwick.

Air travel is also possible from Bristol International airport, which is 15 miles from Bath, with flights from the USA, Europe and North Africa. The nearest seaport is Portsmouth, which is 80 miles away. Portsmouth provides ferry services to the Channel Islands, France and Spain.

Visitors who travel by car are directed to

Park-and-Ride schemes, as the city centre can become congested with traffic. Car parks are available in the centre of Bath but it is often more convenient to use the Park-and-Ride scheme as car access has been limited in some areas. There are three Park-and-Ride schemes that are linked to the city centre by frequent non-stop buses that operate every twelve to fifteen minutes. The journey takes approximately ten minutes.

Availability of attractions and other tourist facilities

There are over 30 museums and visitor attractions in Bath. The most visited are: Roman Baths Museum, Bath Abbey, Museum of Costume, Sally Lunn's Refreshment House and Museum, Royal Photographic Society Galleries and the American Museum. Cultural events bring thousands of people to the city each year, including the International Music Festival and the Literary Festival.

The Roman Baths is the most well-known attraction, receiving nearly 1 million visitors each year. Visitors can experience the Roman Temple, the hot spring water and walk where Romans walked. Audio guides are available in several languages and parts of the Roman Baths have been enhanced by the use of virtual tours revealing what the building once looked like.

Bath is also famous for being the home of the author Jane Austen, who wrote *Pride and Prejudice* and *Sense and Sensibility*. The Jane Austen Centre offers a glimpse of life during Regency times and explores how living in Bath affected Jane Austen's life and writing.

Part of the challenge to tourism managers is to encourage tourists to visit a wide range of attractions in Bath, as many travel to see the Roman Baths which can become very busy during peak times.

There are many tourist facilities within the city, with over 150 restaurants and traditional pubs and bars. There are many independent shops and boutiques and markets, as well as the main high street stores.

In the city and surrounding area there are over 100 hotels and guest houses, over 40 self-catering cottages and apartments, approximately 15 farms offering accommodation and over 10 public houses and inns with guest rooms, as well as local camping and caravan sites. There are very few one- and two-star hotels, with the majority having three- and four-stars, and some being awarded five stars, including the Royal Crescent Hotel and the Bath Spa Hotel.

For those keen on sport, Bath has a premiership rugby club, a racecourse, a local football team and plays host to the Somerset County Cricket Festival, which attracts many people to the city.

Cost of visiting

The cost of visiting Bath can be expensive as it is a destination that prides itself on providing a high-quality visitor experience. Although visitors expect to pay more for higher levels of quality, prices reflect value for money in terms of what visitors can see and do. The cost of visiting varies depending on the attractions visited and the standard of accommodation.

The cost of visiting the Roman Baths in 2005:

Fare	Price
Adult	£9.50
Child	£5.30
Concession price	£8.50
Senior citizen	£8.50

The cost of visiting the Jane Austen Centre in 2005:

Fare	Price
Adult	£5.95
Child	£3.25
Concession price	£4.50
Senior citizen	£4.50
Family price	£16

Change in customer needs and expectations

The Bath Visitor Survey in 2001 revealed that most of the visitors are in the 45–54 age range, whilst people in the 16–24 age group are least likely to be visiting Bath. Most of the staying visitors are employed in managerial or professional occupations.

Bath Visitor Survey

Seventy-five per cent of visitors found the quality of service provided by their accommodation to be 'good' or 'very good' whilst 62 per cent of respondents considered the value for money of their accommodation to have been 'good' or 'very good'.

Eighty-six per cent of those surveyed visited Bath as part of a holiday (overnight stay) or leisure day trip, with 52 per cent of respondents having visited Bath on a previous occasion.

Seventy-seven per cent of respondents were on a short break of between 1 and 3 nights in the city, including 29 per cent who were staying for 1 night.

Two-thirds, 64 per cent, of day visitors spent an average of between 3 and 5 hours in Bath.

When asked what they particularly liked about the city, 37 per cent mentioned architecture, 26 per cent mentioned the atmosphere, and 16 per cent particularly liked the history.

When asked if there was anything they would like to see improved in the city, 70 per cent did not respond or give an answer to this question. Those that did commented on the number of vagrants and beggars, the traffic and the condition of public toilets.

Source: Bath Visitor Survey (2001)

Destination management

Bath Tourism Plus is the destination marketing organisation for the city of Bath and the surrounding area. It aims to rejuvenate the image of Bath and beyond as a leisure and business travel destination. The business travel and conference marketing section of the company trades as Bath Conference Plus.

Bath Tourism Plus began trading on the 1 October 2003, taking over the management of tourism promotion from Bath and North East Somerset Council, and has established partnerships between the public and private sectors.

Bath Tourism Plus is located in Bath city centre and markets Bath and beyond to leisure and business visitors. The company manages the city's tourist information centre, Bath Conference Plus and the Bath Christmas Market.

Image and promotion

Bath promotes itself through brochures, guides, websites and indirectly through travel articles in magazines, radio and television programmes. Its tourist information centre has been refurbished to make it more attractive to visitors.

The Bath Film Office promotes and assists film-making in Bath and North East Somerset. Film-makers have been attracted to Bath for over 50 years to make feature films, commercials, travel programmes, and documentaries. The Film Office provides advice on locations, local crew, media facilities and liaison with all necessary council departments and key local contacts, such as local businesses and the police.

Political factors

Tourism businesses, Bath Tourism Plus and Bath and North East Somerset Council work closely together to enhance the development of tourism in the city. They aim to make the best use of the economic and social benefits of tourism and to increase the profits of businesses involved in providing attractions and facilities to tourists.

The tourism industry has had to respond to external factors beyond its control. Initially, following the terrorist attacks in the USA on 11 September 2001, the number of international tourists fell by one-third. Since then consumer confidence has returned and the opening of a route from Bristol International airport to New York will enable visitors from America to have easier access to the city.

Tourism managers in Bath are working closely with South West Tourism, the South West Regional Development Agency and VisitBritain to make Bath a more sustainable city by reducing any negative effects of tourism.

Recommendations

Bath can further develop its future popularity and appeal in order to receive more incoming visitors. However, as the city is already busy with tourists, tourism managers need to work on strategies so that more visitors stay longer in the city. Not only does this relieve pressure on roads and transport but also benefits the city as visitors spend more money in hotels, bars, restaurants and tourist attractions. Tourism managers may also consider making the city attractive to younger visitors.

The city needs to attract high levels of visitors all-year round. Visitor numbers during Christmas have been increased through the promotion of the Bath Christmas Market. Bath does not have a major conference venue that can accommodate the needs of large international conferences and exhibitions.

Tourism needs to develop, yet at the same time maintain the existing quality of the buildings and the visitor experience with the highest standards of care for the environment. Tourism managers are keen to develop sustainable tourism in Bath with projects such as The Real Bath Breakfast (see page 173).

Part of the strategy to widen the appeal and popularity of the city is to bring visitors closer to the waters of Bath's natural hot springs. The Thermae Bath Spa is expected to offer indoor and open-air bathing on a roof-top pool, with steam rooms, whirlpools and natural health treatments. However, the project has fallen behind schedule as a result of political arguments between the developers, the local council and local residents. Further delays have caused the cost of the project to rise. New developers have been appointed. When open, the Thermae Bath Spa will provide a unique health spa only 100 metres from the Roman Baths, allowing visitors to experience the thermal waters as the Romans did.

For more information visit http://www.visitbath.co.uk

The rooftop pool of the Thermae Bath Spa

ASSESSMENT

Portfolio practice

You will be asked to produce an evaluation of the factors that have affected the popularity and appeal of a selected destination. It could be one of the destinations that you described in the tourist itinerary.

You need to produce a critical evaluation of the main factors that have led to the popularity and appeal of a selected destination in the British Isles. Make sure that the factors that you select are appropriate and that they are covered in detail. Remember to draw conclusions from your research.

You will then be required to make recommendations of how this destination can develop its future popularity and appeal in order to receive more incoming visitors. Your recommendations should be drawn from the conclusions made in the evaluation. The suggestions should be realistic and appropriate for both the destination and the incoming visitor and must be substantiated and justified.

Knowledge check

1 Name the countries that are included in the British Isles.

2 Identify the different travel and tourism organisations that support tourism in the British Isles.

3 Name the six categories that describe the features of destinations in the British Isles.

4 What are the features that make destinations appealing to tourists?

5 Identify six different groups of tourists and briefly describe their needs.

6 Describe what is included in an itinerary.

7 What are the main sources of tourism statistics for the British Isles?

8 Describe the seven factors that affect the popularity and appeal of destinations.

Resources

Automobile Association (2001) *Discover Britain: The Illustrated Walking and Exploring Guide.* Windsor: AA Publishing.

Automobile Association (2001) *Pocket Book of Walks Through Britain's History.* Windsor: AA Publishing.

Dorling Kindersley (2005) *Eyewitness Travel Guides: Great Britain.* London: Dorling Kindersley Limited.

Lonely Planet (2001) *Britain,* 4th ed. London: Lonely Planet Publications.

Norwich, J.J. (ed) (2000) *Everyman Guides England and Wales.* London: Everyman Publishing PLC.

Porter, D. and Prince, D. (2002) *Frommer's Great Britain.* New York: Hungry Minds, Inc.

Riley-Smith, D. (2002) *Days Out Atlas.* Norwich: Paragraph Publishing.

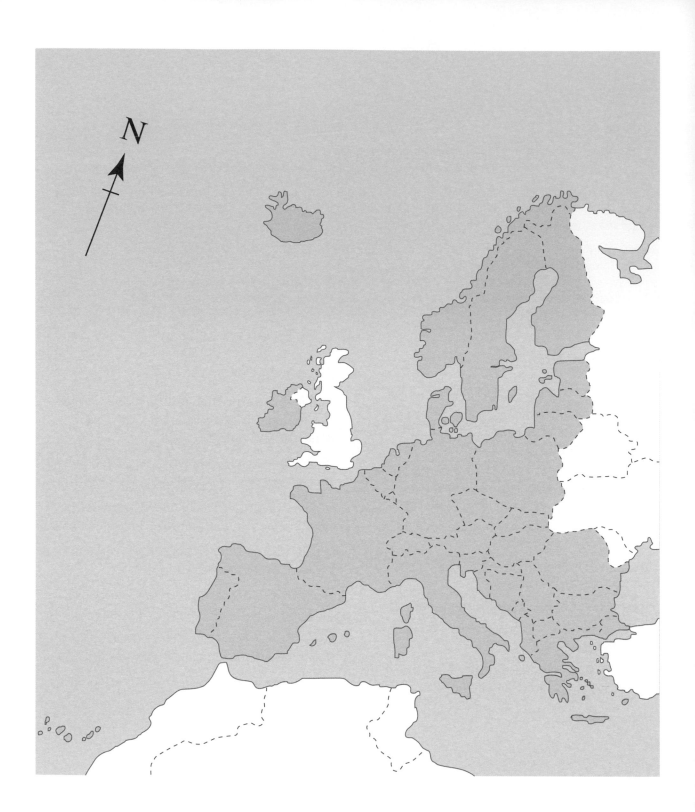

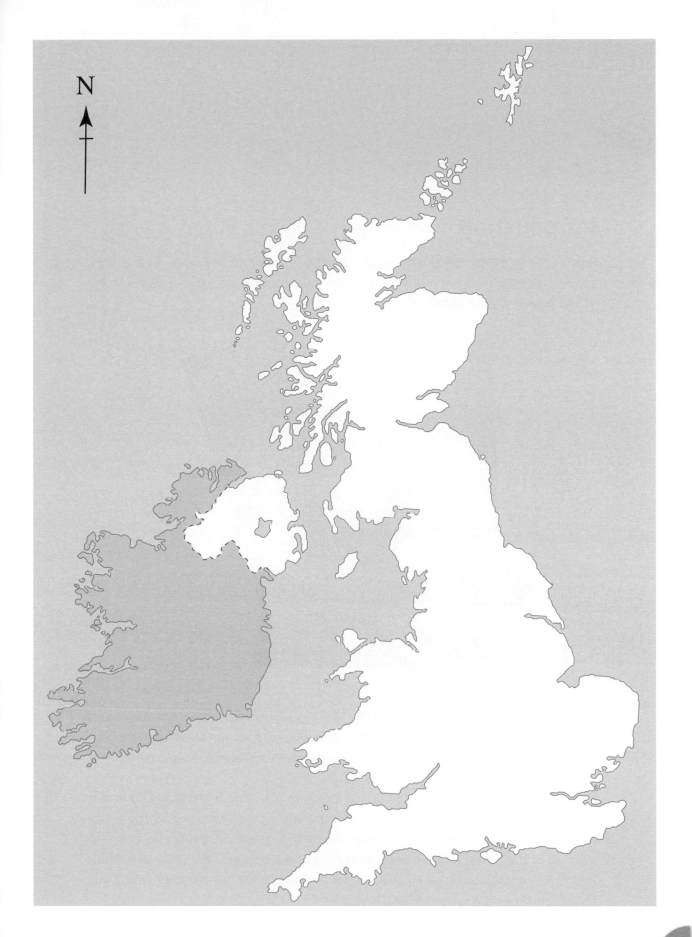

UNIT 5

Travelling safely

Introduction

Being able to travel the world safely is both essential and desirable. In this unit, you will discover how the travel and tourism industry operates to ensure the safety of the traveller, their belongings and their money.

Travelling safely

In the first part, you will learn about the legal and regulatory requirements placed upon organisations by governments and agencies, and by the travel and tourism industry itself, and how they are applied in different situations.

In the second part, you will identify and examine the restrictions many countries place upon the movement of tourists and the implications of these to the travel and tourism industry. Restrictions may exist for political or security reasons, or because of the potential for disease to spread across borders. You will learn about the major contagious diseases, their causes and symptoms, where they are mainly found, and how the spread of risk is limited.

In the final part of this unit, you will explore how the industry deals with emergency situations and can help travellers to deal with such situations, whether they are small scale, such as medical problems encountered by an individual traveller, or large scale, such as hurricanes and volcanic eruptions.

How you will be assessed

This unit is assessed by an external examination of 90 minutes duration.

After completing the unit you will be able to demonstrate and apply your knowledge of:

* Legal and regulatory requirements which are placed upon the travel and tourism industry and travellers

* Restrictions on travel, e.g. for political, health, or security reasons

* Small-scale and major emergency situations and how they are handled by the travel and tourism industry and associated organisations.

5.1 Legal and regulatory requirements

Regulations set by travel and tourism organisations

By this stage of the course, you will appreciate just how large and complex the travel and tourism industry is. A number of organisations exist to make sure it operates smoothly, to standards set within the industry.

There are four main organisations within the industry:

* International Air Transport Association (IATA)
* Civil Aviation Authority (CAA)
* Joint Aviation Authority (JAA)
* Association of British Travel Agents (ABTA).

International Air Transport Association (IATA)

IATA is a remarkable organisation. Founded in Havana, Cuba, in April 1945, it is the prime vehicle for inter-airline co-operation, promoting safe, reliable, secure and economical air services, for the benefit of the world's consumers. The

enormous growth in civil aviation since the Second World War would have been much less spectacular without the standards and procedures developed within IATA. At the time of writing, 265 airlines are members of IATA, accounting for 94 per cent of the world's international scheduled flights. Additionally, thousands of travel agents and freight forwarders across the world have IATA approval, and many suppliers have 'strategic partnership' status.

IATA developed into seven areas:

* Avionics and telecommunications
* Engineering and environment
* Airports
* Flight operations
* Medical
* Facilitation
* Security.

Skills practice

Go to the IATA website and explore what the organisation's functions are. Then write two sentences for each of the seven areas of IATA, describing their functions.

IATA was re-organised on a two-tier basis in October 1979. It became a trade association, dealing with technical, legal, financial, traffic services and most agency matters, and also a tariff co-ordination body, dealing with passenger fares, cargo rates, and related conditions and charges.

Examples of developments in which IATA have been heavily involved include:

* New aircraft and systems
* Inter-airline fare agreements
* Standardised ticketing
* International acceptance of other airlines' tickets
* Financial settlements between members
* Procedures to enhance the ability of passengers and freight to transfer between airlines
* Security and terrorist counter-measures
* Standardised baggage container sizes
* International regulations on the carriage and packaging of dangerous goods and live animals.

Working with the Air Traffic Conference of America, it even developed its own language, which is used in every aspect of the airline industry. This language includes agreed coding for every airline, for example EI for Aer Lingus, QF for Qantas, and a three-letter code for every airport in the world, for example ADL for Adelaide, LAX for Los Angeles, as well as abbreviations for common airline terms, for example PSGR for 'Passenger', NN for 'Need', ARNK for 'Arrival unknown', BBML for 'Baby food'.

Through IATA's work:

* airlines can knit their activities and procedures into a world-wide system
* passenger and cargo agents can be represented and benefit from neutrally applied agency service standards and levels of professional skill
* individual passengers can make one telephone call to reserve a ticket, pay in one currency and then use the ticket on several airlines in several countries – or even return it for a cash refund
* governments can work with airlines and draw on their experience and expertise.

IATA has a major influence on all aspects of air travel

CASE STUDY

IATA clearing house

IATA operates a clearing house to enable airlines and associated companies to settle their inter-company bills. By offsetting their mutual transactions through the clearing house, participating companies can reduce hundreds of bi-lateral, multi-currency transactions for passenger, cargo, baggage, catering, ground handling and other services, to one single amount. Billions of dollars worth of transactions are simplified and cleared through this process every year.

IATA has a number of settlement systems to enable financial settlements to be made to airlines, agents and third-party customers.

1 **The Billing and Settlement Plan (BSP) is for passenger air transportation. Discover what it does. What are the benefits of a BSP, and to whom?**
2 **What is the equivalent system for cargo air transportation?**

Civil Aviation Authority (CAA)

All countries have some form of civil aviation authority. In the UK, the CAA, unusually, is a public corporation. It receives no direct government funding, its costs being met from its charges on those it regulates. It was established by parliament in 1972 as an independent specialist aviation regulator and provider of air-traffic services. It has four main functions:

* **Airspace policy** It is responsible for the planning and regulation of UK airspace. It used to have direct responsibility for air traffic control but National Air Traffic Services took that over in 2001, although the CAA remains the regulatory body. The CAA has to consider all those who wish to pass through UK airspace, whether they are civilian or military. Aircraft cannot fly by any route, at any height they wish. They are generally routed along 'motorways' in the air, at specific heights. Some heights and areas are specifically for military aircraft. UK airspace is very crowded, being the main route into and out of Europe for those aircraft flying to and from the Americas, so the CAA is responsible for finding ways to make the best use of the available airspace.

* **Economic regulation** The CAA regulates airports, air traffic services and airlines, and provides economic advice on aviation policy. It produces and publishes much useful data, such as the volume of traffic handled and punctuality of airlines and UK airports.

* **Safety regulation** This is a major responsibility of the CAA. Its work includes ensuring safety in the airspace, at aerodromes, in airlines, and of aircraft and passengers. It is responsible, for example, for registering all UK aerodromes and UK aircraft, flight crews and engineers. It issues regulations and gives information and advice on safety subjects, for example who can sit in emergency row seats, safety briefings to passengers, use of mobile phones on aircraft, and the carriage of dangerous goods.

CAA poster indicating some of the dangerous items that you must not carry on aircraft

* **Consumer protection** The CAA regulates the finances and fitness of travel organisers selling flights and package holidays in the UK.

Key term

Package This is a pre-arranged combination of at least two of the following components when offered for sale at an inclusive price and when the service covers a period of more than twenty-four hours or includes overnight accommodation: (a) transport, (b) accommodation, (c) other tourist services not ancillary to transport or accommodation and accounting for a significant proportion of the package. (see the Package Travel, Package Holidays and Package Tours Regulations 1992)

The CAA manages the UK's largest system of consumer protection for travellers, known as the Air Travel Organisers' Licence (ATOL).

Over 28 million passengers took ATOL-protected holidays in 2004/5. Forty-three per cent of these passengers used the package holidays of the Big Four tour operators. ATOL protects passengers from losing their money or being stranded abroad. The ATOL is required by all individuals and companies selling packages which include flights. Applicants must show they are fit to hold an ATOL and have adequate financial arrangements. The CAA carries out financial checks on the firms it licenses and requires a guarantee, called a bond, to be lodged with them. If a firm goes out of business, the CAA will make a refund to the passengers, or if the passengers are still abroad, arrange for them to finish their holiday and fly home.

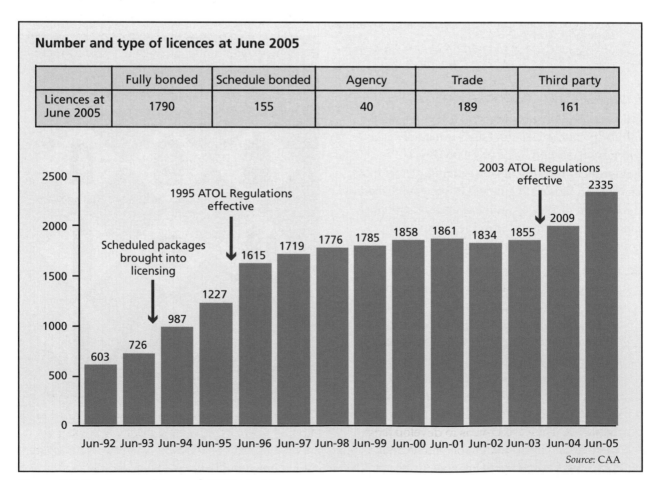

Number and type of licences at June 2005

	Fully bonded	Schedule bonded	Agency	Trade	Third party
Licences at June 2005	1790	155	40	189	161

Figure 5.1 Number and type of ATOLs held

CASE STUDY

Are these covered by ATOL?

- *Jason and Kerry were on a package holiday in Kenya. They were unhappy with their outbound flight, as they had been downgraded due to overbookings.*

  Can an ATOL claim be made?

- *Jasmin, Kim, and Natasha were on a package holiday in Portugal. They booked it directly with the tour operator, Wunderbreak Holidays, an ATOL company. Three days before they were due to fly home, the local Wunderbreak Holidays representative said the company had gone bust.*

  1 **What protection will they have under the ATOL scheme?**

  2 **What will not be covered?**

- *Bob, Wilhelm, Kaz, Francoise and Kirsty booked a weekend in Amsterdam. They booked their flight from Bournemouth on a budget airline by phone, and their hotel through the Internet. On the day they were due to fly from Bournemouth, they got a phone call from the hotel company to say the hotel had burned down and they should make their own accommodation arrangements.*

  Will Bob and his friends be able to claim through the ATOL scheme?

JAR-OPS 1.995 Minimum requirements

(a) An operator shall ensure that each crew member:

   (i)   is at least 18 years of age;

   (ii) has passed an initial medical examination or assessment and is found medically fit to discharge the duties specified in the Operations Manual (See AMC OPS 1.995(a)(2));

   (iii) remains medically fit to discharge the duties specified in the Operations Manual.

(b) An operator shall ensure that each cabin crew member is competent to perform his duties in accordance with procedures specified in the Operations Manual.

Source: JAA

Extract from JAA Requirement: Section 1 – Subpart O – Cabin Crew 01.12.01

The CAA also licenses UK airlines and enforces European Council requirements in relation to their finances, nationality, liability to passengers for death or injury, and insurance. Additionally, it enforces certain other legal requirements and codes of practice for the protection of passengers.

Joint Aviation Authorities (JAA)

The Joint Aviation Authorities (JAA) represents the civil aviation authorities of 39 European states who have agreed to co-operate in developing and implementing common safety standards and procedures. A major objective is to develop Joint Aviation Requirements (JARs) for aircraft design and manufacture, aircraft operations and maintenance, and the licensing of aviation personnel.

However, major changes are being introduced through the creation of the **European Aviation Safety Agency (EASA)**, which became operational in 2003. The JAA achieved improvements through the co-operation and goodwill of the countries involved. The EASA has been given legal powers by the EU to take over responsibility from the JAA, initially to produce common rules for airworthiness and environmental protection. There are proposals for the EASA to progressively have full responsibility for European aviation regulations, including air traffic management and airport requirements. In effect, this would mean that the aviation authorities in each country would act as regional offices of the EASA, and the EASA would delegate issues to them for implementation.

Association of British Travel Agents (ABTA)

In 2005, ABTA's membership consisted of 1052 tour operators' offices and 6310 travel agency offices in the UK, plus 156 organisations associated with the industry who are members of the ABTA Travel Industry Partner Scheme. Approximately 80 per cent of all UK package holidays were sold through ABTA members. It has existed for over 50 years and, through its efforts, has helped the industry grow enormously, in

An ABTA and IATA travel agent

ways which have been of benefit to its members and customers.

ABTA is a self-regulatory body, run by its membership. Its aims are to:

* Promote and develop the general interests of all members of ABTA

* Maintain codes of conduct for the benefit of the travelling public and ABTA members, such that membership will be recognised as a guarantee of integrity, competence and high standards of service

* Maintain liaison with governments and organisations in respect of the development of travel and tourism

* Ensure all members provide financial protection for the travelling public, in the event of any member's failure.

ABTA's codes of conduct regulate all aspects of tour operators' and travel agents' relationships with their customers. The tour operators' code of conduct includes minimum standards for brochures, to ensure they contain clear, comprehensive and accurate descriptions of facilities offered. It details rules that govern booking conditions as they relate, for example, to the cancellation or alteration of tours, holidays or other arrangements by the tour operator.

A similar code of conduct applies to travel agents. This covers all aspects of travel agents' relationships with their customers, regarding the standard of service and information they give to them.

Tour operators and travel agents belonging to ABTA must provide bonds to protect their customers. The bond may be an insurance policy or bank guarantee which offers financial protection in the event of the member's financial failure. This will enable those clients who have started their holidays to complete them as originally planned and secure travel arrangements back to the UK, and those clients whose holidays have not started to have alternative arrangements made for their holidays to proceed, or to be reimbursed.

You will remember that the CAA requires an ATOL to be held by any tour operator intending to operate package tours, using flights. It is a statutory requirement. However, bonding for those organising packages without an air carriage component is provided through the ABTA bonding scheme. As it is not a mandatory requirement to belong to ABTA, non-members can also arrange packages without bonding. In that respect, ABTA bonding for non-flight packages can be seen as being voluntary. However, non-ABTA tour operators offering non-flight packages are required to take out insurance to protect their clients' money, or hold it in a separate account. Local authority trading standards officers monitor these arrangements.

Key points

- The CAA issues ATOLs to organisers of package travel arrangements when there is an element of air travel. This includes a requirement for the travel organiser to have a bond to ensure financial protection.

- ABTA operates a bonding scheme for members who are organising and selling package travel arrangements which do not have an element of air travel.

The ABTA code has strict rules about the handling of complaints. ABTA aims to resolve complaints against members and, if necessary, provide access to the ABTA arbitration scheme, which enables clients to pursue their claim without high legal costs.

Over 19 million package holidays were taken in 2003/4, but ABTA only dealt with 15,700 complaints of which just 1134 were referred to the ABTA arbitration scheme. In that year, less than 2 per cent of ABTA members went out of business and £2.6 million was paid in settlement of claims, including those arising from company failures. All of these measures showed a decrease, in other words an improvement in performance, on previous years. Some of this decrease may be the result of a slight reduction in the number of ABTA members and the increasing trend of the travelling public to book their holidays independently through the Internet.

Skills practice

You are the training officer for a travel agency chain. Prepare a 5-minute presentation for new staff on the history of ABTA, its current aims and functions, and the benefits of ABTA to the industry and the consumer.

There are other organisations representing tour operators and travel agents which encourage and promote the industry and the professional standards of their members. For example:

✱ Association of Independent Tour Operators (AITO)

✱ Federation of Tour Operators (FTO)

✱ Guild of Travel Management Companies (GTMC)

✱ British Incoming Tour Operators' Association (BITOA).

People are increasingly booking the various components of their holiday (e.g. flights and accommodation) independently via the Internet. Consumer and travel organisations are alerting the public to the fact that they may not be protected if any service provider fails to provide services booked independently. Customers may need to seek other legislation to recover their losses.

CASE STUDY

EUjet

Read this article about the demise of EUjet:

EUjet leaves thousands stranded

Last week's failure of EUjet (www.eujet.com) has highlighted the precarious position of travellers when their scheduled airline collapses.

Almost 5500 people were stranded mid-trip, while up to 50,000 hold forward bookings. The majority will have bought direct from the airline; if they paid with a credit card, and the transaction was UK-based and for at least £100, they should apply for a refund through their card provider. However, as this is now peak season, replacement travel is likely to cost more than the original tickets – easyJet and Monarch have offered £25 tickets to holidaymakers stuck abroad, but have limited availability.

Travel insurance is unlikely to help; only a few companies, such as Gosure (0845 222 0020, www.gosure.com) and the Post Office (0800 169 9999, www.postoffice.co.uk), offer cover for scheduled-airline failure.

Otherwise the prospects for refunds are bleak: EUjet has admitted customers stand little chance of seeing any cash back from its administrator.

Source: Sunday Times 31 July 2005

What category of passenger might be able to have their return flight arrangements looked after, and/or get a refund?

Key points

- The International Air Transport Association (IATA) represents the airline industry and is a major worldwide influence in the standardisation and simplification of procedures relating to civil aviation.

- The Civil Aviation Authority (CAA) is the UK's independent aviation regulator. It has four main functions: airspace policy; economic regulation; safety regulation; consumer protection. It issues Air Travel Organisers' Licences (ATOLs), which are required by any organiser of package tours which include air transport.

- The Joint Aviation Authorities (JAA) represents the civil aviation authorities of 39 European states, to implement common safety standards and procedures. It does so through the co-operation of its members.

- The European Aviation Safety Agency (EASA) has been given legal powers by the EU and will progressively take over from the JAA and, in some aviation matters, from the civil aviation authorities in EU countries.

- The Association of British Travel Agents (ABTA) is the major representative of UK tour operators and travel agents. It maintains codes of conduct for its members; liaises with the government and other organisations to promote and protect the travel and tourism industry; and operates a bonding scheme to financially protect those who are buying package holidays which do not have an air travel element.

Legislation

In addition to the regulations imposed by travel and tourism related organisations, there are many legal requirements placed upon the industry by governments.

In this section, the year of initial legislation is quoted, but there may have been amendments in later years.

Some laws are specific to our industry, some are generic, that is they apply to any organisation in any field. Let us first look at two which are specific to our industry.

EU Directive on Package Travel, Package Holidays and Package Tours (90/314/EEC) 1990

This piece of European Union legislation applies to package travel (whether it is for holidays or business, or any other reason). In many respects, it brings together laws and industry codes of practice which already existed. It is a very important Directive which has had a major influence on the industry. The UK enacts this Directive through the Package Travel, Package Holidays and Package Tours Regulations 1992.

The Directive is designed to protect consumers. It has ten main parts:

1 *Misleading descriptive matter* If any organiser or retailer provides misleading descriptive matter about a package, including its price and conditions applying to the contract, they must compensate the client for any loss incurred as a result, including disappointment.

2 *Brochures* The information in organisers' brochures must be legible, comprehensible and accurate. For example, the brochure must clearly describe the type, location and standard of accommodation; what meals are included; the itinerary; the price and how and when it must be paid.

3 *Other information* The organiser must provide the client with information on passports, visas, health formalities, how clients' money is being safeguarded, and arrangements for repatriation in the event of insolvency.

4 *Contract* A written contract must be provided to clients, containing details of a number of issues, including, but not limited to: itinerary; transport; accommodation; meals; names and addresses of the organiser, retailer and, where appropriate, insurer; the price and payment schedule; any special requirements identified by the client; methods and timescales within which clients must make any complaints.

5 *Transfer of bookings* The circumstances under which transferring bookings to other dates, destinations or people, can be made.

6 *Changes in price* These are only permitted if they arise because of changes in transport costs, taxes, fees, or exchange rates, and only if the cost increases by more than 2 per cent. They can only be made before specified deadlines.

7 *Cancellation by the client* Rights are given to the clients if, because of significant changes to the contract (including price), they wish to cancel or change their package.

8 *Failure to provide services* If a significant part of the contracted services cannot be delivered, the organiser must make alternative arrangements at no extra cost to the client. Compensation may also be due.

9 *Liability for proper performance of contract* This is a particularly significant part of the Directive. The organiser is responsible for all obligations of the contract, even though the services may be provided by third parties. So, for example, if a coach excursion which was part of the package was not provided, or a client was

Lake *Como*

7 DAYS FROM £825

Set in an idyllic landscape of mountainous and rugged hillsides, the tranquil waters of Lake Como have for centuries attracted visitors who come here for relaxation and inspiration. Favoured by some of England's most romantic 19th century poets including Wordsworth, Shelley and Byron, it has also attracted numerous royal visitors from Edward III to Prince Charles in addition to Verdi and Liszt who were also inspired by its splendour. Numerous small towns and villages line the shores with their lakeside promenades and cafés. Magnificent villas and gardens can be reached both by water and land and this holiday allows you to progress at your own relaxed pace as each new vista unfolds before you. It provides ample opportunity to sample the delights of Italian cuisine, served with all the flair and mastery expected of Italian chefs.

This holiday includes 6 breakfasts and 6 evening meals

Menaggio is one of Lake Como's most attractive resorts and an ideal base for exploration. Its tree-lined promenade where the gentle blue waters lap at the shores and its narrow cobbled streets ascending towards the fine villas perched on the hillside overlooking the town, makes for a wonderful stay. The tranquil town of **Varenna** is located on Lake Como's eastern shore. With its medieval character and cobbled streets, it houses one of the oldest surviving churches on the lake, its high spire standing majestically above the yellow ochre and rusty red village. A ruined 11th century castle overlooks Varenna's narrow streets and attractive town square. The villas and gardens are the main attraction and also

well worth visiting are Villa dei Cipressi and Villa Monastero, the latter dating from the 13th century. **Tremezzo**, **Bellagio** and **Como** are all within easy reach by ferry from Menaggio. Tremezzo, famous for the Villa Carlotta with its splendidly landscaped gardens, should not be missed. Bellagio, with its elegant lakeside promenade and cafés, and the gardens of Villa Melzi designed by Giocondo Albertolli are a delight to wander through. Como, the provincial capital, is both a tourist resort and the centre of the Italian silk industry. A bustling town with an attractive pedestrianised area dominated by the magnificent façade of the cathedral and the elegant Piazza Cavour.

GRAND HOTEL MENAGGIO **

As its name suggests, the Grand Hotel Menaggio is a first class hotel overlooking the bay of Menaggio. Directly on the waterfront, the hotel is close to the ferry station and only a five-minute walk from the main square and lakeside promenade. The public areas are elegantly furnished in keeping with the traditional 'turn-of-the-century' atmosphere which is still present in this fashionable lakeside resort. Whether it is to discover the surrounding area or to relax, the Grand Hotel Menaggio makes for an excellent choice.

• Lounge • Bar • Terrace • Restaurant • Heated outdoor swimming pool • Fitness room • Rooms with bath or shower, television, radio, telephone, safety deposit box, mini-bar, hairdryer and air conditioning.

▲ Varenna

▲ Bellagio

▼ Lake Como

WHAT IS INCLUDED

- Duration 7 days, 6 nights in hotel in Menaggio.
- **VIP Local Departure Service™** to London Heathrow or Gatwick Airport and from London Heathrow or Gatwick Airport to your front door.
- Check-in service by Titan staff.
- Scheduled British Airways or Alitalia flights from Heathrow or Gatwick to Milan and from Milan to Heathrow or Gatwick.
- Transfers to and from airports.
- Services of a Titan Holiday Manager throughout.
- Accommodation as specified or of a similar standard.
- 6 breakfasts and 6 evening meals.
- Excursion to Villa Carlotta.
- Hotel porterage (1 bag per person).
- All airport taxes, security charges and UK Air Passenger Duty of £5 per person.

WHAT YOU PAY AND WHEN YOU GO

2005		July	
		2	£875
Departure	**Price**	16	£875
May		**September**	
7	£825	17	£895
28	£865	24	£875
Supplement per person for single room:			£195

(247)

Information in brochures must be legible, comprehensible and accurate

Source: Titan Travel

injured at a hotel booked as part of a package, the client could hold the organiser responsible for the proper performance of the obligations of the contract. It is up to the organiser then to take action against their supplier, to recover any losses they experienced as a result of the action against them by the client. Exceptions to the organiser's responsibility are if the failure is (a) due to the client, or (b) attributable to a third party unconnected to the provision of the services and is unforeseeable or unavoidable, or (c) is unforeseeable and beyond the control of the party involved, and could not have been avoided even if due care had been exercised.

10 *Security in case of insolvency* The organiser must provide evidence of security for the refund of money and repatriation of the client in the event of the organiser becoming insolvent. The ABTA and ATOL bonding mentioned earlier are the main methods of doing so.

Think it over …

Collect a range of tour operators' brochures. Work with a colleague to identify where in those brochures the tour operators have covered the requirements of the EU Directive on Package Travel.

EU Regulation (261/2004): Compensation and assistance to passengers in the event of denied boarding, cancellation, or long delay of flights

In 2005, the EU introduced further protection for air travellers, including those on charter flights. The protection applies if the flight is from an EU airport, or to an EU airport from outside the EU when operated by an EU airline. If an airline has overbooked a flight, it must seek volunteers to give up their seats in return for agreed benefits, which must include the choice of either a refund (with a free ticket back to the passenger's original point of departure, if relevant), or alternative transport to their destination. If the passenger who is denied boarding is not a volunteer, the airline must also provide compensation ranging from 250 to 600, depending upon the length of the flight. Refreshments, hotel accommodation

and communication facilities must also be provided as appropriate. Similar arrangements and compensation must be provided if the flight is cancelled, depending upon how much advance notice is given to the passenger. If a passenger is downgraded into a lower-class cabin than paid for, they must be reimbursed by a percentage of the value of the ticket.

Additionally, if there is a delay, the airline must provide refreshments, hotel accommodation and communication facilities as applicable. The delay has to be in excess of a specified number of hours, which vary depending upon the length of the flight. If the delay is over five hours, the airline must also offer to refund the passenger's ticket (with a free flight back to the original departure point).

Think it over …

Obtain a copy of the EU leaflet on Air Passenger Rights or read the legislation on denied boarding, cancellations, delays, and downgrading (www.europa.eu.int/abc/travel/flying/index_en.htm).

1 Discuss with colleagues the implications for those airlines who have charged fares lower than the level of compensation due.

2 Airlines' responsibility is limited or excluded if the cancellation or delay has been caused by extraordinary circumstances. Discuss what you feel those circumstances might be, then refer to clauses 12, 14 and 15 of the EU Regulation. Does your list agree with those clauses?

Other laws are generic, applying to all organisations and people in the UK. The following are some which feature strongly in the travel and tourism industry.

Disability Discrimination Act 1995

One in six people living in the UK are considered to have some form of disability. The Disability Discrimination Act is designed to remove barriers and restrictions for them. The Act has been phased in over several years. It includes rights for disabled people in the areas of buying or renting land or property, employment, and access to goods, facilities and services.

Travel destinations in various parts of the world provide suitable facilities for those who have a disability

Key term

Disability This is defined in the Disability Discrimination Act as a physical or mental impairment that has a substantial and long term effect on a person's ability to carry out normal day-to-day activities.

Employers should consider allowing employment applications to be in braille or large print, or in non-written methods. They should review selection processes and make adjustments to locations, etc. for interviews. Staff with disabilities may need the job to be partially re-designed, or parts of it allocated to others. They may also need flexible hours, furniture to be rearranged and specialist equipment to be provided, etc.

The stage covering access to goods, facilities and services came into effect in 2004. Prior to this, organisations could not refuse to serve, or provide, a lower standard of service to someone with a disability. From 2004, organisations also had to ensure reasonable adjustments to any physical barriers preventing disabled people from using the service provided. This might include improved lighting and signs; greater colour contrasts; disabled toilet facilities; ramps and handrails; induction loops for those with hearing impairment; seating; lower reception desks to assist those in wheelchairs, etc.

Every reasonable measure must be taken to remove any impediment which might cause discrimination of those who are disabled, and to provide assistance to overcome any remaining constraints. For example, is the travel agency shop 'wheelchair friendly'; does the visitor attraction ensure information is available to the deaf and blind; can disabled people get on and off the coach easily?

Skills practice

In pairs, visit two local travel and tourism related venues, for example a rail station, theme park, museum, travel agency. Note what provisions they have made for disabled people. Also note any more provisions you feel they could usefully provide.

Discuss your findings with your main group.

Data Protection Act 1998

The Data Protection Act gives people certain rights over the information held about them. It primarily relates to information held in computer records, but may also apply to some manual records. It places obligations on those processing the information. It applies equally to information about employees and about customers.

Skills practice

Wundertravel is a new travel agency opening in Leatherford. Computers are used to make bookings, keep customer and staff records, write letters and emails, and send mailshots.

You are the manager and are to write a report for your director on how the Data Protection Act may affect your agency and what action you are taking to comply with it. Download a copy of the Data Protection Act fact sheet from www.informationcommissioner.gov.uk, to help you.

Trade Descriptions Act 1968

The Trade Descriptions Act forms part of consumer law and makes it an offence, in respect of supplying a service (e.g. holidays, accommodation, travel), to knowingly or recklessly apply a false description to goods and/or supply goods to which a false trade description has been applied.

It is an offence whether the description is in writing or made verbally. Care must be taken to ensure that what is said and what is written in brochures and anything else distributed is accurate. It would be an offence, for example, if you described a hotel as being 50 metres from the sea, if it was actually 500 metres. It has to be proved that you made that error knowingly or recklessly, but prosecutors could argue that, as a professional, you should have taken action to ensure you knew the accuracy of such a statement. In that example you may be able to show that, even if the statement in the brochure was inaccurate, you were not being reckless because you had inserted an error slip in the brochure and/or that you had directly told the customer of the error. Tour operators must ensure that they have methods to alert them to any changes that might affect the information they previously gave to their clients, and that they advise those who might be affected as quickly as possible.

Make sure your descriptions are accurate

Consumer Protection Act 1987

Parts 1 and 2 of the Act deal with the supply of defective or unsafe products and the protection and safety of consumers. Part 3 covers prices. It is illegal to give misleading price information about any goods, services, facilities or accommodation being sold, that is the true price is greater than shown in promotional material, or is described as being generally available at that price but is actually only available in certain circumstances, or does not clearly and fully state what is included in the price and that surcharges will be payable after the booking.

After the terrorist attacks in September 2001, aviation security charges were introduced to cover the cost of additional security and the insurance costs being experienced by the aviation industry. These costs were passed on to customers travelling by air. In September 2003, the Office of Fair Trading warned the travel industry that such costs had to be included in the basic holiday prices and be shown in brochures within the headline price for a holiday.

Enterprise Act 2002

The Fair Trading Act was effectively replaced by the Enterprise Act. Parts of the Enterprise Act establish the Office of Fair Trading (OFT) as a corporate body giving it a number of powers relating to the consumer. The OFT can enforce certain consumer legislation by means of Enforcement Orders in the event of:

* 'Community infringements' (breaches of UK laws giving effect to specific EU Directives, such as on consumer credit, package holidays and unfair terms in consumer contracts)

* 'Domestic infringements' (breaches of UK laws) which harm the collective interests of consumers in the UK.

Additionally, the Enterprise Act highlights that a key function of the OFT is to promote good practice in respect of consumer interests. One way of doing so is to give approval to consumer codes of practice which are intended to regulate the conduct of businesses that supply goods or services to consumers, with a view to safeguarding or promoting the interests of consumers. Those voluntary codes can be proposed and sponsored by trade associations and others with influence. Of course, we have evidence of such codes in the work of ABTA and others.

Supply of Goods and Services Act 1982

The Supply of Goods and Services Act applies to England, Wales and Northern Ireland, and there is similar legislation for Scotland. When a customer purchases goods or services from the seller, a contract exists which includes implied conditions, such as description of the goods or services, quality and fitness for purpose. The Act requires a supplier to carry out any service contained in that contract with reasonable care and skill. If the supplier fails to do so, the customer can either claim compensation or cancel the contract. It is the seller of the service who is responsible to the customer, not the provider of the service, although the seller may, in turn, have a case against the provider.

CASE STUDY

A legal tangle!

Work with a colleague on this activity.

You work for a tour operator which sells from high street shops. Your manager has come to you in a flustered state! 'I've just received this letter of complaint,' he moaned. 'It looks like a lot of legal problems to me. Help me sort it out.' The following is the background to the complaint.

Mr and Mrs Almond wished to book an inclusive holiday with you. Mrs Almond is blind and has a guide dog, Rosie. When she visited you, she was told that dogs were not allowed in the shop. The next day, she returned with her husband, but without Rosie. They booked a package holiday on a Mediterranean island selecting the Hotel Cretian, which the brochure said was 4-star. They asked for a ground floor room for disabled people and explained that they would be taking Rosie. Next day, the consultant confirmed that this had been booked.

The day before travel, Mr Almond visited the shop to collect the travel documents. He found them on an unattended desk, complete with an invoice showing his name and address. The invoice also included extra charges for airport security, in addition to the package holiday price.

When they tried to check-in at the airport the next day, the passenger agent said the airline knew nothing about Rosie. Fortunately, the airline moved some other passengers so that Mr and Mrs Almond could sit together in the bulkhead seats, which meant Rosie had room to lie down.

When they arrived at the hotel, they were told that, although the ground-floor room for disabled people had been confirmed, it was not available. They were allocated a room on the third floor which had less space and steps into the bathroom and shower. There were no facilities for Rosie. They were surprised that the hotel lacked some of the luxury facilities that they expected of a 4-star hotel. They mentioned this to the hotel staff who said the hotel used to be 4-star but, as some of the facilities had been removed, they had been downgraded to 3-star at the start of the season.

Mr and Mrs Almonds' letter ended by complaining that the small print in the travel documents supplied by your company said they had to lodge any complaint with you within 24 hours of returning to the UK, which they had been unable to do because of personal reasons.

1 **What advice would you give your manager on which pieces of legislation, if any, apply?**
2 **What improvements do you think your company should make to their practices and procedures, to avoid a recurrence of such a problem?**

- Some legislation is general to any industry, but some is specific to the travel and tourism industry.

- The EU Directive on Package Travel is a major piece of legislation for the industry and is enacted in the UK through the Package Travel, Package Holidays and Package Tours Regulations 1992. It brings together aspects of many other laws and is designed to protect consumers' interests. One important feature is that the organiser/seller of the package is responsible for all parts of that package – they cannot claim that they are not responsible because another person or organisation actually provided a particular element.

- The EU also introduced legislation which compensates air passengers in the event of them being offloaded, downgraded or delayed, or having their flights cancelled.

- The Disability Discrimination Act has three parts, the second of which relates to employment rights and the third of which relates to the right of access to goods, facilities and services.

- The Data Protection Act gives people rights over certain information held by them.

- The Trade Descriptions Act covers false trade descriptions.

- Part of the Consumer Protection Act covers prices.

- The Enterprise Act replaced the Fair Trading Act and empowers the Office of Fair Trading to enforce certain consumer legislation on businesses infringing that legislation, through enforcement orders. It also requires the OFT to encourage good consumer practice through using methods such as codes of practice.

- Part of the Supply of Goods and Services Act requires the supplier to carry out any service with reasonable care and skill.

5.2 Restrictions on travel

You might argue that, in an ideal world, we should all have unimpeded access to everywhere and anyone in the world. Sadly, that is not the case. Governments wish to monitor and control those attempting to enter and leave their country. Travel organisations need to ensure the safety and smooth progress of their passengers. Controls need to be in place to minimise the health risks to travellers and the spread of disease. This section takes a closer look at these issues.

Government restrictions

Countries need some control over who can enter and who can leave their country. The simplest method is by the use of an identity card. This may enable travellers to enter or leave their own country, and a country with which the traveller's country has a particularly close relationship, for example nationals of France can enter the UK on presentation of a national identity card.

The next level of restriction is a passport issued by a country to its citizens to enable them to both leave and re-enter that country. It also usually enables travellers to enter and leave other countries, sometimes without a visa. UK passports were first described as 'Safe Conducts' in the 15th century, but it was not until 1915 that passports, as we know them, came into use in the UK. Until 1988 they had blue covers and were known as 'Old Blues'. Since then they have been burgundy red documents and the front cover is headed 'European Union', although they also bear the title 'United Kingdom of Great Britain and Northern

Make sure travel documents are in order

Ireland' and the Royal coat of arms, and so remain British, not European, passports. Most importantly, the new passports are machine readable (known as MRP), enabling speedy and accurate checks to be made by running the passport through a swipe machine. Even now, though, a UK passport carries the impressive statement:

'Her Britannic Majesty's Secretary of State requests and requires in the name of her Majesty all those whom it may concern to allow the bearer to pass freely without let or hindrance, and to afford the bearer such assistance and protection as may be necessary.'

There are several types of UK passport, depending upon the individual's status, for example a Citizen of the British Dependant Territories, or British Overseas Citizen, or British National Overseas, or British Protected Person.

Think it over ...

This is a full group discussion.

1 What nationalities are there in your group?
2 Which of your group have passports?
3 Where did they have to apply for them?
4 Have any of your group had to obtain visas?
5 For which countries?
6 How did they apply for them?

An Old Blue and an MRP

When entering another country, the traveller may have their passport stamped by an immigration official. That stamp shows, amongst other things, the port of entry and the entry date. It may also state how long the traveller is entitled to stay in the country. The passport is stamped again with the port of embarkation and date when the traveller leaves the country.

A further requirement applied by countries wishing to have stricter control over who enters their country, is an entry visa. This enables the vetting of the traveller and the purpose of their travel, before they are given permission to enter that country. Usually, they must be obtained from one of the country's embassies before travelling to a country but occasionally visas can be issued on arrival. Sometimes, the visa takes the form of a stamp in the passport, but sometimes it is on a separate piece of paper. The visa will normally specify the length of validity, but may also specify how many times the country can be entered, what the purpose of the visit is and what areas of the country can be visited. Transit visas are sometimes issued to travellers passing through a country, for example to connect with a further flight, but this is unlikely to allow permission to leave the airport. At the time of writing, nationals of Switzerland are entitled to enter the Russian Federation without a visa, but nationals of Austria are not; Australian citizens do not need a visa to enter the UK as a tourist, but they do if they wish to work; nationals of Vietnam travelling to the UK for any reason need a visa.

A further restriction applied by some countries is placed upon travellers who have visited that country, but wish to leave, for example those who have been in the Yemen for more than one month need an exit permit.

An even tighter restriction is applied by a few countries wishing to control the movement of their own citizens. Those citizens may need permission to leave their own country, for example Cuba.

Some travellers may be exempt from all or some of these restrictions if travelling to or from certain countries:

✱ Infants and children may be allowed to travel if shown in their parent's passport, as long as they travel with that parent. Some school groups can travel without passports, but need other documentation.

✱ Merchant seamen have to relocate between their ships and home. Many countries allow them to transit through their airports without visas, which might normally be required, if they carry supporting documents from their shipping company.

✱ Some passengers are only passing through countries to connect from one flight to another. Some countries will allow them to transit without a visa (TWOV) as long as they catch the first connecting flight. Often, they will not be allowed to leave the airport, although this is sometimes allowed, for example when the connecting flight is not until the following day.

✱ Military personnel travelling to or from their country of duty may be allowed to travel without passports or visas, on condition that they have other specified documents.

✱ Diplomats travelling on diplomatic passports may be allowed to travel without a visa, particularly if they are accredited to the country they are entering.

Tour operators and travel agents should advise their clients of the travel documents they will require, indeed EU legislation requires them to do so when booking packages. There are a number of public and trade sources of travel documentation information, including government and embassy websites. The UK Passport Service's website www.ukpai.gov.uk provides information about obtaining UK passports and www.ukvisas.gov.uk provides information on required travel documents to those wishing to come to the UK.

Using recognised travel industry manuals and/or websites, decide what passports and visas will be required by the following travellers:

• A New Zealand national travelling from Auckland to the USA for a three-week holiday.

• A Canadian national who is travelling as a member of the UN forces to Bosnia.

• A Finnish merchant seaman flying from Helsinki via Moscow to Mumbai to join his ship.

• A German national and his wife who is a Thai national, travelling with their 18-month-old daughter, who has dual nationality, from Frankfurt to Morocco.

Because of the heightened threat of terrorism in the world, the USA has tightened its security. In addition to passport and visa requirements, airlines are required to provide US authorities with details of the passengers on every flight going to the USA, before that aircraft can land there.

This has presented the airlines with a number of procedural and technological challenges, as they must provide an accurate passenger list of those who have actually checked in for the flight, rather than those who booked on the flight (some passengers book and don't travel, others don't book, but standby for flights). Accuracy is vital and the amount of time available is very tight, as passengers may be checking in as late as 30 minutes before departure. The airlines would not want aircraft to become airborne before learning that there is someone on board who is not acceptable to the USA, as this would mean that the aircraft would have to return to its departure point.

These requirements have led to a number of delays to aircraft and a few having to turn back once they were airborne. However, the airlines have become more skilled in obtaining much of the information required at the time the passenger makes their booking, and in using accurate and speedy procedures to advise the US authorities. Most airlines had to extend the check-in deadline and many ask passengers to check in two or two-and-a-half hours before departure.

Countries are always seeking ways to prevent identity and passport fraud and improve processing. Trials are underway in several countries which are leading to improvements, such as machine-readable passports containing biometric chips which store facial, fingerprint and iris data.

Skills practice

The UK and the USA are just two of the countries exploring and introducing new methods of identification and new levels of control on who is entering or leaving their countries.

As an individual exercise:

1 Research the latest methods of identification being explored or introduced by the UK and the USA.

2 Discover what changes there have been since 2001, or are planned, in respect of passport and visa requirements for those travelling to the UK and the USA.

Travel and tourism industry restrictions

Even though the actual immigration authorities of the country you are leaving may not ask to see your passport or visa, it is still necessary to have the right documents. Airlines and airport staff will normally require you to show them:

* *At the check-in point* This is to ensure you are the person named on the ticket, and that you have the necessary travel documents to leave the country and enter the countries you are visiting.

* *At the security control point* Airport staff will want to see your boarding pass or ticket and may ask to see your passport/visa again, to ensure you have it and are entitled to continue through security to the airside area, which is treated as being 'outside' the country.

* *At the boarding gate* You may be asked to show it again, to ensure that you have not given your boarding pass to someone else after you checked in, and to double-check that your documents are in order for the countries you are visiting.

Airlines are particularly careful with these checks because if they fly someone to a country without the proper travel documents that country can refuse the passenger permission to enter the country. They can also require the airline to take the passenger back to the country they left, at the airline's expense, and to bear any other costs involved, for example the overnight detention of a passenger awaiting the first flight back to the country they left. Additionally, the airline may be fined heavily for the error. It is not unusual for an airline to be charged £50 per day detention expenses, plus a £2500 fine per person, plus the cost of flying them back to their point of departure.

In addition to the passport and visa checks, airlines also require travellers to have a ticket and to have a boarding card. The ticket is evidence that the passenger has paid to travel on the flight.

Processes differ between airlines, but the common principle stems from the usual method of processing the passenger, as follows:

* The passenger agent checks the passenger in by computer. The ticket is exchanged for a boarding card which contains the passenger's name, the flight number and, often, the seat number allocated to the passenger, the boarding gate number, and the time the gate will close and the aircraft is due to depart. If the passenger checks in baggage, a computer-produced bar-coded label will be attached to the bag, whilst a tear-off portion will be given to the passenger as their receipt.

* The boarding card enables the passenger to pass through security to 'airside' and continue to the boarding gate where a passenger agent will make a computer entry to record that the passenger has boarded the flight. The passenger keeps the boarding card stub, which shows their name, flight number and seat number, and which they take on board with them.

* Approximately 10 minutes before the aircraft is due to depart, the passenger agent will check their computer for the names of any passengers who have not boarded the aircraft and will start a search for them, including making public address announcements. Often, the passenger

has dallied too long in the airport shops, or has fallen asleep! If the passenger does not arrive at the boarding gate within the following five minutes, staff will start to take action to remove the passenger's bag from the aircraft, as it is a security risk to allow a bag to travel on a flight without the passenger.

Source: Qantas

The boarding card contains useful information and provides access to the flight

Of course, there are alternative procedures also in use. An increasingly frequent one is through the use of e-tickets. Passengers who make their bookings on the Internet or by phone are given a unique reference number at the time of booking which they use at the airport, together with proof of identity, instead of a ticket, to obtain a boarding card. Increasingly, passengers use self-service check-in machines, into which they enter their booking reference to obtain a boarding card. Some budget airlines do not provide seat numbers to passengers. The boarding card may be coloured and passengers are boarded in sequence, by the colour of their boarding card.

Skills practice

Work with a colleague on this activity.

1 Research your local airport and airlines. Discover what control methods they use for their passengers, for example check-in methods, document checks, boarding processes.

2 Research rail companies and ferry companies. What controls and procedures do they operate?

3 Compare your findings with the rest of your group.

Key points

- To travel outside their own country, travellers need identity cards or passports.

- They may also need visas.

- Travel organisers and retailers must ensure they brief their customers accurately on the travel documents they will need.

- Airlines have procedures which control passenger movement, for example the requirement to have a ticket and boarding card and correct travel documents.

Health

With the opportunity to travel comes the opportunity to spread disease! There have been tremendous advances in hygiene, immunisation and treatment, which has eradicated or minimised several contagious diseases. However, there are signs that some diseases are spreading again. This is partially because of the increase in travel, and partially because disease carriers like mosquitoes have become immune to the methods we have been using to protect ourselves.

The United Nations formed the World Health Organisation in 1948 to act as the directing and co-ordinating body on international health matters. It has 192 states as members. Part of its work is in the field of international health regulations and it is a prime source of information regarding international health problems, health legislation, and recommendations for its members. Every country also publishes its health regulations and recommendations to travellers. The UK Department of Health publishes information which details the health risks around the world, the major diseases, the precautions to take, a country-by-country health check, and how to get treatment.

Some diseases are restricted to, or more prevalent in, certain parts of the world, but they can be spread by various means, notably travellers. From time to time, travellers may suffer from relatively minor illnesses, like diarrhoea or sickness. Very occasionally these upsets can indicate more serious illness. The following are some of the major diseases. (*Note*: The following information is a layman's indication of the diseases and should not be taken as professional medical advice.)

Key terms

Vaccination This is the introduction of weakened or dead bacteria which prompt the immune system to produce antibodies to ward off the disease in future.

Immunisation This is the creation of immunity against a disease.

Inoculation This is the introduction, often by needle, of a vaccine to a living body to create immunity.

Cholera

Although it is relatively uncommon in travellers, cholera is an increasing problem in areas of poor sanitation and hygiene, as in parts of South America, the Middle East, Africa and Asia. It is caused by the consumption of contaminated food and water. The main symptoms are severe diarrhoea and dehydration, low body temperature and muscle cramps. In 1973, the World Health Organisation recognised that vaccination was not preventing the spread of cholera, so countries ceased to require travellers to have cholera vaccination certificates. Vaccination is still available, but only provides limited, short-term immunity. Prevention is largely through careful hygiene and using bottled or boiled water and avoiding uncooked food, including vegetables and fruit. Treatment will probably include antibiotics and the replacement of fluid loss. Untreated, it can rapidly lead to death for 35 per cent to 80 per cent of patients, but treatment will lead to recovery in almost every case.

Typhoid

Typhoid occurs throughout Asia, Africa and South America, and less so in other areas. It is notable in areas of poor hygiene, but also reflects lifestyle, for example travelling 'rough' and eating at street stalls. It is primarily caused by eating food which is contaminated by salmonella. Symptoms include fever, cough, abdominal pain and constipation which, after a few days, changes to violent diarrhoea. Immunisation is recommended for most countries apart from Australia, North America and Europe, but also in those countries if the traveller's lifestyle indicates the need.

Prevention is by impeccable care over food and water. Preventative treatment is in the form of tablets or injection. Treatment will probably include antibiotics and intravenous fluids. Untreated, it can lead to death for up to 30 per cent of patients, but treatment will lead to recovery in almost every case.

Malaria

Malaria is a major and increasing health problem throughout tropical regions. It is transmitted to humans by bites from mosquitoes carrying the malaria parasite, injected into the blood stream. There are several types of malaria. General symptoms include chills, fever and vomiting attacks recurring every few days. There can be jaundice and anaemia. There is no vaccine to prevent malaria. Prevention is by taking anti-malaria tablets and by covering the body and using anti-mosquito repellent. Treatment will primarily be by the use of drugs appropriate to the type of malaria. Attacks can recur for many years. Mosquitoes in some areas of the world, for example south-east Asia, have become resistant to the preventative treatments we are using. An estimated 200–300 million malaria infections occur every year, although around 98 per cent of sufferers survive.

Only a relatively small number of those infected are travellers, but this is increasing at an alarming rate. One of the problems is carelessness.

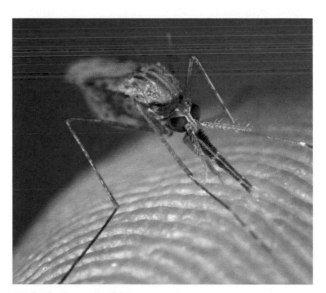

Malaria is carried by mosquitoes

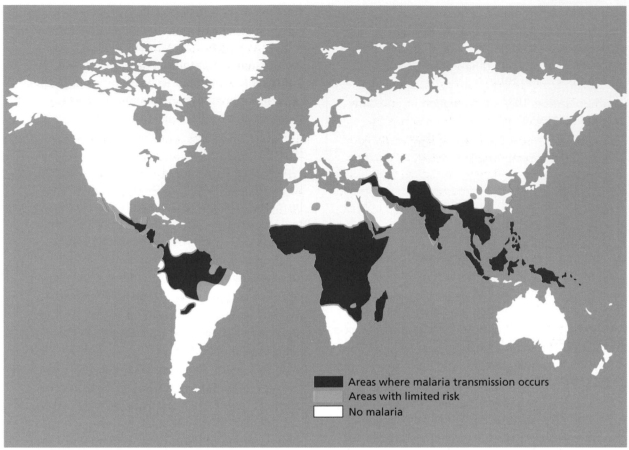

■	Areas where malaria transmission occurs
▨	Areas with limited risk
□	No malaria

Figure 5.2 Worldwide malaria distribution in 2002

Source: WHO global atlas

Most anti-malaria tablets have to be taken daily or weekly, not only during the stay in the infected area, but also for two weeks before and four weeks after being there. Too many people fail to do so. Some travellers also fail to cover their bodies sufficiently at night. It is tempting not to do so when dressing for an evening's open-air entertainment in the tropics. Some who get symptoms weeks after they have been to an infected area dismiss it as a cold and do not visit the doctor, or tell the doctor where they have been, so treatment is delayed.

HIV/AIDS

AIDS (Acquired Immune Deficiency Syndrome) is caused by HIV (Human Immuno-Deficiency Virus). It is believed that it spread from apes to humans in Africa in the early 20th century and was carried to Haiti in the Caribbean before moving on to the USA, although it was only recognised as AIDS around 1981. It has now spread across the world. Some countries have required travellers to produce evidence that they are free from HIV but the World Health Organisation opposes this as it does not believe this is a clinically sound approach.

HIV/AIDS can be transmitted through unprotected sex with an infected person; the use of infected syringes; HIV-infected blood transfusions; and from an infected mother to her baby before or after birth. It cannot be passed on through everyday social contact, insect bites, dirty food or crockery, kissing, or sneezing. It can remain dormant in a person's body for years, although it can be passed on during that time. Sufferers may experience a glandular-like fever and enlargement of the lymph nodes. Over time, it can develop with a wider and more extreme range of symptoms.

The condition can continue for years without worsening, but it cannot recede to a less severe stage. Currently there is no preventative vaccine. Prevention is through avoiding the risks, for example by only having safe sex and not sharing needles. Treatment is primarily through lifestyle, exercise and medication which prolongs the 'steady-state'. More than half of those who are HIV positive do not progress to the most severe stage for more than 10 years, but once they have done so, life expectancy is short. Hopefully, many sufferers will be spared this progression with the discovery of a cure which scientists throughout the world are currently trying to achieve.

Yellow fever

This disease occurs primarily in Central Africa and Central and South America and there are signs of a major increase in cases in the last 25 years. At the time of writing, 15 countries require travellers to have a vaccination certificate before being allowed to enter the country and many others require it if the traveller has been to an infected country.

The disease is transmitted to humans by bites from infected mosquitoes which carry it between humans. Although some infections are mild, it can be a very serious and violent condition which includes vomiting, fever and extensive bleeding as a result of which liver and kidney failure are common. Prevention is through vaccination which lasts for 10 years, by covering the body during the day (mosquitoes carrying yellow fever usually bite during the day) and using mosquito repellent. There is no effective treatment and the mortality rate from severe yellow fever is high.

Hepatitis C

This disease is worldwide. It is a viral condition spread in the same way as HIV/AIDS, by contaminating blood. Prevention is by avoiding risks, as it is for HIV/AIDS. Patients often do not feel unwell, but may start to feel tired, which may be followed by signs of jaundice and liver damage. Some patients get better on their own, but the majority develop long-term problems, sometimes leading to the need for a liver transplant.

Hepatitis C should not be confused with two other types of hepatitis which are also infections of the liver. Hepatitis A is usually caught from contaminated food or water. It can be found worldwide and many of us have built some immunity to it. Symptoms include tiredness and nausea and evidence of jaundice. Personal hygiene is very important. Hepatitis B also occurs worldwide and is spread in the same way as HIV/AIDS. It can take up to six months before symptoms are experienced. It causes fever and affects the liver. However, vaccines are available for both forms.

Key point

Do not let your customers take a risk with their health. It could spoil their holiday. It could cause the spread of disease and it could result in a recurring illness for the rest of their lives. It might even kill them.

Other conditions

The Department of Health also alerts travellers to a number of other conditions which travellers should guard against, for example rabies, dengue, meningitis, tuberculosis. Although very rare and sometimes localised to specific areas, these can be very serious conditions. The Department of Health recommends that all travellers, regardless of destination, should be immunised against diphtheria, polio, and tetanus.

[Note: The sources of the preceding health information are: UK Department of Health, World Health Organisation, *The Complete Family Medical Guide* (Hinkler Books 2004), Directors of Health Promotion and Education (DHPE) USA].

Skills practice

Have a look at your health records. What vaccinations have you had? Are they all up-to-date?

In recent times, there have been substantial concerns regarding outbreaks of 'new' diseases, which could be quickly spread across the world, for example SARS and Avian influenza.

As a travel consultant, and using the recognised governmental and trade sources, what travel and health advice would you give the following travellers:

- A businessman who is a Dutch national travelling non-stop from Amsterdam to Rome, returning in five days.

- A couple with UK passports flying direct from London to Nairobi for a two-week safari holiday.

- A couple with an 18-month-old infant and six-year-old daughter, all of whom are UK citizens, travelling direct from Manchester to Orlando for a 10-day holiday.

- Two 19-year-old students planning a gap year in Australasia. They intend to do casual work whilst in Australia and New Zealand. One is a UK citizen, the other is a Swiss citizen.

- A businessman of Irish nationality with the following itinerary:
  06 June London–Brussels
  09 June Brussels–Monrovia
  16 June Monrovia–Accra
  17 June Accra–Johannesburg
  24 June Johannesburg–London
  He will be visiting the country region of Liberia which, at the time of travel, is a yellow fever affected area.

Having read the last few pages, you may be alarmed and depressed about travelling. Don't be! The vast majority of travellers do not require complex travel documents or fall foul of disease. However, it is vital that the travel industry and its customers do all they can to avoid such problems by having travel documents in order and taking proper health precautions. This can be done by discovering and applying the useful information provided by governments and health organisations.

The Foreign and Commonwealth Office publishes the latest advice on travel matters, including recommendations as to whether to travel to a country, and what the risks are, country-by-country. The travel industry uses the Foreign and Commonwealth Office advice to determine whether the operator should, and whether passengers can, without penalty, cancel travel arrangements to that country.

1 What facilities could a tour operator or travel agent offer customers to enable them to discover for themselves what travel documentation and health requirements they will need?

2 What procedures should the tour operator or travel agent put in place to ensure it has met its legal responsibilities in respect of providing accurate and timely information regarding travel documentation and health requirements?

3 What problems might arise if a tour operator or travel agent has not advised its clients of the travel documents which are required for their journey?

- The World Health Organisation is part of the United Nations and directs and co-ordinates health matters for 192 states.

- There are signs of diseases returning and increasing as the world's population increases and becomes more mobile.

- Certain vaccinations are mandatory to enter some countries, but most are recommendations.

- Travel organisers and retailers must ensure they brief their customers accurately on the health requirements for their travels.

- There are a number of sources of information on international health matters, including the World Health Organisation, the Foreign and Commonwealth Office, the Department of Health, and foreign governments.

- The travel industry uses the advice from the Foreign and Commonwealth Office to determine what action it should take if there are heightened issues of safety or health in any country.

5.3 Emergency situations

Small-scale situations

Regardless of why we are travelling, we all wish for a safe experience without any problems, but problems can arise! Many of these risks can be avoided or reduced by good planning, taking the right preventative action in advance of the trip, and behaving appropriately during our travels. So what advice can we give, as travel and tourism professionals, to our customers?

What could go wrong?

The first stage of avoiding or reducing risk is to have your customers think about what could go wrong. What requirements does the country they are going to visit have of them, for example to have appropriate travel documents? What are the health risks? What is security like? What local laws may particularly affect them? Are there any other risks in that country? A useful source of information is the Foreign and Commonwealth Office (www.fco.gov.uk/travel), which provides travel advice by country and up-to-date information on:

✱ Travel checklists

✱ Passports and visas

✱ Travel insurance

✱ Travel health

✱ Travel money

✱ What the FCO can do to help.

> ### Think it over …
>
> One of your travel agency's clients needs to go to India, Sri Lanka, Thailand and Indonesia. Using Foreign and Commonwealth Office information, what advice would you give her about entry requirements, health, safety and security, and any other issues?

What could possibly go wrong?

The *Travel Information Manual* (TIM), published monthly by IATA Netherlands Data Publications, contains the latest information, country by country, on passports, visas, health, airport tax, customs, currency, etc. The on-line version (TIMATIC) is available through PCs linked to airline and computer reservations systems, so is commonly used by tour operators and travel agents.

Minimising the risk

The second stage is for your customers to consider what they can do to minimise the risks.

Loss

To minimise the loss of money, customers could do the following:

* Carry as little as possible with them and spread what they are carrying around their body, keeping some in a money belt hidden under their clothing

* Keep money in the hotel room safe

* Spread their funds between cash, travellers cheques (which can be replaced if lost or stolen) and credit cards.

A tip for travellers is to write down the details of their tickets, passport, credit card, etc., and keep these details in a safe place, leaving a copy of it with a trusted friend or relative in the UK. There are companies with whom such details can be logged, for example Sentinel. A single call to Sentinel will result in them putting a stop on all missing documents and assisting with their replacement.

Health

The risk of health problems can be substantially reduced by taking action both before and during travels. Travellers can obtain advice and preventative treatment at most doctors' surgeries and travel clinics. Some preventative medications can be obtained without prescriptions at pharmacists. Health advice by country can also be obtained from the World Health Organisation, the Foreign and Commonwealth Office, the Department of Health, and foreign embassies.

Travellers should prepare themselves for their journeys as early as possible. Obtaining passports, visas and vaccinations may take 6–8 weeks. Some immunisations and other preventative medication may take some weeks to become effective.

Apart from the contagious diseases, less major illnesses may also be avoidable by using preventative treatments, for example air/sea sickness tablets and water purification tablets.

Once on their travels, your customers can avoid risks by taking medical advice, for example avoiding water that may be contaminated, applying anti-mosquito sprays, wearing long-sleeved tops and trousers in the evening in mosquito areas. It is sensible for travellers to take a first-aid kit. Its contents may vary depending upon the countries being visited.

If travelling to a European Union country or Iceland, Liechtenstein, Norway or Switzerland, residents of the UK (subject to their nationality) have rights to medical treatment that becomes necessary during their visit. In some countries, treatment is free or partially free, in others the traveller has to pay in full and then reclaim. To obtain these rights, travellers need a European Health Insurance Card (EHIC) issued by the Department of Health.

Insurance

The third stage is for your customers to insure themselves against risk. Tour operators and travel agents will require their customers to take out insurance arranged by the tour operator or travel agent, or show that they have arranged adequate travel insurance themselves.

Insurance is for a fixed period, normally the period of the holiday. However, with travellers increasingly taking frequent breaks, sometimes of short duration, many take out annual insurance plans. These can be cheaper than taking out several short-term policies.

Skills practice

Work in pairs to obtain a selection of travel brochures which contain insurance details, and a selection of travel insurance policies which can be purchased direct from insurance companies or brokers.

* Identify and compare the main features.

* Note what exclusions are identified.

Travellers arranging self-drive car hire should always consider their liability and establish what cover is provided in the car-hire price. What might appear to be a bargain price may not turn out to be so cheap when it is discovered what level of insurance is provided. It might be limited to basic third-party cover against damage or injury to others, which leaves the driver financially responsible for loss or damage to the hired car, injury to the driver or passengers, and loss of contents. The cost of the supplementary insurance could be high. Not surprisingly, these additional insurances can often cost more than the rental of the car itself!

The fastest growing sector of travellers is those aged over 50. Insurance premiums can escalate for them and have far more restrictions applied as to what conditions will be covered. Some insurers will not insure older travellers. Car-hire companies generally apply age limits to renting their cars.

Apart from the advice obtainable from the Foreign and Commonwealth Office, there are many other organisations which might be able to provide advice on preventing and handling emergencies, depending upon the type of problem, including:

* Embassies and consulates
* Insurance companies
* Medical assistance groups
* Tour operators and travel agents
* Airlines, coach, rail and ferry companies.

What if it still goes wrong?

You have helped your customers anticipate and protect themselves against emergency situations, but what if emergencies still arise? Let us look at some examples.

Holiday cancellations

These might arise due to circumstances affecting the traveller, or affecting the tour operator. When customers book their holiday months in advance, they don't know what might befall them by the time they are due to travel. They or a travel companion may be taken ill, or a close relative who is not travelling with them may die. Any of these circumstances may cause them to cancel their holiday.

Can we cancel?

Some tour operators have softened their cancellation policies in the wake of the bombings. Call-centre team leaders at Thomson have been ordered to use discretion when dealing with cancellations, especially where families with young children are concerned. First Choice has confirmed that customers travelling to Sharm can amend bookings free of charge until the end of August. Thomas Cook, however, has stated that cancelled trips will not be refunded 'and we are not waiving the £30 amendment charge'.

Tour operators are by no means obliged to refund clients nervous of terrorist attacks. The Association of British Travel Agents warns: 'If people choose not to go, normal terms and conditions apply.' This means that travellers will only be guaranteed refunds if the Foreign Office issues a formal warning against all non-essential travel to a country, but under the FO's new policy of less proscriptive travel advice, that is unlikely to happen.

'We have not changed the overall level of the advice, just updated the facts,' said the Foreign Office. 'The travel advice was already at a high level, warning people to be extremely vigilant.' That their position might prevent worried travellers from obtaining refunds was, they said, 'completely beyond our remit'.

Insurance cover is unlikely to help. Stuart Wartalski of Endsleigh Insurance said that travel premiums would not rise in the wake of the bombings because 'overwhelmingly, policies do not cover acts of terrorism – host governments usually pick up the bill for emergency healthcare and the FCO takes it from there'. Equally, claims for cancellation due to fear of terrorism would not be accepted. One holidaymaker, who declined to be named, tried to cancel her holiday to the Red Sea resort of Taba, where 34 died in a bombing last October. She was told by First Choice that no refund was available, nor could she transfer her holiday to another resort. On the basis of her fears, she has now obtained a certificate from her GP declaring her unfit for travel and will claim on her insurance policy's cancellation clause.

Source: Sunday Times 31 July 2005

Travellers should be made aware of any restrictions to the flexibility of the arrangements made for them. For example, their air fare may not allow any changes, or there may be a charge for any changes. The ticket may not be refundable, or be only partly refundable. The hotel may withhold some or all of the payment for a traveller's stay. It is common practice for hotels to ask for a credit card number when someone books a hotel room. If the guest does not arrive by a given time, the hotel may release the room to someone else and also charge one night's accommodation to the original guest's credit card. If your customer has booked a package holiday, the cancellation policy should have been given to them in writing and also explained to them. Travel insurance taken as part of the package or arranged independently may reimburse cancellation losses to the customer.

If the cancellation of a package arrangement is caused by the tour operator, the traveller can expect them to provide a refund or an alternative package of equivalent standard and price, plus compensation, depending upon the amount of warning given. These arrangements may not apply if the cancellation is beyond the tour operator's control, for example war, terrorist activity, industrial disputes, weather. Travellers will only be guaranteed full refunds for reasons beyond the control of the tour operator if the Foreign and Commonwealth Office issues a formal warning against all non-essential travel to a country.

Holiday curtailment

This might also arise due to circumstances affecting the traveller or affecting the tour operator. Typical examples include the ill health of the traveller whilst on holiday, or the ill health or death of their travel companion or close relative. Such events are usually covered in travel insurance policies. Travellers should alert their tour operator's local representative and/or travel agent to any problem as soon as possible, to give them the opportunity to resolve the problem or to give their client advice on what action to take.

If the tour operator curtails the package holiday, similar arrangements apply as for holiday cancellations.

If, for any reason, travellers are dissatisfied with the holiday arrangements, they should notify the supplier (or local representative of the package holiday if applicable) as quickly as possible so that they have the opportunity to resolve the problem or give their client advice on what action to take. Travellers should confirm this in writing, providing any supporting evidence, for example photographs. It is rare for complaints not to be resolved before the traveller returns home, but if they are not, they should continue to pursue the matter direct with the supplier and/or through the travel agent. If it was a package travel arrangement, a written complaint is needed, with any supporting evidence. Usually, any outstanding complaints are settled amicably but, in the event of continued dissatisfaction, the traveller can go to independent arbitration, which could be ABTA's own arbitration scheme.

Medical problems

Even if you have taken precautions before and during the holiday or business trip, medical problems can still arise. Medical help should be sought, either by contacting a doctor or by calling the emergency services. Travellers should initially ask their tour operator's local representative or hotel staff for help, as they will know the best and speediest way to get it. Additionally, the tour operator, travel agent and the traveller's insurance company may need to be advised of the situation verbally and in writing, so that they can assist the traveller and their companions and attend to any subsequent arrangements or claims.

Insurers have specialists to advise on and assist with the situation. They will require the traveller to ensure certain action is taken to enable any claim to be met, for example they will need to be advised of the situation within a certain timeframe and may require specified doctors, hospitals and repatriation methods to be used. On medical advice, they may decide to repatriate the traveller. This might involve a journey by private air ambulance, or flying a nurse out to escort the passenger to the UK on a commercial flight. Private ambulances may need to be arranged in both countries, and extra oxygen or a stretcher may be needed on the aircraft.

CASE STUDY

Crisis in Crete

Brian was taken ill whilst on holiday in Crete with his wife. He spent five days in intensive care in a Crete hospital and his travel insurers flew a nurse from the UK to escort him back to England.

1 **What cover would Brian have had under the EHIC scheme?**
2 **What is the EHIC process in Crete?**
3 **Look at a travel insurance policy. What cover would that have provided?**

Key terms

The UK has an overseas network of diplomatic and consular missions.

Diplomatic missions These are either high commissions (in Commonwealth countries), or embassies (in non-Commonwealth countries).

Consular missions These are consulates which have a more limited role: to protect the interests of their nationals in a particular country.

Lost passport

If the traveller has taken your advice, they and a relative or friend in the UK will have a separate record of their passport details, which will make the process of getting a replacement easier and quicker. If their passport is lost or stolen overseas, the traveller should obtain a certificate of loss from the police and take that to the British Consulate, most of which can issue new passports after checks have been conducted. All missions are able to issue emergency passports.

Lost money

If the traveller has kept only the minimum amount of money on their person, and has taken their funds in a variety of forms (e.g. cash, travellers cheques and credit cards), they will have increased their chances of still having some funds available, and of being able to claim for a replacement of any lost funds. Loss or theft of money, in whatever form, should be reported to the police immediately and a report number obtained, to assist any subsequent dealings with the travellers cheques issuer, credit card company or travel insurer. Without the theft report number, insurers are unlikely to accept any claim for replacement.

Take care of your belongings and don't attract attention to yourself!

If the loss is of travellers cheques, they can be replaced by advising the issuing company of the missing cheque numbers (the traveller should have kept a record of the travellers cheques issued and details of when they were used, so they will know which are lost or stolen). A call to the credit card company will ensure a stop is placed upon any missing credit card, to prevent it from being used by anyone. However, the traveller must wait for a new credit card to be issued. If the missing money is cash, this can only be recovered through travel insurance, and it will often exclude the first £50 or more, of the loss.

Theft and muggings

Fortunately, thefts and muggings are rare, but they do happen. Some countries, areas, and environments are particularly prone to thefts and muggings. Travellers should take the precautions mentioned earlier and take advice from the FCO website and other such sources. It makes sense not to wear a lot of jewellery or an expensive watch in public areas, and to keep camera equipment secure. Particular care should be taken in high-risk environments, for example in crowded public transport; whilst watching street entertainers; walking in dark areas at night.

Lost baggage

Travellers are most likely to allow baggage to leave their possession when they are travelling by air. Airline baggage rarely goes missing and even more rarely is permanently lost. The most common cause of baggage going missing is when a passenger and their baggage are transferring between flights. Perhaps the aircraft they are transferring from arrives at the transfer airport a little late. The passenger may be able to run and catch their onward flight, but their baggage doesn't make it in time. The baggage will therefore be 'missing' when the passenger arrives at their final destination. However, staff at the transfer airport will arrange for it to travel on the first available onward flight and, hopefully, will tell staff at the final destination, or even contact the flight, so that the passenger can be put at ease.

Most airlines will deliver the 'missing' baggage to the passenger's hotel without charge. However, many budget airlines require connecting passengers to collect and check in their bags again at the transfer airport, a lengthy and sometimes tiring process, particularly if the passenger has to pass through immigration controls to do so. Some budget airlines will not deliver the baggage to the passenger's home or hotel, but require the passenger to collect it from the airport.

Most airlines have printers that automatically print baggage labels when the passenger checks in. This reduces the risk of the passenger agent handwriting the wrong destination on the baggage label, which results in baggage going missing, for example writing LOS (Lagos, Nigeria) on the baggage label when it should have been LAX (Los Angeles, USA).

Passengers should carefully check that the bags they take off the carousel are definitely theirs. Many bags look alike and are taken in error. Black 'wheelie' bags and black soft bags are very popular and there may be dozens of them on a flight. It is sensible to put some distinguishing feature on the bag, for example a coloured strap or ribbon, and your name and address both on the outside (with the details hidden from casual sight) and inside the bag.

When a passenger reports that their baggage is missing, they will be asked to show the stub of the baggage label, which was given to them when they checked in. This shows where it was labelled to and also carries a unique number. A Baggage Irregularity Report is completed, which includes drawings of types of bags to help identification. This report also records information about the colour of the missing bag, any distinguishing features and details of the contents, as well as the passenger's temporary and permanent contact details.

Many airlines belong to an international baggage tracing system called WorldTracer. It is used at almost 2000 airports around the world. Airlines report details of baggage they are searching for, and unclaimed baggage they have found, to the WorldTracer computer system. These reports are compared and matched, enabling the vast majority of bags to be found and reunited with their owners.

Airlines may provide the passenger with a toiletry kit and authority to purchase essentials,

BRITISH AIRWAYS

LIMITS OF LIABILITY

The applicable limits of liability for your journey on a flight operated by British Airways are as follows:

1. There are no financial limits for death or bodily injury and the air carrier may make an advance payment to meet immediate economic needs of the person entitled to claim compensation;
2. In the case of destruction, loss of, or damage or delay to baggage, 1,000 Special Drawing Rights (approximately £820 or EUR 1,230) and, if the value of your baggage is greater than this limit, you should inform the carrier at check-in or ensure that it is fully insured prior to travel;
3. In the case of delay to your journey, 4,150 Special Drawing Rights (approximately £3,500 or EUR 5,100).

If your journey also involves carriage by other airlines, you should contact them for information on their limits of liability.

This notice conforms to the requirements of European Community Regulation (EC) No. 889/2002.

BA/T1824 ASTRON

British Airways' Limits of Liability leaflet is handed out with every ticket

Source: British Airways

up to a fairly low financial limit, whilst the search for missing baggage is in hand. If the traveller wishes to claim compensation from the airline, they normally must do so in writing within seven days. Liability for loss of baggage is limited by a number of regulations, depending upon the airline and country. It is typically restricted to around £820. Passengers should also advise their travel insurers, who will normally settle the balance of any such claim.

If the luggage is lost or stolen whilst it is in the possession of the traveller, they should report the loss to the tour operator's local representative if on a package holiday and to the location where the baggage was lost (e.g. coach operator or hotel), as well as the police, making sure that a copy of the police report is obtained.

Arrest and imprisonment

It makes good sense to be aware of the laws in foreign countries, for example the local laws about consuming alcohol, drugs (including those which might be considered as medication in the traveller's own country), driving, jay-walking, smoking, and chewing gum in public areas. Such information is readily available from the FCO and other countries' embassies.

If arrested, travellers should follow the instructions of the police and not do anything to inflame the situation. They should ask the police

to immediately contact their embassy or consulate. That is their right. The embassy or consulate can provide a lot of help, including contacting and visiting travellers who have been detained; providing information on the local legal system, prison arrangements, and suitably qualified English-speaking lawyers; and checking that the traveller's medical needs are met and relatives are advised.

The Foreign and Commonwealth Office can provide a tremendous amount of advice and support to its citizens in a variety of circumstances. However, the FCO makes it clear that its consuls cannot:

* get anyone out of prison
* give legal advice or start court proceedings
* get better treatment in hospital or prison than is given to local nationals
* investigate a crime
* pay travellers' bills
* pay travel costs, except in special circumstances
* do the work of travel agents, airlines, banks or motoring organisations
* demand travellers be treated as British if they have dual nationality and are in the country of their second nationality.

> **CASE STUDY**
> **Don't get into a fight!**
> You are the local resort representative for Megabreak Holidays. It is 3 am and one of your clients has called you in a state of panic to say that her boyfriend has been mugged by two people outside a disco. One of the assailants has ran off with her boyfriend's passport, money and air ticket. He had fought with the other mugger, and both the mugger and her boyfriend were arrested. The last she saw of her boyfriend was in a police van, with a bloody head.
>
> 1 What will you do in these circumstances?
> 2 Who will you contact, or advise your clients to contact? Why?

Major situations

Somewhere in the world there are major emergency situations (*force majeure*) happening now. These are either man-made or natural. In this last section we will look at a few such situations.

Wars

Probably nobody alive today will be able to remember a time when there was not an international or civil war somewhere in the world.

> **Think it over ...**
>
> As a group, think about the situation in the world today. List any international conflicts between countries, or civil wars, or unrest within countries, happening now.

Travellers need to be warned if they are considering travelling to places where there is conflict or a major emergency. It may be that the entire country is in conflict, or that there are pockets of unrest and civil disturbance within the country. We need to warn our clients of such situations. The Foreign and Commonwealth Office will provide information and advice, which may be as severe as advising strongly against entry to that country, to the extent that anyone who does so will not have the support there of the British government's representative.

Terrorist attacks

Since the start of the 21st century, terrorist attacks have been very much in the news. These attacks could happen in any country where the terrorists believe their political, religious, ideological or similar interests have been wronged, or even in neutral countries but at locations, buildings, offices, etc. linked to the country the terrorists have a grievance against. Once again, the Foreign and Commonwealth Office monitors countries closely, watching for situations which could make them vulnerable to attack. Since 9/11, insurance companies have become much tougher on the circumstances under which they will provide cover, and most exclude any costs or disruption arising from such events.

Industrial disputes

Travel arrangements can sometimes be disrupted by industrial disputes, particularly if it is travel industry people who are in dispute. Such situations are likely to be covered by travel insurance, but your customers should also expect the organisation involved in the dispute to make the best possible alternative arrangements for them. Tour operators and travel agents will need to play their part in assisting and must have a good communications network so that they are aware of the current situation and can find solutions.

Natural disasters (e.g. volcanic eruptions, flooding)

We know where live volcanoes are and usually there are warnings that they are likely to erupt, so travel industry organisations can work with local authorities to evacuate their clients from the area, and make suitable accommodation and travel arrangements for them. The efficiency of your local travel representative will be crucial to the success of the evacuation. Earthquakes and floods are less predictable, as we know from the terrible events of the Indian Ocean tsunami in December 2004 and the South East Asia earthquake in October 2005.

Severe weather conditions

Weather conditions can be forecast with some success. We know that there is a hurricane season

Tourists in the entertainment district of Patong in Phuket, Thailand, after the devastation by the Asian tsunami in December 2004

in the West Indies and Gulf of Mexico which peaks between August and October; a typhoon season in the western Pacific Ocean and China mostly between July and October; and monsoons which bring torrential rains to India from April to October. What we do not know is how severe these events will be. There is generally a state of preparedness in such regions, and local authorities and businesses will have emergency plans in readiness. Such events may result in transportation being cancelled, cruise ships being diverted, hotels closing facilities, shops and businesses shutting down. Planned evacuation may even be needed.

Major outbreaks of disease

With good sense, our customers will have protected themselves against anticipated diseases and will have paid attention to the Foreign and Commonwealth Office advice. However, outbreaks do occur and it is then a matter of containing the outbreak, and finding and eradicating the cause as quickly as possible.

Skills practice

Here are three diseases which have featured in the news since 2000:

- SARS
- Norwalk virus
- Avian flu.

1 Research these three conditions and find out the following:
   - What they are and what causes them
   - When and where they happened
   - What action was taken to limit or eradicate the outbreaks.

2 Evaluate the effect of these on the travel and tourism industry.

Handling emergency situations

Travel and tourism organisations all have emergency plans which identify key contacts within and outside the organisation, and describe how and when to initiate the emergency plan and what to do during and after the emergency. Many tour operators have crisis centres which they open and man with trained staff in the event of a crisis.

Fortunately, train, aircraft and ship accidents are very rare, but transport organisations have comprehensive arrangements to handle them, and have refresher training events on a regular basis.

Crises can be complex and need a lot of trained staff to handle them calmly. In the event of an aircraft accident, the airline and airport authority, in co-operation with the emergency services, will open a command centre to take strategic control over events and an emergency call centre for the many calls they will receive from anxious friends and relatives. If the accident happens on or near the airport, they will open separate rooms for those who survived the accident, for friends and relatives who were waiting for the flight to arrive and for them to meet the survivors. Staff will also need to man a centre which will look after subsequent arrangements for those affected. They may need to go to survivors in hospitals and hotels. In major emergencies, governmental departments (e.g. the Foreign and Commonwealth Office) will play a key role in determining the size and nature of the problem, deciding on action and implementing it in co-ordination with other organisations which are involved.

Skills practice

As a group of three or four, carry out this activity.

You are the operations manager for the tour operator Island Shores. A hurricane has hit an island on which you have 275 guests staying in three hotels. You operate a charter flight to the island twice a week. You have four initial decisions to make:

- Who will be affected by this event
- What needs to be done
- How to do it
- Who you must involve.

Key points

- There is substantial travel advice and help available for travellers, from a number of official and industry sources.
- Most of the risks of travel can be removed or reduced by good preparation before travelling, and sensible behaviour whilst travelling.
- Government and travel industry organisations have contingencies for handling major emergency situations.

Knowledge check

The following questions will help you check what you have learned in this unit.

1 What changes did IATA make in 1979?
2 What are the four main functions of the CAA?
3 What is a 'Package'?
4 What is an ATOL and who issues it?
5 What are ABTA's aims?
6 What compensation must be provided by an EU airline if a booked passenger is denied boarding on a flight from an EU country, due to overbookings?
7 What requirements were introduced in 2004 under the Disability Discrimination Act?
8 What requirements does the Data Protection Act place upon organisations and their staff?
9 What authority, in addition to a passport, might a traveller need to enter another country? Who issues that additional authority?
10 Why might airline staff check a passenger's travel documents, other than their ticket and boarding card?
11 Name the five major diseases.
12 How is malaria transmitted?
13 Name four ways travellers can minimise the risk to their funds, before or during their travels.
14 Name four things UK embassies/consulates cannot do for their nationals.
15 When is the peak hurricane season in the West Indies and Gulf of Mexico?

Resources

Books

The Traveller's Companion, Think Publishing 2004.
The Complete Family Medical Guide, Hinkler Books Pty Ltd., Australia, 2004.

Websites

Air Transport Users Council: www.auc.org.uk

Association of British Travel Agents (ABTA): www.abta.com

Association of Independent Tour Operators (AITO): www.aito.co.uk

Civil Aviation Authority (CAA): www.caa.co.uk

Directors of Health Promotion and Education, USA: www.dhpe.org

Disability Policy Division, Department of Work & Pensions: www.disability.gov.uk

European Aviation Safety Agency: www.casa.eu.int

European Union: www.europa.eu.int

Federation of Tour Operators (FTO): www.fto.uk

Guild of Travel Management Companies (formerly Guild of British Travel Agents): www.gbta-guild.com

Information Commissioner: www.informationcommissioner.gov.uk

International Air Transport Association: www.iata.org

Joint Aviation Authorities: www.jaa.nl

Office for National Statistics: www.statistics.gov.uk

Office of Public Sector Information: www.opsi.gov.uk

UK Department of Health travellers information: www.dh.gov.uk/travellers

UKinbound (formerly British Incoming Tour Operators): www.UKinbound.org

UK Passport Service: www.ukpa.gov.uk

UK visa information site: www.ukvisas.gov.uk

World Health Organisation: www.who.int.

World Health Organisation Global Atlas: http://globalatlas.who.int.

Resort operations

Introduction

Many of you may wish to work as an overseas representative. The idea of working in a holiday destination for six months at a time may seem like an extended holiday in itself. Sun, parties, beach and getting away from home and the UK may all spring to mind! And certainly it is an exciting life style, but glamorous it is not! Long hours, difficult customers, tired hoteliers, flight delays and endless welcome meetings are also part of the reps role.

This unit will give you an insight into the reality of what happens in resort offices of tour operators. The activities will depend on the size of the tour operator, its products (e.g. summer sun or winter sports) and the location of the resort. You will learn about different types of tour operators, the range of resort staff they employ and how they all contribute towards preparing for and dealing with customers in resorts.

You will research the key duties of a resort representative and develop skills that are required for this role. Many of the skills needed will make use of those customer service skills already explored in Unit 2.

Representatives are the face of tour operators, that is customers will go on holiday and the only person they may meet from the tour operator is the rep. Thus the representative plays a vital role in determining customer satisfaction and repeat business! Tour operators, therefore, spend huge amounts of money ensuring their representatives are customer-focused individuals who are able to manage difficult situations and create 'win win' situations. You will examine how tour operators train their staff as well as the type of information representatives need to know in order to provide the excellent service that is expected of them.

How you will be assessed

Throughout this unit, activities and tasks will help you to develop your knowledge and understanding. Some of these could be used as material for the final assessment. Case studies are included to add industry relevance and demonstrate how aspects of resort operations are carried out in particular tour operators.

After studying this unit you will be able to demonstrate and apply your knowledge of:

* The activities of the resort office
* The duties of a resort representative
* The significance of induction, training and product knowledge in delivering high-quality customer service.

6.1 The activities of the resort office

When you think of a resort representative what comes to mind? Is it summer sun, beaches, welcome meetings, parties and smiling faces? This is the image most people have of the resort representative. It is after all the case that most of us meet reps on our summer sun holiday. These are the people who ensure that we have a smooth holiday, answer our queries and take us on excursions. It all seems so simple. But behind the scenes a lot of hard work is going on. In many resorts, teams of staff are working in a resort office to ensure everything runs smoothly and to provide a back-up service when it does not! In the first part of this unit, we will focus on the activities of the resort office. But before we do, it is important to establish that there are many tour operators, offering many different types of holiday and that they all work in different ways.

Get to know the tour operators!

Many of you will be going on holiday this summer and it is very likely that you will travel with one of the 'Big Four' tour operators (TUI UK, First Choice, Thomas Cook, My Travel) to a summer sun location. These four companies clearly dominate the UK tour operator market, and as a result employ the most overseas personnel. However, we must not forget the other tour operators, the full range of products on offer and the fact that holiday locations include mountainous and countryside locations too. The top 40 UK tour operators are listed in Table 6.1, but there are also many other smaller specialist companies within the UK who also need overseas staff.

Table 6.1 Passengers authorised by top 40 ATOL holders

FOR YEAR FROM...	JUNE 2005	JUNE 2004	% CHG
1 TUI UK	4,753,111	4,822,263	−1
2 First Choice	2,623,449	2,392,116	10
3 Thomas Cook	2,489,495	2,516,061	−1
4 My Travel	2,041,554	2,830,756	−28
5 Expedia	800,633	493,889	62
6 Gold Medal	675,000	654,848	3
7 Avro	618,999	620,089	0
8 Freedom Flights	530,162	251,455	111
9 Direct Holidays	521,296	679,823	−23
10 Trailfinders	490,539	564,974	−13
11 Lotus (Dial-a-Flight)	477,113	414,999	15
12 Travelworld Vacations	457,975	353,046	30
13 Thomas Cook Retail	411,499	406,734	1
14 Panorama Holidays	402,551	409,675	−2
15 Cosmosair	380,000	402,449	−6
16 Virgin Holidays	374,312	359,428	4
17 Kuoni	298,629	271,473	10
18 The Destination Group	279,201	225,812	24
19 Libra Holidays	267,500	283,000	−5
20 Flight Centre (UK)	265,715	182,603	46
21 Kosmar Villa Holidays	255,000	252,000	1
22 Travel 2	233,749	210,364	11
23 Really Great Holiday Co	226,000	230,000	−2
24 Hotelplan (Inghams)	202,500	186,200	9
25 Globespan	196,508	327,150	−40
26 Co-operative Group	186,004	125,708	48
27 Carnival	185,000	275,412	−33
28 Travelcoast	175,060	75,130	133
29 Saga	162,644	161,534	1
30 HCCT (CT2 Holidays)	159,278	282,400	−44
31 Thomas Cook Signature	156,650	144,154	9
32 BCT Travel Group2	144,200	237,500	−39
33 Balkan Holidays	138,150	125,500	10
34 The Airline Seat Co	123,945	81,858	51
35 AirMiles Travel Co	117,174	188,846	−38
36 Future Travel	113,940	66,809	71
37 Travelocity	112,470	141,698	−21
38 STA	107,583	218,316	−51
39 Travelbag	106,291	230,891	−54
40 James Villa Holidays	105,900	100,100	6

Source: Trade Travel Gazette 8 July 2005

The Association of Independent Tour Operators (AITO) is an organisation representing about 160 specialist tour operators. Go to the members list of their website, www.aito.co.uk, to carry out the following tasks.

1 Select four specialist tour operators and for each complete a table similar to the one below. (You may also need to check out each company website.) An example has been given to start you off.

2 Carry out the same activity for one of the Big Four tour operators.

3 Compare your findings with the rest of your group.

4 Do you think the different tour operators need different types of people?

Name of operator	Product (e.g. winter sun, ski, city break, culture)	Destinations	Customer types	I think the role of the rep would involve ...
Alternative Travel Group (ATG)	Adventure/culture (walking and cycling holidays)	Austria Czech Republic France Greece Italy Portugal Spain Turkey Jordan India	Active people Most 40+ Usually couples, some singles and families	Guiding customers each day on their walk between destinations. Sorting out accommodation each night. Providing information (especially about weather), dealing with problems (e.g. injury so guest could not walk), etc.

Think it over ...

TUI UK, First Choice, Thomas Cook, My Travel accounted for approximately 46 per cent of the package market in 2004 – the lowest level since January 1998. The figure compares with 49 per cent in 2003 and 57 per cent in 2001.

1 Why do you think this trend is occurring?

2 What are the implications for overseas reps?

Think it over ...

What has been the impact of recent television programmes focusing on resort representatives? Consider the appeal of the representative's role, the impact on recruitment and the image of reps.

The overseas operation

Holidays are planned and set up in the UK by the operations department of a tour operator. This may take two years! However, once clients have arrived overseas it is the overseas team who deals with all the day-to-day aspects of 'operating' the holiday.

It is clear that the overseas operation will vary from tour operator to tour operator. It will depend on:

✱ *Size of tour operator (number of passengers carried)* The company may be one of the Big Four, with thousands of passengers in hundreds of summer sun resorts from May to October, or a small specialist tour operator with 20 passengers arriving each week to a ski chalet.

✱ *Number of overseas staff needed* Clearly the large tour operators need lots of overseas staff and therefore have teams in their major resorts. The members of the staff teams all have different roles and report to a local manager based in the resort office. The reps will get all their information via the resort office. By contrast, representatives for specialist companies may work alone or just with one other colleague. Their manager may even be based in the UK and their information will come directly from the company's UK operations department.

✱ *Product* The tour operator may be offering beach holidays (summer/winter sun) to which clients travel on a charter or a fly-drive package every week on any day and need to be greeted when they arrive. Ski clients need ski hire, ski lessons and lift passes to be organised – very different to the needs of the summer sun customer!

✱ *Customer types* Families may need the services of a children's rep, be able to book excursions with the resort rep and enjoy having a team of people available if there are any queries. However, some customers may want to be more independent – they may book a villa, hire a car and only want to see the rep if there is a problem.

✱ *Location* Tour operators have overseas staff at beach locations for their summer and winter sun programmes. Some operators have winter staff in mountain resorts looking after their ski clients, while others may have representatives in the same resorts in the summer looking after adventure seekers or even coach tours. Some overseas representatives may be accompanying coach tours and be in a different location each night. Overseas roles can be in Europe, but there are also opportunities in long-haul destinations.

Although the activities of the resort office do vary from tour operator to tour operator, there are many activities that are common to all. The tasks carried out in a typical resort office for one of the large tour operators include.

✱ Receiving hotel rooming lists and any special requests from the UK office. Disseminating this information to hotel reps and hotels.

✱ Passing on information about late bookings and no shows (i.e. amending rooming lists and advising hoteliers/reps).

✱ Organising transfers: booking coaches, organising transfer reps/rotas, checking flight times and advising reps of delays.

✱ Organising optional excursions: setting prices, booking coaches, collating numbers, booking any extras (e.g. meals or rides), organising guides.

✱ Providing resources to staff (e.g. presenters and notice boards, administration forms and IT facilities).

✱ Dealing with administration: the resort office is a central point for reps to collect information, be paid their commissions, and where they can access ICT facilities and meet colleagues.

✱ Dealing with major problems and accidents.

✱ Team management: team leaders, resort and area managers will use the resort office to meet with staff.

The resort office acts as a central point. Senior staff are located here. Team meetings will also be held at the office. All communication from the UK is to this central point, from where all resort staff will collect information, such as rooming lists, flight delays, booking amendments, etc. If the tour operator is small and does not have an office, then all details are sent from the UK directly to the rep. This could be by fax, email or even courier. Small tour operators usually set up an agreement with a hotel that the rep can use their office or even just the fax. The rep then uses their own bedroom as an office!

Think it over ...

Thomson's staff all have pigeonholes in the resort offices. Consider the different types of resort staff and what type of information they might find in their pigeonhole.

We will now investigate in more detail some of the key activities carried out by the overseas operation.

Rooming lists

Rooming lists are downloaded by the administrative staff in the resort office, usually about three days prior to the arrival of the pax (passengers). This list provides detailed information about the passengers who are due to arrive, their rooming requirements and any special requests (e.g. sea view, ground-floor room or balcony). Where a different board basis is offered, the rooming list will also indicate which passengers are booked as bed and breakfast, which want half-board and which want full-board accommodation. You will also be able to work out from the rooming list the number of children arriving and their ages (this is particularly important if you are a children's representative – you will be able to plan the next week's activities!).

Key terms

Rooming list A list of pax and their room requirements. It is usually sent directly to the hotel as well as the resort office.

Pax An industry term for passengers.

Bed and breakfast Accommodation with breakfast.

Half-board Accommodation with dinner.

Full-board Accommodation with breakfast, lunch and dinner.

Much of the information on the rooming lists will either be abbreviated or in a recognised 'code'. Some will be a tour operator's own shorthand, for example 1RO3B is Thomson shorthand for a 1-bedroom apartment that sleeps 3. Many abbreviations are common to all operators. Airports are indicated by three-letter codes that are internationally recognised. You should try learning some!

Skills practice

Rhoda is a transfer rep working in Spain. She has seven flights arriving this week from the UK. Their three-letter codes are below.

ABZ

BHX

EXT

LVL

LGW

NWI

BFS

1 Using information in the table below, find out where Rhoda's pax are coming from.

2 All flights are arriving at AGP. What resources can you use to find out at which airport she will be working?

Code	UK airport
ABZ	Aberdeen
BFS	Belfast
BHX	Birmingham
BRS	Bristol
CWL	Cardiff
EMA	East Midlands
EDI	Edinburgh
EXT	Exeter
GLA	Glasgow
LBA	Leeds/Bradford
LVL	Liverpool
LGW	London Gatwick
LHR	London Heathrow
STN	London Stansted
MAN	Manchester
NCL	Newcastle
NWI	Norwich

Understanding the rooming lists

The following notes indicate the kind of detail that is recorded on the rooming lists used by tour operators.

1 The booking reference should be used on all paperwork. This reference is given to customers when they booked their holiday and all information can be found in the computer by entering this reference number.

2 All passengers' names will be given as they appear on their passport. The first name is the lead name and sometimes only this name appears on additional paperwork.

3 On many rooming lists ages are only given for children aged between 2 and 11. Under 2 they are classed as infants. Over 11 they are charged as adults.

4 Room and facilities columns show everything the guests have booked and paid for. The rep must make sure they receive these!

5 Board options are shown here.

6 Most tour operators automatically provide a cot for infants. If cots are required for two-year-olds these must be requested.

7 Some guests will book the insurance provided by the operator. If so, Y will appear in this column. If they have not, they must advise who their insurers are. This information is sometimes included on rooming lists and sometimes provided separately.

Skills practice

1 The following are common abbreviations used by tour operators to indicate type of room and facilities available:

AC   BL   CS   PB/WC   SH   SV

Research a tour operator's brochure to find out what these abbreviations mean. Are there any others used?

2 You are working as a rep for Seasun Holidays and have just received the rooming list in Figure 6.1. Using this rooming list, the research you did for task 1, and the information in 'Understanding the rooming lists' above, answer the following questions. (**Note**: The Figure 6.1 table heading numbers correspond to the numbered notes in 'Understanding the rooming lists'.)

(a) What facilities have Mr and Mrs Aspin booked?

(b) How many children will be at the hotel and how many are infants?

(c) At what age does an infant become a child?

(d) Who has booked car hire and for how long?

(e) How many guests have not booked Seasun's own insurance?

(f) How do you think the holiday code is formed? (Look carefully at its construction.)

(g) Which airport are guests coming into?

(h) Which airline are they flying with? (You can work this out from the flight number.)

Seasun Holidays: Rooming List

Holiday code   PalReV
Resort: Palma, Mallorca
Accommodation: Belle Vue
Dates: 12–26 June 2006 (14 nights)

Flight details   Arrive 1050 on 23 Jul   BY561   MAN/PMI
                    Depart 1150 on 06 Aug   BY231   PMI/MAN

1 Booking ref.	2 Name	3 Age	4 Room and facilities	5 Board	6 Cot	7 Ins
98345	Mr K Towers	A	Twin PB WC BL SV	BB	0	N
	Mrs H Towers	A	Low floor	BB		
			Car hire 3 days type C			
12376	Mr P Aoday	A		HB	01	Y
	Ms K Dalgo	A	HB			
	Inf. Y Dalgo-Ashday	01				
39548	Mr R Tabecki	A	Twin PB WC BL	HB	02	Y
	Mrs J Tabecki	A	Twin PB WC BL	HB		
	Mstr T Tabecki	02	Adjoining rooms	HB		
	Mr D Thomas	A		HB		
	Ms J Vickery	A		HB		
	Miss F Thomas	01				
30987	Mr R Aspin	A	Twin PB WC BL SV	HB	0	N
	Mrs J Aspin	A	Quiet room	HB		
45374	Ms K Smith	A	Twin PB WC	BB	0	Y
	Ms D Pashay	A	Extra bed	BB		
	Ms R Holker	A	Room overlooking pool	BB		

Total guests: 14 + 2 infants
    09 guests half board
    05 guests bed and breakfast

Figure 6.1 Sample rooming list

There will be one rooming list for each property (e.g. hotel, self-catering apartment block or chalet). A copy will be put in the pigeonholes of those representatives responsible for that accommodation, and a copy will be forwarded to the hotelier/accommodation provider. If the hotelier has email this can be done electronically. However, faxes are still widely used in resorts. The representative may even be responsible for taking the rooming list to small hoteliers or chalet owners personally.

Think it over ...

Do you think it strange that a rooming list is called a rooming list?

Although it does indeed include room requirements, it actually includes a lot of other information. List all the other information that may be included on a rooming list.

Excursions

CASE STUDY

Excursions

Genine works as a tour manager for Cusmar Tours, taking coach parties around Europe. One of the tours she does is a 13-day tour of Europe, which includes 6 nights in St Anton. It is during her stay in St Anton that Genine earns her money! On arrival in St Anton, Genine carries out a welcome meeting where she spends some time telling the guests about the excursions available. She runs an excursion on four of the five days they are in resort. Although the numbers for each day vary, most are very popular. For example, everyone wants to go over the border to Italy, where they can buy fantastic leather goods, and many want to spend a day in Innsbruck. The half-day trip to the glacier is less popular, even though a ride on a ski lift is included. The trip to Liechtenstein (the smallest country in Europe!) also does not sell well – despite the fact that you can buy fantastic chocolate there.

Genine will run the excursions as long as there are 10 people booked. She will be guiding each excursion, so although she earns money if they all sell well, she often hopes one does not run, as it means she gets an extra day off!

When selling the excursions, Genine simply completes a booking chart as she collects the money. This ensures that she won't leave without anyone. The only other thing she has to do is book anything that is included in the price, for example for the glacier trip she telephones the ski lift company to advise of numbers. Of course, she always tells the coach driver which excursions have sold well and on which days he is required. (She doesn't even have to book a coach as she has her own coach and coach driver with her for the 14-day duration of the tour.)

1 **Find out where St Anton is.**
2 **Find a similar coach tour to the one operated by Cusmar Tours. What excursions could Cusmar introduce to replace the less popular excursions to Liechtenstein and the glacier?**
3 **Why do you think Genine does not run an excursion if less than 10 people are booked?**
4 **What are the advantages and disadvantages to herself, the tour operator and the driver of not running excursions?**

As you can see from the case study, the organisation of excursions for reps working by themselves (with their own coach and driver) is relatively straightforward. If they sell enough excursions, they simply book any extras required and then work as a guide on the excursion.

In a large resort office, things are quite different. There may be as many as 20 reps selling the same excursions. Once the welcome meeting (where they sell excursions) is over, reps will take their sales figures to the office where administrative staff will collate the numbers and book coaches as required. Any other bookings will also be done by the administrative staff, for example a local meal or a ride in a telepherique to the top of a mountain may be included in the price. A rota will determine which rep is accompanying each excursion – giving others a chance of a day off!

Liaison with local agencies

As the central administrative point, the resort office will be where any contact with local agencies will be made. The resort manager will deal with more serious issues, while appropriate staff will deal with administrative details. Examples of liaison with local agencies could include:

* A hotelier who is concerned about next week's bookings. He has noticed from the rooming list that a large number of young women have requested to all be on the same floor. He has already asked the operator twice not to send any groups of young women to his hotel – last year he received many complaints from families because of the 'laddish' behaviour of a hen party.

* A ski school contacts the resort office. They are contracted to provide English-speaking instructors, but due to the large number of bookings at February half-term, they are not going to be able to do so.

* The resort manager is concerned by a spate of apparent thefts at the airport. Arriving passengers have received offers of help to take their luggage to the waiting coaches. They presumed these people were either porters or employed by the tour operator. The luggage was taken to the coaches, but never reached the hotel. The resort manager has asked the reps to be vigilant and advise arriving passengers to take care of their own luggage. However, she also wishes to discuss this with the operations manager of the airport.

* A restaurant owner who provides passengers with lunch each Wednesday on their excursion to Rhonda (from Malaga) has been told that it will no longer be required. The owner is dependent upon passing trade and telephones to find out why he is no longer getting this large weekly booking.

Airport transfers

Many of you will have experience of an airport transfer, where you have been met at an overseas airport by a smiling representative with a clipboard, had your name ticked off, and been sent to a specific coach. Once en route, your transfer rep will have given you lots of information before

Holiday reps holding up placards to attract the attention of incoming holidaymakers at Palma airport, Majorca

dropping you at your hotel. Simple enough! However, behind the scenes a lot goes on to make this first impression positive, and to get tired, and maybe stressed, passengers to their accommodation quickly and without fuss.

Key terms

Transfer To tranfer involves taking people from the airport to their accommodation or vice versa.

Arrival transfer Meeting people at the airport and taking them to their accommodation.

Departure transfer Taking people from their accommodation to the airport at the end of their holidays.

Accompanied transfer The transfer has a rep on board.

'See-off' The rep puts everyone on the coach, explains to them what is going to happen and when they will arrive. The pax are then left with the driver to take them to their destination.

Full transfer The rep collects departing passengers from their accommodation and takes them to the airport. Once they have all checked in and gone through to the departure lounge, the rep will go to arrivals to meet the inbound pax (the inbound plane is usually the one that will take the outbound pax back to the UK).

How transfers are operated by the resort office will vary from tour operator to tour operator, but also from resort to resort and week to week. For example, in some resorts a rep may transfer departing pax to the airport, and stay for several hours meeting flights and 'seeing-off' passengers, before getting on the last transfer back to the resort once all the flights have landed. This would be the case in larger arrival destinations, such as Mallorca, Malaga or Ibiza, where flights may be arriving every day from the UK. In other areas, flights could be arriving just once or twice a week.

Each tour operator has its own procedures and paperwork, but a general indication of what is involved in a full transfer is included in the chart below.

Two days before arrival and departure
- *Rep receives rooming lists for arriving pax and departure details for those in resort.*
- *Rep examines rooming lists and advises hotelier.*
- *Rep puts departure details on notice board (flight times and coach pick-up times) and arranges courtesy rooms if necessary.*
- *Rep checks what transfer duties he/she has and if they will be 'on duty' in the hotel as normal.*
- *Leaves message about changed 'duty hours'.*

On the day of arrival and departure
- *Arrives at first pick-up point with all documents and looking smart, at least 15 minutes before scheduled departures.*
- *Meets driver, agrees best pick-up route.*
- *Collects pax from accommodation, checking names as they go along.*
- *Does head count at each stop.*

At airport departure
- *Guides pax to departure check-in desks.*
- *Works with other reps to ensure all checked in smoothly.*
- *Says good-bye to pax.*

At airport arrival
- *Reports to airport manager, and updates on delays, no shows, extras.*
- *Advises colleagues of coach number and where it is.*
- *Greets pax as they arrive.*
- *Directs them to their coaches. (Some reps in coach park to guide pax.)*
- *Does name check and a head count on the coach, once all passengers are on board.*
- *Welcomes pax.*
- *Deals with queries.*

During transfer to resort
- *Establishes rapport with pax.*
- *Advises pax about welcome meeting, weather, etc. as appropriate.*

Arrival at resort/accomodation
- *Accompanies pax to reception.*

Figure 6.2 A flow chart of a full transfer　　　　Source: Adapted from Thomson's training manual

Courtesy rooms These are rooms provided free of charge by the hotel to groups of passengers so that they can leave luggage. Courtesy rooms are often required if guests have to check out of their rooms several hours before their return transfer.

Good organisation is essential for a transfer day to run smoothly. The activities of the resort office in ensuring this involves:

* Booking the right number of coaches

* Devising staff rotas

* Passing on all information about extras and late bookings

* Advising about flight delays

* Providing an excellent back-up service to deal with any problems as they arise (see problems and complaints later in this section).

Overbooking the allocation

Long before the guests book their holidays, hotel contractors will have visited local hotels to contract beds for the following season. Some of these will be taken on guarantee contracts, others on allocation.

Key terms

Contract beds A tour operator will negotiate with a hotelier to agree the number of beds the tour operator will have the following season, the price and the 'conditions', for example half-board, self-catering, all rooms with balconies. Large tour operators will have guarantee and/or allocation contracts.

Guarantee contract Such a contract is where tour operators guarantee to pay for the beds, whether they fill them or not.

Allocation contract This is where a tour operator takes a number of beds per week (e.g. 30). This contract means that the tour operator expects to fill 30 beds, but only confirms with the hotelier the exact numbers a few weeks before customers arrive. The tour operator only pays for those beds used.

Skills practice

Review the advantages and disadvantages of a guarantee contract in the table below and complete the table for allocation contracts:

Guarantee contract	Advantages	Disadvantages
To the hotelier	Money in advance Knows beds are filled for the season	Can become dependent upon one tour operator
To the tour operator	Knows exactly how many beds available	Costly

Allocation contract	Advantages	Disadvantages
To the hotelier		
To the tour operator		

One hotelier may have several allocation contracts, each with a different tour operator. As an example, take the fictional case of the Hotel Belle Vue. It has 110 beds. The hotel manager, Antonio Dalio, however, has signed four allocation contracts for the summer season, each for 30 beds. This means that if all four tour operators fill their contracts, the Hotel Bellevue will be 10 beds short – an overbooking! Antonio will not know that the overbooking is going to occur until the tour operator confirms exact numbers a few weeks before guests arrive.

It is in the resort office's interests to make sure each hotelier gets the exact numbers in good time. As long as this happens, it is usually the responsibility of the hotelier to find alternative accommodation for the customer. However, it is the representative's job to advise the customer about the overbooking. This is a difficult task, and although guests are normally upgraded, advising the guests of the changed situation may need someone more skilled than a representative. This is usually the role of a team leader, guest service manager, or someone else with experience.

All tour operators are aware that hoteliers offer more beds on 'allocation contracts' than they actually have – after all, by ensuring their properties are always full, hoteliers are able to offer tour operators beds at a good price (and so keep holiday costs low). However, this is a sensitive subject. Which guests the hotel manager decides to 'bump' may depend on his relationship with the contractor, the resort manager, or the representative. It is in the resort team's interest that their own guests remain in the allocated hotel – so they must try to maintain a positive rapport with hoteliers.

We will be looking in more detail at dealing with overbooking later in the unit (page 268).

Complaints and emergencies

People on holiday are likely to complain if facilities do not match up to their expectations or if something goes wrong. Reps, with the support of senior staff, are expected to solve as many complaints as they can in resort so that the customer is satisfied and does not pursue the complaint once they get home. Companies do work hard to minimise complaints, but most, if not all, reps will be on the receiving end of complaints whoever they work for, particularly if the weather is poor. ABTA says it receives over 18,000 holiday complaints a year. Theoretically, these are complaints that were not resolved by tour operators, so the customers complained to ABTA. However, some customers may go straight to ABTA without complaining to their tour operator, as ABTA is so well known.

Customers are told in the booking conditions (found in the brochure) that they should report complaints to their rep, so that the rep has an opportunity to resolve the complaint. The following extract from the Thomas Cook Worldwide signature brochure demonstrates this point.

If the complaint remains unresolved, the rep, or a senior member of the resort team, will ask customers to complete a customer report form to record their complaint. Most tour operators have a two-part form. The customer completes the first part of the form and gives it to the rep. The second part of this document is completed by the

If you have a complaint

We aim to provide the best Holiday possible. If you are not satisfied with your holiday please complain as soon as possible to the *relevant* person (for example the hotel management). If they cannot help you must tell your Thomas Cook representative and we will do everything reasonably possible to sort the problem out. If they are not available or you are not satisfied with their response you must contact our UK Duty Manager on 44 1733 411911 straight away. If you are still not satisfied, ask your Holiday rep for a Customer Relations Report Form. Fill this in and return a copy of it to him or her. You will have to keep a copy. When you get back home, send your copy to our offices in the UK, together with a covering letter, within 28 days of returning home. If you have special needs which prevent you from writing to us then, where possible, we will accept details of your complaint over the telephone.

We should point out that failure to follow the above procedures, and/or failure to complain as set out above within 28 days of your return may reduce or extinguish any rights you have to claim compensation from us, or from any relevant supplier. Any such rights will be reduced or extinguished if, had you done so, you or we could have taken steps to reduce the loss or damage suffered or entirely prevented it from being suffered. It is difficult and sometimes impossible to properly investigate a complaint if we are not told about it during the holiday and reasonably quickly once the holiday is over. Your right to compensation may be reduced or extinguished should any delay in your complaint being notified during or after the holiday prevent us from carrying out a proper investigation.

We aim to sort out all complaints ourselves, but if this is not possible your complaint can be considered under a scheme devised by the Association of British Travel Agents and administered by the Chartered Institute of Arbitrators. We will give you details of this scheme if you ask. The scheme does not apply to claims over £15,000 in total or more than £5,000 a person, or to claims mainly about illness or injury. To take advantage of the scheme you must contact the Chartered Institute of Arbitrators within 9 months of returning from your Holiday.

Thomas Cook Signature Limited
17 Coningsby Road
Peterborough PL3 8SB
Registered in England No. 4088652

All rights reserved. No part of this brochure may be produced, stored in a retrieval system or transmitted, in any form or by any means, without prior permission from Thomas Cook Signature Limited.

2nd edition; June 2004

Extract from the booking conditions for Thomas Cook holidays

rep, adding additional information about the actions that have already been taken (e.g. changed room, free excursion offered). This information can then be used by the customer relations department at head office, when dealing with the complaint in the UK. It is essential that it is completed accurately, factually and objectively – it may be used in court and will almost certainly determine whether or not a guest receives compensation.

We will look at the skills to deal with complaints later (page 265). While the rep may be able to deal with the complaint themselves, they must make sure that the manager, and maybe even the head office, is aware of the complaint.

CUSTOMER REPORT FORM

Customer Report Form

FORM NUMBER **343098325**

Tour Operator [   ]

Resort (e.g. Palma Nova) _____ Area (e.g. Majorca) _____

Customer Name _____ **Booking Ref. No** _____

Accommodation _____ UK Departure Date _____

Customer UK Address _____

_____ Postcode _____

Customer Telephone _____ Rep Name _____ Date _____

Please give details below of issues raised (to be completed by the customer or representative)

1 _____
_____
2 _____
_____
3 _____
_____
4 _____
_____
5 _____
_____

Actions taken to resolve the issues raised above

1 _____
2 _____
3 _____
4 _____
5 _____

Customer Signature _____ **Date** _____

Copy received by _____ **on behalf of (Hotelier/Supplier)** _____

Figure 6.3 A complaint form

Think it over ...

One of the most common complaints against overseas tour operators is about the representative. What should managers do if such complaints are received?

Think it over ...

Some tour operators employ specialist people (e.g. guest service managers) to deal with problems and complaints in resorts. This is very expensive, but clearly these operators consider it worthwhile. What do you think are the advantages of employing such specialist staff?

Bear in mind the following and answer the question below:

- It is estimated that tour operators spend more than £3 million a year on refunds.
- Seven out of ten complaining customers will become repeat customers if you solve the complaint in their favour.
- If you resolve a problem on the spot, 95 per cent of customers will travel with the same tour operator again.

What impact do you think these factors have on tour operator training programmes and complaints procedures?

As well as procedures for dealing with complaints, all tour operators will train staff to deal with unexpected emergency situations. Emergency holiday situations include:

✱ Coach crash

✱ Hotel fire

✱ Disease (e.g. typhoid)

✱ Food poisoning

✱ Avalanches

✱ Hurricanes

✱ Terrorism

✱ Tsunami.

Skills practice

Research archived newspapers for any of the above emergencies in holiday destinations. What happened to the tourists? How were they dealt with?

In all such cases, a senior manager in resort will manage guests and UK operations staff may well fly out to support operations. Clearly, in any of the above situations the welfare and safety of injured or ill guests is of prime importance. However, tour operators will also have to deal with guests who may want to return home (but may not be able to do so because of weather, risk of infection, availability of aircraft), clients in the UK who wish to cancel the forthcoming holiday, and, not least of all, the press. It is the representative's role in such a situation to do as much as possible for customers, under the supervision of senior staff. Often, the amount a rep can do is extremely limited. However, they can help keep clients informed at all stages.

In such situations, resort offices will act as a communication point. Depending on the emergency they may:

✱ Contract aircraft to get clients home

✱ Contract hotels and coaches to move clients to a different resort

✱ Liaise with the UK office to keep them up to date and provide accurate information

✱ Establish 24/7 rotas

✱ Deal with local press.

Key points

- The Big Four tour operators dominate the bookings for overseas package holidays. You will find lots of information about them and their staff roles on their websites. But there are also many other tour operators offering a variety of holidays to many destinations.
- The activities of the resort office differ for each tour operator.
- Some tour operators do not have resort offices – overseas reps liaise directly with the UK/head office.
- The rooming list provides far more details than just the type of room required.
- The relationship that tour operators and their reps have with their accommodation suppliers may determine which clients are 'bumped' in an overbooking situation!
- Airport transfers are organised by the resort office – sometimes they are accompanied by transfer reps, sometimes by resort reps. A rota is needed when many flights are due on the same day.
- Allocation contracts are better than guarantee contracts for tour operators. It means that the tour operators only have to confirm number of beds needed a few weeks before guests arrive and only pay for beds used. But hoteliers often take allocation contracts with several tour operators to ensure that their hotels are always full. As a result overbookings sometimes occur.

Overseas staff

Where tour operators have large programmes in an area each season, for example Costa del Sol or Mallorca, Chamonix or Val d'Isere, they will almost always have an established resort office, a resort manager and an overseas team of staff. The size of the resort team will depend on the numbers of guests expected in resort for the season. The type of people employed will depend upon what the tour operator is offering, for example a ski-guiding service will mean ski guides are employed, while children's clubs require children's representatives and nursery nurses, and sports coaches will run activity programmes at some club hotels.

In this section we are going to look at a range of overseas staff who make up the resort team. The organisational chart below (Figure 6.4) is an example of a resort team in the Mediterranean looking after an area (e.g. Costa del sol).

Figure 6.4 Resort team organisational chart

THE OVERSEAS TEAM

THE MANAGEMENT TEAM

- *Regional manager* Oversees entire area. Liaises with UK and recruits senior resort staff.
- *Resort manager* Ensures the smooth running of the resort, liaises with suppliers and occasionally the UK office.
- *Resort trainer* Often moves between resorts, offering training as required and monitoring quality of customer service delivery.
- *Team manager* The key role is to ensure revenue is maximised through selling of excursions and other services.
- *Senior guest service manager* The main role is to resolve (and if possible pre-empt) problems. They aim to improve quality and standards.
- *Administration manager* Oversees the administration team – which is essential to the smooth running of the resort. Establishes appropriate administrative systems.

THE TEAM LEADERS

- *Team leader* Supervises and co-ordinates all representatives. Organises rotas in conjunction with team manager.
- *Children's reps/co-ordinator* Responsible for monitoring children's reps programmes, making sure they are fun, varied and exciting to children. Monitors sales and safety.
- *Nursery nurse in charge* Supervises nursery nurses.

THE ADMINISTRATION TEAM

Examples of responsibilities include making hotel reservations, organising transfers, liaison with insurers, calculating staff commissions and holidays due (for full-time staff).

THE REPRESENTATIVES

- *Resort rep* Ensures a high level of customer satisfaction by providing excellent customer care. Also required to maximise sales of excursions and other services.
- *Entertainment rep* Employed in some resorts to offer a full entertainment programme.
- *Airport rep* Based at the airport, they liaise between the airport, airline staff and other representatives.
- *Transfer rep* Only employed in large resorts. Transfer reps just do airport transfers.
- *Water sports instructors* Manage a water sports activity programme at those resorts offering sailing and windsurfing.
- *Sports coach* Manages a sports activity programme at those resorts offering specialist activities.
- *Children's rep* Provides fun and exciting activities in a safe environment for children aged 3–12 years.
- *Nursery nurse* Cares for children aged under 3 years in specialised crèche facilities.

Source: Adapted from a Thomson's training programme

Figure 6.5 An overseas resort team

Go to a travel agency and collect a number of brochures. Examine the introductory and back pages of each brochure and then answer the following questions:

1 What is each company/brand offering its customers? Make notes on what is included and what optional extras are offered (for which customers will be charged).

2 What staff do you think will be employed by each company?

Overseas representatives

There are many different types of overseas representative. The most common is the resort representative, in uniform and working for one of the Big Four tour operators.

There are many others. Camping and holiday home operators employ many seasonal representatives, who spend their summers under canvas. Some overseas representatives look after customers from several tour operators all at once and are employed by local companies. In this section, we will find out about the roles and responsibilities of the different types of overseas representative employed overseas by UK tour operators.

Resort representative

A resort representative is responsible for customers in a number of different hotels, apartments or villas in a resort. This role typifies that of an overseas representative, and most people employed by the major tour operators have this role. They live in the resort, sometimes in the same accommodation as guests, but sometimes with other representatives in staff accommodation.

Their role involves:

* Representing the tour operator. The holiday representative may be the only person from the tour operating company that the holidaymaker meets. Therefore, the impression presented by the rep is of vital importance. A poor rep can lose many customers and do great harm to the company's image.

* Providing customer service. The rep is there to make sure that the customer has an enjoyable holiday and that any problems are swiftly solved.

Most resort reps will need to:

* Conduct welcome meetings for new arrivals
* Prepare information file about the resort for guests' use
* Keep notice board in the hotel or apartment block updated
* Visit properties every day to answer guests' queries
* Sell and book excursions
* Handle payments
* Keep paperwork up to date
* Book hire cars etc. for guests
* Guide tours
* Handle airport transfers according to a rota
* Participate in entertainment for guests
* Check properties for health and safety
* Liaise with hotel management
* Deal with problems and emergencies.

The representative will receive training and be given a uniform. They are also provided with accommodation and a basic salary. Commission is earned on the excursions sold.

You can see that there is a lot to the job and, of course, the representative has to be on call in case of emergency, although when there are several reps in a resort they have a rota for this. Problems may range from overbookings to serious illness or even death. You will have an opportunity later (page 265) to consider some of the problems that you might face as a rep, and how you would deal with them.

CASE STUDY
First Choice

You'll make sure every customer enjoys a great holiday. You're always around to offer practical advice, or simply to recommend great places to go or fun things to do.

Of course, you'll also deal with unexpected situations coolly and professionally. Every day will be different! You're able to think on your feet, have fantastic problem-solving and communication skills, and be full of initiative.

You'll need to be flexible, over 21, and passionate about delivering excellent customer service. Also important are sales skills and an energetic approach.

This extract from www.firstchoice.co.uk summarises the role of the rep. If you look at the website, you can see all the different types of representative jobs available. Make some brief notes on the different roles.

The roles and responsibilities vary according to the type of resort and holiday brand the representative is working with. We are going to look at some of the variations on the resort representative role.

Holidays representatives for young people

This kind of representative work is often very appealing to young people, as there is a great deal of partying! These representatives have to party almost every night, even when they don't feel like it. In addition to the usual duties of a representative, they are expected to take their guests on pub crawls and to clubs, and to arrange games and drinking competitions so that guests go home having had a wonderful time. They need to have lots of energy and stamina, as there isn't much time for sleep and

they need to be able to keep sober and sensible when all around are not. They must have initiative, because with the kind of nightlife that is going on, there may be many problems of sickness, injury or theft to sort out. They also have to be young so that they fit in with the age group of the clients.

These positions are seasonal and the representatives can expect to be employed from May to October. There is a lot more demand for 18–30 type holidays in the peak summer season, so there are more jobs for reps in that period, which means this job can fit in with studying. These representatives work in major summer holiday resorts all over Western Europe.

Villa representatives

These employees need to be drivers and are usually provided with a company car. Unlucky ones might only get a moped. Villas are likely to be located at considerable distances from each other, so it may be time-consuming reaching them and ensuring that all clients are welcomed. The nature of the job is different, in that the customers' needs are different. Villa holiday customers are less likely to join excursions and are usually more independent and happy to organise their own activities. So the representative may only be called on when there is a problem. The advantage for the representative is that they should have more free time than other kinds of representatives, if all is running smoothly.

Because villas have owners, there may be another dimension to this job, for example the representative may have to mediate between an owner and a customer if there is a problem. As the owners cannot all be expected to speak English, the representative should speak the local language. For this reason some tour operators choose to employ local people as villa representatives. They have excellent local knowledge and so can advise customers. Villa representatives are employed all over Europe, and indeed in further flung destinations, but are likely to be in the less busy holiday resorts.

Young people clubbing at the Paradis nightclub in San Antonio, Ibiza, Spain

Simply Travel

For the past 25 years, Simply Travel has been providing travel solutions for the discerning few who want more from their holiday than the usual package. During that time we have grown into one of the UK's leading specialist tour operators, not through aggressive marketing tactics, but by providing an attractive alternative to mass-market package holidays, which has led our clients to travel with us again and again and to recommend us to others.

At Simply Ski we have gone out of our way to discover quality chalet accommodation full of character and comfort in the best ski resorts in the Alps.

Simply Travel provides properties which are full of character in the more authentic corners of the world. Some of the properties are charmingly simple, others unashamedly luxurious, but they are all a far cry from the mainstream, in character as well as location.

Simply's representatives abroad are employed purely to assist the clients in making the most of their holiday.

Source: www.shgjobs.co.uk

Sovereign Service Executives

Sovereign is renowned for delivering outstanding levels of service. Through acting as a source of information on the local area, offering excursions, or simply advising customers on how they can get the most out of their holidays, you'll exceed our customers' high expectations.

Over 21 with a very mature approach, you have excellent interpersonal and communication skills and ideally a second European language. You can manage your own time easily because of your outstanding organisational ability and will also need a current driving licence.

You'll be independent, interested in culture and history, flexible, over 21 with common sense and ideally a second language.

Source: www.sovereign.co.uk

'Prestige' or 'select' representatives

Most tour operators have brands that are aimed at older or more discerning customers. These customers expect a different kind of holiday to the 18–30 customer, so a different personality of rep is needed. Sovereign, the tour operator, looks for representatives with more maturity, good communication skills and a second language, as shown in the following extract from their website. Although they ask for an age of over 21, it is likely that suitable candidates are much older. Some tour operators deliberately target older people (50-plus) in their recruitment, as they think their older clients will be more comfortable with a more mature representative. Note how Sovereign gives these representatives a special title to give them enhanced status.

Campsite couriers

These reps are often students who want to work abroad for the summer. Besides all the usual tasks that we described above, couriers are responsible for cleaning the tents and holiday homes in between clients. This can be quite a task, depending on how the customers left their accommodation. The couriers are provided with tents in a staff area of the campsite. The downside of this kind of work is that the guests know where you live and will find you!

Ski-resort representatives

If you work successfully as a ski-resort representative, you should not have any problem getting a transfer to warmer climes in the summer – tour operators prefer to keep trained and proven staff. Ski-resort representatives do the same job as other resort representatives. They are allocated a number of hotels or chalets and visit their guests, solve problems and sell excursions in the same way. They are likely to be keen skiers or snowboarders as that is the main activity for them in their free time.

A snowboarder carving a tight turn

In addition to the resort representative, you will find chalet hosts and assistants in the ski resort. These staff are expected to clean daily, order food and cook it for the guests. If they become very efficient, they can get their morning breakfast and cleaning routine finished by late morning. Then they are free until it is time to cook the dinner at about 5 pm. This gives a good few hours skiing most days and is definitely the perk of the job. The chalet hosts are expected to give excellent customer service, but do not book excursions or do airport duty. They can call on the resort representative if they have any problems.

Skills practice

Research two resort jobs that appeal to you. There are careers sections and links to jobs on all the major tour operator websites. Just search for the name of the tour operator that interests you. TUI (Thomson) has a dedicated jobs website for all its brands at www.shgjobs.co.uk

Transfer representative

Transfer representatives meet and greet holidaymakers at the airport and take them by coach to their hotel. If passengers are travelling by taxi or hire car, they are welcomed and sent on their way. The job of the transfer representative is possibly the least appealing of the rep jobs, as the hours are long and there is little variation in the work. You might be interested in this work if you really like a challenge because transfer representatives face the problems and the anger of customers caused by delayed aircraft. Resort representatives often take turns to do airport duty to share the load.

Children's representative

A children's representative usually needs to hold an NNEB or NVQ level 3 in Childcare, have some experience of working with children and a first-aid certificate. This is important to note, as for most holiday representative jobs there are no specific qualifications required, although a good standard of education, equivalent to five GCSEs, is likely to be asked for. The lower age criterion for children's reps is generally lower, at 19 years old.

Duties involve looking after groups of children for several hours a day and organising activities for them. There is usually different provision made for different age groups.

Role Profile

Role Title	CHILDREN'S REPRESENTATIVE
Reporting To:	TEAM MANAGER/TEAM LEADER/CHILDREN'S REPRESENTATIVE CO-ORDINATOR
Role Purpose: *Why the role exists and its contribution*	To provide a varied programme of children's activities to enhance the enjoyment of our customers' holidays.

Role Specification

What the role holder needs to do to achieve the role purpose

Key Responsibilities	Key Elements
• Providing activities within children's club	• Plan a fortnightly programme that is varied and appeals to all ages • Advertise and promote effectively • Control of club stock/equipment • Adhere to signing in/signing out procedures • Adhere to club's ratio • Monitor club attendance • Keep club room clean and tidy
• Customer service	• Provide relevant information via transfers/WOW/guiding excursions as applicable • Answer questions and queries about children's club, hotel and resort • Seek out customers in order to create a positive relationship • Work with our suppliers to enhance customers' holidays
• Quality control	• Complete pre-season health and safety check of children's club • Liaise with suppliers to ensure maximum safety • Carry out fortnightly checks • Report any health and safety issues/incidents to health and safety departments and suppliers • Observe required standards at work
• Problem solving	• Solve problems quickly and efficiently • Know when not to escalate the problem • Pre-empt problems
• Organisation and planning	• Complete weekly reports • Complete company administration forms • Account for money collected for payment of children's club facilities from late deals • Preparation for activities

Source: Thomson

Figure 6.6 A children's rep role profile

Tour manager

A tour manager's role is very different from every other representative's role. A tour manager accompanies a coach tour, offering both representative and guiding services. They usually work alone (with the help of the coach driver) and, as well as all the skills required by a rep, they also need detailed knowledge about many destinations. They will also stay in different hotels every night – and so cannot develop their own

A tour manager acts as a rep and a guide

social life. Many tour managers work on back-to-back tours for a whole season, that is as they drop off one group of passengers they will pick up the next. They only get time off if passengers are guided by a local guide (a legal requirement in some European cities) or if there is a break between tours (see case study on page 277).

Supervisory and management staff

It is important that you realise that there is a career structure within holiday representation, especially in busy resorts. All tour operators want their good staff to stay for the following season and take on more senior roles. As in Figure 6.5, the management team of a resort office may comprise team leaders, team managers, resort managers, trainers and specialist problem-solving staff (guest service manager). Smaller resorts may simply have one resort manager responsible for a handful of reps, reporting to a regional manager in another part of the country.

The responsibilities of management staff are to:

* Manage sales – ensure they are maximised and correctly accounted for
* Co-ordinate operations
* Ensure a high standard of customer service at all times

* Manage the resort office
* Monitor, train and develop the team of reps
* Deal with problems and complaints
* Manage and motivate staff
* Act as the point of contact in the resort in an emergency
* Liaise with head office as required
* Provide head office with statistical and other information.

The roles and responsibilities of each member of the resort management team will depend on numbers of staff employed and where they are located. In resorts where there is a large management team, the guest service manager will take on the role of dealing with problems, and the resort trainer will monitor customer service delivery and provide guidance and training to the representatives team as required.

Management staff usually need to be in resort before reps arrive at the beginning of the season and often have an extra week 'clearing up' at the end of the season. In Figure 6.7 you can see the additional duties managers have at each end of the season.

Administration staff

Administration staff are the 'behind the scenes' staff without whom a resort could not run. The administrative team may vary from one person, working for the resort manager, to a team of five or six, with their own manager. The use of email has enhanced the administrators' roles. IT systems now link directly with head office systems, queries can be quickly solved by email and most information can either be downloaded directly or sent by email. Although some staff working in the administrative team do not come into direct contact with the guests, others do, and so people in these roles also require customer service skills. Languages are often needed, as the administrative staff will be the key point of contact with local hoteliers and coach companies. These staff also need to have excellent organisational and IT skills, be good team players, and they will, ideally, have previous experience in working in an office environment.

JOB DESCRIPTION

Position: RESORT MANAGER
Location: Within the overseas programme, as stated in your covering letter
Reports to: Area Manager

As Resort Manager you will oversee all operational and guest related aspects of the running of the resort, supervise and organise all resort staff and ensure that the high standards that the company expects are maintained.

Your responsibilities and duties:

Pre-season:

- Attend the pre-season management training course.
- Assist the Senior Management team with training the staff at the designated venue.
- Organise and supervise the cleaning and preparation of all chalets, resort office and child care rooms (Esprit).
- Produce detailed inventories of all the chalets, staff accommodation and resort office and child care rooms (Esprit).
- Meet with local suppliers for catering, laundry, lift pass, ski school and equipment hire and confirm the arrangements for orders, deliveries and purchasing.
- Produce Health & Safety, Fire and Hygiene reports for all chalets and child care venues (Esprit).
- Organise effective safe storage and transport of Esprit Children's ski equipment (Esprit).
- Ensure resort personnel files are completed.
- Compile information about your resort and create the chalet notice boards and chalet information files.
- Complete a brochure accuracy report on the resort, all chalets, Nurseries and Snow Clubs (Esprit) and submit to the Marketing Department in the UK.
- Ensure that all staff have the correct uniform and inform the Area Manager if any additional items are required.
- Prepare both an Après Ski and Ski Escorting programme.

Post-season:

- Oversee and organise the cleaning and closing down of all the chalets, Nurseries, Snow Clubs (Esprit) and staff accommodation in the resort.
- Produce detailed inventories of all the chalets, Nurseries, Snow Club rooms (Esprit), staff accommodation and resort office, and cross reference with those completed pre-season, detailing any breakages or damage.
- Ensure that all company property is correctly packaged and stored.
- Liaise with owners over the hand-over of the chalets and staff accommodation, ensuring that hand-over reports are completed and signed off.
- Collect all staff manuals, chalet signs, notice boards, and information files.
- Ensure that the resort vehicle logbook is complete and the vehicle is clean inside and out.
- Complete the end of season resort report and submit to the Area Manager.
- Complete end of season staff appraisals and submit to the Area Manager.
- Ensure that all staff uniforms are returned, clean and inventoried.
- Complete staff clearance forms and send to Overseas Personnel Department in the UK.
- Liaise with the Regional Office regarding the arrangements for the transport of all staff back to the UK.
- Ensure that all invoices and bills have been settled before the close down of resort accounts.
- Sign off accounts with the Regional Office resolving any discrepancies before your departure.
- Ensure that all reports, accounts and property are signed over to the Regional Office before your departure.

Source: Esprit Holidays

Figure 6.7 Extracts from a job description of a resort manager

RESORT ADMINISTRATORS

Making sure everything works like clockwork will be down to you. You'll provide an efficient support system by helping to download, process and distribute rooming and transfer lists, liaising with hoteliers, suppliers and resort staff.

Good organisational skills are vital, and you should be computer literate, over 21 and have good knowledge of a second European language.

Source: Extract from www.justchoice.co.uk

Qualities required of resort administrators

OFFICE STAFF (SUMMER/WINTER)

We have occasional vacancies for general administrative and accounts-based staff to join us at our overseas offices – including qualified accountants and people with a financial/accounts background who have good PC and telephone skills. We also need general office staff with strong customer service skills to deal with customers and resort staff on an everyday basis. Language skills and knowledge of database packages would be an advantage.

Source: www.shgjobs.co.uk

Qualities required of general administrative and accounts staff

Skills practice

Look at the job profile for the children's rep (page 253). Use this format to write a similar job profile for a resort administrator.

Skills practice

To find out more about seasonal work overseas, go to the FAQ on the website www.shgjobs.co.uk

Skills practice

The following extract is taken from the Esprit website. It details tasks that candidates have to complete as part of their job application. Select a job that you would like to do and complete the application task.

Resort Manager
You have a week to prepare your resort for guests. Prepare a schedule for your staff.

Resort Representative
Prepare a welcome briefing for your guests on their arrival.

Hotel Manager/Assistant Manager
Outline the different tasks within a hotel team and say how you would maintain a smooth operation.

Chalet Manager/Chalet Trainer
Detail specific points to check in a chalet on inspection and how you would maintain standards.

Chef & Chalet Host/Cook
Prepare a six-day menu plan to dinner party standard, including afternoon tea and a three-course evening meal with canapés.

Chalet Housekeeper and Hotel/Chalet Assistant
Describe what you think your daily duties will involve and what the transfer day will entail.

Resort Child Care Manager
Present a set-up week plan to ensure that all child care rooms are ready for first arrivals.

Nanny/Nursery Assistant
Prepare a timetable for a six-day nursery from 8.30am–5.00pm

Snow/Alps Ranger
Prepare a schedule of activities to occupy children aged 3–11 for six afternoons, to include bad weather options for two afternoons.

Kitchen/Night Porter
List the additional duties you think may be included as part of your Night Porter shift.

Source: Extract from www.Esprit-holidays.co.uk

Key points

- Where tour operators have many clients, they employ teams of staff and have an established resort office.

- The term 'resort rep' covers many different roles.

- Tour operators need different types of staff for their different brands, for example the party animal for the 2wenties brand and a mature and discerning person for Simply Travel and Sovereign customers.

- There are several supervisory and management roles within most resort teams.

- These senior staff have usually been reps in previous seasons.

- Tour operators want to keep their staff for several seasons – it saves on training costs and usually helps provide better customer service.

ASSESSMENT

Portfolio practice

Read the following scenario of an adventure holiday specialist and do the tasks that follow.

You work for Let's Go, a small tour operator specialising in adventure holidays to France. Ten years ago the usual customer for these holidays was aged under 30. In the last 10 years, the company has grown — it now operates throughout Europe and turnover has doubled. However, Josh Dalio, the operations director, has also noticed two other things: the age profile of customers is now higher than five years ago and the number of complaints has doubled.

The management team is keen to expand the organisation further, but at the last management meeting it was decided that this expansion could not go ahead until the number of complaints was reduced.

It is clear that Let's Go is not offering the high standard of service that it did when it was smaller. At present an overseas resort manager is employed in each resort. All overseas staff deal directly with Josie in the UK office in Skipton. Josie does the administration for all trips – she emails rooming lists, advises of cancellations/late bookings, deals with resort managers' (RMs) problems, and supports the RMs when they need advice. Josh wonders if the operation is now too big for one person. Does Josie need an assistant or should he set up an overseas office in one of the French resorts, from where all the RMs could be managed? In fact he fancies a year overseas himself.

Josh asks you to carry out some research for him. He needs to present a plan at the next management meeting in two weeks. He asks you to carry out the following tasks:

1 Prepare a short report describing how resort offices operate. Give examples of how this works in the case of other tour operators.

2 Decide whether Josie would still be needed. Give examples of situations where the overseas staff would still need to liaise with the UK office. (If you give enough examples, Josh may be able to keep her on.)

6.2 Duties of the resort representative

The duties of the resort representatives are many and varied. The key role is to provide guests with an excellent standard of customer care and represent the tour operator at all times. Exact duties will vary according to the tour operator, the reps role (e.g. holiday rep, transfer rep or children's rep) and the resort in which they work. However, the following is a list of the main duties:

* Conduct a welcome meeting
* Sell excursions
* Deal with problems
* Administration
* Liaise with suppliers, for example hoteliers, coach companies (although some of this may be done by the resort manager or administration staff).

We will now look in more detail at these duties.

Welcome meeting

The welcome meeting is one of the most important activities carried out by the rep. In some cases (if the rep has not done the transfer), this is when the representative meets their guests for the first time. It is also the 'golden opportunity' to sell excursions. For guests it is a chance to gain information about the resort, hotel and area – and find out about possible excursions. All representatives receive training on the delivery of the welcome meeting. The training will include presentation skills as well as selling skills.

To be successful, a welcome meeting must take place when the guests are relaxed and have had a chance to settle in. So, if they have arrived on a morning flight, a late afternoon or early evening welcome meeting is appropriate, whereas if they have arrived late at night, the next morning is the most suitable time. Reps must also sort out a suitable venue. In some resorts, welcome meetings will take place in the hotels in which the guests are all staying, in others it may be in a local bar (e.g. if people are all staying in different self-catering apartments). Free drinks are usually provided.

Think it over …

When welcome meetings take place, reps usually set up an arrangement with a bar owner – they take the guests there and the bar owner provides free drinks. What are the advantages of such an arrangement to the tour operator, the guests and the bar owner?

Think it over …

People are increasingly confident about travelling overseas independently. Many prefer to book their own flights and hotels over the Internet, rather than book a package holiday. Others may prefer package holidays, but 'do their own thing' while at the resort.

How do you think this changes the reps role (and income)?

The main aim of the welcome meeting is to:

* Establish a positive rapport with the guests and ensure they know who to go to if there are problems
* Sell excursions
* Provide information (about the resort, hotel, local amenities and health and safety) so that guests can have an enjoyable holiday.

The introduction and welcome

Once guests are settled and all have their drinks, reps should welcome them to the resort and introduce themselves and other members of the team as appropriate. For example, if working in a ski resort, representatives may introduce ski guides, whereas in beach resorts offering children's clubs, they may have children's representatives at the welcome meeting, ready to meet the kids and persuade them to come to the kids clubs!

During this first part of the welcome session, the reps need to establish a rapport with their guests. Guests in turn need to know that the rep is friendly, approachable and knowledgeable. Reps therefore need to be well prepared and have information to hand. They should arrive early, be professionally presented and well organised – remember first impressions count!

In Unit 2 the following points about first impressions were stressed:

- It takes 10 seconds to make a first impression
- You never get a second chance to make a first impression.

Using your customer service knowledge from Unit 2, write guidelines for new reps about the preparation required for their welcome meeting. Include information about personal presentation (e.g. uniform, name badges, first impressions, company image, body language), venue (size, complementary drinks), and the product knowledge needed.

Key terms

Rapport This means to establish a positive relationship with other people.

Body language This is how we communicate without using words, for example through our facial expressions and gestures.

Health and safety information

Health and safety training will be given to all representatives, and they will be advised what to include in their welcome meeting. This may include:

✱ The dangers of the sun

✱ Fire risks (especially for those staying in tents)

✱ Local risks/crime levels (especially in long-haul destinations)

✱ Safety on the slopes (ski resorts only!)

✱ Swimming pool guidance (e.g. depth, life guard arrangements)

✱ Local emergency numbers (fire, police, ambulance)

✱ How to contact the rep/resort office in an emergency.

Other information

The rep should aim to provide information that will help guests enjoy their holiday. The rep will know the resort well, whereas guests may be only there for a week, and it would be unfortunate to miss out on a great restaurant or the best club, just because they didn't find it until the last day. Local information about the destination or amenities and general information about the property in which guest are staying, will all help guests enjoy their holidays to the maximum – and reps must consider carefully what to include and, of course, ensure it is appropriate to their resort. Examples could include:

✱ *Property information*: safety boxes and costs; swimming pool rules; reception closing time and arrangements for coming in late at night.

✱ *Destination information*: local sights and attractions; best beaches (distance, cost of chairs, umbrellas); shopping facilities; local transport; local regulations/customs; festivals and bank holidays; language basics (if appropriate); recent weather and forecasts.

✱ *Local amenities*: medical information (nearest doctor and hospital); sports facilities; and personal recommendations of bars, clubs and restaurants.

Reps will normally find out most of this information once they arrive in resort and start to carry out local research. They will visit the local tourist office, talk to the hoteliers, and other locals. If working as part of a resort team, experienced reps will be able to pass on their local knowledge.

Reps may be able to gather local maps and information leaflets about local amenities that they can hand out at the welcome meeting. Local tourist offices may provide these free of charge.

Selling excursions

One of the key functions of the welcome meeting is to sell excursions. Tour operators make money from excursions and reps earn commission from the sales. Many guests like to go on an excursion to see more of their holiday destination or to take part in an activity (e.g. whitewater rafting). Excursions are not the only things reps sell. Car hire is usually available and some tour operators also sell children's clubs.

The excursions that are available are, of course, particular to each destination. A rep working in a ski resort may offer only evening entertainments, such as curling or ice skating, whereas a rep based at a beach may offer beach barbecues and island tours, as well as excursions to local cities and attractions.

PARIS EXCURSIONS

Complete City Tour   FPCE01

The perfect way to start any Paris trip – a comprehensive luxury coach tour of Paris: Eiffel Tower, Notre Dame, Bastille, Concorde and much more. Fascinating English commentary with individual headphones.

Paris City First Tour   FPCE08/13

As above with pick up and drop off at your hotel and free time to explore Notre Dame and Montmartre.

Versailles Apartments   FPCE02/15

Your guide will enthral you with the life of the French Royals as you visit the Queen's apartments. See the Hall of Mirrors, the reception area and the magnificent Palace Gardens. The Palace is closed on some French Bank Holidays.

Paris City First Versailles   FPCE09/14

As Versailles Apartments but with free visit (no guided tour) and with pick up and drop off at your hotel and entrance to the State Departments.

Giverny   FPCE38

Monet at home! A guided visit of the wonderful flower gardens and famous Japanese bridge. Free time to visit Monet's home and former studio.
The afternoon finishes with either shopping or a stroll up to the Museum of American Art.

Paris City First Giverny   FPCE11

As above but as a free visit (no guided tour) and with pick up and drop off at your hotel. All entrance fees are included. You may visit the house and studio and stroll along the lily pond at your own leisure. Entrance fee to the Museum of American Art is also included.

Illuminations of Paris   FPCE03/19

Discover the beauty of Paris at night with this guided tour of magnificently floodlit sights, including the Eiffel Tower, Arc de Triomphe, the Opéra and much more. Recorded commentary on the curiosities and magic of the capital after dark. Every evening (except 21 Jun & 14 Jul & 31 Dec).

City First Illuminations   FPCE10/18/24

As above with pick up and drop off at your hotel and tour in an air-conditioned minibus, and live commentary.

Source: Cresta

These Paris excursions are the kind of excursions that a rep would sell at a welcome meeting for tourists to the city

CASE STUDY

Selling children's activities at Thomson resorts

A what's on welcome (WOW!) normally lasts about 30 minutes. During that time the holiday rep will give information about the hotel, the resort, and the top 10 highlights. As a children's representative, you are given a few minutes (about five minutes into the meeting) to give the children and their parents information they need about the children's clubs. (Some of this information may be in written format and handed out to families – in order to keep the speech as short as possible.) The speech should include:

- An introduction to the team and an explanation of what you do

- Safety information

- Meeting times and places, signing-in procedures

- An enthusiastic description of the fun activities you organise.

You can lead the children out of the welcome, and return them to their parents at the end of the general welcome meeting.

You now have about 20 minutes to 'sell' the children's club to the children themselves, to make them feel comfortable with you, and excited about what they will do in the children's club. You will know from the rooming list how many children you will have at the welcome meeting, so you should have the right number of T-shirts, hats and badges ready to hand out. You may want to get the children involved in a game and try on their T-shirts.

When you return the children to their parents make sure you have the parental agreement form to hand, for them to fill in giving their consent to the children attending the club. Children cannot attend the club unless you have these forms of consent from the parents. It is a good idea to fill in the details yourself from the rooming list (the names, ages and booking references) in advance, to save the time parents would spend filling them in.

Source: Adapted from Thomson's children's representatives programme.

1 Why do you think a parental agreement form is needed?
2 What safety information do you think the children's rep will include in their speech?

Reps need good selling skills in order to maximise their sales. They should:

✱ Present the excursions in a lively and enthusiastic way

✱ Make personal recommendations (e.g. 'This tour is particularly popular' or 'If you like seafood, I would really recommend coming on this day trip, as we have lunch at a fabulous restaurant')

✱ Hand out a leaflet with all excursion details, costs and times – so that people can book later if they wish to

✱ Make sure they know the features and present the benefits of each tour/excursion

✱ Tell guests how to book, for example at the end of the welcome meeting or at any time the rep visits their hotel/property

✱ Finish their welcome meeting with 'I am taking bookings now if you would like to come and see me.'

Feature This is a particular aspect of an excursion, for example half-day, lunch included, free time available, guided.

Benefit This is what the customer gains from the feature.

The following are examples of features of excursions and the benefits they offer that help a rep to sell them to holidaymakers.

Feature	Benefit
Half-day	'You will be back by midday, so you will still have time to get some sun in the afternoon.'
Lunch included	'A great lunch is included at a local restaurant, so you won't lose time looking for somewhere to eat.'
Free time	'You have two hours free, so you will be able to shop or go to the beach, or even the Picasso museum – whatever takes your fancy.'
Guided	'The city tour will be guided, so you will certainly gets lots of local information.'
An evening dinner with reps cabaret	'Come to be wined, dined, and then entertained by us, we are good – honest!'
Beach BBQ with music	'After a delicious BBQ, you can dance under the stars on the golden sands.'

Skills practice

Choose a tour operator and select a resort from their brochure. Imagine you are a new rep in this report. Prepare notes for a welcome meeting. You must include:

- An introduction and welcome
- Health and safety information appropriate to the resort and product
- Property information
- Resort/local information
- Information about two excursions or activities that you can sell.

Note: Choose your tour operator and resort carefully. For example, a rep delivering a welcome meeting for 2wenties guests in Ibiza, will have a very different style to a Prestige rep delivering a welcome meeting in Florence! Select the role you think suits you most!

Documentation

All reps have some administration to do. Reps earn commission from their excursion sales, so all sales must be carefully recorded and accounted for. Receipts must be given to clients, booking forms passed to the resort office, and liquidation reports completed each week. Administration tasks vary according to the rep's role and the tour operators' practices. For example, Thomson's reps do not have to do much administration and no accounting – the administrators in the resort office use the sales activities sheets (completed by each rep to indicate what they have sold) to calculate how much money (commission) is due to each rep. In smaller companies, reps will do their own accounts. This involves completing a liquidation report, working out how much commission they have earned, withholding this money, and banking the rest of the money they have collected from their guests.

Key terms

Liquidation report This is a simple accounting form which reconciles income and expenditure. Reps are required to complete one of these each week.

Commission This is a percentage (usually 7–10%) of the sales a rep makes.

Liquidation Report

Representative ...Telly Finegan............   Tour reference ..BX109..............

Resort ...Santa Pensa............   Date ex UK ..15/6/200X..........

Number of pax ..20....................   Currency ....

EXCURSIONS FEATURED IN FINAL ITINERARY

Name of excursion	Selling price (€)	No. of pax (€)	Total income (€)
Package			
Beach BBQ	15	12	180
City Tour – Palma	20	14	280
Cabaret	18	10	180
		Sub-total =	640

First Deduct bridge/tunnel tolls etc.   (0)

(Attach receipts for all deductions and give details overleaf)   Sub-total =   640

Then Deduct reps commission at 10%   (64)

     Balance (1) =   576

PAYMENT DETAILS

Total amount paid in   € 576

Name and address of bank   Santander Casa

Date paid in   23/6/200X

© Worldwide Tour Management (March 99)

Figure 6.8
A liquidation report

CASE STUDY

Weekly administration tasks for a Thomson rep

At the end of each week, Thomson's reps have to sit down and spend time doing their weekly administrative duties. As a minimum they have to submit to their resort office the following:

- *A weekly report* This will detail number of clients, weather, unusual activities/events (e.g. fire alarm went off, local festival or a fight between guests). This report may be similar each week. However, it must still be completed. If a client complains once they get back home, the resort and UK office will already have details of the week and anything that might have contributed to the complaint – after all, a rainy week in Spain is more likely to result in a complaint than a sunny one!

- *Sales activities report* Each rep must detail how many excursions they have sold. This form is used at the resort office to:
  - check that monies received are correct
  - calculate commission due to the rep (usually around 7–10% of each excursion price)
  - analyse the popularity of each excursion
  - analyse the selling skills of each rep.

  Source: Thomson

1 Why does a rainy week result in more complaints?
2 Why does Thomson head office always want a weekly report – even if it has been a 'normal' week?
3 What action might be taken if a rep does not sell many excursions?

Genine, the tour manager for Cusmar Tours, takes coach parties around Europe. She has just handed in her excursion booking form for the last tour. Genuine earns £1 from all pre-sold excursions and £2 on all excursions sold in resort.

Examine the optional excursion report below and work out how much she has earned in commission on this trip. (**Note**: A circle around the numbers means she sold these in resort; the others were pre-booked with head office.)

CUSMAR TOURS

Optional Excursion Report

Tour: _European Highlights - 13 days_   Tour Manager: _Genine Godfrey_

Tour code: _MM6PPT02_   Departure date: _06/12/06_

Excursion	e.g.	Italy	Innsbruck	1/2 day Glacier	1/2 day Lichtenstein
	Pre-sold price	£12.50	£12.00	£10.00	£10.50
	Price in resort	£15.50	£15.50	£12.00	£12.50
Lead name	Number of pax				
JEFFRIES	2	2	2	2	
ATHORN	2		2	2	
HAMPSON	2		2	2	
ELLISON	2	2		②	
TIPLADY	4				④
DAWSON	4		4		④
WILSON	2	2	2	②	
ADDISON	2		2	②	
BOTTOMLEY	2		②	2	
Total numbers on all tours	Pre-sold	6	14	8	0
	Sold in resort	⓪	②	⑥	⑧

Please return this form with your Original Pre-Booked List

Figure 6.9 Optional excursion report

Key points

- All records, for example complaint forms and weekly reports, can be used as legal documents. It is important to be aware of this when completing documentation, so make sure all paperwork is accurate, legible and objective.
- When dealing with customers' problems, you must:
  - listen actively
  - stay calm
  - use positive body language
  - consider the customer's point of view
  - if you say you will do something, do it!

Think it over ...

Thomson and My Travel employ senior staff to act as troubleshooters in resort. They are called in to deal with problems that a rep cannot solve straight away. This leaves the rep free to concentrate on his/her other guests and normal duties that could otherwise be neglected.

CASE STUDY

Thomson snapped up Sue Bullifent when she applied to be a rep in Turkey four years ago. Now a guest service manager, she spends her summers working in the Turkish resort of Fethiye and the winters working in Los Christianos, Tenerife.

Although being a rep had its good parts, Ms Bullifent admits she tired of it after a while, and that the role of guest service manager is challenging and different.

Thomson's programmes to Turkey and Tenerife differ and Ms Bullifent's roles vary in each place.

As the resort in Turkey is much smaller, she deals with welfare concerns.

She is faced with getting people to hospital, sorting out clients with no insurance, organising speedy flights home and dealing with emergencies as calmly and efficiently as possible.

But as she sits sipping a glass of water in the shade of a bougainvillea bush, Ms Bullifent doesn't seem the highly strung type.

'I once had to tell a poor lady in Turkey that her husband had died in a paragliding accident. It was terrible', she says.

But she dealt with it because she had to.

Thomson has more hotels in Tenerife, so the team is bigger. It has a separate welfare department so there are less dramas to deal with than in Turkey.

Ms Bullifent says: 'I like the variation of the two places. I am most fond of Turkey, but it is nice to keep myself fresh by not being there all year round.'

She uses ideas from the larger, Tenerife-based hotels to improve standards in Turkey.

She says: 'Things like leaving a card in the hotel room saying that it has been cleaned helps to improve customer scores.

'I like to keep my eyes open and see how we can do things differently in Turkey.'

Ms Bullifent thinks all young reps would benefit from the chance to travel.

'If young reps have never had the experience of living abroad before they start working with Thomson, the day-to-day problems they come across can be too much,' she says.

There is a lot to be said for starting a job with a tour operator later in life.

Ms Bullifent is looking forward to returning to Turkey and taking up the role of 'team leader'.

Her phone rings and she excuses herself.

She says calmly: 'I have to go and get a last-minute flight home for a recently widowed man who is missing his wife too much to enjoy his holiday.'

Source: Travel Trade Gazette 4 December 2000

1 List all the problems mentioned that Sue has had to deal with in the four years that she has been a guest service manager.
2 List the personal skills and qualities that she has that enable her to deal with such problems so professionally.

Now that we have examined the personal skills needed to deal with problems (whatever they may be), we must look at possible solutions for specific problems.

Accidents

Clearly, accidents need immediate action. Depending on the seriousness of the accident the rep would have to act accordingly, for example they may need to apply first aid and/or advise the client to go to the hospital, or call an ambulance. The rep must be clear, organised (have appropriate telephone numbers to hand) and calm. Depending on their role, the rep may need to accompany the injured person to the hospital. All accidents will need to be recorded.

A dirty room

A dirty room is unacceptable. The rep will need to inspect the room and speak to the hotelier to request either a room change or a thorough clean, whichever is appropriate to the situation. The reaction of the hotelier may determine the next stage of action required. For example, if the hotelier is genuinely apologetic and explains that the room was missed because of a new member of cleaning staff, this may not need to be taken further. However, if the hotelier is dismissive, this matter will need reporting to the local resort manager, who may need to discuss this with the hotelier and possibly review future contracts.

Noise

People go on holiday to relax and not to be bothered by noise. If building works are planned for the resort, or nearby, tour operators should advise customers beforehand. This is a requirement of the EC Package Travel, Package Holidays and Package Tours Regulations. While these regulations should eliminate the problem, it still occurs, for example if the hotelier had not advised the tour operator. This matter should be referred to the resort management team. They would either seek compensation from the hotelier (so that they could offer this to guests) or move the clients (at the hotelier's expense.)

Noise from other guests is another matter! Always approach such situations carefully.

Chatting informally to the offending guests and telling them they were a 'bit loud' when they came home the previous night from the booze cruise, is more likely to get them 'onside' than a more formal 'telling off'. The rep needs to speak carefully to both parties and try and get them to appreciate the other customers' situation. This is a case where a cooling-off time can be very helpful while you investigate the matter. As a last resort, a change of room may be needed.

Lost or stolen passport

Passengers cannot fly home from an overseas destination without a passport. Lost or stolen passports are a fairly common problem. The rep will know procedures for handling this. They should advise the guest to report the loss to the police and then send them to the appropriate embassy for help. The rep should know where the nearest British embassy, or consulate, is. They should also know where other embassies or consulates are, as some guests may not be British passport holders. Temporary travel passports (valid for just 24 hours) can normally be issued on the spot providing a police report of the loss is presented.

Overbooking

We have already looked at why overbookings occur. It is usually the responsibility of the hotelier to find alternative accommodation when they have too many guests for the beds available. Tour operators obviously want their clients to be well looked after, and will usually require upgraded accommodation to be provided. This will be stated in the accommodation contract. However, it is the rep, or a senior member of the resort team, who has to advise guests of the change in accommodation as soon as they arrive at the airport.

This is not an easy task. Clients may have travelled a long way and be tired. They will obviously be disappointed, or annoyed, about such a change. When telling clients about the changes, resort staff should try to take the clients to a quiet area away from other guests – it is not in their interests for other clients to hear what is being said, particularly if the overbooked client becomes angry! Such scenes do not create a good first impression. Reps need to be apologetic, reassuring and very positive about the upgraded accommodation. Company procedures should be followed: some tour operators may offer a complimentary excursion, or something similar, as a gesture of good will.

Skills practice

In groups of 3–4, role-play the following scenarios. Take it in turns to be the rep, the guest and the observers. Add your own scenarios to those suggested.

Observers should grade each rep according to the following criteria:

- Active listening
- Apology
- Reassuring the customer
- Appropriate questioning
- Staying calm
- Offering solutions
- Suitability of solutions
- Agreement of solution
- Body language
- Confident manner
- Calmness throughout the role-play.

Scenario 1

Jane Jones was waiting for an excursion. While waiting outside the hotel she suddenly realised that she had forgotten her sun hat. She returned to her room to get it and the coach went without her. She is distressed, as this excursion to the local temples was to have been the highlight of her holiday.

Scenario 2

Jim and Josh had a heavy night on the town last night. This morning the people in their neighbouring apartment woke them with loud music before 7 am. They think this is really rude. (They claim they came home very quietly!).

Scenario 3

Mr Millington walks with a frame. He has been allocated a room on the first floor. While this is not normally a problem, the lift is being serviced today and he cannot get back to his room.

Scenario 4

Sue and Joe Bryan have two young children. They want a babysitter for tonight so that they can go and celebrate their tenth wedding anniversary. This service is advertised in the brochure. However, they have been told that the service has been withdrawn. They are really disappointed.

You may be able to use this activity as preparation for your assessment.

Key points

- A rep's income is partly made up by commission, which they earn by selling excursions.
- Excursion sales also contribute towards a tour operator's profits, and so some set sales targets for reps.
- Welcome meetings are a good opportunity to sell excursions.
- When selling, it is important to focus on benefits.
- Reps must carry out their own research once in resort in order to be able to provide local information.
- All reps must do simple administration, and possibly some basic accounts.
- It is important that reps try to pre-empt problems and avoid them becoming complaints.
- When dealing with difficult situations, reps must always remain calm and professional.

ASSESSMENT

Portfolio practice

Below are two scenarios that require you to carry out tasks that will help you prepare for your assessment.

Scenario 1

You have been recruited as a high season rep for a small tour operator. The operator has had a spate of late bookings and needs extra staff. You will go out to resort in two weeks' time for the peak season. You have been allocated to the resort you requested on your application form. Your guests will be arriving the day after you arrive in resort. It is therefore essential that you do as much research as possible now. You will need to provide information to guests on the resort, the hotel and the local area. You must also provide information about two excursions so that you are able to sell them at the welcome meeting.

You must carry out research, prepare your welcome meeting and be ready to deliver it once you arrive in resort.

Scenario 2

You have been in resort now for three weeks and it is really going quite well. You are feeling quite pleased with yourself. Your team leader has seen that you are competent and has this morning asked you to deal with two problems.

- You must visit Asha and Andy Roberts. They have just got married and are clubbing every night to celebrate. The family in the next-door apartment get up at 6 am every day. The children make lots of noise, run up and down the stairs and bang doors. Asha and Andy have complained about the noise. The family have complained that they are woken every night when Asha and Andy come home! You need to visit both parties and sort this out.

- You must accompany the transfer rep and deal with an overbooking problem. Either a group of four young men or a family of four will have to be moved from the hotel for the week. You have to offer them alternative accommodation. Your team leader knows this will be difficult. Although the alternative hotel is an upgrade, it is out of town. If the guests really complain, you may have to offer complimentary car hire, however your manager wants you to avoid this if at all possible, because of the cost. She does not mind which group you move.

6.3 The significance of induction, training and product knowledge of staff in delivering high-quality customer service

The resort representative is the face of the company. Many holidaymakers will not have met anyone from the tour operator until they step off the plane and meet the rep at the airport. The rep's skills at this and at every other point in the holiday are vital. Their product knowledge is also significant. They need to answer questions, give accurate information and provide an interesting commentary on the excursions. Not only will they determine customer satisfaction levels, but they will also affect the image of the company and whether guests choose to travel with that tour operator again. We know from Unit 2 how important excellent service is.

So, to be successful, tour operators need to invest heavily in recruiting the right staff and then training them to a high standard. How long the training is and what kind of training is required varies with the tour operator, depending on their size, products and the number of staff employed. For example, the Big Four tour operators, who employ hundreds of staff in their overseas resort teams, all offer thorough UK and overseas training for several days. By contrast, smaller operators, who only recruit tour managers to accompany coach tours, may only offer a one-day induction training in the UK before sending staff on one of their tours to experience first hand how it is done!

CASE STUDY

Getting the right staff at Thomson Holidays

Fiona Groutage, overseas recruitment manager at Thomson Holidays, is the person responsible for ensuring that the right people are recruited as reps in Thomson resorts. She knows that the success of Thomson Holidays is partially dependent upon her and her team's abilities to:

- Recruit the right number of people
- Carry out rigorous interviews to ensure the candidates have suitable skills
- Train them (both in the UK and overseas)
- Motivate them sufficiently – so that the reps stay with Thomson for several seasons.

The summer reps recruitment process starts seven months before the season, in October. This is when Fiona places advertisements in the national press, magazines (such as *Company* and *Cosmopolitan*) and on Thomson's Internet website. All applications are scrutinised by the overseas HR department. HR staff will look for evidence of service or sales experience and check whether applicants are over 21 years of age and that they have presented a neat and informative application. They also like to see some evidence of travel experience and proof of flexibility (e.g .shift work, irregular hours).

In November the interviews start. From mid-November to mid-December Fiona travels the country carrying out interviews in different towns every day – and using overseas team leaders to help her out. The initial interview has two stages. The first stage, held in the morning, is a group interview, involving individual and team exercises. These will involve sales and customer service activities, assessment of problem-solving skills and testing basic maths. The second stage, held in the afternoon, is when one-to-one interviews are carried out. By the end of the day, the recruitment team will have identified suitable candidates and will fax the list through to head office in London, from where appropriate letters to candidates are sent out.

The successful applicants must attend rigorous training sessions. The first is a five-day course, which will take place between February and March just outside London. The aim of this course is to develop skills that will be required for overseas work in the holiday industry. The focus will be on:

- Customer service
- Sales
- Problem solving
- Presentations
- First aid
- Working with suppliers/ensuring quality.

Although an employment contract will have been issued to successful candidates after the interview, one of the conditions for employment is the successful completion of the training. If the candidates are not able to demonstrate suitable skills, the offer of employment can be withdrawn at this stage. Although this is unusual, candidates can be dismissed for unsuitable behaviour!

Once accepted for employment the reps must prepare to be away from home for six months. Medical and dental checks are recommended before they leave. Mid-April is when they go to resort. Before the first guests arrive (around 1 May), the final training will take place. The resort team will run this for between 5 and 10 days. It will cover:

- How the resort is operated
- The resort office
- Reporting procedures
- Emergency procedures
- Local excursions
- Local suppliers.

At this stage, the rep is allocated their hotel/apartment, and they must ensure everything is ready for guests.

Although this is the end of the initial training, team managers conduct ongoing training throughout the season.

Fiona wants good staff to stay. In July she is already sending out notifications to resort, asking staff to apply for promotions. She will go out to resort towards the end of the season, in September or October, to interview existing staff for next year's team leader positions.

And then it is time to start advertising again.

Source: Thomson Holidays

1 **What sort of exercises will be carried out during the morning of the initial training (the group interview)? Can you name some exercises?**

2 **List some of the questions that may be asked at the one-to-one interviews.**

3 **How could candidates fail after the initial training? Can you identify some examples of 'unsuitable behaviour'?**

4 **Why does Fiona want reps to stay for several seasons?**

5 **The resort training takes between 5 and 10 days. Write a training programme for the first two days of this course.**

Induction training

Induction training is the first part of all training and is offered by all tour operators to staff, whether working in the UK or overseas. The information provided at this stage will be general information about the company and specific information about jobs. Induction programmes can last for one day or up to 15 days (e.g. Thomson's overseas reps). Longer programmes are usually divided into two sessions: the first five days being in the UK, and the second session in resort.

The induction programmes will usually cover:

* A welcome
* Background to the company
* Company structure and who's who
* Resort structure – who does what
* Reporting structure and lines of responsibility
* The reps role and its importance
* Customer service skills
* What goes on in resort
* Welcome meetings
* Sales skills
* Basic administration.

Some induction programmes also cover first aid.

At the first stage of induction reps are provided with manuals and are usually required to study these before the next stage of training. Tour operators treat their training manuals as confidential documents, so these need to be returned to the company at the end of each season. Most of those on induction training believe they already have the job, however they are still being scrutinised by training staff as to whether they are suitable. Many induction programmes last several days, at the end of which there will be a party to celebrate. If you are ever on one of these training programmes, it is important to remember that your ability to handle your drink and remain professional at all times are some of the skills required by the rep, so you will be assessed as to how you behave at the party!!

Some tour operators follow up their UK induction training with work shadowing, while others offer overseas training in resort. Both of these are part of the induction – in fact it is not until reps have done this second part of the induction that they are ready to do the job.

The overseas part of the induction training is more job specific. Resort reps need to get to know their property, transfer reps need further training on procedures and administrative staff need to set up their systems. All staff must settle in, become familiar with the resort, the suppliers used, and local practices and procedures. The team needs to 'gel' and any differences ironed out before guests arrive.

Key terms

Induction training The first training that new employees receive.

In-house training Training carried out by the tour operator.

External training Training carried out by other organisations, for example colleges or training organisations.

Work shadowing

The overseas part of the induction training is often carried out through work shadowing. Work shadowing involves watching somebody doing his or her job. This will provide the rep with an insight into what goes on and will help in understanding the role and how to do it at a later stage. For some roles this is an excellent way to learn. For example, the tour manager taking clients on a weekend tour of Paris can only learn so much about the role in a training room in the company's head office in the UK!

CASE STUDY

Training at Cusmar Tours

Genine applied for her job as tour manager at Cusmar Tours after she had completed her travel and tourism course at college. She had done a couple of seasons in summer and ski resorts and now felt she had enough customer service experience to manage a tour. Anyway, she knew she would earn good money and wanted to see something of Europe. Genine's application was successful.

Her training involved a one-day training programme in London. Cusmar only employs experienced reps, so the purpose of this day was really just to provide information on polices and practices, introduce key personnel, and make sure reps knew what to do in the most common everyday situations and problems. Genine then accompanied Trash on a European coach tour. He had been a tour manager for 10 years and really knew the ropes. After a week touring France, Switzerland and Austria with him, she felt as though she could deal with any situation! She was also now familiar with many of the destinations that she would also go to on her tour – and she had been writing loads of notes to help with her commentary. She was ready to go!

What are the benefits of work shadowing as a training method?

In-house training or external training

There are many external qualifications offered for resort representatives by colleges, travel associations and private companies. Your local college may offer such programmes. The aim of these courses is to provide candidates with an insight into the role of the overseas representative, and to provide some of the generic skills, such as customer service, sales skills, and how to run a welcome meeting. They will help develop candidates' awareness of the type of problems encountered as a resort representative.

Tour operators welcome candidates who have been on such programmes – they have gained some idea of what goes on in resorts, will not view the role as glamorous, and will have already acquired some of the essential skills. However, this does not mean that candidates are already trained and ready to start work as a rep! They still need to learn how each tour operator operates their overseas programmes and company procedures for all eventualities. So all tour operators run their own in-house induction programmes and many will provide further in-house training appropriate to each role.

Chalet Cookery Courses

Ever wanted to do a Ski season as a Chalet Host but unsure of your cookery skills?

Well SHG have the Answer.

Throughout the Summer 2005 SHG will be running a series of cookery courses.

These 5-day cookery courses are designed to ensure your season is both successful and enjoyable.

The courses are residential and will be run by our own fully trained chefs.

We will offer everyone who successfully completes the course a position with ourselves.

A training course on cookery for ski chalet hosts

Some training is offered as part of the application process, especially for those overseas positions where there is a shortage of staff with suitable skills.

Mentoring

Mentoring schemes are becoming increasingly popular. A mentor is someone who offers guidance to a new employee. Usually they have greater experience and are a willing listener and advisor. The mentor and the mentee will meet regularly to discuss any areas that the mentee is finding problematic, or that they just need to talk through. The mentor is not a line manager – they just 'look out for' the mentee during the early days in a new job, when it is easy to get things wrong!

Visits

As part of their induction, all new overseas staff will need to visit all suppliers to introduce themselves and establish a positive relationship. The resort rep needs to know where all their properties are, how to contact the owners (e.g. of villas) or managers (e.g. hotels, coach companies). In ski resorts, reps need to meet the key personnel at the ski school, the ski shop and lift pass company. They should not wait until there is a problem before they meet these people. A rep who is guiding excursions will have to visit the towns, theme parks or other excursion destinations to ensure they are familiar with them. They can then develop a commentary to make an excursion informative and interesting. In larger tour operators, new reps will simply work shadow experienced reps on excursions before they are left in charge of a coach full of tourists expecting a guided tour!

The content of representatives' training programmes

Every tour operator has its own method of training overseas staff. Most of the information will be specific to the company. However, wherever it is carried out and whether through induction, mentoring or work shadowing, all reps will receive the following information at some stage.

Company profile

All staff need to know a little about the company for which they are working. This is normally included in induction training. A profile of the company would typically include: size of company, areas in which it operates/programmes (e.g. winter sun, ski, long haul, cruise), numbers of staff employed, sister/parent companies and key personnel. Most tour operators' websites provide a brief company profile.

> **Key terms**
>
> **Company profile** A brief outline of the organisation.

Resort, property and excursion information

Specific resort information would only be given at the final phase of training, after reps have been allocated their resorts. In the larger tour operators, information about the resort, the excursions and specific properties would all be provided by the resort management team once staff were in resort – after all, it is much easier to learn about the layout of a resort or hotel by walking around it and about excursions by going on them.

> **Skills practice**
>
> You have just been appointed as a Club 18–30 rep to Palma. Access the company's website and obtain a copy of its brochure (or download extracts from www.club18-30.com). Then investigate the company profile, the resort, one hotel and two excursions you need to sell.

Company policies and practices

At induction training all reps are given a manual that covers all company policies and practices. Much of the training programme will enforce this. However, as we will never remember everything, the manual is an invaluable source of reference during the season! For most tour operators, their manuals are confidential and they insist that these are returned at the end of the season. This is to guard against their competitors getting to know their policies and procedures. Examples of policies and practices detailed at training and in the reps manual include:

* What to do on arrival in resort
* Uniform requirements
* Administration and reporting
* Sales
* How to run excursions (commentary, delays, no shows)
* Working with coach drivers
* Reporting structures
* Dealing with complaints
* Emergencies.

Below is an extract from a tour manager's manual. The extract details company policies and provides clear advice to tour managers about how to deal with specific situations.

The tour managers at Newmarket Holidays collect their passengers at local departure points in the UK before heading off in their coaches across the Channel. They work alone (with the help of their coach driver) and need clear instructions on how to deal with issues such as 'no shows'!

B. UPON DEPARTURE

Upon boarding the coach, please check that it is in good working order. Check that there is a microphone and that it works, the video, toilet and tea and coffee-making facilities (where applicable) are functioning.

If there is a problem, please deal with it prior to departure. **Contact Newmarket if a problem is beyond your control**.

Do not allow passengers to board the coach until you have satisfied yourself that it is prepared properly.

Ensure that you introduce yourself to the coach driver(s), and AT THE OUTSET, establish your position as Tour Manager with him/her (them). SEE ADDITIONAL NOTES ON "WORKING WITH COACH DRIVERS".

Before departure, do a **name check** as well as **a head count**. This is especially important when there is more than one coach departing from a particular point.

ALSO, ON A FOREIGN HOLIDAY, PLEASE CHECK THAT EACH PASSENGER TAKES HIS/HER PASSPORT AND INSURANCE DOCUMENTATION ON BOARD THE COACH. WE INSIST THAT ALL PASSENGERS TAKE INSURANCE ON OVERSEAS HOLIDAYS.

"NO SMOKING"

Newmarket has a policy of no-smoking on coaches. Tour managers are required to strictly enforce this rule, WHICH ALSO APPLIES TO TOUR MANAGERS AND DRIVERS THEMSELVES!

The only occasions upon which smoking will be allowed are on Newmarket Travel Service Coaches consisting of a single group where a Group Organiser has requested it.

"NO SHOWS"

Wait exactly fifteen minutes after the stated departure time from any pick-up for any late passengers to arrive.

Then proceed to the last pick-up point and, AT THE EARLIEST "REASONABLE" HOUR, inform Newmarket of the names of "missing" passengers. (There is little point in dragging a duty executive out of bed at 5.30 a.m. to let him know that Mr and Mrs Davies didn't show up in Wrexham three hours earlier!).

Figure 6.11 Extract from the Newmarket Group's manual for their tour managers

Legal and regulatory requirements

Tour operators have legal commitments that will be outlined in training programmes, so that overseas staff are clear about the legal consequences of their actions. Reps need to understand what a tour operators' responsibilities are under the:

* Trade Descriptions Act 1967
* Consumer Protection Act 1987
* EC Directive on Package Travel, Package Holidays and Package Tours 1992.

Trade Descriptions Act 1968

The key point of this Act is that products and services must be correctly described. So, hotel descriptions must be accurate and brochures must contain 'warts and all' information. As brochures are put together a long time before the customers go on holiday, the resort staff have an important role in updating head office staff about any changes. They in turn must advise their customers of the relevant changes, for example that the swimming pool has closed or water sports are no longer available.

Consumer Protection Act 1987

The EC Directive on Package Holidays has now superseded much of this Act. The key requirement of the Act is that prices for products and services are correctly displayed. So a sales promotion, for example, might offer a free child place if accompanied by two full paying adults. However, tour operators could not insist that they all share one room, unless this had been clearly stated in the promotion.

EC Directive on Package Travel, Package Holidays and Package Tours 1992

Under these regulations tour operators are accountable for their suppliers. (For example, if a coach company is negligent and causes injury to a client, the tour operator is liable.) Furthermore, there are many requirements to ensure brochures are 'legible, comprehensible and accurate'. Precise details of the package have to be included in the contract, for example excursions, itinerary, price and payment schedule. Complaints have to be answered within a specific time frame. The implications of these regulations is that reps must report anything that would make the tour operator liable, such as:

* Poor suppliers or negligent suppliers (e.g. a hotel fire door locked, coach company not adhering to drivers' hours regulations)
* Brochure inaccuracies (e.g. sea view no longer available because a new building blocks it)
* Services not available (e.g. use of swimming pool).

Other legislation with which tour operators need to be familiar include health and safety legislation (see page 277). Tour managers and reps escorting tours or guiding excursions, need to be aware of the regulations that affect the numbers of hours a coach driver can drive without a break.

Drivers' hours regulations

The regulations on drivers' hours state that a driver is entitled to a 45-minute break after $4\frac{1}{2}$ hours of driving or 15-minute breaks totalling at least 45 minutes during a $4\frac{1}{2}$-hour period. There is a maximum of 9 hours actual driving per day; this can be increased to 10 hours twice a week. A rest period between working days is normally 11 hours, but there are variations on this allowing for split rest periods. The rules are complicated and can be found in full at www.coach-tours.co.uk.

As far as the overseas representative is concerned, they need not know drivers' hours rules in detail, but should have them available for reference should they need them. The rep must be aware that excursions must be planned, incorporating the required driver rest periods and that delays might take a driver over the hours allowed.

Key term

Tachograph This is an instrument that measures speed and distance travelled (it works when a vehicle is stationary and when it is moving – so can also record rest periods). It is used to ensure that drivers comply with the law and the police can demand to check it at any time.

CASE STUDY

A tour manager's responsibilities

Jo is a full-time travel and tourism student. Before doing the course, she used to work in a Spanish resort as a transfer rep. She then worked in a travel agency for a few years. She misses her life of travel – and is short of money – so she now does occasional weekends for a travel company, taking weekend tours to Paris.

While doing her training course in Manchester, she was surprised by the amount of legislation that now affects the tour operator. The trainer made it very clear that her role was really important, and that her actions and reports could affect the company if they were sued for anything.

On every weekend tour to Paris Jo is required to:

- Check that the hotels used and facilities available are as described in the brochure. As the brochure went out about 18 months before the holidays take place, some details are sometimes not accurate. One week the lift was not working (and this is significant as most clients are elderly). She rang head office straight away and clients booked on the following week's holiday were told immediately (and many offered ground floor rooms).

- Keep accurate records of delays and keep passengers informed. If there are long delays, she has to inform the duty officer, who may authorise refreshments.

- Ensure all the services booked by clients are provided. For example, one week a special champagne breakfast had been booked by a group – but not provided. Jo spoke to the hotel manager and her own boss. The champagne breakfast was provided the following day. Jo was aware that under the EC Directive on Package Travel 1992 the tour operator was liable for any deficiencies of the supplier (the hotel).

- Write a report for every complaint passengers make. She sends this to head office as soon as the tour is over (under the EC Directive on Package Holidays, her boss has 28 days in which to respond to the complaint). When completing the report she is careful to be factual and not show any bias – she knows that if the complaint goes to court or arbitration, copies of her report will be seen by many others!

1 **Name the legislation relevant to the reps role.**
2 **What are the risks associated with brochures being published so long before the customers go on holiday?**
3 **What does 'liable for the deficiencies of any supplier' mean?**
4 **Why must Jo's records be accurate and factual?**

Health and safety

Health and safety is of paramount importance to all tour operators. This is for three reasons:

* Every tour operator has a legal responsibility (under the Health and Safety at Work Act 1974 and the EC Directive on Package Travel, Package Holidays and Package Tours 1992) to ensure the health and safety of its customers and employees

* We all have a moral responsibility to protect life

* Tour operators want to avoid any negative publicity that could damage their reputation (guests are more than likely to sue than ever before).

Tour operators' training programmes will, therefore, cover health and safety, and the content may vary so that it is appropriate to the rep's role.

For example, a Canvas Holiday rep (see case study on page 279) will have different concerns to ski reps, whose training will cover safety on the slopes and how to deal with accidents, getting injured people off the slopes, and the hospitalisation of guests. All reps must continuously be aware of the need to ensure that the environment (whether it be the hotel, swimming pool, kids club or campsite) is safe for guests. While regular checks may be carried out by resort management, smaller operators may provide checklists for reps to complete and send a copy back to the UK (see Figure 6.12).

HOTEL HEALTH & SAFETY CHECKLIST

Hotel	Resort	Check date

Area inspected	Standards OK?	If no, action taken
Balconies		
Fire exit doors		
Extinguishers		
Lighting		
Notices		
Elevators		
Public stairs		
Room electrics		
Reception area		
Pool depths		
Life guards		

Comments:

Signature _____

Date _____

Figure 6.12 Health and safety checklist

CASE STUDY

Health and safety at Canvas Holidays

Canvas Holidays is a leading self-drive tour operator. While health and safety is certainly an issue for all tour operators, Canvas feels that the nature of its holidays makes an awareness of health and safety even more vital. It therefore forms a substantial part of the induction training for all new couriers. Particular focus is given to the following health and safety risks:

- Guests cooking using naked gas flames
- The high risk of using fire around tents
- The risks in sites where cars move in and out within the sites
- The risks presented by the use of products used by reps for cleaning the sites.

Canvas's couriers are made aware that everyone within the company is responsible for health and safety. All staff are required to ensure that safe practices are adhered to at all times – and they must report anything that they feel could risk their own or their guest's health and safety. They are asked to pay particular attention to the following areas:

- Swimming pools
- Children's play areas
- Fire
- Electricity
- Campsite road safety
- Campsite activities
- Gas and carbon monoxide
- Manual handling and cleaning products
- Infectious diseases/hygiene (there are risks if cleaning is not thorough)
- Vehicles and road safety.

In order to improve health and safety on European campsites, the major operators in the self-driver camping industry have agreed to work together. These operators have staff on many campsites throughout Europe – and in many cases they are on the same sites, working alongside each other and using the same facilities. They have all agreed that health and safety is not a competitive issue – and that they should pool resources to ensure that risks in all these sites are reduced as far as is possible.

Source: Canvas Holidays

1 **Identify the potential health and safety risks associated with each of the areas listed above.**
2 **Write guidelines for the Canvas Holidays couriers for two of the potential risk areas.**

CASE STUDY

Hourmont Total Ski

Hourmont Total Ski is a small specialist tour operator whose niché market is holidays for school and college groups. Its main programme is skiing holidays to the Alps, but it also has a small summer educational programme.

Hourmont is different from other school-group operators – it is the only company whose head office is in the Alps. It operates all its Austrian ski resorts from its head office in Innsbruck, while a second resort office in Bolzano (in Italy) supports Italian resorts. Sixteen office staff are employed in the Alps to run the entire ski programme.

Hourmont employs resort reps to work in its ski resorts for the winter season. However, they

HOURMONT SCHOOL TOURS

e-mail: hstsales@chs-tour.com
www.hourmontschooltours.com

are called resort managers (RMs) as they work by themselves in resorts, with back-up support from the resort office. Some of the RMs are employed for the entire winter season, but many are temporary staff employed just for Christmas, February half-term and Easter. These are peak seasons for school-tour operators, when the UK schools and colleges take their ski trips, and so

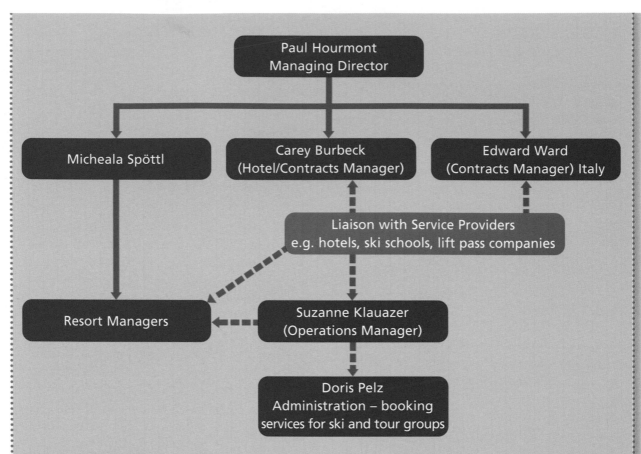

Figure 6.13 Hourmont organisational chart

temporary high-season resort staff are recruited. These temporary staff have to be trained to the same high standard as staff who work an entire season.

All resort managers undergo a two-phase training programme in the Alps. The first part is a three-day induction programme that takes place in the Innsbruck office. The second phase takes place in resorts in the three- or four-day period prior to the arrival of holiday groups, and is less formal. Once resort managers have settled themselves into their accommodation, they are expected to spend this time visiting their suppliers and ensuring everything is set up for the following week. They will need to undertake visits to the hotel, ski school, ski hire, lift company and any other suppliers involved in evening entertainment. The following tasks are just some of the duties to be carried out in those three days:

- Hotelier: liaise with hotelier; check final numbers and room breakdown (i.e. how many doubles, singles, triples and four-bedded rooms are to be used); check lunch arrangements (all groups have full-board and the rep must check whether the hotels provide a packed lunch to be eaten on the slopes or if groups return for a hot lunch).
- Ski school: check final numbers and amount of ski lessons booked (some schools will have 2 hours per day, some 4 and some may even have 6); ensure appropriate number of ski school instructors are booked; check lesson times.
- Ski hire: the resort manager needs to ensure they know where the ski hire is and that it will be open when required. Many of the schools will be arriving by coach late at night and their equipment needs to be ready so that they can be on the slopes first thing in the morning.

- Lift company: check final numbers and when lift passes can be collected.
- Evening entertainment suppliers: many schools will have pre-booked an evening entertainments programme which may include bowling, ice-skating, a disco and a trip to a local pizzeria. The RM will need to organise days, times and check final numbers with each supplier/venue.

While setting up the resort, the RMs have full support from the Innsbruck office. A member of the resort office team will visit to ensure everything is set up and offer guidance where required. All RMs are given a mobile phone and two of the resort office staff are on duty 24/7. The support the RMs receive ensures a high level of service.

'Our resort managers are, with few exceptions, Austrians and Italians. Hourmont Total Ski operates an incomparable resort management system. We have permanent resort managers based in seven locations. During an average February half-term, we employ some 25 resort managers who are equipped with 20 mobile phones and 14 cars, and enjoy the full back-up of the Innsbruck and Bolzano office teams.'

Source: www.hourmonttotalski.com

1 **What type of tour operator is Hourmont Total Ski?**

2 **What do you think is the impact of giving resort staff the title 'resort managers'?**

3 **Who do the RMs report to?**

4 **What are the advantages to the groups and to the hotels of being given a packed lunch?**

5 **Who will provide the RMs with all their information?**

6 **Which staff do you think are most likely to be on 24/7 telephone duty?**

7 **Why do you think Austrians and Italians are predominantly recruited for the high season jobs?**

Skills practice

Research the Hourmont Total Ski website. Make notes for the training manager to deliver to the new resort managers to be recruited next season. You should cover:

- Company profile
- Health and safety (especially on the slopes)
- Company policies (e.g. only using licensed suppliers, ski school hours)
- Evening entertainment (what is included, and why bumboarding is not included!)
- An outline of insurance cover.

Some of this information could be used in your final assessment.

Key points

- All tour operators will offer some form of induction training for new staff. How long it is will vary according to the tour operator.
- Some parts of the induction may be carried out overseas, either in resort offices or through work shadowing.
- Work shadowing is a good way of training tour managers who work by themselves guiding coach tours.
- All tour operators provide overseas staff with a manual outlining policies and procedures.
- There are many external training programmes now available for overseas staff. These provide an excellent insight into the overseas roles – however, tour operators will still want their new staff to go through their own training programmes.

1 Who are the Big Four tour operators?

2 Identify five pieces of information you may find on a rooming list.

3 Give the airport codes for London Heathrow, Newcastle, Belfast, Palma, Palermo and Barcelona.

4 Give five examples of local agencies with whom resort offices may have contact.

5 What is a full transfer?

6 Outline an allocation contract and its advantages to the tour operator.

7 Identify six different resort roles that may be found in a resort team.

8 Why are sales such a focus for many tour operators?

9 Outline the structure of a welcome meeting.

10 What is a liquidation report?

11 State five things you must do when dealing with a problem situation.

12 What would be included in a typical induction training programme?

13 Why is work shadowing a good form of training?

14 What sort of training goes on in resorts?

15 Why must reps not accept liability?

16 Why must all documentation be completed clearly and accurately?

ASSESSMENT

Portfolio practice

Read the following scenario and carry out the task below.

All the staff at Let's Go are impressed by the report you gave outlining the activities of an overseas resort office. Josh has now decided that the resort office is to be set up in France for next season (and he is going to be the area manager!).

He has started the recruitment process for his overseas team, but needs advice on training. It appears that he is not thinking of doing anything formal. The managing director of Let's Go knows this is a mistake and has approached you to provide advice to the management team. He wants you to give a presentation at the next management meeting. You must include the following:

- The importance of induction, training and product knowledge for overseas staff

- Examples of how other operators train their staff

- Suggested content of the training programmes to ensure that representatives have excellent product knowledge.

Index